Microsoft®

1CAD/MCSD
f-Paced Training Kit

2
Second Edition

VELOPING
WINDOWS®-BASED
APPLICATIONS
WITH MICROSOFT®
VISUAL BASIC® .NET
AND MICROSOFT
VISUAL C#® .NET

Exams
70-306 and 70-316

Matthew A. Stoecker
with Microsoft Corporation

rosoft®
net™

PUBLISHED BY
Microsoft Press
A Division of Microsoft Corporation
One Microsoft Way
Redmond, Washington 98052-6399

Library of Congress Cataloging-in-Publication Data
Stoecker, Matthew A.
     MCAD/MCSD Self-Paced Training Kit: Developing WIndows-Based Applications with
     Microsoft Visual Basic .NET, and Microsoft Visual C# .NET/ Matthew A. Stoecker with
     Microsoft Corporation. --2nd ed.
          p. cm.
     First ed. was entered under title. c2002.
     Includes index.
     ISBN 0-7356-1926-3
     1. Electronic data processing personnel–Certification.   2. Microsoft
software--Examinations--Study guides.   3. Microsoft Visual Basic.   4. C# (Computer
program language)   5. Microsoft .NET.   I. Title: Developing Windows-Based Applications
with Microsoft Visual Basic .NET, and Microsoft Visual C# .NET.   II. Microsoft
Corporation.   III. MCAD/MCSAD self-paced training kit   IV. Title

     QA76.3.S749835   2003
     005.7'2--dc21   2003042020

Printed and bound in the United States of America.

2 3 4 5 6 7 8 9   QWT   8 7 6 5 4 3

Distributed in Canada by H.B. Fenn and Company Ltd.
A CIP catalogue record for this book is available from the British Library.

Microsoft Press books are available through booksellers and distributors worldwide. For further information about international editions, contact your local Microsoft Corporation office or contact Microsoft
Press International directly at fax (425) 936-7329. Visit our Web site at www.microsoft.com/mspress. Send
comments to *tkinput@microsoft.com*.

Acquisitions Editor: Kathy Harding
Project Editor: Aileen Wrothwell
Technical Editor: Robert Brunner

Body Part No. X09-46539

Contents

About This Book

Welcome to MCAD/MCSD Training Kit—Developing Windows-Based Applications with Microsoft Visual Basic .NET and Microsoft Visual C# .NET. By completing the lessons and associated exercises in this course, you will acquire the knowledge and skills necessary to develop Windows-based solutions using Visual Basic .NET or Visual C# .NET.

This book also addresses the objectives of the Microsoft Certified Professional Exam 70-306 and Exam 70-316. This self-paced course provides content that supports the skills measured by these exams.

Note For more information about becoming a Microsoft Certified Application Developer (MCAD) or a Microsoft Certified Solution Developer (MCSD), see the section titled "The Microsoft Certified Professional Program" later in this introduction.

The "Getting Started" section of this introduction provides important setup instructions that describe the hardware and software requirements to complete the procedures in this course. It also provides information about the networking configuration necessary to complete some of the hands-on procedures. Read through this section thoroughly before you start the lessons.

Intended Audience

This book was created for software developers who need to design, plan, implement, and support Windows-based applications or who plan to take the related Microsoft Certified Professional exams:

- Developing and Implementing Windows-Based Applications with Microsoft Visual Basic .NET and Microsoft Visual Studio .NET (Exam 70-306)
- Developing and Implementing Windows-Based Applications with Microsoft Visual C# .NET and Microsoft Visual Studio .NET (Exam 70-316)

Prerequisites

This course requires that students meet the following prerequisites:

- Be able to create a simple application using Visual Basic .NET or Visual C# .NET.
- Be able to describe the purpose and use of basic controls and menus in a Visual Basic .NET or Visual C# .NET application.

- Be able to describe the relationship between controls and events.
- Have a moderate understanding of basic Structured Query Language (SQL) syntax.

About the CD-ROM

The Supplemental Course Materials CD-ROM contains a variety of informational aids that can be used throughout this book. This includes

- **eBook**   A complete electronic version of this training kit.
- **Completed labs**   Each chapter in this training kit concludes with a lab containing a series of exercises that reinforce the skills you learned. Completed versions of these applications are included so that you can compare your results. You can also use these completed applications as a reference if you get stuck while completing an exercise.
- **Required files**   Practice files that are required to perform the hands-on procedures. You should use these files when indicated in the exercises.
- **Sample exam questions**   To practice taking a certification exam, you can use the sample exam questions provided on the CD-ROM. The sample questions help you assess your understanding of the materials presented in this book.

About the DVD

The DVD contains a 60-day evaluation edition of Microsoft Visual Studio .NET Professional.

Note   The 60-day evaluation edition provided with this training is not the full retail product and is provided only for the purposes of training and evaluation. Microsoft Technical Support does not support this evaluation edition.

For additional support information regarding this book and the CD-ROM and DVD (including answers to commonly asked questions about installation and use), visit the Microsoft Press Technical Support Web site at *www.microsoft.com/mspress/support/*. You can also email TKINPUT@MICROSOFT.COM, or send a letter to Microsoft Press, Attn: Microsoft Press Technical Support, One Microsoft Way, Redmond, WA 98502-6399.

Features of This Book

Each chapter contains sections that are designed to help you get the most educational value from the chapter:

- Each chapter opens with a "Before You Begin" section, which prepares you for completing the chapter.
- The chapters are then divided into lessons. Each lesson contains the reference and procedural information used for a specific skill.
- The lessons and exercises offer step-by-step procedures that are identified with a bullet symbol like the one to the left of this paragraph.
- At the end of each lesson is the "Lesson Summary" section, which identifies the key concepts from the lesson.
- The "Lab" section provides hands-on exercises that reinforce each of the skills taught in each of the chapter lessons. The exercises give you an opportunity to use the skills being presented or explore the part of the application being described. Wherever possible, the exercises in a lab build on each other to create a complete application by the end of that lab.
- At the end of each chapter is the "Review" section that you can use to test what you have learned.

Appendix A, "Questions and Answers," contains all of the questions asked in each chapter with their corresponding answers.

Notes

Two types of Notes appear throughout the lessons.

- Notes marked **Note** contain supplemental information.
- Notes marked **Caution** contain warnings about the possible loss of data.

Notational Conventions

The following notational conventions are used throughout this book.

- Characters or commands that you type appear in **bold** type.
- *Italic* in syntax statements indicates placeholders for variable information. *Italic* is also used for book titles and program elements in text.
- Names of files and folders appear in initial capital letters except when you are to type them directly. Unless otherwise indicated, you can use lowercase letters when you type a filename in a dialog box or at a command prompt.
- Filename extensions, when they appear without a filename, are in lowercase letters.
- Acronyms appear in all uppercase letters.

- `Monospace` type represents code samples, examples of screen text, or entries that you might type at a command prompt or in initialization files.

- Angle brackets < > are used in syntax statements to enclose optional items. For example, <filename> in command syntax indicates that you can choose to type a filename with the command. Type only the information within the brackets, not the brackets themselves.

- When Visual Basic and Visual C# terms are mentioned together in text, the Visual Basic term appears first, followed by the C# term in parentheses.

- Icons represent specific sections in the book as follows:

Icon	Represents
	Supplemental course materials. You will find these materials on the Supplemental Course Materials CD-ROM.
	A hands-on exercise. You should perform the exercise to give yourself an opportunity to use the skills being presented in the lesson.
	Chapter review questions. These questions at the end of each chapter allow you to test what you have learned in the chapter. You will find the answers to the review questions in Appendix A, "Questions and Answers" at the end of the book.

Keyboard Conventions

- A plus sign (+) between two key names means that you must press those keys at the same time. For example, Press Alt+Tab means that you hold down Alt while you press Tab.

- A comma (,) between two or more key names means that you must press each of the keys consecutively, not together. For example, Press Alt, F, X means that you press and release each key in sequence. Press Alt+W, L means that you first press Alt and W at the same time, and then release them and press L.

- You can choose menu commands by using the keyboard. Press the Alt key to activate the menu bar, and then sequentially press the keys that correspond to the highlighted or underlined letter of the menu name and the command name. For some commands, you can also press a key combination listed on the menu.

- You can select or clear check boxes or option buttons in dialog boxes with the keyboard. Press the Alt key, and then press the key that corresponds to the underlined letter of the option name. Or you can press Tab until the option is highlighted, and then press the Spacebar to select or clear the check box or option button.

- You can cancel the display of a dialog box by pressing the Esc key.

Chapter and Appendix Overview

This self-paced training kit combines notes, hands-on procedures, and review questions to teach you how to create Windows-based applications with Visual Basic .NET and Visual C# .NET. It is designed to be completed from beginning to end, but you can choose a customized track and only complete the sections that interest you. (See the next section, "Finding the Best Starting Point for You," for more information.) If you choose the customized track option, see the "Before You Begin" section in each chapter. Any hands-on procedures that require preliminary work from preceding chapters refer to the appropriate chapters.

The book is divided into the following sections and chapters:

- The "About This Book" section contains a self-paced training overview and introduces the components of this training kit. Read this section thoroughly to get the greatest educational value from this self-paced training and to plan which lessons you will complete.

- Chapter 1, "Introduction to the .NET Framework," introduces the .NET Framework, the common language runtime, and the .NET base class library. It describes how memory is managed using garbage collection. It explains how to create a class and a structure, and how to implement and scope methods.

- Chapter 2, "Creating the User Interface," describes the elements of the user interface and the steps you take in creating it. It explains controls, menus, using form and control events, and validating user input.

- Chapter 3, "Types and Members," explains in detail how to implement and use custom types. It explains how to create arrays and collections, and how to implement properties and events.

- Chapter 4, "Object-Oriented Programming and Polymorphism," introduces the concepts of object-oriented programming. It describes how to create overloaded members and how to implement polymorphism through inheritance and interface implementation.

- Chapter 5, "Testing and Debugging Your Application," describes how to use the tools provided by Visual Studio .NET to debug your application. It explains how to use the Trace and Debug classes to get real-time feedback from your application, and how to throw and handle exceptions. This chapter also describes how to develop a unit test plan for your application.

- Chapter 6, "Data Access Using ADO.NET," explains in detail how to use Microsoft ADO.NET to access data from a variety of sources. Connected and disconnected data access is explained, and binding data to the user interface is examined as well. This chapter also provides a sampling of XML data topics.

- Chapter 7, "Creating Controls Using the .NET Framework," describes how to use the .NET Framework to create user controls, custom controls, and inherited controls. It describes how to render visual elements with GDI+ technology, and how to accomplish some common tasks with controls.

- Chapter 8, "Advanced .NET Framework Topics," describes several advanced development topics. It explains how to create localizable applications, and how to implement printing in your application. It describes how to access COM components, the Windows API, and Web Services. It also explains how to implement help and set accessibility properties for your application.

- Chapter 9, "Assemblies, Configuration, and Security," explains how to create assemblies and use resources. It describes how to retrieve values from the configuration file and use them in your application. This chapter also explains how to implement role-based and code access security in your application.

- Chapter 10, "Deploying Your Application," explains how to create and configure a setup project for your application and how to plan a deployment scheme for your program.

- Appendix A, "Questions and Answers," lists all of the review questions from the book, showing the page number for each question and the suggested answer.

- The Glossary provides definitions for many of the terms and concepts presented in this training kit.

Finding the Best Starting Point for You

Because this book is self-paced, you can skip some lessons and revisit them later. Use the following table to find the best starting point for you:

If you	Follow this learning path
Are preparing to take the Microsoft Certified Professional Exam 70-306 or Exam 70-316	Read the "Getting Started" section. Then work through the remaining chapters in any order.
Want to review information about specific topics from the exam	Use the "Where to Find Specific Skills in This Book" section that follows this table.

Where to Find Specific Skills in This Book

The following table provides a list of the skills measured on certification Exam 70-306, Developing and Implementing Windows-Based Applications with Microsoft Visual Basic .NET and Microsoft Visual Studio .NET, and Exam 70-316, Developing and Implementing Windows-Based Applications with Microsoft Visual C# .NET and Microsoft Visual Studio .NET. The table provides the skill and where in this book you will find the lesson relating to that skill.

Note   Exam skills are subject to change without prior notice and at the sole discretion of Microsoft.

Table A.1. Creating User Services

Skill Being Measured	Location in Book
Create a Windows Form by using the Windows Form Designer	Chapter 2, Lesson 2
Add controls to a Windows Form	Chapter 2, Lesson 3
Implement navigation for the user interface	Chapter 2, Lesson 2
Validate user input	Chapter 2, Lesson 5
Implement error handling in the UI	Chapter 5, Lesson 4
Implement online user assistance	Chapter 8, Lesson 4
Display data from a data source	Chapter 6, Lesson 4
Incorporate existing code into a Microsoft Windows-based application	Chapter 8, Lesson 2
Instantiate and invoke Web Services and components	Chapter 8, Lesson 2
Implement globalization	Chapter 8, Lesson 5
Create, implement, and handle events	Chapter 3, Lesson 4
Implement print capability	Chapter 8, Lesson 1
Implement accessibility features	Chapter 8, Lesson 3

Table A.2. Creating and Managing Components and .NET Assemblies

Skill Being Measured	Location in Book
Create and modify a .NET assembly	Chapter 9, Lesson 1
Create a Windows control	Chapter 7, Lesson 2

Table A.3. Consuming and Manipulating Data

Skill Being Measured	Location in Book
Access and manipulate data from a Microsoft SQL Server database by creating and using ad hoc queries and stored procedures	Chapter 6, Lessons 1, 2, 3
Access and manipulate data from a data store	Chapter 6, Lessons 1, 2, 3
Handle data errors	Chapter 6, Lesson 3

Table A.4. Testing and Debugging

Skill Being Measured	Location in Book
Create a unit test plan	Chapter 5, Lesson 3
Implement tracing	Chapter 5, Lesson 2
Debug, rework, and resolve defects in code	Chapter 5, Lesson 1

Table A.5.   Deploying a Windows-Based Application

Skill Being Measured	Location in Book
Plan the deployment of a Windows-based application	Chapter 10, Lesson 1
Create a setup program that installs an application and allows for the application to be uninstalled	Chapter 10, Lesson 1
Deploy a Windows-based application	Chapter 10, Lesson 1
Add assemblies to the Global Assembly Cache	Chapter 9, Lesson 1; Chapter 10, Lesson 2
Verify security policies for a deployed application	Chapter 10, Lesson 2

Table A.6.   Maintaining and Supporting a Windows-Based Application

Skill Being Measured	Location in Book
Optimize the performance of a Windows-based application	Chapter 5, Lesson 2; Chapter 9, Lesson 2
Diagnose and resolve errors and issues	Chapter 5, Lesson 1; Chapter 9, Lesson 2

Table A.7.   Configuring and Securing a Windows-Based Application

Skill Being Measured	Location in Book
Configure a Windows-based application	Chapter 9, Lesson 2
Configure security for a Windows-based application	Chapter 9, Lesson 3
Configure authorization	Chapter 9, Lesson 3

Getting Started

This self-paced training kit contains hands-on procedures to help you learn about developing Windows-based applications with Visual Basic .NET and Visual C# .NET.

Hardware Requirements

Each computer must have the following minimum configuration. All hardware should be on the Microsoft Windows XP or Microsoft Windows 2000 Hardware Compatibility List.

- Pentium II class processor, 450 megahertz (MHz).
- 160 MB physical memory, 256 MB recommended.
- CD-ROM or DVD drive, 12x or faster recommended.

> **Note** A DVD drive is required to install the Visual Studio .NET Professional Evaluation Edition software.

- 3.5 gigabytes (GB) on installation drive, which includes 500 megabytes (MB) on system drive.
- Super VGA (800 x 600) or higher-resolution monitor with 256 colors.
- Microsoft Mouse or compatible pointing device.

Software Requirements

The following software is required to complete the procedures in this course.

- Microsoft Windows 2000 or Microsoft Windows XP Professional Edition
- Microsoft Visual Studio .NET, Professional Edition, Enterprise Developer Edition, or Enterprise Architect Edition
- Microsoft Access 2000 or later with the Jet 4.0 data engine

Setup Instructions

Set up your computer according to the manufacturer's instructions.

The Exercise Files

The Supplemental Course Materials CD-ROM contains a set of exercise files and solution files, some of which you will need to copy to your hard disk drive to complete the exercises in this book.

To install the exercise files to your hard disk drive

1. Insert the Supplemental Course Materials CD-ROM into your CD-ROM drive.

> **Note** If AutoRun is disabled on your machine, refer to the Readme.txt file on the CD-ROM.

2. Select Labs Folder on the user interface menu, and then select the exercise file you want to view. If required for the exercise, copy the files to a working folder on your hard disk drive.

The eBook

The CD-ROM also includes an electronic version of the book that you can view using a Hypertext Markup Language (HTML) browser.

To use the eBook

1. Insert the Supplemental Course Materials CD-ROM into your CD-ROM drive.

   Note   If AutoRun is disabled on your machine, refer to the Readme.txt file on the CD-ROM.

2. Click eBook on the user interface menu and follow the prompts.

   Note   You must have the Supplemental Course Materials CD-ROM inserted in your CD-ROM drive to run the eBook.

Sample Exam Questions

To install the sample exam questions to your hard disk drive

1. Insert the Supplemental Course Materials CD-ROM into your CD-ROM drive.

   Note   If AutoRun is disabled on your machine, refer to the Readme.txt file on the CD-ROM.

2. Click Sample Exam Questions on the user interface menu and follow the prompts.

The Microsoft Certified Professional Program

The Microsoft Certified Professional (MCP) program provides the best method to prove your command of current Microsoft products and technologies. Microsoft, an industry leader in certification, is on the forefront of testing methodology. Microsoft exams and corresponding certifications are developed to validate your mastery of critical competencies as you design and develop, or implement and support, solutions with Microsoft products and technologies. Computer professionals who become Microsoft certified are recognized as experts and are sought after industry-wide.

The Microsoft Certified Professional program offers multiple certifications based on specific areas of technical expertise including:

- **Microsoft Certified Application Developer (MCAD) for Microsoft .NET**   Qualified to develop and maintain department-level applications, components, Web or desktop clients, or back-end data services.
- **Microsoft Certified Solution Developer (MCSD)**   Qualified to design and develop custom business solutions with Microsoft development tools, technologies, and platforms and Microsoft Windows architecture.

- **Microsoft Certified Professional (MCP)**   Individuals who have demonstrated in-depth knowledge of at least one Microsoft Windows operating system or architecturally significant platform. An MCP is qualified to implement a Microsoft product or technology as part of a business solution for an organization.

- **Microsoft Certified Systems Engineer (MCSE) on Microsoft Windows 2000**   Qualified to effectively analyze the business requirements, and design and implement the infrastructure for business solutions based on the Microsoft Windows 2000 platform and Microsoft .NET Enterprise Servers.

- **Microsoft Certified Systems Administrator (MCSA) on Microsoft Windows 2000**   Individuals who implement, manage, and troubleshoot existing network and system environments based on the Microsoft Windows 2000 and Windows .NET Server operating systems.

- **Microsoft Certified Database Administrator (MCDBA) on Microsoft SQL Server 2000**   Individuals who derive physical database designs, develop logical data models, create physical databases, create data services by using Transact-SQL, manage and maintain databases, configure and manage security, monitor and optimize databases, and install and configure Microsoft SQL Server.

- **Microsoft Certified Trainer (MCT)**   Instructionally and technically qualified to deliver Microsoft Official Curriculum through a Microsoft Certified Technical Education Center (CTEC).

Microsoft Certification Benefits

Microsoft certification, one of the most comprehensive certification programs available for assessing and maintaining software-related skills, is a valuable measure of an individual's knowledge and expertise. Microsoft certification is awarded to individuals who have successfully demonstrated their ability to perform specific tasks and implement solutions with Microsoft products. Not only does this provide an objective measure for employers to consider, it also provides guidance for what an individual should know to be proficient. And as with any skills-assessment and benchmarking measure, certification brings a variety of benefits to the individual and to employers and organizations.

Microsoft Certification Benefits for Individuals

As a Microsoft Certified Professional, you receive many benefits:

- Industry recognition of your knowledge and proficiency with Microsoft products and technologies.

- A Microsoft Developer Network subscription. MCPs receive rebates or discounts on a one-year subscription to the Microsoft Developer Network (*www.msdn.microsoft.com/subscriptions/*) during the first year of certification. (Fulfillment details will vary depending on your location; please see your Welcome Kit.)

- Access to technical and product information direct from Microsoft through a secured area of the MCP Web site (go to *www.microsoft.com/traincert/mcp/ mcpsecure.asp/*).

- Access to exclusive discounts on products and services from selected companies. Individuals who are currently certified can learn more about exclusive discounts by visiting the MCP secured Web site (go to *www.microsoft.com/ traincert/mcp/mcpsecure.asp/* and select the "Other Benefits" link).

- MCP logo, certificate, transcript, wallet card, and lapel pin to identify you as a Microsoft Certified Professional (MCP) to colleagues and clients. Electronic files of logos and transcript can be downloaded from the MCP secured Web site (go to *www.microsoft.com/traincert/mcp/mcpsecure.asp/*) upon certification.

- Invitations to Microsoft conferences, technical training sessions, and special events.

- Free access to Microsoft Certified Professional Magazine Online, a career and professional development magazine. Secured content on the Microsoft Certified Professional Magazine Online Web site includes the current issue (available only to MCPs), additional online-only content and columns, an MCP-only database, and regular chats with Microsoft and other technical experts.

- Discount on a membership to PASS (for MCPs only), the Professional Association for SQL Server. In addition to playing a key role in the only worldwide, user-run SQL Server user group endorsed by Microsoft, members enjoy unique access to a world of educational opportunities (go to *www.microsoft.com/ traincert/mcp/mcpsecure.asp/*).

An additional benefit is received by Microsoft Certified System Engineers (MCSEs):

- A 50-percent rebate or discount off the estimated retail price of a one-year subscription to TechNet or TechNet Plus during the first year of certification. (Fulfillment details will vary depending on your location. Please see your Welcome Kit.) In addition, about 95 percent of the CD-ROM content is available free online at the TechNet Web site (*www.microsoft.com/technet/*).

Additional benefits are received by Microsoft Certified Database Administrators (MCDBAs):

- A 50-percent rebate or discount off the estimated retail price of a one-year subscription to TechNet or TechNet Plus during the first year of certification. (Fulfillment details will vary depending on your location. Please see your Welcome Kit.) In addition, about 95 percent of the CD-ROM content is available free online at the TechNet Web site (*www.microsoft.com/technet/*).

- A one-year subscription to SQL Server Magazine. Written by industry experts, the magazine contains technical and how-to tips and advice—a must for anyone working with SQL Server.

A list of benefits for Microsoft Certified Trainers (MCTs) can be found at *www.microsoft.com/traincert/mcp/mct/benefits.asp/*.

Microsoft Certification Benefits for Employers and Organizations

Through certification, computer professionals can maximize the return on investment in Microsoft technology. Research shows that Microsoft certification provides organizations with:

- Excellent return on training and certification investments by providing a standard method of determining training needs and measuring results.
- Increased customer satisfaction and decreased support costs through improved service, increased productivity, and greater technical self-sufficiency.
- Reliable benchmarks for hiring, promoting, and career planning.
- Recognition and rewards for productive employees by validating their expertise.
- Retraining options for existing employees so they can work effectively with new technologies.
- Assurance of quality when outsourcing computer services.

Requirements for Becoming a Microsoft Certified Professional

The certification requirements differ for each certification and are specific to the products and job functions addressed by the certification.

To become a Microsoft Certified Professional, you must pass rigorous certification exams that provide a valid and reliable measure of technical proficiency and expertise. These exams are designed to test your expertise and ability to perform a role or task with a product, and are developed with the input of professionals in the industry. Questions in the exams reflect how Microsoft products are used in actual organizations, giving them "real-world" relevance.

- Microsoft Certified Professional candidates are required to pass one operating system exam. Candidates can pass additional Microsoft certification exams to further qualify their skills with other Microsoft products, development tools, or desktop applications.
- Microsoft Certified Systems Engineers are required to pass five core exams and two elective exams.
- Microsoft Certified Systems Administrators are required to pass three core exams and one elective exam that provide a valid and reliable measure of technical proficiency and expertise.
- Microsoft Certified Database Administrators are required to pass three core exams and one elective exam that measure technical proficiency and expertise.

- Microsoft Certified Solution Developers are required to pass three core Microsoft Windows operating system technology exams and one BackOffice technology elective exam.

- Microsoft Certified Trainers are required to meet instructional and technical requirements specific to each Microsoft Official Curriculum course they are certified to deliver. The MCT program requires on-going training to meet the requirements for the annual renewal of certification. For more information about becoming a Microsoft Certified Trainer, visit *www.microsoft.com/ traincert/mcp/mct/* or contact a regional service center near you.

Technical Training for Computer Professionals

Technical training is available in a variety of ways including instructor-led classes, online instruction, or self-paced training available at thousands of locations worldwide.

Self-Paced Training

For motivated learners who are ready for the challenge, self-paced instruction is the most flexible, cost-effective way to increase your knowledge and skills.

A full line of self-paced print and computer-based training materials is available direct from the source—Microsoft Press. Microsoft Official Curriculum courseware kits from Microsoft Press are designed for advanced computer system professionals and are available from Microsoft Press and the Microsoft Developer Division. Self-paced training kits from Microsoft Press feature print-based instructional materials along with CD-ROM–based product software, multimedia presentations, lab exercises, and practice files. The Mastering Series provides in-depth, interactive training on CD-ROMs for experienced developers. They're both great ways to prepare for the Microsoft Certified Professional (MCP) exams.

Online Training

For a more flexible alternative to instructor-led classes, turn to online instruction. It's as near as the Internet, and it's ready whenever you are. Learn at your own pace and on your own schedule in a virtual classroom, often with easy access to an online instructor. Without ever leaving your desk, you can gain the expertise you need. Online instruction covers a variety of Microsoft products and technologies. It includes options ranging from Microsoft Official Curriculum to choices available nowhere else. It's training on demand with access to learning resources 24 hours a day. Online training is available through Microsoft Certified Technical Education Centers (CTECs).

Microsoft Certified Technical Education Centers

Microsoft Certified Technical Education Centers (CTECs) are the best source for instructor-led training that can help you prepare to become a Microsoft Certified Professional. The Microsoft CTEC program is a worldwide network of qualified technical training organizations that provide authorized delivery of Microsoft Official Curriculum courses by Microsoft Certified Trainers to computer professionals.

For a listing of CTEC locations in the United States and Canada, visit *www.microsoft.com/traincert/ctec/*.

Technical Support

Every effort has been made to ensure the accuracy of this book and the contents of the companion disc. If you have comments, questions, or ideas regarding this book or the companion disc, please send them to Microsoft Press using either of the following methods:

E-mail:
TKINPUT@MICROSOFT.COM

Postal Mail:

Microsoft Press
Attn: Editor MCAD/MCSD Training Kit—Developing Windows-Based Applications with Microsoft Visual Basic .NET and Visual C# .NET
One Microsoft Way
Redmond, WA 98052-6399

The Microsoft Press Web site (*www.microsoft.com/mspress/support/*) provides corrections for books. Please note that product support is not offered through this Web site. For further information regarding Microsoft software support options, please connect to *www.microsoft.com/support/* or call Microsoft Support Network Sales at (800) 936-3500.

For information about ordering the full version of any Microsoft software, please call Microsoft Sales at (800) 426-9400 or visit *www.microsoft.com*.

C H A P T E R   1

Introduction to the .NET Framework

About This Chapter

This chapter discusses the Microsoft .NET Framework and the common language runtime. It also provides an introduction to the syntax of class, structure, and method declaration.

Before You Begin

There are no prerequisites to completing the lessons in this chapter.

Lesson 1: The .NET Framework and the Common Language Runtime

The Microsoft .NET Framework is an integrated and managed environment for the development and execution of your code. This lesson is an introduction to the .NET Framework, the philosophy behind it, and how it works.

After this lesson, you will be able to

- Describe the elements of the .NET Framework
- Describe the parts of an assembly and identify what is contained in each part
- Describe how a .NET application is compiled and executed

Estimated lesson time: 20 minutes

Overview of the .NET Framework

The .NET Framework is a managed type-safe environment for application development and execution. The .NET Framework manages all aspects of your program's execution. It allocates memory for the storage of data and instructions, grants or denies the appropriate permissions to your application, initiates and manages application execution, and manages the reallocation of memory from resources that are no longer needed. The .NET Framework consists of two main components: the common language runtime and the .NET Framework class library.

The common language runtime can be thought of as the environment that manages code execution. It provides core services, such as code compilation, memory allocation, thread management, and garbage collection. Through the common type system (CTS), it enforces strict type-safety and ensures that code is executed in a safe environment by also enforcing code access security.

The .NET Framework class library provides a collection of useful and reusable types that are designed to integrate with the common language runtime. The types provided by the .NET Framework are object-oriented and fully extensible, and they allow you to seamlessly integrate your applications with the .NET Framework. The .NET base class library is discussed further in Lesson 2 of this chapter.

Languages and the .NET Framework

The .NET Framework is designed for cross-language compatibility, which means, simply, that .NET components can interact with each other no matter what supported language they were written in originally. So, an application written in Microsoft Visual Basic .NET might reference a dynamic-link library (DLL) file written in Microsoft Visual C#, which in turn might access a resource written in managed Microsoft Visual C++ or any other .NET language. This language interoperability extends to full object-oriented inheritance. A Visual Basic .NET class might be derived from a C# class, for example, or vice versa.

This level of cross-language compatibility is possible because of the common language runtime. When a .NET application is compiled, it is converted from the language in which it was written (Visual Basic .NET, C#, or any other .NET-compliant language) to Microsoft Intermediate Language (MSIL or IL). MSIL is a low-level language that the common language runtime can read and understand. Because all .NET executables and DLLs exist as MSIL, they can freely interoperate. The Common Language Specification (CLS) defines the minimum standards to which .NET language compilers must conform. Thus, the CLS ensures that any source code successfully compiled by a .NET compiler can interoperate with the .NET Framework.

The CTS ensures type compatibility between .NET components. Because .NET applications are converted to IL prior to deployment and execution, all primitive data types are represented as .NET types. Thus, a Visual Basic *Integer* and a C# *int* are both represented in IL code as a *System.Int32*. Because both languages use a common type system, it is possible to transfer data between components and avoid time-consuming conversions or hard-to-find errors.

Visual Studio .NET ships with languages such as Visual Basic .NET, Visual C#, and Visual C++ with managed extensions, as well as the JScript scripting language. You can also write managed code for the .NET Framework in other languages. Third-party tools and compilers exist for Fortran, Cobol, Perl, and a host of other languages. All of these languages share the same cross-language compatibility and inheritability. Thus, you can write code for the .NET Framework in the language of your choice, and it will be able to interact with code written for the .NET Framework in any other language.

The Structure of a .NET Application

To understand how the common language runtime manages code execution, you must examine the structure of a .NET application. The primary unit of a .NET application is the *assembly*. An assembly is a self-describing collection of code, resources, and metadata. The *assembly manifest* contains information about what is contained within the assembly. The assembly manifest provides:

- Identity information, such as the assembly's name and version number
- A list of all types exposed by the assembly
- A list of other assemblies required by the assembly
- A list of code access security instructions, including permissions required by the assembly and permissions to be denied the assembly

Each assembly has one and only one assembly manifest, and it contains all the description information for the assembly. However, the assembly manifest can be contained in its own file or within one of the assembly's *modules*.

An assembly contains one or more modules. A module contains the code that makes up your application or library, and it contains metadata that describes that code. When you compile a project into an assembly, your code is converted from high-level code to IL. Because all managed code is first converted to IL code, applications written in different languages can easily interact. For example, one developer might write an application in Visual C# that accesses a DLL in Visual Basic .NET. Both resources will be converted to IL modules before being executed, thus avoiding any language-incompatibility issues.

Each module also contains a number of types. Types are templates that describe a set of data encapsulation and functionality. There are two kinds of types: reference types (classes) and value types (structures). These types are discussed in greater detail in Lesson 2 of this chapter. Each type is described to the common language runtime in the assembly manifest. A type can contain fields, properties, and methods, each of which should be related to a common functionality. For example, you might have a class that represents a bank account. It contains fields, properties, and methods related to the functions needed to implement a bank account. A field represents storage of a particular type of data. One field might store the name of an account holder, for example. Properties are similar to fields, but properties usually provide some kind of validation when data is set or retrieved. You might have a property that represents an account balance. When an attempt is made to change the value, the property can check to see if the attempted change is greater than a predetermined limit. If the value is greater than the limit, the property does not allow the change. Methods represent behavior, such as actions taken on data stored within the class or changes to the user interface. Continuing with the bank account example, you might have a *Transfer* method that transfers a balance from a checking account to a savings account, or an *Alert* method that warns users when their balances fall below a predetermined level.

Compilation and Execution of a .NET Application

When you compile a .NET application, it is not compiled to binary machine code; rather, it is converted to IL. This is the form that your deployed application takes—one or more assemblies consisting of executable files and DLL files in IL form. At least one of these assemblies will contain an executable file that has been designated as the entry point for the application.

When execution of your program begins, the first assembly is loaded into memory. At this point, the common language runtime examines the assembly manifest and determines the requirements to run the program. It examines security permissions requested by the assembly and compares them with the system's security policy. If the system's security policy does not allow the requested permissions, the application will not run. If the application passes the system's security policy, the common language runtime executes the code. It creates a process for the application to run in and begins application execution. When execution starts, the first bit of code that needs to be executed is loaded into memory and compiled into native binary code from IL by the common language runtime's Just-In-Time (JIT) compiler. Once compiled, the code is executed and stored in memory as native code. Thus, each portion of code is compiled only once when an application executes. Whenever program execution branches to code that has not yet run, the JIT compiler compiles it ahead of execution and stores it in memory as binary code. This way, application performance is maximized because only the parts of a program that are executed are compiled.

Lesson Summary

■ The .NET Framework is a foundation for software development. The .NET Framework consists of the common language runtime, which provides many of the core services required for program execution, and the .NET base class library, which exposes a set of pre-developed classes to facilitate program development. The CLS defines a minimum set of standards that all languages using the .NET Framework must support, and the CTS ensures type compatibility between components developed in different languages.

■ The primary unit of a .NET application is the assembly, which includes an assembly manifest. The assembly manifest describes the assembly and one or more modules, and the modules contain the source code for the application.

■ A .NET executable is stored as an IL file. When loaded, the assembly is checked against the security policy of the local system. If it is allowed to run, the first assembly is loaded into memory and JIT compiled into native binary code, where it is stored for the remainder of the program's execution.

Lesson 2: The .NET Base Class Library

The .NET base class library is a collection of object-oriented types and interfaces that provide object models and services for many of the complex programming tasks you will face. Most of the types presented by the .NET base class library are fully extensible, allowing you to build types that incorporate your own functionality into your managed code. This lesson introduces some of the .NET base class library namespaces and describes how to reference the library and use its types and methods.

After this lesson, you will be able to

- Describe the .NET base class library
- Explain the difference between value types and reference types
- Create a reference to a namespace
- Create an instance of a .NET Framework class and value type

Estimated lesson time: 30 minutes

The .NET Framework base class library contains the base classes that provide many of the services and objects you need when writing your applications. The class library is organized into *namespaces*. A namespace is a logical grouping of types that perform related functions. For example, the *System.Windows.Forms* namespace contains all the types that make up Windows forms and the controls used in those forms.

Namespaces are logical groupings of related classes. The namespaces in the .NET base class library are organized hierarchically. The root of the .NET Framework is the *System* namespace. Other namespaces can be accessed with the period operator. A typical namespace construction appears as follows:

```
System
System.Data
System.Data.SQLClient
```

The first example refers to the *System* namespace. The second refers to the *System.Data* namespace. The third example refers to the *System.Data.SQLClient* namespace. Table 1.1 introduces some of the more commonly used .NET base class namespaces.

Table 1.1.   Representative .NET Namespaces

Namespace	Description
System	This namespace is the root for many of the low-level types required by the .NET Framework. It is the root for primitive data types as well, and it is the root for all the other namespaces in the .NET base class library.
System.Collections	This namespace contains classes that represent a variety of different container types, such as *ArrayList*, *SortedList*, *Queue*, and *Stack*. You also can find abstract classes, such as *CollectionBase*, which are useful for implementing your own collection functionality.
System.ComponentModel	This namespace contains classes involved in component creation and containment, such as attributes, type converters, and license providers.
System.Data	This namespace contains classes required for database access and manipulations, as well as additional namespaces used for data access.
System.Data.Common	This namespace contains a set of classes that are shared by the .NET managed data providers.
System.Data.OleDb	This namespace contains classes that make up the managed data provider for OLE DB data access.
System.Data.SQLClient	This namespace contains classes that are optimized for interacting with Microsoft SQL Server.
System.Drawing	This namespace exposes GDI+ functionality and provides classes that facilitate graphics rendering.
System.IO	In this namespace, you will find types for handling file system I/O.
System.Math	This namespace is home to common mathematics functions such as extracting roots and trigonometry.
System.Reflection	This namespace provides support for obtaining information and dynamic creation of types at runtime.
System.Security	This namespace is home to types dealing with permissions, cryptography, and code access security.
System.Threading	This namespace contains classes that facilitate the implementation of multithreaded applications.
System.Windows.Forms	This namespace contains types involved in creating standard Windows applications. Classes that represent forms and controls reside here as well.

The namespace names are self-descriptive by design. Straightforward names make the .NET Framework easy to use and allow you to rapidly familiarize yourself with its contents.

Reference Types and Value Types

Types in the .NET Framework come in two varieties: *value types* and *reference types*. The primary difference between value types and reference types has to do with the way variable data is accessed. To understand this difference, a little background on memory dynamics is required.

Application data memory is divided into two primary components, the *stack* and the *heap*. The stack is an area of memory reserved by the application to run the program. The stack is analogous to a stack of dinner plates. Plates are placed on the stack one on top of another. When a plate is removed from the stack, it is always the last one to have been placed on top that is removed first. So it is with program variables. When a function is called, all the variables used by the function are *pushed* onto the stack. If that function calls additional functions, it pushes additional variables onto the stack. When the most recently called function terminates, all of its variables go out of scope (meaning that they are no longer available to the application) and are *popped* off the stack. Memory consumed by those variables is then freed up, and program execution continues.

The heap, on the other hand, is a separate area of memory reserved for the creation of reusable objects. The common language runtime manages allocation of heap memory for objects and controls the reclamation of memory from unused objects through garbage collection.

Note   Garbage collection is discussed further in Lesson 6 of this chapter.

All the data associated with a value type is allocated on the stack. When a variable of a value type goes out of scope, it is destroyed and its memory is reclaimed. A variable of a reference type, on the other hand, exists in two memory locations. The actual object data is allocated on the heap. A variable containing a pointer to that object is allocated on the stack. When that variable is called by a function, it returns the memory address for the object to which it refers. When that variable goes out of scope, the object reference is destroyed but the object itself is not. If any other references to that object exist, the object remains intact. If the object is left without any references, it is subject to garbage collection. (See Lesson 6 of this chapter.)

Examples of value types include primitives, such as *Integer* (*int*), *Boolean* (*bool*), *Char* (*char*), and so on, as well as user-defined types such as *Structure* (*struct*) and *Enumeration* (*enum*). Classes represent the majority of reference types. Other reference types include the interface, delegate, and array types. Classes and structures are discussed in Lesson 3 of this chapter, and other reference and value types are discussed in Chapter 3.

Note   Throughout this book, when Visual Basic and Visual C# terms are mentioned together, the Visual Basic term appears first, followed by the C# term in parentheses.

Using .NET Framework Types in Your Application

When you begin writing an application, you automatically begin with a reference to the .NET Framework base class library. You reference it so that your application is aware of the base class library and is able to create instances of the types represented by it.

Value Types

In Visual Basic .NET, you use the *Dim* statement to create a variable that represents a value type. In C#, you create a variable by declaring its type and then the variable name. The following code is an example:

Visual Basic .NET

```
Dim myInteger As Integer
```

Visual C#

```
int myInteger;
```

This line tells the runtime to allocate the appropriate amount of memory to hold an integer variable. Although this line creates the variable, it does not assign a value to it. You can assign a value using the assignment operator, as follows:

Visual Basic .NET

```
myInteger = 42
```

Visual C#

```
myInteger = 42;
```

You can also choose to assign a value to a variable upon creation, as shown in this example:

Visual Basic .NET

```
Dim myInteger As Integer = 42
```

Visual C#

```
int myInteger = 42;
```

Note   Although declaration and initialization on a single line was discouraged in Visual Basic 6, there is no performance drawback to single-line declaration and initialization in Visual Basic .NET.

Reference Types

Creating an instance of a type is a two-step process. The first step is to declare the variable as that type, which allocates the appropriate amount of memory for that variable but does not actually create the object. The following syntax declares an object:

Visual Basic .NET

```
Dim myForm As System.Windows.Forms.Form
```

Visual C#

```
System.Windows.Forms.Form myForm;
```

This line tells the runtime to set aside enough memory to hold a *Form* variable and assigns it the name *myForm*, but it does not actually create the *Form* object in memory. The second step, called *instantiation*, actually creates the object. An example of instantiation follows:

Visual Basic .NET

```
myForm = New System.Windows.Forms.Form()
```

Visual C#

```
myForm = new System.Windows.Forms.Form();
```

This line makes a call to the constructor method of the type *System.Windows.Forms.Form* by way of the *New* (*new*) keyword. The constructor is a special method that is invoked only at the beginning of an object's lifetime. It contains any code that must be executed for the object to work (assigning values to properties, for example). If any parameters were required by the constructor, they would be contained within the parentheses at the end of the line. The following example shows declaration and instantiation of a hypothetical *Widget* class that requires a string as a parameter in the constructor. For further discussion of the constructor, see Lesson 4 in this chapter.

Visual Basic .NET

```
Dim myWidget As Widget
myWidget = New Widget("This string is required by the constructor")
```

Visual C#

```
Widget myWidget;
myWidget = new Widget("This string is required by the constructor");
```

If desired, you can also combine both declaration and instantiation into a single statement. By declaring and instantiating an object in the same line, you reserve the memory for the object and immediately create the object that resides in that memory. Although there was a significant performance penalty for this shortcut in previous versions of Visual Basic, Visual Basic .NET and Visual C# are optimized to allow this behavior without any performance loss. The following example shows the one-step declaration and instantiation of a new *Form*:

Visual Basic .NET

```
Dim myForm As New System.Windows.Forms.Form()
```

Visual C#

```
System.Windows.Forms.Form myForm = new
    System.Windows.Forms.Form();
```

Both value types and reference types must be initialized before use. For class and structure fields in Visual Basic .NET, types are initialized with default values on declaration. Numeric value types (such as *integer*) and floating-point types are assigned zero; Boolean variables are assigned *False*; and reference types are assigned to a null reference.

In C#, variables of a reference type have a default value of null. It is recommended that you do not rely on the default value. These variables should not be used until they have been initialized.

Using Value Type and Reference Type Variables

A variable that represents a value type contains all the data represented by that type. A variable that represents a reference type contains a reference to a particular object. This distinction is important. Consider the following example:

Visual Basic .NET

```
Dim x, y As integer
x = 15
y = x
x = 30
' What is the value of y?
```

Visual C#

```
int x, y;
x = 15;
y = x;
x = 30;
// What is the value of y?
```

In this example, two integer variables named x and y are created. X is assigned a value of 15, and then y is assigned the value of x. Next the value of x is changed to 30, and the question is posed: what is the value of y? The answer to this question might seem obvious, and it is y = 15 because x and y are two separate variables and have no effect on each other when changed. When the line y = x is encountered, the value of x is copied to the value of y, and there is no further connection between the two variables.

This situation changes, however, in the case of reference types. Let's reconsider the previous example using a reference type (*Form*) instead of a value type.

Visual Basic .NET

```
Dim x, y As System.Windows.Forms.Form
x = New System.Windows.Forms.Form()
x.Text = "This is Form 1"
y = x
x.Text = "This is Form 2"
' What value does y.Text return?
```

Visual C#

```
System.Windows.Forms.Form x,y;
x = new System.Windows.Forms.Form();
x.Text = "This is Form 1";
y = x;
x.Text = "This is Form 2";
// What value does y.Text return?
```

What value does *y.Text* return? This time, the answer is less obvious. Because *System.Windows.Forms.Form* is a reference type, the variable x does not actually contain a *Form*; rather, it points to an instance of a *Form*. When the line y = x is encountered, the runtime copies the reference from variable x to y. Thus, the variables x and y now point to the same instance of *Form*. Because these two variables refer to the same instance of the object, they will return the same values for properties of that object. Thus, *y.Text* returns "This is Form 2".

The Imports and Using Statements

Up to this point of the chapter, if you wanted to access a type in the .NET Framework base class library, you had to use the full name of the type, including every namespace to which it belonged. For example:

```
System.Windows.Forms.Form
```

This is called the *fully-qualified name*, meaning it refers both to the class and to the namespace in which it can be found. You can make your development environment "aware" of various namespaces by using the *Imports* (Visual Basic .NET) or *using* (Visual C#) statement. This technique allows you to refer to a type using only its generic name and to omit the qualifying namespaces. Thus, you could refer to *System.Windows.Forms.Form* as simply *Form*. In Visual Basic .NET, the *Imports* statement must be placed at the top of the code window, preceding any other statement (except *Option*). In Visual C#, the *using* statement must occur before any other namespace element, such as a class or struct. This example demonstrates use of this statement:

Visual Basic .NET

```
Imports System.Windows.Forms
```

Visual C#

```
using System.Windows.Forms;
```

When two types of the same name exist in more than one imported namespace, you must use the fully qualified name to avoid a naming conflict. Thus, if you are using *MyNameSpaceOne* and *MyNameSpaceTwo*, and each contains a *Widget* class, you would have to refer to *MyNameSpaceOne.Widget* or *MyNameSpaceTwo.Widget* to ensure the correct result.

In C#, you can resolve namespace conflicts such as these by creating an alias. An alias allows you to choose one name to refer to another class. You create an alias using the *using* keyword, as shown below:

Visual C#

```
using myAlias = MyNameSpaceTwo.Widget;
```

After implementing an alias, you can use it in code to represent the aliased class. For example:

Visual C#

```
// You can now refer to MyNameSpaceTwo as myAlias. The
// following two lines produce the same result:
MyNameSpaceTwo.Widget anotherWidget = new MyNameSpaceTwo.Widget() ;
myAlias anotherWidget = new myAlias() ;
```

You cannot create aliases for types in this manner in Visual Basic .NET.

Referencing External Libraries

You might want to use class libraries not contained by the .NET Framework, such as libraries developed by third-party vendors or libraries you developed. To access these external libraries, you must create a reference.

To create a reference to an external library

1. In the Solution Explorer, right-click the References node of your project.

2. From the pop-up menu, choose Add Reference. The Add Reference dialog box appears.

3. Choose the appropriate tab for the library you want to reference. .NET libraries are available on the .NET tab. Legacy COM libraries appear on the COM tab, and local Visual Studio projects appear on the Projects tab.

4. Locate the library you want to reference, and double-click it to add it to the Selected components box. Click OK to confirm the choice of that reference.

Lesson Summary

- The .NET Framework base class library is a library of code that exposes functionality useful for application building. The base class library is organized into namespaces, which contain types and additional namespaces related to common functionality.

- Types can be either value types or reference types. A variable of a value type contains all the data associated with that type. A variable of a reference type contains a pointer to an instance of an object of that type.

- Non-user-defined value types are created on declaration and remain empty until they are assigned a value. Reference types must be instantiated after declaration to create the object. Declaration and instantiation can be combined into a single step without any loss of performance.

- When a value type variable is assigned to another value type variable, the data contained within the first variable is copied into the second. When a reference type variable is assigned to another reference type variable, only the reference to the object is copied, and both variables will refer to the same object.

- You can use the *using* or *Imports* statements to allow references to members of a namespace without using the fully qualified name. If you want to use an external library, you must create a reference to it.

Lesson 3: Using Classes and Structures

You have seen how the .NET Framework base class library provides a plethora of standard types to help you in the development of your applications. You can also create user-defined types that implement custom behaviors. Classes and structures represent the two principal user-defined types.

After this lesson, you will be able to

- Create a new class or structure
- Create an instance of a class or a structure
- Explain the difference between a class and a structure
- Create a nested type

Estimated lesson time: 30 minutes

Classes are templates for *objects*. They describe the kind and amount of data that an object will contain, but they do not represent any particular instance of an object. A real-world example of a class might be "Car"—the abstract idea of what a car is. You know that a car has an engine, four wheels, a body color, an individual fuel efficiency, and a dozen other properties. Although the *Car* class would describe all these properties, as well as have descriptions of actions that the car might perform (roll forward, turn on windshield wipers, and so on), the class would not represent any particular car. Your car, on the other hand, is an object. It has a specific color, a specific fuel efficiency, a specific engine, and four specific wheels. A different car might have different values for each of these properties, but both would be recognizable as being an instance of the *Car* class.

Members

Classes describe the properties and behaviors of the objects they represent through members. Members are methods, fields, properties, and events that belong to a particular class. Fields and properties represent the data about an object—the color of the car, its fuel efficiency, and whether it has an automatic or manual transmission, for example. A method represents something the object can do, such as move forward or turn on headlights. An event represents something interesting that happens to the object, such as overheating or crashing.

Note   This chapter discusses fields and methods. Properties and events are covered in Chapter 3.

Creating Classes

You create a new class by using the *Class* (Visual Basic .NET) or *class* (C#) key-word. For example:

Visual Basic .NET

```
Public Class Widget
' Class member implementation goes here
End Class
```

Visual C#

```
public class Widget
{
    // Class member implementation goes here
}
```

In this example, you use the *Class* (*class*) keyword to create a user-defined class. *Widget* is the name of the class, and the *Public* (*public*) keyword specifies the access level. Access levels are examined in greater detail in Lesson 5 of this chapter.

Creating Structures

Creating structures is very similar to creating classes. You use the *Structure* (Visual Basic .NET) or *struct* (C#) keyword. For example:

Visual Basic .NET

```
Public Structure Vector
    ' Structure implementation goes here
End Structure
```

Visual C#

```
public struct Vector
{
    // Structure implementation goes here
}
```

Adding Members

In Visual Basic .NET, a class comprises everything between the *Class* keyword and the *End Class* keyword. In C#, a class comprises everything within braces (*{}*). Structures are similar. Within the bounds of a class or a structure, you add the members. The following example demonstrates adding a member field to your *Widget* class:

Visual Basic .NET

```
Public Class Widget
    Public Spin As Integer
End Class
```

Visual C#

```
public class Widget
{
    public int Spin;
}
```

Your *Widget* class now contains a member variable named *Spin*. This variable has a *Public* (*public*) access level and can contain an *Integer* (*int*) value. Adding methods as members of your class or structure is discussed in Lesson 4 of this chapter.

Nested Types

Types can contain other types. Types within types are called *nested types*. Using classes as an example, a nested class usually represents an object that the parent class might need to create and manipulate, but which an external object would never need to create independently. An abstract example might be a *Wheel* class. A *Wheel* class might need to create and maintain a collection of *Spoke* objects internally, but outside users would probably never need to create a *Spoke* object independent of a wheel. A more realistic example might be an *AccountManager* class that controls all the interaction with *Account* objects. You might not want to allow *Account* objects to be created independently of the *AccountManager* class, so you would make *Account* a nested class inside *AccountManager*. This does not mean that outside objects can never instantiate objects based on nested classes—this depends on the access level of both the parent class and the nested class. See Lesson 5 of this chapter for more detail. An example of a nested class follows:

Visual Basic .NET

```
Public Class Widget
    ' Widget Class code goes here
    Private Class Widgurt
    ' Widgurt class code goes here
    End Class
End Class
```

Visual C#

```
public class Widget
{
    // Widget class code goes here
    private class Widgurt
    {
        // Widgurt class code goes here.
    }
}
```

Instantiating User-Defined Types

You declare and instantiate a user-defined type the same way that you declare and instantiate a .NET Framework type. For both value types (structures) and reference types (classes), you need to declare the variable as a variable of that type and then create an instance of it with the *New* (*new*) keyword. Examples are as follows:

Visual Basic .NET

```
Public Class Demo
    Public Structure ValueDemo
        Public X As Integer
    End Structure
    Public Class RefDemo
        Public Y As Integer
    End Class
    Public Sub InstantiateTypes()
        ' This line declares a ValueDemo variable
        Dim DemoStructure As ValueDemo
        ' This line creates an instance of ValueDemo on the stack
        DemoStructure = New ValueDemo()
        ' The variable is ready to receive data.
        DemoStructure.X = 15
        ' This line declares a RefDemo variable, but doesn't
        ' create an instance of the class
        Dim DemoClass As RefDemo
        ' This line actually creates the object
        DemoClass = New RefDemo()
        ' And you can now assign value to its members
        DemoClass.Y = 15
    End Sub
End Class
```

Visual C#

```
public class Demo
{
    public struct ValueDemo
    {
        public int X;
    }
    public class RefDemo
    {
        public int Y;
    }
    public void InstantiateTypes()
    {
        // This line declares a ValueDemo variable
        ValueDemo DemoStructure;
        // This line creates an instance of ValueDemo on the stack
        DemoStructure = new ValueDemo();
```

```
    // The variable is ready to receive data
    DemoStructure.X = 15;
    // This line declares a RefDemo variable, but doesn't create
    // an instance of the class
    RefDemo DemoClass;
    DemoClass = new RefDemo();
    // And you can now assign value to its members
    DemoClass.Y = 15;
  }
}
```

Classes vs. Structures

On the surface, classes and structures appear to be very similar. Both can contain members such as fields and methods, both require a constructor to create a new instance of themselves, and like all types in the .NET Framework, both inherit from *Object*. The key difference between classes and structures is that classes are reference types and structures are value types. On a low level, this means that the instance data for classes is allocated on the heap, whereas the instance data for structures is allocated on the stack. Access to the stack is designed to be light and fast, but storage of large amounts of data on the stack can impede overall application performance.

In practical terms, *that* structures are best used for smaller, lightweight objects that contain relatively little instance data or for objects that do not persist for long. Classes are best used for larger objects that contain more instance data and are expected to exist in memory for extended periods.

Lesson Summary

- User-defined types include classes and structures. Both can have members, which are fields, properties, methods, or events. Classes are reference types, and structures are value types.

- The *Class* keyword is used to create new classes in Visual Basic .NET and the *class* keyword is used for Visual C#. Structures are created by using the *Structure* keyword in Visual Basic .NET and the *struct* keyword in Visual C#. Both classes and structures can contain nested types.

- User-defined types are instantiated in the same manner as predefined types, except that both value types and reference types must use the *New* (*new*) keyword upon instantiation.

Lesson 4: Using Methods

Methods do the work of classes and structures. They calculate values, update data, receive input, and perform all the manipulations that make up the behavior of a type. In this lesson, you will learn how to create methods, use parameters, and create constructors and destructors for your class.

After this lesson, you will be able to

- Create a new method
- Specify return types for your method
- Specify input and output parameters for your method
- Create a constructor and a destructor for your class

Estimated lesson time: 45 minutes

Adding Methods

You can add methods as members to your classes. Methods represent actions your class can take. Methods generally come in two varieties: those that return a value (functions in Visual Basic) and those that do not return a value (subs in Visual Basic). The following code shows an example of both kinds of methods:

Visual Basic .NET

```
Public Sub MySub()
    MessageBox.Show("This is a non-value returning method")
End Sub

' Note that the underscore symbol ( _ ) is used in
' Visual Basic .NET to continue a line from one line to the next.
Public Function Add(ByVal first as Integer, ByVal second as _
    Integer) As Integer
    Dim Result as Integer
    Result = first + second
    Return Result
End Function
```

Visual C# makes no distinction between methods that return a value and methods that do not. In either case, you must specify the return value type. If the method does not return a value, its return type is *void*. Here are examples of C# methods:

Visual C#

```
public void myVoidMethod()
{
    MessageBox.Show("This method doesn't return a value");
}
```

```
 public int Add(int first, int second)
{
   int Result;
   Result = first + second;
   return Result;
}
```

Calling Methods

A method does not execute until it is called. You can call a method by referencing its name along with any required parameters. For example:

Visual Basic .NET

```
' This line calls the Rotate method, with two parameters
Rotate(45, "Degrees")
```

Visual C#

```
// This line calls the Rotate method, with two parameters
Rotate(45, "Degrees");
```

The *Main* method is a special case. It is called upon initiation of program execution. Destructors, another special case, are called by the runtime just prior to destruction of an object. Constructors, a third special case, are executed by an object during its initialization. These methods are discussed further later in this lesson.

Method Variables

Variables declared within methods are said to have *method scope*, which means that once the methods complete execution, they are destroyed and their memory reclaimed. They are said to have gone *out of scope*.

Variables within smaller divisions of methods have even more limited scope. For example, variables declared within a *For-Next* (*for*) loop are accessible only within the loop. The following example demonstrates this because the variable *Y* has gone out of scope:

Visual Basic .NET

```
Public Sub myMethod()
   Dim X as Integer
   For X = 1 to 100
     Dim Y as Integer
     Y = X
   Next X
   ' This line causes an error
   Console.WriteLine(Y.ToString)
End Sub
```

Visual C#

```
public void myMethod()
{
   int X;
   for (X = 1; X < 101; X++)
   {
      int Y;
      Y = X;
   }
   // This line causes an error
   Console.WriteLine(Y.ToString());
}
```

Visual Basic allows you to create method variables that are not destroyed after a method finishes execution. These variables, called *static method variables*, persist in memory and retain their values through multiple executions of a method. You declare a static variable with the *Static* keyword as follows:

Visual Basic .NET

```
Public Sub myMethod()
   Static Iterations as Integer
   ' This variable will be incremented every time this method
   ' is run.
   Iterations += 1
End Sub
```

Although this variable persists in memory, it is still available only during execution of this method. You would use a *Static* variable for a method that needed to keep track of how many times it had been called.

Note   This feature is not available in Visual C#, and the *Static* keyword in C# has a different meaning, which is discussed in Lesson 5 of this chapter.

Parameters

A method can take one or more parameters. A parameter is an argument that is passed to the method by the method that calls it. Parameters are enclosed in parentheses after the method name in the method declaration, and types must be specified for parameters. Here is an example of a method with parameters:

Visual Basic .NET

```
Public Sub DisplayName(ByVal name As String, ByVal age As Byte)
   Console.WriteLine("Hello " & name & ". You are " & _
      age.ToString & " years old.")
End Sub
```

Visual C#

```
public void DisplayName(string name, byte age)
{
   Console.WriteLine("Hello " + name + ". You are " +
     age.ToString() + "years old.");
}
```

This method requires two parameters: a *String* parameter, which is given the local name *name*, and a *Byte* parameter, which is given the local name *age*. These variables have scope only for the duration of the method, and they cannot be used after the method returns. For a further discussion of scope, see Lesson 5 of this chapter.

Parameters can be passed in two ways, *by value* or *by reference*. In the .NET Framework, parameters are passed by value by default. By value means that whenever a parameter is supplied, a copy of the data contained in the variable is made and passed to the method. Any changes made in the value passed to the method are not reflected in the original variable. Although it is the default setting, you can explicitly indicate that a variable be passed by value in Visual Basic with the *ByVal* keyword.

When parameters are passed by reference, on the other hand, a reference to the memory location where the variable resides is supplied instead of an actual value. Thus, every time the method performs a manipulation on that variable, the changes are reflected in the actual object. To pass a parameter by reference in Visual Basic .NET, you use the keyword *ByRef*. In Visual C#, the keyword *ref* is used. The following example demonstrates passing parameters by value or by reference:

Visual Basic .NET

```
Public Sub Demo1()
   Dim x, y As Integer
   x = 15
   y = 20
   ' This line calls the Demo2 method (see below)
   Demo2(x, y)
   ' What values will x and y have now?
   MessageBox.Show("X = " & x.ToString & " Y = " & y.ToString)
End Sub
Public Sub Demo2(ByVal p1 As Integer, ByRef p2 As Integer)
   p1 = p1 + p2
   p2 = p2 + p1
End Sub
```

Visual C#

```
public void Demo1()
{
    int x,y;
    x = 15;
    y = 20;
```

```
    // This line calls the Demo2 method (see below)
    Demo2(x, ref y);
    // What values will x and y have now?
    System.Windows.Forms.MessageBox.Show("X = " + x.ToString() +
        " Y = " + y.ToString());
}
public void Demo2(int p1, ref int p2)
{
    p1 = p1 + p2;
    p2 = p2 + p1;
}
```

In this example, two variables named x and y are created and assigned values. The variables x and y are then passed to the second method. X is passed by value, y is passed by reference, and both are represented in the second method as the variables p1 and p2. Because p1 is passed by value, it represents a copy of the data stored in x, and the manipulations performed on it are for naught. Once the method ends, the variable goes out of scope and its memory is reclaimed. The parameter p2, on the other hand, does not contain a value at all; rather, it contains a reference to the actual data stored in the variable y. Thus, when the line p2 = p2 + p1 is reached, the value stored at the memory location represented by p2 is changed. Therefore, when the final line of the *Demo1* method is reached, the value of x will be unchanged at 15, but the value of y will have changed and will be equal to 55.

Note that if your parameter is a reference type, it makes no difference if the parameter is passed by value or by reference—the behavior will be the same. In both cases, any manipulations done on the parameter will be reflected in the object passed as a parameter.

Output Parameters

In Visual C#, you can also use output parameters. This feature is not available in Visual Basic .NET. An output parameter is a parameter that is passed from a called method to the method that called it—that is, in the reverse direction. Output parameters are useful if you want a method to return more than a single value. An output parameter is specified by using the *out* keyword. Output parameters are always passed by reference and do not need to be initialized before use. The following example demonstrates output parameters:

Visual C#

```
public void aWord (out string Word)
{
    Word = "Mambo";
}
public void ShowWord()
{
    string Word;
    aWord(out Word);
    Console.Writeline("The word of the day is " + Word);
}
```

Here the *ShowWord* method calls the *aWord* method with the output parameter *Word*. The *aWord* method assigns a value to the output parameter *Word*, thereby assigning a value to the *Word* variable.

Optional Parameters

In Visual Basic .NET, you are able to specify optional parameters for your methods. This feature is not available in Visual C#. You specify a parameter as optional using the *Optional* keyword. Optional parameters must be the last parameters in a method declaration, and you must supply default values for optional parameters. The following example demonstrates the use of optional parameters:

Visual Basic .NET

```
Public Sub Cook(ByVal time As Integer, Optional ByVal temp As _
    Integer = 350)
    ' Implementation code goes here
End Sub
```

Constructors and Destructors

The constructor is the first method that is run when an instance of a type is created. In Visual Basic, the constructor is always *Sub New*. In Visual C#, it is a method with the same name as the class. You use a constructor to initialize class and structure data before use. Constructors can never return a value and can be overridden to provide custom initialization functionality. Chapter 4 discusses how to override methods. A constructor can also contain calls to other methods. An example of a constructor follows:

Visual Basic .NET

```
Public Class aClass
    Public Sub New()
        ' Class initialization code goes here
    End Sub
End Class
```

Visual C#

```
public class aClass
{
    public aClass()
    {
        // Class initialization code goes here
    }
}
```

Similarly, a destructor is the last method run by a class. A destructor (known as a *finalizer* in Visual Basic) contains code to "clean up" when a class is destroyed. This cleanup might include decrementing counters or releasing resources. A finalizer in Visual Basic .NET is always *Sub Finalize()*, and a destructor in Visual C# is a method with the same name as the class preceded by a tilde (~). Examples of destructors follow:

Visual Basic .NET

```
Public Class aClass
    Protected Overrides Sub Finalize()
        ' Clean up code goes here
    End Sub
End Class
```

Visual C#

```
public class aClass
{
    ~aClass()
    {
        // Clean up code goes here
    }
}
```

Note   In Visual Basic, the finalizer must use the *Overrides* keyword. The meaning and usage of this keyword is discussed in Chapter 4.

Because garbage collection does not occur in any specific order, it is impossible to determine when a class's destructor will be called.

Lesson Summary

- Methods perform the data manipulation that gives classes and structures their associated behavior. Methods can return a value, but they do not have to. In Visual Basic .NET, methods that return values are called *Functions*, and non-value-returning methods are called *Subs*. In Visual C#, if a method doesn't return a value, it has a return type of *void*. Methods are called by placing the name of the method in the code along with any required parameters.

- Methods can have parameters, which are values required by the method. Parameters are passed by value by default. You can pass parameters by reference with the *ref* keyword (Visual C#) or with the *ByRef* keyword (Visual Basic .NET). For parameters of reference types, the behavior is the same whether passed by value or by reference. Visual C# allows you to specify output parameters from your method. Visual Basic .NET allows you to designate optional parameters.

- The constructor is the first method called on instantiation of a type. The constructor provides a way to set default values for data or perform other necessary functions before the object is available for use. Destructors are called just before an object is destroyed and can be used to run clean-up code. Since object cleanup is controlled by the common language runtime, you cannot control when a destructor is called.

Lesson 5: Scope and Access Levels

Access levels define how types are instantiated and how members are accessed. You use access levels to encapsulate data and methods in your types, and to expose functionality to outside objects. In this lesson, you will learn how access modifiers control code access and how to use them in your types.

After this lesson, you will be able to

- Explain the meanings of different access levels and how they affect access to classes, variables, and nested types
- Explain what scope is and how it affects program execution

Estimated lesson time: 20 minutes

You can control how elements of your application are accessed by using access modifiers. Access modifiers are keywords such as *Public* (*public*), *Private* (*private*), and *Friend* (*internal*) that precede a variable or type declaration. The keyword that is used controls the level of access the member is allowed. When an access modifier precedes a member declaration, it affects the scope of that member, meaning it controls what code can access it. When a modifier precedes a type declaration, it determines both the scope of its members and how that type is instanced.

Member Access Modifiers

Type members can have modifiers to control their scope. Table 1.2 summarizes the different access levels.

Table 1.2.   Access Levels

Access Modifier	Effect on Members
Public (Visual Basic .NET), *public* (Visual C#)	Can be accessed from anywhere.
Private (Visual Basic .NET), *private* (Visual C#)	Can be accessed only by members within the type that defines it.
Friend (Visual Basic .NET), *internal* (Visual C#)	Can be accessed from all types within the assembly, but not from outside the assembly.
Protected (Visual Basic .NET), *protected* (Visual C#)	Can be accessed only by members within the type that defines it or types that inherit from that type.
Protected Friend (Visual Basic .NET), *protected internal* (Visual C#)	Can be accessed from all types within the assembly or from types inheriting from the owning type. This is the union of *Protected* (*protected*) and *Friend* (*internal*) access.

Any member with the *Public* (*public*) modifier is visible to all code outside the class. Thus, other objects can access and modify public fields and can call public methods. Conversely, *Private* (*private*) methods are visible only inside the type to which they belong and cannot be accessed from the outside. A third access modifier, *Friend* (*internal*), indicates that members can be accessed by other types in the same assembly but cannot be accessed from types outside the assembly. The *Protected* (*protected*) modifier allows access from within the type to which the member belongs and to any types that inherit that type. The *Protected Friend* (*protected internal*) level provides the union of *Protected* (*protected*) and *Friend* (*internal*) access. For member variables, the access modifier can replace the *Dim* statement. If the *Dim* statement is used (in Visual Basic .NET) or no access modifier is used (in Visual C#), the variable is considered *private* in Visual C# and Visual Basic .NET classes, *Public* in Visual Basic .NET structures, and *private* in Visual C# structures. Methods do not require an access modifier. If no access modifier is specified, the method is *Private* (*private*) by default in a class or structure in C#, and *Public* (*public*) in a class or structure in Visual Basic .NET.

Note   Inheritance is discussed in depth in Chapter 4.

The following example demonstrates how to use the access modifiers and illustrates how they control access:

Visual Basic .NET

```
Public Class aClass
    ' This field can be accessed unconditionally by external
    ' code
    Public anInteger As Integer

    ' This method can be called by members of this class and
    ' assembly, but not by external code

    Friend Sub myMethod()
    End Sub

    ' This field can only be accessed by members of this class
    Private aString As String

    ' This method may be called by members of this class and any
    ' inheriting classes
    Protected Function Return1() As Integer
        Return 1
    End Function

    ' This field may be accessed by members of the assembly or
    ' inheriting classes
    Protected Friend aLong As Long

End Class
```

Visual C#

```
public class aClass
 {
    // This field can be accessed unconditionally by external
    // code
    public int anInteger;

    // This method can be called by members of this class and
    // assembly, but not by external code

    internal void myMethod()
    {
    }

    // This field can only be accessed by members of this class
    private string aString;

    // This method may be called by members of this class and
    // any inheriting classes
    protected int Return1()
    {
       return 1;
    }

    // This field may be accessed by members of the assembly or
    // inheriting classes
    protected internal long aLong;

}
```

Type Access Modifiers

Structures and classes can also have access modifiers. Access modifiers control how a type can be instantiated and are similar to access modifiers for members. A *Public* (*public*) class can be instantiated by any object in the application. A *Friend* (*internal*) class can be created by other members of the assembly but cannot be created by objects external to the assembly. The *Private* (*private*) and *Protected* (*protected*) modifiers can be used only on nested types. A private class can be created only by objects of its own type or by types in which it is nested. Nested types also can be *Protected* (*protected*) or *Protected Friend* (*protected internal*), which allows classes inheriting the parent class to have access to them. *Protected Friend* (*protected internal*) classes are also visible to other members of the namespace. If no access modifier is specified for a class or a structure, it is considered *Public* (*public*).

Note Protected members are discussed in greater detail in Chapter 4.

Access Modifiers for Nested Types

In general, a nested type is a type that is used exclusively by the type that contains it. Thus, it is usually a good practice to assign the *Private* (*private*) access modifier to a nested type. Under rare circumstances, you might want to create a nested type that can be created by other types and assign it a different access modifier. Although you can assign any access modifier to a nested type, the behavior will never be greater than the access modifier of the type that contains it. Consider the following example:

Visual Basic .NET

```
Friend Class ParentClass
    Public Class NestedClass
    End Class
End Class
```

Visual C#

```
internal class ParentClass
{
    public class NestedClass
    {
    }
}
```

In this example, the nested class is declared *Public* (*public*) but is contained within a class that is marked *Friend* (*internal*). Although the nested class is public, it will not be visible to any classes outside the assembly by virtue of the parent class being marked *Friend* (*internal*). Thus, the nested class has a practical access level of *Friend* (*internal*).

Shared (static) Members

Regular members are unique to each object instance as shown in the following pseudocode:

Visual Basic .NET

```
Dim Object1 as New DemoClass()
Dim Object2 as New DemoClass()
Object1.MyField = 15
Object2.MyField = 20
```

Visual C#

```
DemoClass Object1 = new DemoClass();
DemoClass Object2 = new DemoClass();
Object1.MyField = 15;
Object2.MyField = 20;
```

The *MyField* field holds a different value, depending on which instance of the class is referenced. It is also possible to have members that are common to all instances of a class. These members are called *Shared* (*static*) members. Only one instance of a *Shared* or *static* member can exist, no matter how many instances of a particular type have been created.

You can create a *Shared* (*static*) field by using the *Shared* (Visual Basic .NET) or *static* (Visual C#) keyword. For example:

Visual Basic .NET

```
Public Class Demo
    Public Shared MyField As Integer
End Class
```

Visual C#

```
public class Demo
{
    public static int MyField;
}
```

Even though multiple instances of the *Demo* class might be instantiated, there will be only one copy of the *MyField* field. Note that the *Shared* (*static*) keyword is not an access modifier; rather, it specifies the member's shared nature. *Shared* members can still be *Public* (*public*), *Private* (*private*), *Friend* (*internal*), and so on.

Methods can be shared as well as fields. Whereas regular methods belong to instances of types, shared methods belong to the type itself. Because shared methods belong to the type itself, they cannot access instance data from any objects. They can only utilize shared variables, variables declared within the method, or parameters passed into the method.

Accessing Shared Members

Because *Shared* members belong to the type but not to object instances of a type, they should be accessed using the class name rather than the instance name. Although Visual Basic .NET allows you to access *Shared* members through the object, there is still only one instance of the *Shared* members. Visual C# is stricter in this regard and does not allow you to access *static* members through an object instance. An example is shown in the following code sample:

Visual Basic .NET

```
' This example uses the Demo class from the previous example
Dim Object1 as New Demo()

' This is incorrect syntax. You should not access shared
' members through the object name, though it will not cause an
' error.
```

```
Object1.MyField = 15
' This syntax is correct-accessing the field through the class
' instead of the object.
Demo.MyField = 15
```

Visual C#

```
// This example uses the Demo class from the previous example
Demo Object1 = new Demo();

// This is incorrect syntax. You cannot access shared
// members through the object name with Visual C#
Object1.MyField = 15;

// This syntax is correct-accessing the field through the class
// instead of the object.
Demo.MyField = 15;
```

Because *Shared* members belong to the type instead of any one instance of a type, it is not necessary to instantiate a type before accessing *Shared* members. Thus, you can call shared methods or retrieve shared fields before an instance of a type exists.

Lesson Summary

- Access modifiers are used to control the scope of type members. There are five access modifiers: *Public (public)*, *Friend (internal)*, *Private (private)*, *Protected (protected)*, and *Protected Friend (protected internal)*. Each provides varying levels of access.

- If an access modifier is not specified for a method, it has a default access level of *private* in Visual C# classes and structures and *public* in Visual Basic .NET classes and structures. If an access modifier is not specified for a member variable, it has a default access level of *private* in a class or *public* in a structure.

- Access modifiers also can be used on types to control how a type is instantiated. Access levels for types are as follows: *Public (public)* types can be instantiated from anywhere. *Friend (internal)* types can be instantiated only by members of the assembly, and *Private (private)* types can be instantiated only by themselves or within a containing type.

- If no access modifier is specified for a class or a structure, it is considered *Public (public)*.

- Nested types obey the same rules as non-nested types, but in practice, they can never have an access level greater than that of their parent type.

- *Shared (static)* members belong to the type but not to any instance of a type. They can be accessed without creating an instance of the type and are accessed using the type name instead of the instance name. Shared methods cannot refer to any instance data.

Lesson 6: Garbage Collection

The automatic memory management scheme employed by the .NET Framework is called *garbage collection*. Memory from objects that are no longer used is traced and reclaimed without any action required by the application. In this lesson, you learn how garbage collection works.

After this lesson, you will be able to

- Describe how garbage collection manages the reclamation of unused memory
- Describe how garbage collection deals with circular references

Estimated lesson time: 15 minutes

The .NET Framework employs automatic memory management, which means that when an object is no longer being used, the .NET Framework automatically reclaims the memory that was being used by that object. This process is called garbage collection. Consider the following example:

Visual Basic .NET

```
Sub GarbageCollectionExample1()
    Dim myWidget As New Widget()
End Sub
```

Visual C#

```
void GarbageCollectionExample1()
{
    Widget myWidget = new Widget();
}
```

When this procedure ends, the variable *myWidget* goes out of scope and the object it refers to is no longer referenced by any application variable. The garbage collector continuously traces the reference tree in the background and identifies objects that no longer have references. When it finds one, such as the *Widget* in the previous example, it deletes it and reclaims the memory. Because the garbage collector is always running, you do not have to explicitly destroy objects when you are finished with them.

The garbage collector is a low-priority thread under normal circumstances. It operates when processor time is not consumed by more important tasks. When memory becomes limited, however, the garbage collector thread moves up in priority. Memory is reclaimed at a more rapid pace until it is no longer limited, at which point the priority of garbage collection is again lowered.

This non-deterministic approach to memory reclamation seeks to maximize application performance and supplies a less bug-prone application environment. There is a cost, however. Because of the mechanism by which garbage collection operates, you cannot be certain when an object will be reclaimed. Thus, you have no control over when a class's destructor (Visual C#) or finalizer (Visual Basic .NET) is executed. These methods should not contain code that you rely on being run at a given time. Instead, classes that appropriate expensive resources usually implement a *Dispose()* method to explicitly free those resources when the class is no longer needed.

Circular References

Garbage collection also manages circular references, previously a common form of memory leak. Consider the following example:

Visual Basic .NET

```
Class Widget
    Public ChildWidget As Widget
    Public Parent As Widget
End Class
Class aClass
    Public GrandParent As Widget
    Sub Demo()
        Dim Parent As Widget
        Dim Child As Widget
        GrandParent = New Widget()
        GrandParent.ChildWidget = New Widget()
        Parent = GrandParent.ChildWidget
        Parent.ChildWidget = New Widget()
        Child = Parent.ChildWidget
        Child.Parent = Parent
        GrandParent = Nothing
    End Sub
End Class
```

Visual C#

```
class Widget
{
    public Widget ChildWidget;
    public Widget Parent;
}
class aClass
{
    Widget GrandParent;
    void Demo()
    {
        Widget Parent;
        Widget Child;
        GrandParent = new Widget();
```

```
GrandParent.ChildWidget = new Widget();
Parent = GrandParent.ChildWidget;
Parent.ChildWidget = new Widget();
Child = Parent.ChildWidget;
Child.Parent = Parent;
GrandParent = null;
   }
}
```

The *Widget* class consists of two fields: a *ChildWidget* field that holds a reference to a *Widget* object and a *Parent* field that holds a reference to another *Widget* object. In this example, a *Widget* object is created and assigned to the variable *GrandParent*. This object then spawns another *Widget* object and assigns it to its *ChildWidget* field. The *Parent* variable is also assigned to point to this object. *Parent*, in turn, creates a third *Widget*, which is assigned to both the *ChildWidget* field of *Parent* and to the *Child* variable. The *Parent* field of the *Child* variable is assigned to *Parent*, thus creating a reference from *Child* to *Parent*. When the *GrandParent* variable is set to nothing, the *Widget* objects represented by *Parent* and *Child* are left referring only to each other—a circular reference.

Although circular references can create difficult-to-locate memory leaks in other development platforms, the .NET Framework garbage collector is able to trace and remove such memory leaks. Thus, if a pair of objects are only referenced by each other, they will be marked for garbage collection.

Lesson Summary

- The .NET Framework provides automatic memory reclamation through the garbage collector. The garbage collector is a low-priority thread that always runs in the background of the application. When memory is scarce, the priority of the garbage collector is elevated until sufficient resources are reclaimed.

- Because you cannot be certain when an object will be garbage collected, you should not rely on code in finalizers or destructors being run within any given time frame. If you have resources that need to be reclaimed as quickly as possible, provide a *Dispose( )* method that gets called explicitly.

- The garbage collector continuously traces the reference tree and disposes of objects containing circular references to one another in addition to disposing of unreferenced objects.

Lab 1: Classes and Garbage Collection

In this lab, you will practice creating classes and members, and you will create a demonstration of how garbage collection automatically manages memory. You will create a class that interacts with a pre-made user interface. This class will have a shared variable that keeps track of the number of instances that currently exist in memory. Additionally, you will add code to the constructor and destructor of this class to increment and decrement this variable. You will then create multiple instances of this class and watch as their memory is reclaimed by garbage collection. The solution to this lab is available in the \Labs\Ch01\Solution folder on the Supplemental Course Materials CD-ROM.

Note   For this and all of the labs in this book, you will find Visual Basic .NET and Visual C# solutions in their respective folders in \Labs\Ch*xx*\Solutions, where *xx* stands for the appropriate chapter number.

Before You Begin

There are no prerequisites to complete this lab.

Estimated lesson time: 20 minutes

Exercise 1.1: Making the Demo Class

In this exercise, you will create the Demo class that interacts with the DemoTest project. The DemoTest project is available in the \Labs\Ch01\Partial folder on the Supplemental Course Materials CD-ROM.

▶ **To make the Demo class**

1. Open the DemoTest.sln solution in \Labs\Ch01\Partial. This solution contains all of the front-end code you will need for your project.
2. From the Project menu, choose Add Class.
3. In the Add New Item dialog box, name your class **Demo**.
4. Add a public, shared field named **Instances** to *Demo*. This field will track the number of instances of *Demo* that are currently in memory. The following line shows an example:

Visual Basic .NET

```
Public Shared Instances As Long
```

Visual C#

```
public static long Instances;
```

5. Create a constructor for this class (Visual Basic .NET), or add to the default constructor created by Visual Studio (Visual C#). In the constructor, you will add code to increment the *Instances* variable. The following code shows an example:

Visual Basic .NET

```
Public Sub New()
    Instances += 1
End Sub
```

Visual C#

```
public Demo()
{
    Instances++;
}
```

6. Create a destructor (finalizer) for this class. In the destructor, add code to decrement the *Instances* variable. For example:

Visual Basic .NET

```
Protected Overrides Sub Finalize()
    Instances -= 1
End Sub
```

Visual C#

```
~Demo()
{
    Instances--;
}
```

Note   In Visual Basic .NET, you must use the *Overrides* keyword in the finalizer. The meaning and use of the *Overrides* keyword is discussed in Chapter 4.

---

7. From the File menu, choose Save All to save your work.

Exercise 1.2: Demonstrating Garbage Collection

The front end provided in the DemoTest project contains a form that displays two controls: a button and a label. Additionally, there is an invisible timer component that updates the label control every second. You will run the application and observe how instances of your class are created and garbage collected.

▶   **To create the garbage collection demo**

1. In the Designer, examine Form1. You can open the designer by double-clicking Form1 in Solution Explorer. Note that it has a *Button* control, a *Label* control, and a *Timer* component in the component tray.

Note   Controls are examined further in Chapter 2.

---

2. Double-click the Button to open the code window to the click event handler.

3. Find *Private Sub Button1_Click* (Visual Basic .NET) or *private void button1_Click* (Visual C#). Add the following code:

Visual Basic .NET

```
Dim Counter As Integer
Dim aDemo
For Counter = 1 to 1000
    aDemo = New Demo()
Next
```

Visual C#

```
int Counter;
Demo aDemo;
for (Counter = 0; Counter < 1000; Counter++)
{
    aDemo = new Demo();
}
```

This code declares two variables, a *Counter* and a variable of the *Demo* class. It then enters an iteration loop. One thousand loops are iterated, and in each loop, the *aDemo* variable is assigned to a new instance of the *Demo* class. Recall that creating a new instance of *Demo* will cause the class's constructor to execute, incrementing the shared variable *Instances*. As the loop ends and restarts, the *aDemo* variable is assigned to another new instance of *Demo*, and all the references to the previous instance of the *Demo* class are released, thus marking the class for garbage collection. This loop will execute 1000 times for every click of the button.

4. Press F5 to build and run your application. You should see a button and a label indicating how many instances of *Demo* exist in memory. Click this button once.

   The label now reads "There are 1000 instances of Demo in memory". Wait for a while. After a measurable interval, perhaps even as long as a couple minutes, the label will indicate zero instances again, indicating that the 1000 instances of *Demo* have been garbage collected and their destructors executed, decrementing the *Instances* variable.

   The label did not revert instantly because garbage collection is a relatively low-priority thread under normal circumstances. However, when memory gets scarce, the priority of the thread is increased.

5. Click the button several times in succession. See how many instances you can put into memory. If your machine has a large amount of memory, you might be able to create tens of thousands of instances before garbage collection is performed. Once memory gets scarce, though, garbage collection rapidly and efficiently reclaims the memory used by these unreferenced objects.

Review

The following review questions are intended to reinforce key concepts and information presented in this chapter. If you are unable to answer a question, return to the appropriate lesson and review, and then try the lesson again. Answers to the questions can be found in Appendix A.

1. Briefly describe the major components of the .NET Framework, and describe what each component does.

2. Briefly explain what is meant by a reference type and a value type.

3. How do you enable your application to use .NET base class library members without referencing their fully qualified names?

4. Briefly describe how garbage collection works.

5. Briefly describe what members are, and list the four types of members.

6. Explain what constructors and destructors are, and describe their use.

7. Briefly explain the difference between *Public* (*public*), *Friend* (*internal*), and *Private* (*private*) access levels as they apply to user-defined types and members.

8. Do you need to instantiate a class before accessing a *Shared* (*static*) member? Why or why not?

9. Briefly describe how a class is similar to a structure. How are they different?

C H A P T E R   2

Creating the User Interface

About This Chapter

This chapter describes how to create a user interface for your form. Essential design elements such as composition, controls and menus, and working with forms will be covered. Additionally, you will learn how to validate user input.

Before You Begin

There are no prerequisites to completing the lessons in this chapter.

Lesson 1: User Interface Design Principles

The user interface provides a mechanism for users to interact with your applicatio Therefore, an efficient design that is easy to use is of paramount importance. Thi lesson presents guidelines for designing user-friendly, elegant, and simple user interfaces.

When designing the user interface, your primary consideration should be the peo ple who will use the application. They are your *target audience*. Knowing your ta get audience makes it easier for you to design a user interface that helps users lear and use the application. A poorly designed user interface, on the other hand, can lead to frustration and inefficiency if it causes the target audience to avoid or evel discard your application.

Forms are the primary element of a Microsoft Windows application. As such, the provide the foundation for each level of user interaction. Controls and menus can be added to forms to supply specific functionality. In addition to being functional your user interface should be attractive and inviting to the user. The .NET Frame work supports a variety of graphic effects that aid in the visual presentation of yo application, including shaped forms and controls, transparent or translucent ele ments, and complex shading effects.

After this lesson, you will be able to

- Describe the importance of the user interface
- Explain the role of forms, controls, and menus in the user interface
- Explain the importance of composition and color in your user interface
- Explain the use of images, icons, and fonts in the interactive design

Estimated lesson time: 30 minutes

Forms, Controls, and Menus

Forms generally contain a set of related information or options that provide users with information they need to proceed. Every form is also a *class*, and you can create multiple instances of a form or inherit from a form. These topics are discussed further in Lesson 2 of this chapter and in Chapter 4.

Controls make information and options accessible to users. Controls such as labels and picture boxes can display information. Controls such as text boxes, list boxes, or combo boxes can both display information and accept user input. Controls such as buttons can allow the user to select a course of action. The use of controls is examined in Lesson 3 of this chapter.

Menus and toolbars provide a structured way to expose available commands to the users of your application. Menus are often incorporated to provide access to higher-level commands that might be common to all the forms of an application, such as commands to save data or exit the application. Menus can present options in a logical, consistent manner that enhances the user experience and enables rapid mastery of the application. Menu elements can be enabled or disabled to customize options available to the user at different points in the application. The use of menus is discussed in Lesson 4 of this chapter.

Composition

Composition drives the "look and feel" of your user interface. How your user inter-face is composed influences how rapidly your application can be learned and adopted. Primary composition considerations include:

- Simplicity
- Position of controls
- Consistency
- Aesthetics

Simplicity

Simplicity is an important aspect of a user interface. A visually "busy" or overly complex user interface makes it harder and more time-consuming to learn the application. A user interface should allow a user to quickly complete all interac-tions required by the program, but it should expose only the functionality needed at each stage of the application.

When designing your user interface, you should keep program flow and execution in mind, so that users of your application will find it easy to use. Controls that dis-play related data should be grouped together on the form. Controls such as list boxes, combo boxes, and check boxes can be used to display data and allow users to choose between preset options. The use of a *tab order* (an order by which users can cycle through controls on a form by pressing the Tab key) allows users to rap-idly navigate fields.

Trying to reproduce a real-world object is a common mistake when designing user interfaces. For instance, if you want to create a form that takes the place of a paper form, it is natural to attempt to reproduce the paper form in the application. This approach might be appropriate for some applications, but for others, it might limit the application and provide no real user benefit because reproducing a paper form can limit the functionality of your application. When designing an application, think about your unique situation and try to use the computer's capabilities to enhance the user experience for your target audience.

Default values are another way to simplify your user interface. For example, if 90 percent of the users of an application will select Washington in a State field, make Washington the default choice for that field. (You should always make it easy to override the default value when necessary.)

Information from your target audience is paramount when designing a user inter-face. The best information to use when designing a user interface is input from the target audience. Tailor your interface to make frequent tasks easy to perform. After your application is complete, additional user input will facilitate continued improvement.

Position of Controls

The location of controls on your user interface should reflect their relative importance and frequency of use. For example, if you have a form that is used to input both required information and optional information, the controls for the required information are more important and should receive greater prominence. In Western cultures, user interfaces are typically designed to be read left-to-right and top-to-bottom. The most important or frequently used controls are most easily accessed at the top of the form. Controls that will be used after a user completes an action on a form, such as a Submit button, should follow the logical flow of information and be placed at the bottom of the form.

It is also necessary to consider the *relatedness* of information. Related information should be displayed in controls that are grouped together. For example, if you have a form that displays information about a customer, a purchase, or an employee, you can group each set of controls on a tab control that allows a user to easily move back and forth between displays.

Aesthetics is also an important consideration in the placement of controls. You should try to avoid forms that display more information than can be understood at a glance. Whenever possible, controls should be adequately spaced to create visual appeal and ease of accessibility.

Consistency

Your user interface should exhibit a consistent design across each form in your application. An inconsistent design can make your application seem disorganized or chaotic, hindering adoption by your target audience. Don't ask users to adapt to new visual elements as they navigate from form to form.

Consistency is created through the use of colors, fonts, size, and types of control. Before any actual application development takes place, you should decide on a visual scheme that will remain consistent throughout the application. Avoid the temptation to show off. Extraneous use of controls or flashy visual elements only distracts users and makes your application less efficient.

Aesthetics

Whenever possible, a user interface should be inviting and pleasant. Although clarity and simplicity should not be sacrificed for the sake of attractiveness, you should endeavor to create an application that will not dissuade users.

Color

Judicious use of color helps make your user interface attractive to the target audience and inviting to use. It is easy to overuse color, however. Loud, vibrant colors might appeal to some users, but others might have a negative reaction. When designing a background color scheme for your application, the safest course is to use muted colors with broad appeal.

Always research any special meanings associated with color that might affect user response to your application. If you are designing an application for a company, you might consider using the company's corporate color scheme in your application. When designing for international audiences, be aware that certain colors might have cultural significance. Maintain consistency, and do not overdo the color.

Always think about how color might affect usability. For example, blue text on a black background can be difficult to read and, thus, impairs usability. Also, be aware of usability issues related to colorblindness. Some people, for example, are unable to distinguish between red and green. Therefore, red text on a green background is invisible to a user with this condition. Do not rely on color alone to convey information. Contrast can also attract attention to important elements of your application.

Fonts

Usability should determine the fonts you choose for your application. For usability, avoid fonts that are difficult to read or highly embellished. Stick to simple, easy-to-read fonts such as Palatino or Times New Roman. Also, as with other design elements, fonts should be applied consistently throughout the application. Use cursive or decorative fonts only for visual effects, such as on a title page if appropriate, and never to convey important information.

Images and Icons

Pictures and icons add visual interest to your application, but careful design is essential to their use. Images that appear "busy" or distract the user will hinder use of your application. Icons can convey information, but again, careful consideration of end-user response is required before deciding on their use. For example, you might consider using a red octagon similar to a U.S. stop sign to indicate that users might not want to proceed beyond that point in the application. A red octagon is not a universally recognized symbol of "stop," however, so its significance might be lost on an international audience. Know your target audience, and tailor the use of icons and visual elements to the audience.

Whenever possible, icons should be kept to simple shapes that are easily rendered in a 16-by-16-pixel square. Complex pictures can suffer a severe loss of resolution (and thus become unusable) when degraded.

Shapes and Transparency

The .NET Framework provides tools for creating forms and controls with varying levels of opacity, using shapes other than the traditional rectangle. These tools can create powerful visual effects, but they should not be overused. For example, although it might be interesting and unique to have a text box shaped like a doughnut, such a text box might be inefficient or detract from the usability of your application. Always keep the end user in mind when applying these effects. Similarly, translucent forms can be used to allow a user to manipulate a form in the foreground while monitoring action on a background form. However, these aspects of the aesthetics of your application should always serve the ultimate purpose—usability.

Lesson Summary

- Interface design is important because a visually consistent and logical interface is easier to learn and more efficient to use.
- Major elements of a user interface include forms, controls, and menus.
- A good user interface pays attention to the following considerations:
  - Simplicity
  - Positioning of Controls
  - Consistency
  - Aesthetics
- Make design decisions that invite the target audience to use your application. Be aware of the cultural significance of your choices, and keep the ideas of consistency and simplicity foremost in your mind when designing your interface.

Lesson 2: Using Forms

As noted in Lesson 1, forms are the fundamental unit of your user interface. They provide a backdrop that hosts the controls, and they allow you to present your application in a consistent and attractive manner. Forms can display data and receive user input. Although it is possible to create an application, such as a Windows service or a console application, that has no forms at all, applications designed for frequent user interaction usually contain at least one form. Applications that are more complex often require several forms to allow the program to flow in a consistent and logical manner.

After this lesson, you will be able to

- State the role of forms in an application
- Explain how to add forms to your application
- Explain how to set the start-up form and the start-up location
- Explain how to set the visual appearance of your form
- Explain how to use form methods
- Explain how to use form events

Estimated lesson time: 30 minutes

Adding Forms to Your Project

Forms enable interaction between your application and a user. When you create a new Windows Forms project, an initial form, named Form1, is added by default. Form1 is not an actual instance of a form, however, but rather a class that represents the code behind an instance of a form. You can edit Form1 by adding controls, menus, and other visual elements in the designer. The designer is a graphic representation of the designable component (usually a form) that you are creating, and it provides the ability to add controls to your form by dragging them from the tool box to the design surface represented on the screen. While designing a form or other component, you are said to be at design-time. As your application grows in size, you will want to add additional form classes to your project.

To add a new form to a project

1. On the Project menu, click Add Windows Form. The Add New Item dialog box opens.
2. Click Windows Form, and click Open. A new form is added to the development environment.

You can also add a new form using code. In this case, you declare a variable that represents a type of form and creates an instance of that form. This form can be used and displayed during execution of your application. Note that you will be unable to use any design tools to create this form, and it will be unavailable at design time. The code method is often employed when you want to display a form that already exists.

To add a form to your application at run time

Declare and instantiate a variable representing your form in the same manner as you would any other class. For example:

Visual Basic .NET

```
' This example assumes that you have already designed a form
' called DialogForm
Dim myForm As DialogForm
myForm = New DialogForm()
```

Visual C#

```
// This example assumes that you have already designed a form
// called DialogForm
DialogForm myForm;
myForm = new DialogForm();
```

Visual Inheritance

Visual inheritance is a means of creating forms that are closely related. The technique allows you to create a form that incorporates all the members, controls, menus, and code associated with an existing form, and to use the new form as a base for additional functionality. Thus, you can create a single form that incorporates elements common to the entire interface and then individually tailor each form for its specific purpose. You can use either the Inheritance Picker or code to create the inheritance relationship. Inheritance is discussed in greater detail in Chapter 4.

To create an inherited form with the Inheritance Picker

1. From the Projects menu, select Add Inherited Form. The Add New Item dialog box opens.
2. In the left pane of the dialog box, choose Local Project Items. In the right pane, select Inherited Form. Name this form in the Name box, and click Open to open the Inheritance Picker.
3. The forms in your project are displayed in the Inheritance Picker. If the form from which you want to inherit is one of these forms, choose it and click OK. A new inherited form is added to your project.

If you want to inherit from a form outside of your project, click Browse. Navigate to the project containing the form you want. Click the DLL file containing the form, and click Open.

You now return to the Inheritance Picker dialog box, where the selected project is now listed. Choose the appropriate form, and click OK. A new inherited form is added to your project.

Note   To use the Inheritance Picker, the form from which you want to inherit must be in the project or compiled in an EXE or DLL file.

To create an inherited form in code

1. From the Projects menu, select Add Windows Form. A new form class is added to your project.

2. Open the code editor for your new form by right-clicking the form in Solution Explorer and choosing View Code. Modify the class declaration (Visual C#) or use the *Inherits* keyword (Visual Basic .NET) to specify the inherited form, as indicated by the following example:

Visual Basic .NET

```
' This example assumes that you are inheriting from a form class
' named MainForm and that that form resides in your project
Public Class myForm
    Inherits MainForm
    ' Additional class implementation omitted
End Class
```

Visual C#

```
// This example assumes that you are inheriting from a form class
// named MainForm, and that that form resides in your project
public class myForm : MainForm
{
    // Additional class implementation omitted
}
```

Note   To use inheritance in code, as shown in the preceding example, your project must be able to refer to that form. Thus, it must include either a reference to the assembly that contains the form from which you want to inherit (in this example, *MainForm*), or that form must be a member of your project.

Setting the Start-Up Form

If your Windows Forms application contains multiple forms, you must designate one as the start-up form. The start-up form is the first form to be loaded on execution of your application. In Visual Basic .NET, you can designate a form as the start-up form by setting the start-up object for your application, which is done in the Properties window, as shown in Figure 2.1.

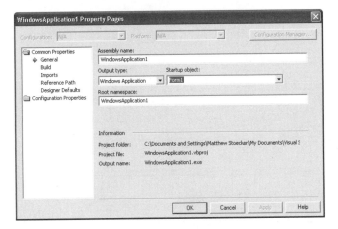

Figure 2.1.   The Visual Basic .NET project Properties window.

To set the start-up form in Visual Basic .NET

1. In Solution Explorer, click the name of your project. The project name is high-lighted.
2. From the Project menu, choose Properties.
3. Under Startup Object, choose the appropriate form from the drop-down menu.

Setting the start-up form in Visual C# is slightly more complicated. To act as a start-up object, your form must have a method named *Main* that serves as the starting point for the application. The *Main* method specifies the application start-up form. For example, a *Main* method that specifies a form named myForm looks like this:

Visual C#

```
static void Main()
{
    Application.Run(new myForm());
}
```

From the project Properties window, you can choose any form that has an appropriate *Main* method as the start-up form, as shown in Figure 2.2.

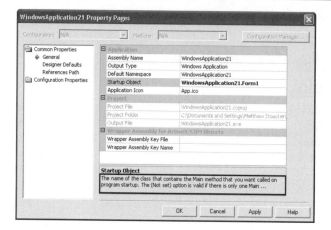

Figure 2.2.   The Visual C# project Properties window.

To set the start-up form in Visual C#

1. In Solution Explorer, click the name of your project. The project name is high-lighted.

2. From the Project menu, choose Properties.

3. Under Startup Object, choose the appropriate form from the drop-down menu. The selected form must contain a suitable *Main* method that specifies the correct start-up object.

Setting the Start-Up Location

You can use the form's *StartPosition* property to determine where on the computer screen the form will open when first displayed. The *StartPosition* property can be set to any of the values contained within the *FormStartPosition* enumeration. The *FormStartPosition* enumeration values are listed in Table 2.1.

Table 2.1.   *FormStartPosition* **Property Settings**

FormStartPosition Setting	Effect
Manual	The form opens at the location determined by the form's *Location* property.
CenterScreen	The form opens centered in the screen.
WindowsDefaultLocation	The form opens at the Windows default location.
WindowsDefaultBounds	The form opens at the Windows default location and at the Windows default bounding size.
CenterParent	The form opens centered on its parent form.

To set the start-up position for a form

In the project's Properties window, change the *StartPosition* property to the desired setting.

Changing the Appearance of Your Form

The way your user interface looks is an important part of your application. A user interface that is poorly designed is correspondingly difficult to learn and, therefore, increases training time and expense. The use of properties allows you to manipulate the appearance of your forms.

A form has many inherent properties that affect its appearance. You can view and change these properties in the Properties window of the designer, as shown in Figure 2.3.

Figure 2.3.   Change inherent properties in the Properties window.

Some properties, such as *Font*, are actually structures with several values that affect the behavior of a form. You can see each of these values and change them as desired by clicking the plus sign (+) next to the *Font* property in the Properties window. Some properties, such as *BackColor* and *ForeColor*, supply an editor to assist in choosing a value.

A form's properties also can be changed at run time in code. For example, if you want the background color to change to red, you would add the following line to your code:

Visual Basic .NET

```
' This assumes that you want to change the color of a previously
' created form called MyForm
MyForm.BackColor = System.Drawing.Color.Red
```

Visual C#

```
// This assumes that you want to change the color of a previously
// created form called MyForm
MyForm.BackColor = System.Drawing.Color.Red;
```

Properties follow the same general syntax as other class members. You use the assignment operator (=) to assign a value to a property, and you use the property name to reference its value.

BackColor, ForeColor, and Text Properties

Users will be immediately aware of *BackColor*, *ForeColor*, and *Text* properties. The *Text* property indicates the caption of the form. The *BackColor* and *ForeColo* properties represent the colors of a form. *ForeColor* is the color of text in the fore ground. Most controls have their *ForeColor* set to the *ForeColor* of the form whe they are added to the form. *BackColor* represents the background color of the form Many controls, such as *Button* and *Label*, have their *BackColor* set to match the form when they are added in the designer. Other controls, such as *TextBox*, have independent settings that must be changed manually.

Use caution when choosing colors. Red text on a blue background might look attractive while you're designing, but it can be hard to read once your application i deployed. High-contrast color schemes offer the best choice for readability.

Font, Cursor, and BackGroundImage

The *Font*, *Cursor*, and *BackGroundImage* properties are tools to help you vary the look of your interface in additional ways. The *Font* property allows you to specify the font you want to use for your form. Once set, the font is applied to the form controls to give the form a consistent look and feel. The *Cursor* property allows you to specify the icon that appears when a mouse pointer is over your form. *Back GroundImage* allows you to set the background as an image instead of a color. If you set a background image, changing the *BackColor* property will not affect the form itself, but it will change the *BackColor* of any form controls.

Opacity

You can create striking visual effects for your form by altering its transparency with the *Opacity* property controls. *Opacity* values range between 0 and 1. A value of 1 indicates that a form is completely opaque, and a value of 0 creates a com-pletely transparent form. Any value between the two settings results in a partially transparent form. An *Opacity* of 1 (fully opaque) is the default value. The *Opacity* property is useful when it is necessary to keep one form in the foreground but mon itor action in a background form. Generally, a control inherits the opacity of the form that hosts it.

To create a transparent or translucent form

Set the *Opacity* property to a value less than 1.

Visual Basic .NET

```
' Creates a half-transparent form
MyForm.Opacity = .5
```

Visual C#

```
// Creates a half-transparent form
MyForm.Opacity = .5;
```

In the Properties Window (as opposed to code), *Opacity* is represented as a percentage value. Thus, when setting *Opacity*, you should select a value between 0 percent and 100 percent.

Using Form Methods

A method performs an action, and classes incorporate member methods that perform functions relevant to that class. Every form encapsulates a base set of functionality inherited from the *System.Windows.Forms.Form* class. Included in this functionality are several methods for managing how your forms are displayed and accessed in the user environment. Some of these methods are

- *Form.Show*
- *Form.ShowDialog*
- *Form.Activate*
- *Form.Hide*
- *Form.Close*

In order to use any of these methods, you must have a reference to a form available, which means that the form must be already instantiated and must exist in memory. In addition to instances of forms you create in code, your application also creates an instance of your start-up form when program execution begins.

When writing code inside a form class, you can refer to the current instance of that form by using the *Me* (Visual Basic .NET) or *this* (Visual C#) keyword. For example, suppose you want to write a method that changes your form's *Text* value. Because you are writing code that will affect a particular instance of the form, the only way to refer to it is with the special keyword, as shown in the following code:

Visual Basic .NET

```
' This line changes the text of the current instance
Me.Text = "This is the active form"
```

Visual C#

```
// This line changes the text of the current instance
this.Text = "This is the active form";
```

Show and ShowDialog

For a form to be useful, it must be visible. To make a form visible, you can call the *Form.Show* method. This method causes an instance of a form class to load into memory, display on the screen, and receive the focus of the application. The *Visible* property is set to *true* when *Form.Show* is called. If a form is already loaded into memory and is simply not visible (if the *Visible* property has been set to *false*, for instance), calling *Form.Show* has essentially the same effect as setting the *Visible* property to *true*.

Form.ShowDialog accomplishes everything that *Form.Show* does, and it displays the form as a modal dialog box, which means that the form must be closed before any other form can receive the focus. Displaying your form modally allows you to force the user to complete any tasks on that form before continuing with the rest of the program. This method of displaying a form should be used when it is crucial that the user completes a specific action. For example, you might use *Form.Show-Dialog* to inform the user that a floppy drive is inaccessible, or to prompt for a password. The following code demonstrates the use of these methods:

Visual Basic .NET

```
' This example assumes that you have created a Form class called
' DialogForm
Dim myForm as New DialogForm()
' Shows the form regularly
myForm.Show()
' Shows the form modally
myForm.ShowDialog()
```

Visual C#

```
// This example assumes that you have created a Form class called
// DialogForm
DialogForm myForm = new DialogForm();
// Shows the form regularly
myForm.Show();
// Shows the form modally
myForm.ShowDialog();
```

Activate

If a form is already visible but does not currently have the focus, you can use the *Form.Activate* method. When called in the active application, the *Form.Activate* method moves the form to the front of the application and assigns it the focus. If this method is called in an application that is not currently active in the user inter-face, it causes the window caption to flash in the taskbar. The form must be visible for this method to have any effect. If called on a form that is not yet visible, this method will do nothing at all.

Visual Basic .NET

```
myForm.Activate()
```

Visual C#

```
myForm.Activate();
```

Hide

The *Form.Hide* method removes a form from view. Although the form still exists in memory, it is no longer be visible until the *Form.Show* method is called or the form's *Visible* property is set to *true* in code. Calling this method sets the form's *Visible* property to *false* and essentially has the same effect.

Visual Basic .NET

```
myForm.Hide()
```

Visual C#

```
myForm.Hide();
```

Close

When you are finished with a form, you can call the *Form.Close* method to close the form and remove it from memory. This method closes all resources contained within the form and marks them for garbage collection (discussed in Chapter 1). Once you have called *Form.Close*, you cannot call *Form.Show* to make the form visible again because the resources for the form are no longer available. If you call *Form.Close* on the start-up form of your application, the application closes.

Visual Basic .NET

```
myForm.Close()
```

Visual C#

```
myForm.Close();
```

Using Form Events

An event represents something interesting happening in the program. When an event takes place, the application *raises* that event and other components of the application have the opportunity to *handle* that event. Each of the aforementioned methods raises one or more events when called. As a developer, you are afforded the opportunity to write code that allows your application to respond to that event and execute code (also known as *handling* the event). Although events and event handlers are discussed in greater detail in Chapter 3, now is a good time to introduce creating and using event handlers.

Each control and form can raise a variety of different events that correspond to events in application execution. For example, when the *Form.Hide* method is called, the form raises the *Deactivate* event and the *VisibleChanged* event. If you want the application to take any kind of action when an event occurs, you can create an *event handler*, which is a method that executes in response to a raised event. You might, for example, place code in a *Deactviate* event handler to ensure that all required fields on a form have been filled in.

You can create an event handler using the Visual Studio .NET user interface. You can also create an event handler directly in code, but this method is more complicated and will be covered in Chapter 3. Visual Basic .NET and Visual C# use slightly different methods for creating an event handler.

To create an event handler with Visual Basic .NET

1. In the Code Editor view, choose (Base Class Events) from the Class Name drop-down menu at the top of the code editor.

   Note   If you want to create an event handler for a control on the form, you should choose that control instead of (Base Class Events).

2. In the Method Name drop-down menu, choose the event for which you want to write code.

   A default event handler is added to your code editor. You can now write code in this method, which will execute when this event is raised. Figure 2.4 shows the Class Name and Method Name lists.

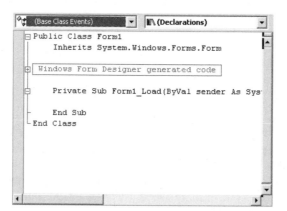

Figure 2.4.   Adding an event handler in Visual Basic .NET.

To create an event handler with Visual C#

1. In Design view, use the mouse to select the form or control for which you want to create an event handler.

2. In the Properties window, click the Events button. A list of available events is displayed in the Properties window.

3. Find the event for which you want to write a handler, and double-click it.

   The Code Editor view opens to a newly created event handler for that event. You can now add code to this method, which will execute when the event is raised. Figure 2.5 shows the events in the Properties window. Note the Events button, which looks like a lightning bolt or spark.

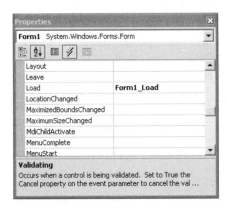

Figure 2.5.   Adding an event handler in Visual C#.

Event Arguments

As with every method, each event handler has a signature. For example, consider the following method:

Visual Basic .NET

```
Private Sub Form1_Load(ByVal sender As System.Object, ByVal e As _
    System.EventArgs) Handles MyBase.Load
    ' Code for the method goes here
End Sub
```

Visual C#

```
private void Form1_Load(object sender, System.EventArgs e)
{
    // Code for the method goes here
}
```

In this method, two arguments are passed to the method by the object (*Form1* in this case) that raises the event. The arguments are *sender*, which is an object that contains a reference to the object that raised the event, and *e*, which is an instance of the *EventArgs* class. If you know the type of object that raised the event, you can obtain a reference to it by explicitly casting *sender* to the correct type. For example:

Visual Basic .NET

```
Dim myForm As Form1
myForm = CType(sender, Form1)
```

Visual C#

```
Form1 myForm;
myForm = (Form1)sender;
```

The *EventArgs* argument represents any other arguments that need to be passed from the object to the event handler. In many cases, the *EventArgs* parameter contains no programmatically useful information. In some cases, however, arguments that are useful or even required by the method will be passed in this parameter. For example, as you will see shortly, the *Form.Closing* event passes an instance of *CancelEventArgs* to its event handler, which can be used to cancel the form's closing. All events raised by forms and controls pass a *sender* reference and some variety of *EventArgs* to their event handler.

Form Lifetime Events

Various events are raised throughout a form's lifetime. In this section, we will examine some of the events that are raised as a form is created, manipulated, and destroyed. The events we will examine are

- *Load*
- *Activated/Deactivate*
- *VisibleChanged*
- *Closing*
- *Closed*

Although this list is not exhaustive of the events a form can raise, it is representative of the normal events that typically occur during a form's lifetime.

Load

The *Load* event is fired when an instance of a form is first loaded into the program. This event is raised the first time that the *Form.Show* or *Form.ShowDialog* method is called for each instance of a form. Consider the following example:

Visual Basic .NET

```
Dim myForm as New Form()
myForm.Show()                    ' The Load event fires here
myForm.Hide()                    ' Form is now invisible
myForm.Show()                    ' The Load event doesn't fire again
myForm.Close()                   ' Closes and disposes the form
myForm.Show()                    ' Throws an exception because myForm
                                 ' is no longer available
```

Visual C#

```
Form myForm = new Form();
myForm.Show();                   // The Load event fires here
myForm.Hide();                   // Form is now invisible
myForm.Show();                   // The Load event doesn't fire again
myForm.Close();                  // Closes and disposes the form
myForm.Show();                   // Throws an exception because myForm
                                 // is no longer available
```

This example demonstrates when the *Load* event is raised. Note that it is raised only once in the lifetime of a particular form object. If you have multiple instances of a single form, the *Load* event is raised once per instance. You can use a handler for the *Load* event to initialize variables for a form and prepare it for use.

Activated/Deactivate

The *Activated* event can fire several times in a form's lifetime. It is raised whenever the form receives the focus. Thus, it is raised when *Form.Show* or *Form.ShowDialog* is called, as well as when *Form.Activate* is called or when a form is brought to the front of the application. You might use the *Activated* event handler to set the focus to a particular control on a form or to change the color to indicate that the form is active.

The *Deactivate* event is raised whenever the current form loses the focus. A form can lose the focus through user interaction with the interface or when the *Form.Hide* or *Form.Close* methods are called (although *Form.Close* raises this event only if the form being closed is the active form). You might use this event to validate user input.

Both the *Activated* and *Deactivate* events fire only when the focus is changed within the program. If you click another application and then return to your .NET program, neither event fires.

VisibleChanged

As the name implies, the *VisibleChanged* event is raised whenever the visible property of the form is changed. Thus, this event is raised whenever the form is made visible or invisible. The form methods that cause this event to be raised include *Form.Show*, *Form.ShowDialog*, *Form.Hide*, and *Form.Close*.

Closing

The *Closing* event is raised when the current form is in the process of closing but has not yet fully closed. This event is raised by calling the *Form.Close* method or by the user clicking the Close button on the form. You can use this event to verify that all tasks required by a particular form have been completed. For example, it can verify that all the fields of a form have been filled out.

The *Closing* event handler signature includes an instance of *CancelEventArgs*. You can abort the form closing and cause the form to remain open by setting the *Cancel* property of this instance to *True*, as shown in the following example:

Visual Basic .NET

```
Private Sub Form1_Closing(ByVal sender As Object, ByVal e As _
    System.ComponentModel.CancelEventArgs) Handles MyBase.Closing
    e.Cancel = True
End Sub
```

Visual C#

```
private void Form1_Closing(object sender,
    System.ComponentModel.CancelEventArgs e)
{
    e.Cancel = true;
}
```

Closed

The *Closed* event is raised after a form has been closed. Like the *Closing* event, this event is raised by calling *Form.Close* or by the user manually closing a form. The *Closed* event is raised after the *Closing* event is raised and any handlers for the *Closing* event are executed. Use the *Closed* event to provide any necessary cleanup code.

Lesson Summary

- Forms are the primary unit of the user interface for a Windows Forms program. You should manage your forms in such a manner as to present a consistent, complete, and attractive visual interface to the end user. You can add forms to your application at design time or at run time, and you can use visual inheritance to create several forms with similar looks and layouts.

- Forms have properties that control their appearance. Changing these properties changes the appearance of the form and sometimes the controls hosted by the form. These properties include

  - *BackColor*
  - *ForeColor*
  - *Text*
  - *Font*
  - *Cursor*
  - *BackGroundImage*
  - *Opacity*

- Forms have several intrinsic methods that you can use to control their lifetime and how they are displayed. Among them are

  - *Form.Show*
  - *Form.ShowDialog*
  - *Form.Activate*
  - *Form.Hide*
  - *Form.Close*

- Each of these methods causes change in the visual interface and raises various events. These events include

  - *Load*
  - *Activated/Deactivate*
  - *VisibleChanged*
  - *Closing*
  - *Closed*

- You can create specialized methods called event handlers that respond to events. These methods are executed whenever the corresponding event is raised.

Lesson 3: Using Controls and Components

Controls are the second element of the visual interface. These graphical tools, also known as Windows Forms controls, are used to create or enhance the functionality of an application. Tools are added to the form from the Visual Studio Toolbox. Some, such as *Button* and *TextBox*, are designed to receive user input and carry out basic tasks associated with user interaction. Others are specialized components designed to manage complex interactions with other parts of the application. Components are similar to controls in that they are existing units of code that encapsulate specific functionality. The main difference between components and controls is that controls have a visual representation, whereas components do not. This lesson provides information on using controls and components when building a user interface.

After this lesson, you will be able to

- Define the role of controls in your application
- Explain the difference between controls and components
- Explain how to set the control tab order
- Describe which controls can contain other controls and how they are used
- Describe docking and anchoring, and explain their use with controls
- Explain how to dynamically add controls to your form
- Describe the process for adding controls to the Toolbox
- Describe how to create event handlers for controls
- Explain what an extender is and how to use one

Estimated lesson time: 45 minutes

Working with Controls

The Visual Studio Toolbox contains a variety of preset controls that you can use to develop your applications. Controls are hosted in forms and implement most of the actual functionality in the user interface. Take the *Button* control, for example. It can be placed on a form and will be displayed, usually with a title that provides some kind of information as to its function. When the user clicks the button with the mouse, an event handler responds to the click and causes code to execute. Other controls, such as the *Label* control and *PictureBox* control, are primarily used to display data to the user. Controls such as *TextBox* and *ListBox* serve a dual purpose: both display information and allow the user to input information.

You can add controls to the forms in your application by using the designer. The designer displays the form you are composing in a graphical state, similar to how the form will look at run time. The Toolbox allows you to select a control with the mouse and add it to the form surface in the designer. All the code associated with the control is also added to your application. You can reposition controls by clicking and dragging them with the mouse. You can resize most controls by grabbing their edge with the mouse and adjusting them as desired. Because an in-depth discussion of the different controls and their functionality is beyond the scope of this book, you should familiarize yourself with the controls in the Toolbox and how they work.

To add a control to your application

1. From the Toolbox, select the control you want to add.
2. Click the form in the location where you want the control to appear. While holding down the left mouse button, draw the control to the size you want it to be on the form.

   Alternatively, you can drag the control from the Toolbox onto the form, or double-click the desired control in the Toolbox. The control will be added to the form with default values for size and position, if appropriate.
3. Use the mouse to set the size and position of the control as desired. You can also use the arrow keys to position the control.

The Properties window displays the properties of the selected control and allows you to edit them. Setting a property during the design stage creates its default value, which can still be changed in the course of code execution. Moving the control on the form in the designer sets the position properties of the control. Although you can accomplish these same tasks in code, the designer allows you to rapidly set control start-up properties rather than spend valuable development time hand-coding values.

To edit properties of a control

1. Right-click a control, and select Properties.
   You can also left-click the control and press F4, or choose Properties from the View menu.
2. Edit the value in the appropriate property box.

To edit properties for multiple controls

1. Click and drag the mouse over the controls to select the controls you want to edit.

   Alternatively, hold down the Ctrl key and click the controls you want to edit. The Properties window displays the properties that are common to all controls selected.
2. Edit the value in the appropriate property box.

Components are also in the Toolbox. Components are similar to controls in that they are pre-assembled units of functionality that you can incorporate into your application. The primary difference between controls and components is that com ponents are not visible in the user interface. An example of a component is the *Timer*, which raises an event at a specified interval. Because they have no visual interface, components are not added to the form when you add them to your appli cation in the designer. Instead, they are added to the *component tray*, a graphical region near the bottom of the designer that allows you to manipulate the propertie of your application's non-visual components. Components are added to an applica tion in the same way controls are added; likewise, the Properties window is used to edit component properties.

Setting the Control Tab Order

The users of your application can use the Tab key to quickly move the focus from one control to another. The tab order sets the order in which controls on the form receive the focus. Tab order is specified by the *TabIndex* property. To change the order in which a control receives the focus, simply set the *TabIndex* property to a different value. Lower values receive the focus first and proceed numerically through higher values. In the event of a tie between *TabIndex* values, the focus firs goes to the control closest to the front of the form. You can bring a control to the front or send it to the back of the form by right-clicking it and choosing Bring To Front or Send To Back, respectively.

Visual Studio contains a tool for setting the tab order. Under the View menu, choose Tab Order. A box containing a number appears inside each control on the designer. To set the tab order, all you have to do is click the controls in the order that you want them to receive the focus.

Note   Some controls, such as *PictureBox*, cannot receive the focus and thus do no have a *TabIndex* property.

To set the tab order using the TabIndex property

1. In the designer, select each control capable of receiving the focus.
2. In the Properties window, set the *TabIndex* property to an appropriate value. The focus passes from control to control in the order of lowest to highest value

To set the tab order with Visual Studio .NET

1. From the View menu, choose Tab Order. Boxes containing the current tab order appear in each control.
2. Click each control in the desired tab order.
3. From the View menu, choose Tab Order again to resume editing.

Controls That Can Contain Other Controls

Some controls, known as *container controls*, allow you to place other controls inside of them. Container controls include *Panel*, *GroupBox*, and *TabControl*. You can use these controls to logically organize groups of controls or a form. For example, you might group a set of related radio buttons in a *GroupBox* control. Using these controls allows logical groupings of controls that you can manipulate programmatically. These controls also help to create a sense of style or information flow in your user interface, and they provide visual cues to the user.

Note   A container control acts as a host for other controls but is independent of those controls. Contrast this with user controls, which can bind multiple controls together into a single interdependent unit. User controls will be discussed in detail in Chapter 7.

When a control contains another control, changes to properties of the container control can affect the contained controls. For example, if the *Enabled* property of a *GroupBox* control is set to *false*, all the controls contained within this control are disabled. Likewise, changes to controls related to the user interface, such as *BackColor*, *ForeColor*, *Visible*, and *Font*, are also applied to contained controls. This allows you to easily create a consistent look for your user interface. The *Anchor* and *Dock* properties of contained controls also function relative to the containing control. These properties are discussed further in the section "Docking and Anchoring Controls" later in this lesson.

Note   Changes in the visual properties of a container control will change the corresponding property in contained controls, but you can still manually change any of these properties on a contained control. If the container control is disabled, however, there is no way to enable a contained control short of re-enabling the containing control.

Using the GroupBox and Panel Controls

The *GroupBox* and *Panel* controls are similar. Both provide a logical and physical grouping of controls. These controls can be thought of as physical subdivisions of a form. Changes in the properties of a *Panel* or *GroupBox* affect all the controls contained within. Controls contained within a *Panel* or *GroupBox* can be moved and repositioned as a single unit during the design stage. At run time, you can disable the entire group by setting the *Enabled* property of the containing control to *false*.

The *GroupBox* control provides a caption for labeling the group of controls within it. You can set this caption using the *Text* property. The *Panel* control is a scrollable container, but it does not provide a caption. By setting the *AutoScroll* property to *true*, you enable scroll bars within the panel.

Using the TabControl Control

The *TabControl* control is a way to group controls on a set of tabs, rather like files in a filing cabinet or dividers in a notebook. The *TabControl* is a host for a number of *TabPages* that host other controls. An example of the *TabControl* might be property pages for an application, with each tab representing properties related to a specific component of the application.

The most important property of *TabControl* is *TabPages*. The *TabPages* property is a collection of *TabPage* controls, each with its own set of properties. A collection is a logical organization of objects similar to an array. Collections are discussed in detail in Chapter 3. You can access each *TabPage* by clicking the tab that represents it, as shown in Figure 2.6.

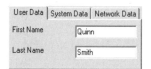

Figure 2.6.   *TabPages* in a *TabControl.*

Individual *TabPages* are similar to *Panel* controls. They provide a scrollable form subdivision that can host a set of other controls. By setting the *Autoscroll* property to *true*, you enable the scroll bars for each *TabPage.*

TabPages are added to the *TabControl* by setting the *TabPages* property. When the *TabPages* property is selected in the designer, the *TabPage* collection editor appears. From this window, you can add *TabPages* to your control and set the properties for each. Once added, you can click the appropriate tab in the designer and add controls to the design surface represented by the *TabPage.* At run time, the user is able to move between different tab pages by clicking the appropriate tabs.

Docking and Anchoring Controls

The *Anchor* and *Dock* properties of a control dictate how it behaves inside its form or parent control. The *Anchor* property allows you to define a constant distance between a control and one or more edges of a form. Thus, if a user resizes a form at run time, the control will always maintain a specific distance from the edges indicated. The *Dock* property allows you to attach a control to an edge of the form or to completely fill the form. A docked control will resize itself when the form is resized.

Using the Anchor Property

You can set the *Anchor* property for any control in the same way you set any other property. In the Properties window, choose *Anchor*. When the drop-down button is clicked, you are presented with a visual interface to help choose anchoring properties, as shown in Figure 2.7.

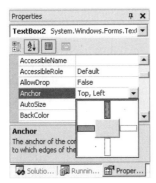

Figure 2.7.   Choosing the *Anchor* property.

You can use the window shown in Figure 2.7 to choose the edges to which you want to anchor your control. The default value for this property is Top, Left, which causes the control to maintain a constant distance between the form's top and left edges. Because forms are resized from the lower-right corner, the net result of this setting is a control that always maintains its position.

In this exercise, you add a button to a form and set the *Anchor* property to a variety of values to observe the effect the *Anchor* property has on control location and sizing.

To demonstrate the Anchor property

1. In Visual Studio, create a new Windows Forms project.
2. In the designer, add a button to the form.
3. Click the button once, and in the Properties window, select the *Anchor* property.

    The *Anchor* property window appears. Note that the top and left bars are darkened, indicating that the control is currently anchored to the top and left edges of the form.

4. In the designer, resize the window by grabbing the lower-right corner with the mouse and dragging. Note that the button maintains its position relative to the top and left edges.

5. In the *Anchor* property window, click both bars. The button is no longer anchored.

6. In the designer, resize the form again. Now the button *floats* on the screen in response to resizing.

    If a control has an *Anchor* property setting of *None*, it will maintain a proportional distance between the edges instead of an absolute distance.

7. Next set the *Anchor* property to *Top*, and resize the form.

    Although the button maintains a constant distance from the top edge, it floats relative to the left and right edges.

8. In the anchor designer window, click the bottom bar, setting the *Anchor* property to Top, Bottom.

9. Resize the window once more. The button still floats relative to the left and right edges, but now it maintains a constant distance between the top and bottom edges. To do this, it must resize itself.

The *Anchor* property allows you to manage how controls respond to resizing the form. You can allow controls to remain fixed in the form by anchoring them to the top and left edges, cause them to stretch when resized by anchoring them to opposite edges, or allow them to float freely by releasing the anchor. Use of the *Anchor* property allows you to implement a variety of resize and relocation behaviors.

Using the Dock Property

Docking refers to attaching your control to the edge of a parent control. The parent control is usually a form, but it can include other container controls such as the *Panel* or *Tab* control. An example of a docked control might be a menu bar at the top of a form.

You can set the *Dock* property of a control at design time in the Properties window. After selecting the *Dock* property, a graphic interface appears that allows you to choose the docking characteristics of your control. The interface is shown in Figure 2.8.

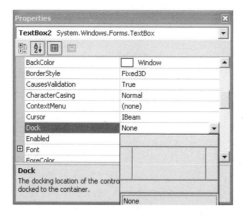

Figure 2.8. Setting the *Dock* property.

To set the *Dock* property, simply click on the section of the interface that corresponds to where you want your control to dock. For example, if you want your control to dock at the top of the form, click the bar at the top of the interface. To release docking, choose None. Clicking the center square of the *Dock* property interface causes the control to fill the form in which it lives. If you set docking for a control, the *Anchor* property is set to Top, Left.

To set docking characteristics for your control

1. In the Properties window, choose the *Dock* property. The *Dock* property visual interface appears.

2. Click the section of the interface you want to use as your dock setting.

Using the Controls Collection

Every container control, including forms, exposes a collection of all the controls it contains. This collection is called the controls collection. The controls collection exposes a *Count* property, which returns the number of items contained within it, and an *Item* property, which returns a specific item. The controls collection also has member methods that can be used to add and remove controls to and from the collection.

In Visual Basic .NET, the *Item* property returns a specific control based on the *Index* of the item. In Visual C#, the property indexer is used. For example:

Visual Basic .NET
```
' Assumes the presence of a form called myForm
Dim aControl As Control
aControl = myForm.Controls.Item(3)
```

Visual C#
```
// Assumes the presence of a form called myForm
Control aControl;
aControl = myForm.Controls[3];
```

Note   In Visual Basic .NET, because the *Item* property is the default property of the controls collection, you can omit the word *Item* when using it. Thus, the preceding example is equivalent to the following code.

Visual Basic .NET
```
Dim aControl As Control
aControl = myForm.Controls(3)
```

You can dynamically add and remove controls to and from the controls collection using the *Add* and *Remove* methods. The following example creates a label control and adds it to the controls collection of a form named myForm:

Visual Basic .NET
```
Dim aLabel As New Label()
aLabel.Text = "This label is being added dynamically"
myForm.Controls.Add(aLabel)
```

Visual C#

```
Label aLabel = new Label();
aLabel.Text = "This label is being added dynamically";
myForm.Controls.Add(aLabel);
```

Likewise, the *Remove* method removes a control from a controls collection. The *RemoveAt* method is useful for removing a control located at a specific index in the collection. Examples follow:

Visual Basic .NET

```
myForm.Controls.Remove(Button1)
myForm.Controls.RemoveAt(3)
```

Visual C#

```
myForm.Controls.Remove(Button1);
myForm.Controls.RemoveAt(3);
```

Similar syntax is used to add and remove controls to and from the controls collection of a container control, such as a *Panel* or a *GroupBox* control. The following example demonstrates how to dynamically add a control to a *TabPage* in a *Tab-Control*:

Visual Basic .NET

```
' This example assumes the existence of a control called
' myTabControl
Dim aButton As New Button()
' This line adds a new button to the tab page located at index 1
' of the TabPages collection in the TabControl
myTabControl.TabPages(1).Controls.Add(aButton)
```

Visual C#

```
// This example assumes the existence of a control called
// myTabControl
Button aButton = new Button();
// This line adds a new button to the tab page located at index 1
// of the TabPages collection in the TabControl
myTabControl.TabPages[1].Controls.Add(aButton);
```

Adding Controls to the Toolbox

You are not limited to the controls provided by the .NET Framework base class library. Third-party developers might supply additional controls for you to use in your development, or you might create your own controls, as you will see in Chapter 7. These controls can be added to the Toolbox for use in the development environment.

To add a control to the Toolbox

1. Choose the Toolbox tab to which you want to add a control. The tab opens.

2. Right-click the Toolbox within that tab area, and choose Customize Toolbox.

   The Customize Toolbox window appears. The Customize Toolbox window displays all components registered on your system. These components are divided between two tabs—a tab that lists all the available .NET components and a tab that lists earlier COM components.

Note   If the Toolbox is not visible, choose Toolbox from the View menu to make it appear.

---

3. If the control you want to add is already registered on the system, select it from the appropriate list and click OK.

4. The control is added to the Toolbox.

5. If the control you want to add is on a floppy disk or in another location, click Browse and browse to the directory location of the file.

6. Select the file, and click OK.

   The control is added to the Toolbox. Note that to add a control to the Toolbox, it must be recognizable as an ActiveX Control, COM component, or .NET assembly.

Creating Event Handlers for Controls

Events represent incidents that happen in the course of program execution. Each control can raise a variety of events that correspond to user interaction. A familiar example is clicking a button. When a button is clicked, the application raises the *Button.Click* event and determines if any methods handle that event. If one or more methods are found to handle that event, those methods are executed. These methods are called *event handlers*.

You can create event handlers to allow your application to respond to user input. Every control has a default event, which represents the event that a control is most likely to raise. For example, the *Button* default event is *Click*, and the *Checkbox* default event is *CheckChanged*. You can easily create an event handler for the default event of a control by double-clicking the control in the designer.

To create an event handler for your control's default event

1. In the designer, double-click the control. The code window opens to a blank event handler for the control's default event.

2. Place the appropriate code in the event handler.

Controls have many other events that can be used for a variety of purposes. You might use the *MouseOver* event, for example, to change the control text when the mouse passes over it. The *Validate* and *Validating* events provide support for validating user input, as is discussed in Lesson 5 of this chapter. Other events can be used to enhance the user interface and provide information to the user. The names of these events indicate when they are raised. You can write event handlers for events in the same manner in which you write event handlers for form events.

To create an event handler with Visual Basic .NET

1. In the Code Editor view, choose the appropriate control from the Class Name drop-down menu at the top of the code editor.

2. In the Method Name drop-down menu, choose the event for which you want to write code.

   A default event handler is added to your code editor. You can now write code in this method, which will execute when this event is raised.

To create an event handler with Visual C#

1. In Design view, use the mouse to select the control for which you want to create an event handler.

2. In the Properties window, click the Events button. A list of available events is displayed in the Properties window.

3. Find the event for which you want to write a handler, and double-click it.

   The Code Editor view opens to a newly created event handler for that event. You can now add code to this method, which will execute when the event is raised.

4. Alternatively, a list of available methods will appear in a drop-down menu to the right of the event name. If you have already written an event handler, you can choose one of these methods to handle your event by selecting it from this menu.

Interacting with the Mouse

Windows Forms controls are capable of raising events that signal interaction with the mouse. Forms raise events in response to mouse clicks, for example, or when the mouse pointer simply passes over a control.

The *Click* and *DoubleClick* events are raised by controls in response to mouse clicks and double-clicks, respectively. These events are generally used to execute code based on a user choice, such as code executed when a user clicks a button. They pass an instance of the *EventArgs* class to their event handlers, along with a reference to the *sender*.

Controls are also capable of raising events in response to interaction with the mouse pointer. Depending on their actual type, controls might be capable of raising the mouse-related events detailed in Table 2.2.

Table 2.2.   Mouse-Related Events

Event	Description	Type of *EventArgs*
MouseEnter	This event is raised when the mouse pointer enters a control.	*System.EventArgs*
MouseMove	This event is raised when the mouse pointer moves over a control.	*System.MouseEventArgs*
MouseHover	This event is raised when the mouse pointer hovers over a control.	*System.EventArgs*
MouseDown	This event is raised when the mouse pointer is over a control and a button is pressed.	*System.MouseEventArgs*
MouseWheel	This event is raised when the mouse wheel moves while the control has focus.	*System.MouseEventArgs*
MouseUp	This event is raised when the mouse pointer is over a control and a button is released.	*System.MouseEventArgs*
MouseLeave	This event is raised when the mouse pointer moves off a control.	*System.EventArgs*

The *MouseEnter*, *MouseHover*, and *MouseLeave* events represent notification that the mouse pointer is in the region of a control. They pass relatively little information to their event handlers. By contrast, the *MouseMove*, *MouseDown*, *Mouse-Wheel*, and *MouseUp* events can be used to implement more substantial interactions between the user and the interface. Each of these events passes an instance of *MouseEventArgs* to the event handler. The *MouseEventArgs* object contains information about the state and location of the mouse, as summarized in Table 2.3.

Table 2.3.   *MouseEventArgs* Properties

Property	Description
Button	This property returns which, if any, mouse buttons are pressed.
Clicks	This property returns the number of times the mouse button was clicked.
Delta	This property returns the number of notches the mouse wheel rotated. This number can be either positive or negative, with positive representing forward rotation and negative representing reverse rotation. Each notch adds or subtracts 120 from the value returned.
x	This property returns the *x* coordinate of a mouse click.
y	This property returns the *y* coordinate of a mouse click.

Using Extender Provider Components

Extender providers are components that impart additional properties to controls. Take the *ToolTipProvider*, for example. When you place an instance of a *ToolTip-Provider* on a form, every control on that form receives a new property. This property can be viewed and set in the Properties window, where it appears as *ToolTip on n*, where *n* is the name of the *ToolTipProvider*. At run time, the value of this property is displayed in a yellow box when the mouse hovers over a control.

Extender providers are usually used to provide information to the users at run time. As we've seen, the *ToolTipProvider* can be used to provide Tool Tips at run time. Other extender providers include the *HelpProvider* and the *ErrorProvider*.

To use an extender provider in your project

1. Add a component of the appropriate extender type (such as *ErrorProvider*) to your form. The component appears in the component tray.

2. In the Properties window, set appropriate values for the properties provided by the extender provider.

The properties provided by extender providers actually reside in the extender providers themselves, not within the controls they extend. Thus, they are not true properties of the component and cannot be accessed in code at run time. The extender provider implements methods that can be used to access the properties it provides. By convention, these methods are always called *Getn* and *Setn*, where *n* is the name of the property provided. Thus, the *ToolTipProvider* implements methods named *GetToolTip* and *SetToolTip*, which can be used in code to access or dynamically change the value of the Tool Tip stored for a particular control. Both methods take a reference to the appropriate control as an argument, and the *Set* methods require a value to which the property is to be set.

To access the value of an extender property at run time

Use the *Get* method implemented for that property. You must supply a reference to the appropriate control.

Visual Basic .NET

```
' This example demonstrates how to retrieve the ToolTip for a
' Button called Button1
Dim myToolTip as String
myToolTip = ToolTip1.GetToolTip(Button1)
```

Visual C#

```
// This example demonstrates how to retrieve the ToolTip for a
// Button called button1
string myToolTip;
myToolTip = toolTip1.GetToolTip(button1);
```

To set the value of an extended property at run time

Use the *Set* method implemented for that property. You must supply a reference to the appropriate control and a new value for that property.

Visual Basic .NET

```
' This example demonstrates how to set the ToolTip for a Button
' called Button1
ToolTip1.SetToolTip(Button1, "Click this button for help")
```

Visual C#

```
// This example demonstrates how to set the ToolTip for a Button
// called button1
toolTip1.SetToolTip(button1, "Click this button for help");
```

Lesson Summary

- You can set the tab order of the controls on your form by setting the *TabIndex* property or by choosing Tab Order from the View menu and clicking on your controls to set the tab order.

- Some controls can contain other controls, which can be used to create logical and visual subdivisions of your form. Examples of controls that can contain other controls include

  - *Panel*

  - *GroupBox*

  - *TabPage*

- The *Dock* and *Anchor* properties implement automatic resizing or repositioning of the controls on your form. Setting the *Dock* property fixes a control to an edge of your form. Setting the *Anchor* property specifies whether your control remains fixed, floats, or changes size in response to the form resizing.

- You can use the controls collection of a form to dynamically add controls at run time. To add a control, you must declare and create an instance of it, and you must add it to the controls collection of the appropriate form.

- Additional controls can be added to the Toolbox by right-clicking the appropriate section of the Toolbox and then selecting the appropriate control, or by browsing to the DLL that contains that control.

- You can create methods that handle events for controls in the same manner you create methods that handle events for forms. These methods execute whenever the event they handle is raised.

- Extender provider components allow you to add more properties to the controls on a form. At run time, these properties are commonly used to provide information to the user, such as a Tool Tip or Help.

Lesson 4: Using Menus

Menus allow your users to easily access critical application functions and tools. Proper menu design and planning ensure proper functionality and accessibility of your application.

After this lesson, you will be able to

- Explain the importance of menus in interface design
- Describe the process of creating a menu using the *MainMenu* component
- Describe the process of creating a context menu using the *ContextMenu* component
- Explain how to enable or disable a menu item
- Explain how to create shortcut keys for menu items
- Explain how to display a check mark or a radio button on a menu item
- Explain how to make menu items invisible
- Explain how to dynamically add items to a menu
- Explain how to dynamically clone a menu

Estimated lesson time: 30 minutes

Menus allow users to access top-level commands and functions in a familiar, easy-to-understand interface. A well-designed menu that exposes your application's functionality in a logical, consistent manner makes your application easier to learn and use. A poorly designed menu, on the other hand, will be avoided and used only when necessary.

When designing menus, you should consider the logical flow of the application. Menu items should be grouped according to related functionality. Using access keys to enable keyboard shortcuts to menu items also makes your application easier to use.

Creating Menus During Design

Main menus are created during the design stage with the *MainMenu* component. The *MainMenu* component contains and manages a collection of *MenuItem* controls, which form the visual element of a menu at run time. With the *MainMenu* component, you can rapidly and intuitively create menus for your forms.

Using the MainMenu Component

The *MainMenu* component allows you to do the following:

- Create new menus and menu bars
- Add new menu items to existing menus
- Modify the properties of menus and menu items via the Properties window
- Create event handlers to handle the *Click* event and other events for menu items

To create a new menu, all you have to do is add a *MainMenu* component to your form. The component appears in the component tray, and a box with the text *Type Here* appears in the menu bar of the form. To create a new menu item, type in the box where indicated. The menu appears on your form as it would at run time. As you type, additional boxes are created beneath and to the right of the first menu item. Submenus are created the same way. If you want to create a submenu, simply type an entry to the right of the menu item that you want to expand. Figure 2.9 shows how to use the *MainMenu* component to create menus.

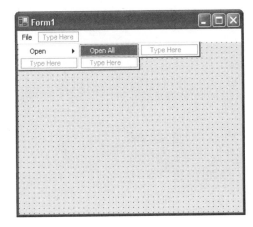

Figure 2.9.   Creating menus with the *MainMenu* component.

When an item is added to a menu, the designer creates an instance of a *MenuItem* object. Each *MenuItem* object has its own properties and members that can be set in the Properties window. The *Text* property represents the text that will be displayed at run time and is set to the text that you type. The *Name* property indicates how you will refer to this object in code and receives a changeable default value.

To create main menus at design time

1. In the Toolbox, add a *MainMenu* component to the form by double-clicking the *MainMenu* tool or by dragging it onto the form. A *MainMenu* component appears in the component tray.

2. In the designer, type the text for the first menu item in the box presented on the form's menu bar. As additional boxes appear, add additional menu items until the structure of your menu is complete. Note that the order in which you add menu items will be reflected in the menu layout.

3. In the Properties window, set any menu-item properties that you want to change, by first selecting the menu item in the designer, and then changing the desired properties.

4. In the Properties window of the form, make sure that the *Menu* property is set to the menu you want to display. If you have multiple menus on a form, only the designated menu will be displayed.

Separating Menu Items

You can separate menu items with a separator. A separator is a horizontal line between items on a menu. You can use separator bars to divide menu items into logical groups on menus that contain multiple items, as shown in Figure 2.10.

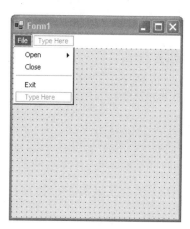

Figure 2.10.   Separator bars on menus.

You can add a separator to your menus by entering a hyphen as the text of a menu item. The hyphen will be displayed as a separator.

To create a separator bar on your menu

1. Select the menu item that represents where you want to place a separator.
2. Type a hyphen (-). At run time, this hyphen will be displayed as a separator bar.

Menu Access and Shortcut Keys

You can enable keyboard access to your menus with access and shortcut keys.

Access Keys

Access keys allow users to open a menu by pressing the Alt key and typing a designated letter. When the menu is open, you can select a menu command by pressing the Alt key and the correct access key. For example, in most programs, the Alt+F key opens the File menu. Access keys are displayed on the form as an underlined letter on the menu items.

You can use the same access key for different menu items as long as the menu items are contained in different menu groups. For example, you can use Alt+C to access the Close command on the File menu group as well as the Copy command on the Edit menu group. You should avoid using the same access key for multiple items on a menu group—for example, avoid using Alt+C for both the Cut and the Copy commands of an Edit menu group. If you do use the same access key combination for two items on a menu group, the access key lets you toggle your selection between the items, but you will be unable to select the item without first pressing the Enter key.

To assign an access key to a menu item

1. In the designer, click the menu item to which you want to assign an access key.

2. Type an ampersand (&) in front of the desired letter for the access key.

Shortcut Keys

Shortcut keys enable instant access to menu commands, thus providing a keyboard shortcut for frequently used menu commands. Shortcut key assignments can be single keys, such as Delete, F1, or Insert, or they can be key combinations, such as Ctrl+A, Ctrl+F1, or Ctrl+Shift+X. When a shortcut key is designated for a menu item, it is shown to the right of the menu item. The shortcut key combination will not be displayed if the *ShowShortcut* property of the menu item is set to *false*.

To assign a shortcut key

1. Select the menu item for which you want to enable a shortcut key.

2. In the Properties window, select the *Shortcut* property.

3. Choose the appropriate shortcut key combination from the drop-down menu.

Using Menu Item Events

You can create event handlers for menu items in the same way that you create event handlers for other controls. The most frequently used event is the *Click* event. The *Click* event handler should contain the code to be executed when the menu item is clicked. This code will also execute when a shortcut key combination is pressed.

The *Select* event is raised when a menu item is highlighted, either with the mouse or with access keys. You might create an event handler that provides detailed help regarding use of a menu command when selected.

The *Popup* event is raised just before a menu item's list is displayed. You can use this event to enable and disable menu items at run time.

See Lesson 2 of this chapter for information on creating an event handler.

Creating Context Menus

Context menus are menus that appear when an item is right-clicked. Context menus are created with the *ContextMenu* component. The *ContextMenu* component is edited in exactly the same way as the *MainMenu* component is edited. The *ContextMenu* appears at the top of the form, and you can add menu items by typing them on the control.

Context menus are very similar to main menus in many respects. Both contain and manage a collection of menu-item controls. You can enable shortcut keys, but not access keys for menu items in a context menu. To associate a context menu with a particular form or control, set the *ContextMenu* property of that form or control to the appropriate menu.

To create a context menu

1. In the Toolbox, add a *ContextMenu* component to the form, either by double-clicking the *ContextMenu* tool or by dragging it onto the form. A *ContextMenu* component appears in the component tray.

2. In the designer, type the text for the first menu item in the box presented on the form's menu bar. As additional boxes appear, add additional menu items until your menu structure is complete.

3. In the Properties window, set any properties and events (for Visual C#) that you want to change for your menu items.

4. Select the form or control with which you want to associate the context menu. In the Properties window for the control, set the *ContextMenu* property to your context menu. The context menu is displayed at run time when the control is right-clicked. You can associate a single context menu with several controls, but only one context menu can be associated per control.

Modifying Menus at Run Time

You can manipulate your menus to dynamically respond to run-time conditions. For example, if your application is unable to complete a certain command, you can disable the menu item that calls that command. You can display a check mark or a radio button next to a menu item to provide information to the user. You can make menu items invisible at times when it would be inappropriate to choose them. You can add menu items at run time, and menus can be cloned or merged with one another at run time.

Enabling and Disabling Menu Commands

Every menu item has an *Enabled* property. When this property is set to *false*, the menu is disabled and cannot respond to user actions. Access and shortcut key actions are also disabled for this menu item, which appears dimmed on the user interface. The following example demonstrates how to disable a menu item at run time:

Visual Basic .NET

```
MenuItem1.Enabled = False
```

Visual C#

```
menuItem1.Enabled = false;
```

Displaying Check Marks on Menu Items

You can use the *Checked* property to display a check mark next to a menu item. You might display a check mark to indicate that a particular option has been selected. The following example demonstrates how to select and clear a menu item:

Visual Basic .NET

```
' Checks the menu item
MenuItem1.Checked = True
' Unchecks the menu item
MenuItem1.Checked = False
```

Visual C#

```
// Checks the menu item
menuItem1.Checked = true;
// Unchecks the menu item
menuItem1.Checked = false;
```

Displaying Radio Buttons on Menu Items

You can display a radio button instead of a check mark. To display radio buttons, set the *RadioCheck* property for the menu item to *true*. The menu item will then display a radio button instead of a check mark. When the *Checked* property is *false*, neither a check mark nor a radio button will be displayed. Note that radio buttons frequently are used to display exclusive options, such as the choice of background colors. If you want to display radio buttons next to mutually exclusive options, you must write code that clears other options when one option is selected.

Making Menu Items Invisible

You can make your menu items invisible by setting the *Visible* property to *false*. You can use this property to modify your menus at run time in response to changing conditions. The following code demonstrates how to make a menu item invisible:

Visual Basic .NET

```
MenuItem1.Visible = False
```

Visual C#

```
menuItem1.Visible = false;
```

Note that making a menu item invisible at run time removes it from the menu bar. Any submenus contained by that menu item will also be inaccessible.

Cloning Menus

You can make a copy of existing menu items at run time. For example, you might want to clone an Edit menu item (and its associated submenus) from a main menu to serve as a context menu for a control. You can create a new menu item by using the *CloneMenu* method. The *CloneMenu* method creates a copy of the specified menu item and all of its members. This includes contained menu items, properties, and event handlers. Thus, all events that are handled by the original menu item will be handled in the same way by the cloned menu item. The newly created context menu can then be assigned to a control. The following example demonstrates how to clone a menu item as a new context menu at run time:

Visual Basic .NET

```
' The following example assumes the existence of a menu item called
' fileMenuItem and a control called myButton
' Declares and instantiates a new context menu
Dim myContextMenu as New ContextMenu()
' Clones fileMenuItem and fills myContextMenu with the cloned item
myContextMenu.MenuItems.Add(fileMenuItem.CloneMenu())
' Assigns the new context menu to myButton
myButton.ContextMenu = myContextMenu
```

Visual C#

```
// The following example assumes the existence of a menu item called
// fileMenuItem and a control called myButton
// Declares and instantiates a new context menu
ContextMenu myContextMenu = new ContextMenu();
// Clones fileMenuItem and fills myContextMenu with the cloned item
myContextMenu.MenuItems.Add(fileMenuItem.CloneMenu());
// Assigns the new context menu to myButton
myButton.ContextMenu = myContextMenu;
```

Merging Menus at Run Time

There might be times when you want to display multiple menus as a single menu. The *MergeMenu* method allows you to combine menus and display them as a single menu at run time. You can merge multiple main or context menus with each other, merge menus with menu items, or merge multiple menu items.

To merge menus at run time

Call the *MergeMenu* method of the menu or menu item that will be displayed. Supply the menu or menu item to be incorporated as the argument.

Visual Basic .NET

```
fileMenuItem.MergeMenu(myContextMenu)
```

Visual C#

```
fileMenuItem.MergeMenu(myContextMenu);
```

Adding Menu Items at Run Time

You can dynamically add new items to an existing menu at run time. For example, you might add menu items that display the pathnames of the most recently opened files. New menu items will not have event handlers associated with them, but you can specify a method to handle the *Click* event as an argument to the constructor of the new menu item. This method must be a *Sub* (*void*) method and have the same signature as other event handlers. An example follows:

Visual Basic .NET

```
Public Sub ClickHandler (ByVal sender As Object, ByVal e As _
    System.EventArgs)
    ' Implementation details omitted
End Sub
```

Visual C#

```
public void ClickHandler (object sender, System.EventArgs e)
{
    // Implementation details omitted
}
```

To add menu items at run time

1. Declare and instantiate a new menu item. You can specify a method to handle the *Click* event at this time if you choose. For example:

   Visual Basic .NET

   ```
   ' This example assumes the existence of a method called
   ' ClickHandler which has the correct event handler signature
   Dim myItem As MenuItem
   myItem = New MenuItem("Item 1", _
       New EventHandler(AddressOf ClickHandler))
   ```

   Visual C#

   ```
   // This example assumes the existence of a method called
   // ClickHandler which has the correct event handler signature
   MenuItem myItem;
   myItem = new MenuItem("Item 1",
       new EventHandler(ClickHandler));
   ```

2. Add the new method to the *MenuItems* collection of the menu you want to modify.

Visual Basic .NET

```
fileMenuItem.MenuItems.Add(myItem)
```

Visual C#

```
fileMenuItem.MenuItems.Add(myItem);
```

Lesson Summary

■ Menus allow you to enable access to high-level commands of your application through an easy-to-use interface. The *MainMenu* control allows you to rapidly create menus for your applications. Features that enhance menus include separator bars, access keys, and shortcut keys.

■ Context menus are useful for enabling access to commands in a variety of contextual situations. Context menus can be created with the *ContextMenu* control and are created at run time in the same manner as main menus.

■ At run time, menus can dynamically provide customized interaction between your application and its users. You can enable and disable menu items, make menu items invisible, and display a check mark or a radio button next to a menu item. You can also dynamically change the structure of menus by creating new menus with the *CloneMenu* method, merging multiple existing menus, or adding new menu items to existing menus.

Lesson 5: Validating User Input

In most applications, the user enters information for the application through the user interface. Data validation ensures that all data entered by a user falls within acceptable parameters before proceeding with program execution. For example, you might have a field where a user enters a zip code as part of an address. Using validation, you could verify that the field contained five and only five characters, all of which were numeric, before proceeding. Validating user input reduces the chance of an input error and makes your application more robust.

In this lesson, you will learn how to use events to validate user input and direct the focus on your forms. You will learn to use field-level validation, which validates entries as they are made, and form-level validation, which validates all the entries on a form at once. You will learn to use control properties to help restrict input, and you will use the *ErrorProvider* component to provide error messages to your users.

After this lesson, you will be able to

- Explain the difference between form-level and field-level validation
- Direct the focus using control methods and events
- Implement form-level validation for your form
- Implement field-level validation for your form

Estimated lesson time: 30 minutes

You can choose between two different types of validation for user input: form-level validation and field-level validation. *Form-level validation* verifies data after the user has filled in all the fields. For example, a user might be directed to fill in a name, address, and phone number, and then click OK. With form-level validation, all the fields on the form would be validated when the user clicked OK.

Field-level validation, on the other hand, verifies that the data in each field is appropriate. For example, if a user fills in a field that holds a phone number, field-level validation can verify that the number contains a valid area code before moving to the next field. As each digit is entered, control events can verify that only numbers are entered.

Field-Level Validation

You might want to validate data as it is entered into each field. Field-level validation gives you control over user input as it occurs. In this section, you will learn how to use control events to validate user input and how to use *TextBox* control properties to help restrict input to appropriate parameters.

Using TextBox Properties

The *TextBox* control is the most common control for user input. Several *TextBox* control properties let you restrict user input values to only those that are acceptable. Some of these properties include

- *MaxLength*
- *PasswordChar*
- *ReadOnly*
- *MultiLine*

Setting the MaxLength Property

The *MaxLength* property limits the number of characters that can be entered into a text box. If the user attempts to exceed the number returned by *MaxLength*, the text box will accept no further input and the system will beep to alert the user. This property is useful for text boxes that always contain data of the same length, such as a zip code field.

Using the PasswordChar Property

The *PasswordChar* property allows you to hide user input at run time. For example, if you set the *PasswordChar* property to an asterisk (*), the text box will display an asterisk for each character, regardless of user input. This behavior is commonly seen in password logon boxes.

Although an asterisk is the character most commonly used for passwords, you can choose any valid character—semicolons or ampersands, for example. The *Text* property value is always set to the value the user enters, regardless of the password character.

Setting the ReadOnly Property

The *ReadOnly* property determines whether a user can edit the value displayed in a text box. If *ReadOnly* is set to *true*, the text cannot be changed by user input. If *ReadOnly* is set to *false*, the user can edit the value normally.

Using the MultiLine Property

The *MultiLine* property determines whether a text box can accept multiple lines. When set to *true*, the user can enter multiple lines in the text box, each separated by a carriage return. The individual lines are stored as an array of strings in the *TextBox.Lines* collection and can be accessed by their index.

Using Events in Field-Level Validation

Field-level keyboard events allow you to immediately validate user input. Controls that can receive keyboard input raise the following three keyboard events:

- *KeyDown*
- *KeyPress*
- *KeyUp*

KeyDown and KeyUp

The *KeyDown* and *KeyUp* events are raised when a key is pressed and a key is released, respectively. The control that has the focus raises the event. When these events are raised, they package information about which key or combination of keys were pressed or released in an instance of *KeyEventArgs*, a class that describes the key combination. A method that handles the *KeyDown* or *KeyUp* event must include a *KeyEventArgs* parameter in its signature. Properties of *KeyEventArgs* are summarized in Table 2.4.

Table 2.4. *KeyEventArgs* Properties

Property	Description
Alt	Gets a value describing whether the Alt key was pressed
Control	Gets a value describing whether the Ctrl key was pressed
Handled	Gets or sets a value indicating whether the event was handled
KeyCode	Returns an enum value representing which key was pressed
KeyData	Returns data representing the key that was pressed, together with whether the Alt, Ctrl, or Shift key was pressed
KeyValue	Returns an integer representation of the *KeyData* property
Modifiers	Gets the modifier flags for the event, indicating what combination of Alt, Ctrl, or Shift keys was pressed
Shift	Gets a value describing whether the Shift key was pressed

The *KeyUp* and *KeyDown* events are most commonly used for determining if the Alt, Ctrl, or Shift key has been pressed. This information is exposed through properties in the *KeyEventArgs* reference that is passed to the handler. The *KeyEventArgs* properties—Alt, Control, and Shift—are properties that return a Boolean value, which indicates whether those keys are down. A value of *true* is returned if the corresponding key is down, and *false* is returned if the key is up. The following code demonstrates a *KeyUp* event handler that checks whether the Alt key is pressed:

Visual Basic .NET

```
Private Sub TextBox1_KeyUp(ByVal sender As Object, ByVal e As _
    System.Windows.Forms.KeyEventArgs) Handles TextBox1.KeyUp
    If e.Alt = True Then
        MessageBox.Show("The ALT key is still down")
    End If
End Sub
```

Visual C#

```
private void textBox1_KeyUp(object sender,
    System.Windows.Forms.KeyEventArgs e)
{
    if (e.Alt == true)
    MessageBox.Show("The ALT key is still down");
}
```

You also can use the *KeyEventArgs.KeyCode* property to examine the actual key that triggered the event. This property returns a *Key* value that represents the key that was pressed (in the case of a *KeyDown* event) or released (in the case of a *KeyUp* event). The following code shows a simple event handler that displays a message box containing a string representation of the key that was pressed:

Visual Basic .NET

```
Private Sub TextBox1_KeyDown(ByVal sender As Object, ByVal e As _
    System.Windows.Forms.KeyEventArgs) Handles TextBox1.KeyDown
    MessageBox.Show(e.KeyCode.ToString())
End Sub
```

Visual C#

```
private void textBox1_KeyDown(object sender,
    System.Windows.Forms.KeyEventArgs e)
{
    MessageBox.Show(e.KeyCode.ToString());
}
```

KeyPress

When a user presses a key that has a corresponding ASCII value, the *KeyPress* event is raised. Keys with a corresponding ASCII value include any alphabetic or numeric characters (alphanumeric a–z, A–Z, and 0–9), as well as some special keyboard characters, such as the Enter and Backspace keys. If a key or a key combination does not produce an ASCII value, it will not raise the *KeyPress* event. Examples of keys that do not raise this event include Ctrl, Alt, and the function keys.

This event is most useful for intercepting keystrokes and evaluating them. When this event is raised, an instance of *KeyPressEventArgs* passes to the event handler as a parameter. The *KeyPressEventArgs* instance contains information about the keystroke that can be used for validating user input. The *KeyPressEventArgs.KeyChar* property contains the ASCII character represented by the keystroke that raised the event. If you want to make sure that the key pressed was a numeric key, for example, you can evaluate the *KeyChar* property in your *KeyPress* event handler. The *KeyPressEventArgs.Handled* property can be used to set whether this event has been handled.

Validating Characters

The *Char* data type contains several *Shared* (*static*) methods that are useful for validating characters trapped by the *KeyPress* event. These methods include

- *Char.IsDigit*
- *Char.IsLetter*
- *Char.IsLetterOrDigit*
- *Char.IsPunctuation*
- *Char.IsLower*
- *Char.IsUpper*

Each of these methods, with their descriptive names, evaluates a character and returns a Boolean value. The *Char.IsDigit* function returns *true* if a character is a numeric digit and *false* if it is not. The *Char.IsLower* function returns *true* if a character is a lowercase letter, *false* otherwise. The other methods behave similarly. The following code uses the *Char.IsNumber* method to test whether the key pressed was a numeric key:

Visual Basic .NET

```
Private Sub TextBox1_KeyPress (ByVal sender As Object, ByVal e As _
    System.Windows.Forms.KeyPressEventArgs) Handles TextBox1.KeyPress
    If Char.IsDigit(e.KeyChar) = True Then
        MessageBox.Show("You pressed a number key")
    End If
End Sub
```

Visual C#

```
private void textBox1_KeyPress (object sender,
    System.Windows.Forms.KeyPressEventArgs e)
{
    if (Char.IsDigit(e.KeyChar) == true)
        MessageBox.Show("You pressed a number key");
}
```

Handling the Focus

Focus is the ability of an object to receive user input through the mouse or the keyboard. Although you can have several controls on your form, only one can have the focus at any given time. The control that has the focus is always on the active form of the application.

Every control implements the *Focus* method. This method sets the focus to the control that called it. The *Focus* method returns a Boolean value that indicates whether the control was successful in setting the focus. Disabled or invisible controls cannot receive the focus. You can determine whether a control can receive the focus by checking the *CanFocus* property, which returns *true* if the control can receive the focus and *false* if it cannot.

Visual Basic .NET

```
' This example checks to see if TextBox1 can receive the focus and
' sets the focus to it if it can.
If TextBox1.CanFocus = True Then
   TextBox1.Focus()
End If
```

Visual C#

```
// This example checks to see if textBox1 can receive the focus and
// sets the focus to it if it can.
if (textBox1.CanFocus == true)
   textBox1.Focus();
```

Focus events occur in the following order:

1. *Enter*
2. *GotFocus*
3. *Leave*
4. *Validating*
5. *Validated*
6. *LostFocus*

The *Enter* and *Leave* events are raised when the focus arrives at a control and whe the focus leaves a control, respectively. *GotFocus* and *LostFocus* are raised when control first obtains the focus and when the focus leaves the control, respectively. Although you can use these events for field-level validation, the *Validating* and *V* *idated* events are more suited to that task.

The Validating and Validated Events

The easiest way to validate data is to use the *Validating* event. The *Validating* even occurs before a control loses the focus. This event is raised only when the *Causes* *Validation* property of the control that is about to receive the focus is set to *true*. Thus, if you want to use the *Validating* event to validate data entered in your con-trol, the *CausesValidation* of the next control in the tab order should be set to *true* To use *Validating* events, the *CausesValidation* property of the control to be vali-dated also must be set to *true*. By default, the *CausesValidation* property of all co trols is set to *true* when controls are created at design time. Typically, the only controls that have *CausesValidation* set to *false* are controls such as Help buttons.

The *Validating* event allows you to perform sophisticated validation on your con-trols. For example, you can implement an event handler that tests whether the valu entered corresponds to a specific format. Another possible use is an event handle that disallows the focus to leave the control until a suitable value has been entere

The *Validating* event includes an instance of the *CancelEventArgs* class. This class contains a single property, *Cancel*. If the input in your control does not fall within required parameters, you can use the *Cancel* property within your event handler to cancel the *Validating* event and return the focus to the control.

The *Validated* event fires after a control has been successfully validated. You can use this event to perform any actions based on the validated input.

The following code demonstrates a handler for the *Validating* event. This method requires an entry in *TextBox1* before it will allow the focus to move to the next control.

Visual Basic .NET

```
Private Sub TextBox1_Validating(ByVal sender As Object, ByVal e As _
    System.ComponentModel.CancelEventArgs) Handles TextBox1.Validating
    ' Checks the value of TextBox1
    If TextBox1.Text = "" Then
        ' Resets the focus if there is no entry in TextBox1
        e.Cancel = True
    End If
End Sub
```

Visual C#

```
private void textBox1_Validating(object sender,
    System.ComponentModel.CancelEventArgs e)
{
    // Checks the value of textBox1
    if (textBox1.Text == "")
        // Resets the focus if there is no entry in TextBox1
        e.Cancel = true;
}
```

To use the Validating event of a text box

1. Add a text box to a form.
2. Create an event handler to handle the *Validating* event for the text box. In the event handler, set the *e.Cancel* property to *true* to cancel validating and return the focus to the text box.
3. Set the *CausesValidation* property to *false* for any controls for which you do not want the *Validating* event to fire.

Form-Level Validation

Form-level validation is the process of validating all fields on a form at once. A centralized procedure implements form-level validation and is usually called when the user is ready to proceed to another step. Implementing a form-level keyboard handler is a more advanced method of form-level validation.

The following code demonstrates how to create a form-level validation method. When a button named *btnValidate* is pressed, the sample tests whether all the text boxes on a form have received input and then resets the focus to the first text box it encounters with no input.

Visual Basic .NET

```
Private Sub btnValidate_Click(ByVal sender As System.Object, ByVal e _

    As System.EventArgs) Handles btnValidate.Click
    Dim aControl As System.Windows.Forms.Control
    ' Loops through each control on the form
    For Each aControl In Me.Controls
        ' Checks to see if the control being considered is a Textbox and
        ' if it contains an empty string
        If TypeOf aControl Is TextBox AndAlso aControl.Text = "" Then
            ' If a textbox is found to contain an empty string, it is
            ' given the focus and the method is exited.
            aControl.Focus()
            Exit Sub
        End If
    Next
End Sub
```

Visual C#

```
private void btnValidate_Click(object sender, System.EventArgs e)
    {
    // Loops through each control on the form
    foreach (System.Windows.Forms.Control aControl in this.Controls)
    {
        // Checks to see if the control being considered is a Textbox
        // and if it contains an empty string
        if (aControl is System.Windows.Forms.TextBox & aControl.Text
            == "")
        {
            // If a textbox is found to contain an empty string, it is
            // given the focus and the method is exited.
            aControl.Focus();
            return;
        }
    }
}
```

Form-Level Keyboard Handler

A keyboard handler is a somewhat more sophisticated technique for form-level validation. A centralized keyboard handler allows you to manage data input for all fields on a form. For example, you can create a method that enables command buttons only after appropriate input has been entered into each field and that performs specific actions with each keystroke.

The *KeyPress*, *KeyDown*, and *KeyUp* events are used to implement a form-level keyboard handler. If a form has no visible or enabled controls, it will raise keyboard events. If the form has controls, however, these events will not be raised. For the form to raise these events, the *KeyPreview* property of the form must be set to *true*. When set to *true*, the form raises keystroke events before the control that has the focus. For example, assume that there is a *KeyPress* handler for the form, that there is a *KeyPress* handler for a text box on that form, and that the *KeyPreview* property of the form is set to *true*. When a key is pressed, the form raises the *KeyPress* event first and the form's *KeyPress* event handler executes first. When execution is complete, the text box's *KeyPress* event handler will execute.

If you are using form-level validation, you can prevent a control's *KeyPress* event handler from executing by setting the *KeyPressEventArgs.Handled* property to *True*, as shown in the following example:

Visual Basic .NET

```
Private Sub Form1_KeyPress(ByVal sender As Object, ByVal e As _
   System.Windows.Forms.KeyPressEventArgs) Handles MyBase.KeyPress
   ' This handles the event and prevents it from being passed to
   ' the control's KeyPress event handler
   e.Handled = True
End Sub
```

Visual C#

```
private void Form1_KeyPress(object sender,
   System.Windows.Forms.KeyPressEventArgs e)
{
   // This handles the event and prevents it from being passed to
   // the control's KeyPress event handler
   e.Handled = true;
}
```

Providing User Feedback

When invalid input is entered into a field, the user should be alerted and given an opportunity to correct the error. There are many ways to inform the user of an input error. If the error is obvious and self-explanatory, an audio cue can alert the user to the problem. In Visual Basic .NET, the *Beep* method produces an attention-getting sound.

Visual Basic .NET

```
' This line causes an audible beep
Beep()
```

Note   Visual C# does not have an inherent beep function.

Other ways to draw a user's attention to an error include changing a control's *Back-Color* or *ForeColor*. For example, a text box with invalid input could have its *Back-Color* changed to red.

If a more detailed message is required, you can use the *MessageBox.Show* method. This method displays a small, modal dialog box with an informative message. Because the dialog box is displayed modally, it halts program execution and is impossible for the user to ignore. The following example shows how to call the *MessageBox.Show* method, along with an informative message:

Visual Basic .NET

```
MessageBox.Show("That value is not valid for this control")
```

Visual C#

```
MessageBox.Show("That value is not valid for this control");
```

The ErrorProvider Component

The *ErrorProvider* component provides an easy way to communicate validation errors to your users. The *ErrorProvider* allows you to set an error message for each control on your form whenever the input is invalid. An error message produces an error icon next to the control, and error message text is shown as a Tool Tip when the mouse hovers over the affected control. The *ErrorProvider* component is found in the Windows Forms tab of the Toolbox.

Displaying an Error

To cause an error condition to be displayed next to a control, you use the *SetError* method of the *ErrorProvider* component. The *SetError* method requires the name of the control to be set and the text to be provided. The method is invoked as shown:

Visual Basic .NET

```
' This example assumes the existence of a control named nameTextBox
' and an ErrorProvider named myErrorProvider
myErrorProvider.SetError(nameTextBox, "Name cannot be left blank!")
```

Visual C#

```
// This example assumes the existence of a control named nameTextBox
// and an ErrorProvider named myErrorProvider
myErrorProvider.SetError(nameTextBox, "Name cannot be left blank!");
```

You can also set an error at design time. In the Properties window, you will see that once you add an *ErrorProvider* control to your form, each control has a new property named *Error on x* where *x* is the name of the *ErrorProvider*. You can set this property to a value in the Properties window. If a value is set for the error, the control immediately shows an error at run time.

Different properties of the *ErrorProvider* component affect how the information is displayed to the user. The *Icon* property controls which icon is displayed next to the control. You might want to have multiple error providers on a single form—one that reports errors and one that reports warnings. You could use different icons for each to provide visual cues to the user. Another property is the *BlinkStyle* property. This property determines whether the error icon blinks when displayed. The *BlinkRate* property determines how rapidly the icon blinks.

To create a validation handler that uses the ErrorProvider component

1. Create your form, and add an *ErrorProvider* component. The *ErrorProvider* component appears in the component tray.

2. Set the *CausesValidation* property of the control for which you want to provide errors to *true* if it is not *true* already.

3. In the event handler for that control's *Validating* event, test the value. Use the *SetError* method to set the error to be displayed when an error condition occurs. The following code demonstrates a validation handler for a text box named pswordTextBox and an error provider named myErrorProvider:

Visual Basic .NET

```
Private Sub pswordTextBox_Validating(ByVal sender As Object, _
   ByVal e As System.ComponentModel.CancelEventArgs) _
   Handles pswordTextBox.Validating
   ' Validate the entry
   If pswordTextBox.Text = "" Then
      ' Set the error for an invalid entry
      myErrorProvider.SetError(pswordTextBox, _
         "Password cannot be blank!")
   Else
      ' Clear the error for a valid entry-no error will be displayed
      myErrorProvider.SetError(pswordTextBox, "")
   End If
End Sub
```

Visual C#

```
private void pswordTextBox_Validating(object sender,
   System.ComponentModel.CancelEventArgs e)
{
   // Validate the entry
   if (pswordTextBox.Text == "")
      // Set the error for an invalid entry
      myErrorProvider.SetError(pswordTextBox,
         "Password cannot be blank!");
   else
      // Clear the error for a valid entry-no error will be displayed
      myErrorProvider.SetError(pswordTextBox, "");
}
```

Lesson Summary

- Form-level validation validates all fields on a form simultaneously. Field-level validation validates each field as data is entered. Field-level validation provides a finer level of validation control.

- The *TextBox* control contains several properties that restrict the values users can enter. These include

  - *MaxLength*

  - *PasswordChar*

  - *ReadOnly*

  - *MultiLine*

- Keyboard events allow you to validate keystrokes; these events are raised by the control that has the focus and is receiving input. The form also raises these events when the *KeyPreview* property is set to *true*. These events are

  - *KeyDown*

  - *KeyUp*

  - *KeyPress*

- The *Char* structure contains several static methods that are useful for validating character input. These methods are

  - *Char.IsDigit*

  - *Char.IsLetter*

  - *Char.IsLetterOrDigit*

  - *Char.IsPunctuation*

  - *Char.IsLower*

  - *Char.IsUpper*

- The *Validating* event occurs before the control loses focus and should be used to validate user input. This event occurs only when the *CausesValidation* property of the control that is about to receive the focus is set to *true*. To keep the focus from moving away from the control in the *Validating* event handler, set the *CancelEventArgs.Cancel* property to *true* in the event handler.

- The *ErrorProvider* component allows you to set an error for a control at run time that displays a visual cue and an informative message to the user. To display an error at run time, use the *ErrorProvider.SetError* method.

Lab 2: The Virtual Doughnut Factory

In this lab, you will create the user interface for a Virtual Doughnut Factory application in either Visual Basic .NET or Visual C#. Your application will serve as a storefront and control panel for an automated doughnut factory. You will add controls, menus, and implement validation. The solution to this lab is available on the Supplemental Course Materials CD-ROM in the \Labs\Ch02\Solution folder.

Before You Begin

There are no prerequisites to completing this lab.

Estimated lesson time: 60 minutes

Exercise 2.1: Creating the User Interface

In this exercise, you will create the user interface by adding controls to the Virtual Doughnut Factory inventory form.

▶ **To create a new project**

1. Select Visual Basic .NET or Visual C# as your preference. Open a new Windows Application project, and name it Virtual Doughnut Factory.

2. The project is opened with one form. In Solution Explorer, click Form1. The Properties window displays the *File* properties for Form1. Change the File Name property to *frmMain.vb* or *frmMain.cs* as appropriate.

3. Set the properties listed in Table 2.5.

Table 2.5.   Properties of the Initial Form

Object	Property	Value
Form1	*Name*	frmMain
	Text	Virtual Doughnut Factory
	Size	480, 400 (approximately)
Virtual Doughnut Factory (Visual Basic .NET only)	*Startup Object*	frmMain

4. If you are using Visual C#, locate *static void Main()* and change it so that it reads as follows:

Visual C#

```
static void Main()
{
    Application.Run(new frmMain());
}
```

5. Add the controls listed in Table 2.6 to the form.

Table 2.6.   Controls and Properties for *frmMain*

Control	Control Type	Property	Value
Label1	Label	*Name*	lblTitle
		Text	Current Inventory
		Font.Size	14
		Font.Bold	True
Label2	Label	*Name*	lblRaised
		Text	Raised
Label3	Label	*Name*	lblCake
		Text	Cake
Label4	Label	*Name*	lblFilled
		Text	Filled
Label5	Label	*Name*	lblGlazedRaised
		Text	Glazed
TextBox1	TextBox	*Name*	txtGlazedRaised
		Text	<blank>
		ReadOnly	True
Label6	Label	*Name*	lblSugarRaised
		Text	Sugar
TextBox2	TextBox	*Name*	txtSugarRaised
		Text	<blank>
		ReadOnly	True
Label7	Label	*Name*	lblChocolateRaised
		Text	Chocolate
TextBox3	TextBox	*Name*	txtChocolateRaised
		Text	<blank>
		ReadOnly	True
Label8	Label	*Name*	lblPlainCake
		Text	Plain
TextBox4	TextBox	*Name*	txtPlainCake
		Text	<blank>
		ReadOnly	True
Label9	Label	*Name*	lblChocolateCake
		Text	Chocolate

Table 2.6.   Controls and Properties for *frmMain*

Control	Control Type	Property	Value
TextBox5	TextBox	*Name*	txtChocolateCake
		Text	\<blank\>
		ReadOnly	True
Label10	Label	*Name*	lblSugarCake
		Text	Sugar
TextBox6	TextBox	*Name*	txtSugarCake
		Text	\<blank\>
		ReadOnly	True
Label11	Label	*Name*	lblLemonFilled
		Text	Lemon
TextBox7	TextBox	*Name*	txtLemonFilled
		Text	\<blank\>
		ReadOnly	True
Label12	Label	*Name*	lblGrapeFilled
		Text	Grape
TextBox8	TextBox	*Name*	txtGrapeFilled
		Text	\<blank\>
		ReadOnly	True
Label13	Label	*Name*	lblCustardFilled
		Text	Custard
TextBox9	TextBox	*Name*	txtCustardFilled
		Text	\<blank\>
		ReadOnly	True
Label14	Label	*Name*	lblSale
		Text	Current Sale
Label15	Label	*Name*	lblQuantity
		Text	Quantity
Label16	Label	*Name*	lblType
		Text	Type
Label17	Label	*Name*	lblPrice
		Text	Price
TextBox10	TextBox	*Name*	txtQuantity
		Text	0

Table 2.6.   Controls and Properties for *frmMain*

Control	Control Type	Property	Value
ComboBox1	ComboBox	*Name*	cmbType
		Text	\<blank>
TextBox11	TextBox	*Name*	txtPrice
		Text	\<blank>
		ReadOnly	True
ListBox1	ListBox	*Name*	lstSale
Label18	Label	*Name*	lblTotal
		Text	Total
TextBox12	TextBox	*Name*	txtTotal
		Text	\<blank>
		ReadOnly	True
Button1	Button	*Name*	btnAddToSale
		Text	Add To Sale
Button2	Button	*Name*	btnRemoveItem
		Text	Remove Item
Button3	Button	*Name*	btnCheckOut
		Text	Check Out

6. In the Properties window, add the following strings to the *Items* collection of *cmbType*: Raised-Glazed, Raised-Sugar, Raised-Chocolate, Cake-Plain, Cake-Chocolate, Cake-Sugar, Filled-Lemon, Filled-Grape, Filled-Custard.

When all of the controls have been added, position them in logical groupings according to function. Figure 2.11 represents a possible layout for your controls.

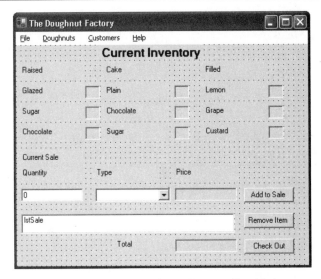

Figure 2.11.   The user interface with controls added.

Exercise 2.2: Adding a Menu

In this exercise, you will use the *MainMenu* component to add a menu bar to your form and create an event handler for the *Click* event of the Exit menu item.

▶ **To add a menu to the project**

1. In the Toolbox, double-click the *MainMenu* component. A *MainMenu* component is added to the component tray of the designer, and a menu box is added to the form.

2. In the menu box, type **&File**.

3. A menu item is added to the menu bar, and new menu boxes are added below and to the right of the menu item. The ampersand (&) provides an access key to the menu. In the Properties window, name this menu item **mnuFile**.

4. Repeat Step 2 to create the menu structure shown in Table 2.7. Indented items are subordinates of the item in the preceding step.

Table 2.7.   Menu Item Properties

Menu Item	Name
&File	mnuFile
E&xit	mnuExit
&Doughnuts	mnuDoughnuts
&Make	mnuMake
&Remove Stale	mnuRemoveStale

Table 2.7.   Menu Item Properties

Menu Item	Name
&Customers	mnuCustomers
&Add a Customer	mnuAddaCustomer
&View Customers	mnuViewCustomers
&Help	mnuHelp
&About	mnuAbout
&Contents	mnuContents

▶ **To create an event handler for the Exit menu item**

1. In the designer, double-click the Exit menu item. The code window opens to the *mnuExit_Click* event handler.

2. Call the *Close* method of the form to create the event handler. For example:

Visual Basic .NET

```
Private Sub mnuExit_Click(ByVal sender As System.Object, _
    ByVal e As System.EventArgs) Handles mneExit.Click
    Me.Close()
End Sub
```

Visual C#

```
private void mnuExit_Click(object sender, System.EventArgs e)
{
    this.Close();
}
```

3. Save and test the application.

Exercise 2.3: Creating Validation Handlers

In this exercise, you will use the *ErrorProvider* component to implement simple validation handlers for *txtQuantity*. In future labs, you will add additional validation to your form.

▶ **To create validation handlers with Visual Basic .NET**

1. In the Toolbox, double-click the *ErrorProvider* component. An *ErrorProvider* is added to the component tray in the designer.

2. Right-click the designer, and choose View Code to open the code editor. In the code editor, select *txtQuantity* in the left drop-down menu and *KeyPress* in the right drop-down menu. An empty event handler for *txtQuantity_KeyPress* appears in the code editor.

3. Write code that will display an error if non-numeric characters are entered into the text box.

Visual Basic .NET

```
Private Sub txtQuantity_KeyPress(ByVal sender As Object, _
    ByVal e As System.Windows.Forms.KeyPressEventArgs) _
    Handles txtQuantity.KeyPress
    If Char.IsDigit(e.KeyChar) = False Then
        ErrorProvider1.SetError(txtQuantity, _
        "Please enter a numeric value")
    Else
        ErrorProvider1.SetError(txtQuantity, "")
    End If
End Sub
```

4. In the drop-down menu on the left, choose *txtQuantity*, and in the drop-down menu on the right, choose *Validating*. An empty event handler is added to the code editor.

5. Add code to validate that the *txtQuantity* field is not empty and has no other errors on it. For example:

Visual Basic .NET

```
Private Sub txtQuantity_Validating(ByVal sender As System.Object, _
    ByVal e As System.ComponentModel.CancelEventArgs) _
    Handles txtQuantity.Validating
    ' Tests that the textbox is not empty
    If txtQuantity.Text = "" Then
        ErrorProvider1.SetError(txtQuantity, _
        "Please enter a quantity")
        e.Cancel = True
        ' Tests that there are no other errors on the textbox.
    ElseIf ErrorProvider1.GetError(txtQuantity) <> "" Then
        e.Cancel = True
    Else
        ErrorProvider1.SetError(txtQuantity, "")
    End If
End Sub
```

6. Press F5 to build and test your code.

▶ **To create validation handlers with Visual C#**

1. In the Toolbox, double-click the *ErrorProvider* component. An *ErrorProvider* is added to the component tray in the designer.

2. In the designer, select *txtQuantity*. In the Properties window, press the Events button. Double-click the entry for *KeyPress*. An empty event handler for *txtQuantity_KeyPress* appears in the code editor.

3. Write code that will display an error if non-numeric characters are entered into the text box.

Visual C#

```csharp
private void txtQuantity_KeyPress(object sender,
    System.Windows.Forms.KeyPressEventArgs e)
{
    if (Char.IsDigit(e.KeyChar) == false)
        errorProvider1.SetError(txtQuantity,
        "Please enter a numeric value");
    else
        errorProvider1.SetError(txtQuantity, "");
}
```

4. In the Solution Explorer, right-click *frmMain* and choose View Designer. Selec *txtQuantity*. In the Properties window, press the Events button and double-click the entry for *Validating*. An empty event handler is added to the code editor.

5. Add code to validate that the *txtQuantity* field is not empty and has no other errors on it. For example:

Visual C#

```csharp
private void txtQuantity_Validating(object sender,
    System.ComponentModel.CancelEventArgs e)
{
    // Tests that the textbox is not empty
    if (txtQuantity.Text == "")
    {
        errorProvider1.SetError(txtQuantity,
            "Please enter a quantity");
        e.Cancel = true;
    }
    // Tests that there are no other errors on the textbox.
    else if (errorProvider1.GetError(txtQuantity) != "")
        e.Cancel = true;
    else
        errorProvider1.SetError(txtQuantity, "");
}
```

6. Press F5 to build and test your code.

Review

The following review questions are intended to reinforce key concepts and information presented in this chapter. If you are unable to answer a question, return to the appropriate lesson and review, and then try the lesson again. Answers to the questions can be found in Appendix A.

1. You are creating an application for a major bank. The application should integrate seamlessly with Microsoft Office XP, be easy to learn, and instill a sense of corporate pride in users. Name two ways you might approach these goals in the user interface.

2. You are writing an application that needs to display a common set of controls on several different forms. What is the fastest way to approach this problem?

3. If you wanted to prompt a user for input every time a form received the focus, what would be the best strategy for implementing this functionality?

4. Describe two ways to set the tab order of controls on your form.

5. What is an extender provider, and what does it do?

6. Explain when you might implement a context menu instead of a main menu.

7. Describe what is meant by field-level validation and form-level validation.

8. Describe how to retrieve the ASCII key code from a keystroke. How would you retrieve key combinations for non-ASCII keys?

9. Describe in general terms how to add a control to a form at run time.

C H A P T E R   3

Types and Members

About This Chapter

This chapter describes how to use different data types, constants, enums, arrays, and collections. Additionally, this chapter explains how to implement properties and events.

Before You Begin

There are no prerequisites to complete the lessons in this chapter.

Lesson 1: Using Data Types

The Microsoft .NET Framework provides a robust system of primitive types to store and represent data in your application. Data primitives represent integer numbers, floating-point numbers, Boolean values, characters, and strings. This type system enforces type-safety so that implicit casts occur only when no loss of data is possible. Explicit conversions can be performed in situations that might cause a loss of data. The .NET data types contain functionality to perform a variety of type-related conversions and tasks.

After this lesson, you will be able to

- Describe the data types provided by the .NET Framework
- Explain how to perform implicit and explicit conversions between types
- Describe the functionality provided by types of the .NET Framework
- Describe string manipulation functions with the *String* class methods

Estimated lesson time: 30 minutes

The .NET Framework provides an extensive system of types that allow you to store, manipulate, and pass values between members of your application. The .NET languages are *strongly typed*. Strongly typed means that objects of one type cannot be freely exchanged with objects of a different type. A call will fail if method and property parameters are not the appropriate type. Implicit and explicit conversions allow you to convert data types when necessary. Such conversions are possible because all types in the .NET Framework derive from *Object*, the base type of all classes and structures.

The .NET Data Types

The .NET data types store your data. They are value types and can be broken down into the following subcategories: Integer types, floating-point types, the Boolean type, and the Char type. Two built-in reference types, the String type and the Object type, are an integral part of your application.

Integer Types

The .NET Framework provides a variety of Integer types. Table 3.1 summarizes these types and lists their corresponding Visual Basic .NET and Visual C# types.

Table 3.1.   Integer Types in the .NET Framework

Type	Visual C# Name	Visual Basic .NET Name	Description	Range
System.Byte	byte	Byte	8-bit unsigned integer	0 to 255
System.Int16	short	Short	16-bit signed integer	−32768 to 32767
System.Int32	int	Integer	32-bit signed integer	-2^{31} to $2^{31}-1$
System.Int64	long	Long	64-bit signed integer	-2^{63} to $2^{63}-1$
System.SByte	sbyte	(Not implemented)	8-bit signed integer	−128 to 127
System.UInt16	ushort	(Not implemented)	16-bit unsigned integer	0 to 65535
System.UInt32	uint	(Not implemented)	32-bit unsigned integer	0 to $2^{32}-1$
System.UInt64	ulong	(Not implemented)	64-bit unsigned integer	0 to $2^{64}-1$

You can assign values to the Integer types using either decimal or hexadecimal notation. To use hexadecimal notation in an integer literal, it should be prefixed with &H for Visual Basic .NET and 0x for Visual C#. For example:

Visual Basic .NET

```
Dim myInteger As Integer
myInteger = &H32EF
```

Visual C#

```
int myInteger;
myInteger = 0x32EF;
```

Floating-Point Types

Three floating-point types can be used to represent numbers that have a fractional component. They are summarized in Table 3.2.

Table 3.2.   Floating-Point Types in the .NET Framework

Type	Visual C# Name	Visual Basic .NET Name	Description	Precision	Range (Approximate)
System.Single	float	Single	32-bit floating-point variable	7 significant digits	$+/-1.4 \times 10^{-45}$ to $+/-3.4 \times 10^{38}$
System.Double	double	Double floating-point variable	64-bit significant digits	15–16	$+/-5.0 \times 10^{-324}$ to $+/-1.7 \times 10^{308}$
System.Decimal	decimal	Decimal floating-point variable	128-bit digits	28 significant	$+/-1.0 \times 10^{-28}$ to $+/-7.9 \times 10^{28}$

The System.Single type is appropriate for floating-point calculations that require a lower degree of precision than normal floating-point operations. It provides seven significant digits of precision. For a much greater degree of precision, you can use the System.Double type, which also has the ability to handle vastly larger values. The System.Decimal type is specifically designed to facilitate financial calculations and is an ultra-high-precision variable. Although it cannot hold values as great as System.Double, it has a much higher level of precision, providing 28 significant digits.

Non-Numeric Types

Four additional types do not represent numbers: System.Boolean, System.Char, System.String, and System.Object.

System.Boolean

The System.Boolean type is used to represent a value that is either *true* or *false*. It is called Boolean in Visual Basic .NET, and bool in Visual C#. The values that are valid for Boolean variables are *True* and *False* (Visual Basic .NET) or *true* and *false* (Visual C#).

System.Char

The System.Char type represents a single instance of a 16-bit Unicode character. It is called Char in Visual Basic .NET and char in Visual C#. You can assign a character literal to a variable of this type by enclosing the literal in double quotes using the suffix "c" (Visual Basic .NET) or in single quotes (Visual C#), as follows:

Visual Basic .NET

```
Dim myChar As Char
myChar = "W"c
```

Visual C#

```
char myChar;
myChar = 'W';
```

You can also use the numeric value of the Unicode character to make the assignment to a Char variable. In Visual Basic .NET, you must use the Chr or ChrW function to make the assignment. In Visual C#, you can provide a four-digit hexadecimal Unicode character. Examples follow:

Visual Basic .NET

```
Dim myChar As Char
myChar = Chr(521)
```

Visual C#

```
char myChar;
myChar = '\u01fe';
```

System.String

The System.String type is a reference type that represents a series of Char data types. In everyday terms, a string can represent a word, a paragraph, a key value, or any other string of characters. In Visual Basic .NET, this type is called String, and in Visual C#, it is called string. You can assign string literals to a string variable by enclosing them in double quotes, as follows:

Visual Basic .NET

```
Dim myString As String
myString = "This is a String! Wow!"
```

Visual C#

```
string myString;
myString = "This is a String! Wow!";
```

The *String* class contains a good deal of built-in functionality, which is discussed later in this lesson.

System.Object

The Object type is the supertype of all types in the .NET Framework. Every type, whether value type or reference type, derives from System.Object. In Visual Basic .NET, it is called Object, and in Visual C#, it is called object. You can assign any object or value to an object variable as follows:

Visual Basic .NET

```
Dim myObject As Object
myObject = 543
myObject = New System.Windows.Forms.Form()
```

Visual C#

```
object myObject;
myObject = 543;
myObject = new System.Windows.Forms.Form();
```

If an object of a particular type is stored in an *Object* variable, it must be explicitly converted back to that type to access any of its inherent functionality.

Converting Types

At times, you will need to convert data from one type to another. Data can be converted in two ways: *implicitly*, which means that the conversion is performed automatically, and *explicitly*, which means that you must specifically ask for the conversion to be performed.

Implicit Conversions

Implicit conversions between types are performed whenever the conversion can occur without the loss of data. For example:

Visual Basic .NET

```
Dim anInteger As Integer = 100
Dim aLong As Long
' Because a long can be assigned to every possible value of integer,
' there is no chance of losing data
aLong = anInteger
```

Visual C#

```
int anInteger = 100;
long aLong;
// Because a long can be assigned to every possible value of integer,
// there is no chance of losing data
aLong = anInteger;
```

If a type can be implicitly converted to another type, you can use the first type any where that the second is required without special syntax. For example, in method calls:

Visual Basic .NET

```
' This example assumes that the TakesADouble method requires a
' Double as a parameter
Dim I As Integer = 100
' I is implicitly converted to Double and used in the method call
TakesADouble(I)
```

Visual C#

```
// This example assumes that the TakesAdouble method requires a
// double as a parameter
int I = 100;
// I is implicitly converted to double and used in the method call
TakesAdouble(I);
```

Table 3.3 shows the implicit conversions that are supported by Visual Basic .NET and Visual C#.

Table 3.3.   Implicit Conversions in Visual Basic .NET and Visual C#

From	To
Byte (Visual Basic .NET)	Short, Integer, Long, Single, Double, Decimal
byte (Visual C#)	short, ushort, int, uint, long, ulong, float, double, decimal
Short	Integer, Long, Single, Double, Decimal
short	int, long, float, double, decimal

Table 3.3.   Implicit Conversions in Visual Basic .NET and Visual C#

From	To
Integer	Long, Single, Double, Decimal
int	long, float, double, decimal
Long	Single, Double, Decimal
long	float, double, decimal
Single	Double
float	double
Char	Integer, Long, Single, Double, Decimal
char	int, uint, long, ulong, float, double, decimal
sbyte (Visual C# only)	short, int, long, float, double, decimal
ushort (Visual C# only)	int, uint, long, ulong, float, double, decimal
uint (Visual C# only)	long, ulong, float, double, decimal
ulong (Visual C# only)	float, double, decimal

Explicit Conversions

When performing a conversion where types cannot be implicitly converted, you must explicitly convert the types. This conversion is called a *cast*. Explicit conversions are accomplished in Visual Basic .NET using the *CType* function and using a special syntax in Visual C#. Examples follow:

Visual Basic .NET

```
Dim aLong As Long = 1000
Dim anInteger As Integer
anInteger = CType(aLong, Integer)
```

Visual C#

```
long aLong = 1000;
int anInteger;
anInteger = (int)aLong;
```

Explicit conversions can be risky. In the preceding example, the conversion was accomplished without any difficulty because both a Long and an Integer can hold a value of 1000. However, consider the following example:

Visual Basic .NET

```
Dim anInteger As Integer = 100000
Dim aShort As Short
aShort = CType(anInteger, Short)
```

Visual C#

```
int anInteger = 100000;
short aShort;
aShort = (short)anInteger;
```

The code in this example will compile and execute without raising an error. However, when you examine the value of *aShort*, you find that it contains −31072. Because the maximum value of *aShort* is smaller than the value that you attempted to convert, the conversion could not be performed and a different value was returned.

Note Because explicit casts are inherently dangerous, you should use them only when absolutely necessary, and you should always provide a system for handling failed casts and handle any exceptions that might be thrown. Exception handling will be discussed in Chapter 5.

Option Strict in Visual Basic .NET

Visual Basic .NET provides a programming option called Option Strict. When Option Strict is on, strong typing is enforced and only conversions that can be performed without loss of data are allowed. When Option Strict is off, however, strong typing is not enforced and all conversions are performed implicitly. The default setting for Visual Basic .NET is Option Strict Off. To set Option Strict On, use the *Option* keyword in the first line of your code file. For example:

Visual Basic .NET

```
Option Strict On
```

The primary purpose of Option Strict Off is backward compatibility with previous versions of Visual Basic. Whenever possible, you should program with Option Strict On. This will allow you to catch many errors during compilation that would be extremely difficult to track down at run time.

To convert types

- If the conversion is of a type where no data can be lost, it will be performed implicitly and no explicit declaration is needed.
- If the conversion potentially could cause a loss of data, you must perform an explicit cast to convert your types. Use the *CType* function in Visual Basic .NET, and the cast syntax function in Visual C#.

Using Data Type Functionality

All data types have built-in functionality. At the very least, they all support the following four methods:

- *Equals.* Determines whether two instances are equal
- *GetHashCode.* Serves as a hash function for a particular type
- *GetType.* Returns the type object for the current instance
- *ToString.* Returns a human-readable form of the object

You have seen that the data types are small. How, then, are they able to implement these methods?

Boxing

The secret is called boxing. Boxing is the implicit conversion of value types to reference types. All classes and types derive from *Object*, and each of these four methods is a method of the *Object* class. Because each class derives from *Object*, each class can be implicitly converted to that type. When you call one of these methods, the Common Language Runtime creates a temporary reference for your value type variable and allows you to treat it as a reference type.

You also can box value types manually. To do this, you simply assign your value to a variable of the *Object* type. An example follows:

Visual Basic .NET

```
Dim I As Integer = 100
Dim O As Object
O = I
```

Visual C#

```
int I = 100;
object O;
O = I;
```

Unboxing is the conversion of a boxed variable back to a value type. To unbox a variable, you must perform an explicit cast on the object to convert it to the appropriate type. Only objects that have been boxed can be unboxed.

Data Type Member Methods

Data types also have methods that do not derive from *Object*. These methods usually involve functionality specific to the type. For example, in Chapter 2, you were introduced to some of the comparison functions of the Char data type. Although a detailed discussion of all these methods is beyond the scope of this lesson, summaries of some of the more useful methods are provided.

Parse

All of the value data types implement a *Parse* method. *Parse* is used to create a numeric value from a string. The *Parse* method is extremely useful when developing user interfaces. Controls that accept user input, such as *TextBox*, do so in the form of a string. The *Parse* method can be used to convert that string to usable data. Note that if a string cannot be read as a numeric value, an error will result. In all implementations, *Parse* is a *static* (*Shared*) method and must be called from the type object rather than from an instance.

To convert a string to a numeric data type

Call the *Parse* method of that data type on that method. An example follows:

Visual Basic .NET

```
Dim I As Integer
Dim S As String
S = "1234"
' I = 1234
I = Integer.Parse(S)
```

Visual C#

```
int I;
string S;
S = "1234";
// I = 1234
I = int.Parse(S);
```

String Functions

String manipulations are keenly important for many applications—converting strings to display formats, for instance, or extracting substrings from existing strings. The *String* class exposes a variety of member methods for the manipulation of strings. Tables 3.4 and 3.5 summarize some of these methods. The tables are divided into instance methods, which return a string based on the instance of the string they are called from, and static methods, which must be called from the String type.

Table 3.4. Some Useful Instance String Methods

Name	Description
String.Insert	Inserts a specified string into the current instance
String.PadLeft, *String.PadRight*	Adds characters to the left and right of the string, respectively
String.Remove	Deletes a specified number of characters from the string, beginning at a specified character
String.Replace	Replaces all occurrences of a specified character in the string with another specified character
String.Split	Returns an array of substrings that are delimited by a specified character
String.Substring	Returns a substring from the specified instance
String.ToCharArray	Returns an array of the characters that make up the string
String.ToLower, *String.ToUpper*	Returns the string converted to all lowercase or all uppercase, respectively
String.TrimEnd, *String.TrimStart*, *String.Trim*	Removes trailing, leading, or both characters from the string, respectively

Table 3.5.   Some Useful *Static* (*Shared*) String Methods

Name	Description
String.Compare	Compares two specified string objects
String.Concat	Returns a string that is the result of the concatenation of two or more strings
String.Format	Returns a string that has been formatted according to a specified format
String.Join	Returns a string that is the result of the concatenation of a specified array of strings, with a specified separation string between each member of the array

Lesson Summary

- The .NET Framework provides a robust, strongly typed data system. Different types represent integer numbers, floating-point numbers, Boolean values, characters, and strings.

- Conversion between types can take one of two forms:

  - Implicit conversions, which are performed automatically by the Common Language Runtime. Implicit conversions can only occur where there is no possible loss of data, such as a conversion from a lower precision type to a higher precision type.

  - Explicit conversions are performed explicitly in code and can lead to the loss of data. Explicit conversions should be undertaken with caution.

- In Visual Basic .NET, *Option Strict On* enables type checking at design time and prevents type mismatch bugs that could be time-consuming to find otherwise. Whenever possible, you should develop with *Option Strict On*.

- Boxing allows you to treat a value type the same as a reference type. Unboxing converts a boxed reference type back to a value type.

- The .NET types provide built-in functionality specific to the type. The *Parse* method is implemented by all the built-in value types and is useful for converting strings to value types. The *String* class exposes several useful functions that allow you to easily manipulate strings.

Lesson 2: Using Constants, Enums, Arrays, and Collections

In this lesson, you will learn how to use the user-defined Constant and Enum types and the Array type. The lesson also describes how to implement advanced array functionality with the *Collection* classes.

After this lesson, you will be able to

- Create constants and enumerations, and use them in methods
- Describe how to create and use arrays
- Explain what a collection is and how to use one
- Describe how to enumerate through the members of a collection or an array

Estimated lesson time: 40 minutes

When working with objects, it is frequently necessary to organize groups of objects into some kind of structure. For example, groups of similar or dissimilar objects might need to be accessed in sequence and will require syntax to keep track of their organization. Arrays allow you to organize groups of similar objects and refer to them by an index rather than by a name. Collections are similar to arrays but implement advanced functionality and can be used to organize dissimilar groups of objects as well. Constants can have user-friendly names to represent frequently used values. Enumerations (enums) allow you to organize sets of related integral constants and use the sets to help make your application easy to read and debug.

Constants and Enumerations

You might find that you frequently use certain values in your application. Constants allow you to assign user-friendly names to these values and refer to them in code. Enumerations are user-defined sets of integral constants that correspond to a set of friendly names. Using constants and enumerations makes your code easier to read, easier to debug, and less prone to errors caused by typographical errors.

Using Constants

Constants allow you to refer to frequently used values by friendly names. The *Const (const)* keyword defines a constant. For example:

Visual Basic .NET

```
Public Const Pi As Double = 3.14159265
```

Visual C#

```
public const double Pi = 3.14159265;
```

Constants can be of any intrinsic or enumerated type, but they cannot be of a user-defined type or an array. As the name implies, constants have a fixed value that, once set, cannot be changed or redefined. Once a constant is defined, you can use its name in code in place of the value it represents. For example:

Visual Basic .NET

```
Public Const Pi as Double = 3.14159265
Public Function CalculateCircleArea(ByVal r as Double) as Double
    Return Pi * r ^ 2
End Function
```

Visual C#

```
public const double Pi = 3.14159265;
public double CalculateCircleArea(double r)
{
    // In C#, ^ is a binary operator and not the exponent operator
    return Pi * r * r;
}
```

Like variables, constants can be of any access level. If you want your constant to be available to all users of your application or component, you can declare it with the *Public* (*public*) keyword, as shown in the preceding examples. To create a constant for use only by the class, use the *Private* (*private*) keyword. The *Friend* (*internal*) keyword specifies assembly level access, and the *Protected* (*protected*) keyword allows access by inheriting types. Access levels are discussed in greater detail in Chapter 2.

Using Enumerations

Enumerations allow you to work with sets of related constants and to associate easy-to-remember names with those sets. For example, you could declare a set of enumeration constants associated with the days of the week and then refer to them by name in your code. The following code demonstrates how to declare an enumeration:

Visual Basic .NET

```
Public Enum DaysOfWeek
    Monday = 1
    Tuesday = 2
    Wednesday = 3
    Thursday = 4
    Friday = 5
    Saturday = 6
    Sunday = 7
End Enum
```

Visual C#

```
public enum DaysOfWeek
{
    Monday = 1,
    Tuesday = 2,
    Wednesday = 3,
    Thursday = 4,
    Friday = 5,
    Saturday = 6,
    Sunday = 7
}
```

The default data type for enumerations is Integer (int), but it can be any of the inte
gral numeric data types (in Visual Basic .NET: Byte, Short, Integer, and Long; and
in Visual C#: byte, short, int, and long). To define an enum as a different data type
you must specify it in the declaration line. For example:

Visual Basic .NET

```
Public Enum DaysOfWeek As Byte
' Additional code omitted
```

Visual C#

```
public enum DaysOfWeek : byte
// additional code omitted
```

It is not necessary to supply values for the members of your enum. If you choose
not to designate specific values, the members will be assigned default values num
bered sequentially starting from zero. For example:

Visual Basic .NET

```
Public Enum Numbers
    zero        ' equals zero
    one         ' equals one
    two         ' equals two
End Enum
```

Visual C#

```
public enum Numbers
{
    zero, // equals zero
    one,  // equals one
    two   // equals two
}
```

Once you define the members of your enumeration, you can use them in code. In Visual Basic .NET, enumeration members convert to the value that they represent and can be used as constants in code. For example:

Visual Basic .NET

```
' This uses the Numbers enum from the previous example
MessageBox.Show((Numbers.two * 2).ToString()) ' Displays 4
```

In Visual C#, however, you must explicitly convert enums to the correct integral type to access the value they represent. For example:

Visual C#

```
// This uses the Numbers enum from the previous example
MessageBox.Show(((int)Numbers.two * 2).ToString()); // Displays 4
```

Because enumerations are user-defined types, you can create methods that require enumeration members as values instead of numeric values. By requiring enum members as parameters instead of numbers, you create code that is less prone to errors from inaccurate typing. The following example uses the DaysOfWeek enum from the previous example and demonstrates how to create a method that requires an enum member as a parameter:

Visual Basic .NET

```
Public Sub ScheduleDayOff(ByVal day As DaysOfWeek)
   Select Case day
      Case DaysOfWeek.Monday
         ' Implementation code omitted
      Case DaysOfWeek.Tuesday
         ' Implementation code omitted
      ' Additional cases omitted
   End Select
End Sub
```

Visual C#

```
public void ScheduleDayOff(DaysOfWeek day)
{
   switch(day)
   {
      case DaysOfWeek.Monday:
         // Implementation code omitted
         break;
      case DaysOfWeek.Tuesday:
         // Implementation code omitted
         break;
      // Additional cases omitted
   }
}
```

Arrays

Arrays are a way to manage groups of similarly typed values or objects. With arrays, you can group a series of variables and refer to them with an index. You can loop through all or part of the variables and examine or affect each in turn. You also can create arrays with multiple dimensions. Arrays in the .NET Framework have built-in functionality to facilitate many tasks.

Declaring and Initializing Arrays

Arrays can be declared and initialized in the same statement. When declaring an array in this manner, you must specify the type and number of the array elements. All arrays in Visual Basic .NET and Visual C# are zero-based—meaning the index of the first element is zero—and numbered sequentially. In Visual Basic .NET, you must specify the number of array elements by indicating the *upper bound* of the array. The upper bound is the number that specifies the index of the last element of the array. When declaring an array in Visual C#, however, you must indicate the number of array elements by specifying the number of elements in the array. Thus, the upper bound of an array in Visual C# is always one less than the number used in the declaration statement. The following example demonstrates how to declare an array of integers:

Visual Basic .NET

```
' This line declares and initializes an array of 33 integers, with
' indexes ranging from 0 to 32
Dim myIntegers(32) As Integer
```

Visual C#

```
// This line declares and initializes an array of 32 integers, with
// indexes ranging from 0 to 31
int[] myIntegers = new int[32];
```

Arrays can be declared and initialized in separate steps. In Visual C#, you can declare an array with one line and dynamically allocate it in another line, as shown in the following example:

Visual C#

```
// This line declares the array
int[] myIntegers;
// This line initializes the array with 32 members
myIntegers = new int[32];
```

You can dynamically initialize arrays in Visual Basic .NET as well, but the syntax is somewhat less flexible. If you declare an array without specifying the number of elements on one line, you must provide values for each element when initializing the array. Initial values can be provided for an array by enclosing them in braces ({ }) and separating them with commas, as the following example demonstrates:

Visual Basic .NET

```
' This line declares the array
Dim myIntegers() As Integer
' This line initializes the array to six members and sets their values
myIntegers = New Integer() {0,1,2,3,4,5}
```

You can redefine your array to change its size at run time. In Visual C#, redefinition is as simple as reinitializing the array as follows:

Visual C#

```
// This line declares and initializes the array
int[] myIntegers = new int[32];
// This line reinitialized the array
myIntegers = new int[45];
```

In Visual Basic .NET, you must use the *ReDim* statement to change the number of elements in an array. An example follows:

Visual Basic .NET

```
Dim myIntegers(32) As Integer
' This line reinitializes the array
ReDim myIntegers(45)
```

In the previous examples, any data contained within an array is lost when the array is reinitialized. There is no way to preserve data when reinitializing arrays in Visual C#. In Visual Basic .NET, you can preserve existing data when reinitializing an array by using the *Preserve* keyword, as shown in the following example:

Visual Basic .NET

```
' Declares the array and initializes it with four members
Dim myIntegers() As Integer = {0,1,2,3}
' Resizes the array, but retains the data in elements 0 through 3
ReDim Preserve myIntegers(10)
```

When creating an array of reference types, declaring and initializing an array does not create an array filled with members of that type. Rather, it creates an array of null references that can point to that type. To fill the array with members, you must assign each variable in the array to an object, which can be either a new object or an existing object. For example:

Visual Basic .NET

```
' This example creates an array of Widgets, then assigns each variable
' to a Widget object
Dim Widgets(10) As Widget
' Assigns Widgets(0) to a new Widget object
Widgets(0) = New Widget()
' Assigns Widgets(1) to an existing Widget object
Dim aWidget As New Widget()
```

```
Widgets(1) = aWidget
' Loops through Widgets and assigns 2 through 10 to a new object
Dim Counter As Integer
For Counter = 2 to 10
    Widgets(Counter) = New Widget()
Next
```

Visual C#

```
// This example creates an array of Widgets, then assigns each
// variable to a Widget object
Widget[] Widgets = new Widget[11];
// Assigns Widgets[0] to a new Widget object
Widgets[0] = new Widget();
// Assigns Widgets[1] to an existing Widget object
Widget aWidget = new Widget();
Widgets[1] = aWidget;
// Loops through Widgets and assigns 2 through 10 to a new object
for (int Counter = 2; Counter < 11; Counter++)
{
    Widgets[Counter] = new Widget();
}
```

Multidimensional Arrays

The arrays discussed thus far are linear arrays, that is, arrays with only one dimension. The .NET Framework supports two kinds of multidimensional arrays: rectangular arrays and jagged arrays. The next two sections will discuss each type of multidimensional array.

Rectangular Arrays

Rectangular arrays are arrays in which each member of each dimension is extended in each other dimension by the same length. For example, a two-dimensional array can be thought of as a table, consisting of rows and columns. In a rectangular array, all the rows have the same number of columns.

You declare a rectangular array by specifying additional dimensions at declaration. The following code demonstrates various ways to declare a multidimensional rectangular array:

Visual Basic .NET

```
' Declares an array of 5 by 3 members
Dim intArrays(4, 2) As Integer
' Declares a two-dimensional array and sets initial values
Dim intArrays2( , ) As Integer = {{1, 2, 3}, {4, 5, 6}}
' Declares a cubical array and sets initial values
Dim cubeArray( , , ) As Integer = {{{7, 2}, {1, 4}}, {{3, 5}, {4, 4}}}
' Declares a complex array of 3 x 3 x 4 x 5 x 6 members
Dim complexArray(2, 2, 3, 4, 5) As Integer
```

Visual C#

```
// Declares an array of 5 by 3 members
int[ , ] intArrays = new int[5, 3];
// Declares a two-dimensional array and sets initial values
int[ , ] intArrays2 = {{1, 2, 3}, {4, 5, 6}};
// Declares a cubical array and sets initial values
int[ , , ] cubeArray = {{{7, 2}, {1, 4}}, {{3, 5}, {4, 4}}};
// Declares a complex array of 3 x 3 x 4 x 5 x 6 members
int[ , , , , ] complexArray = new int[3, 3, 4, 5, 6];
```

Jagged Arrays

The other type of multidimensional array is the jagged array. A two-dimensional jagged array can be thought of as a table where each row can have a different number of columns. For example, consider a table where families are the rows and family members are the columns. Unless each family has the same number of members, each row will have a variable number of columns. You can use a jagged array to represent such a table.

A jagged array is really an array of arrays. To create a jagged array, you declare the array of arrays with multiple sets of parentheses or brackets, and you indicate the size of the jagged array in the first set of brackets (parentheses). The following example demonstrates how to create a simple jagged array:

Visual Basic .NET

```
' Declares an array of 3 arrays
Dim Families(2)() As String
' Initializes the first array to 4 members and sets values
Families(0) = New String() {"Smith", "Mom", "Dad", "Uncle Phil"}
' Initializes the second array to 5 members and sets values
Families(1) = New String() {"Jones", "Mom", "Dad", "Suzie", _
   "Little Bobby"}
' Initializes the third array to 3 members and sets values
Families(2) = New String() {"Williams", "Earl", "Bob"}
```

Visual C#

```
// Declares an array of 3 arrays
string[][] Families = new string[3][];
// Initializes the first array to 4 members and sets values
Families[0] = new string[] {"Smith", "Mom", "Dad", "Uncle Phil"};
// Initializes the second array to 5 members and sets values
Families[1] = new string[] {"Jones", "Mom", "Dad", "Suzie",
   "Little  Bobby"};
// Initializes the third array to 3 members and sets values
Families[2] = new string[] {"Williams", "Earl", "Bob"};
```

Collections

Collections provide advanced functionality for managing groups of objects. A col
lection is a specialized class that organizes and exposes a group of objects. Like
arrays, members of collections can be accessed by an index. Unlike arrays, however, collections can be resized dynamically, and members can be added and
removed at run time.

Note   This section deals specifically with the collection types found in the *Sys-
tem.Collections* namespace. It is technically possible to create a collection class
that does not display this behavior by implementing only some of the interfaces
usually implemented by collection types. Interfaces and their implementation will
be discussed further in Chapter 4.

Collections are useful for managing groups of items that are dynamically created at
run time. For example, you might create an application that analyzes a group of
Customer objects, each representing a set of data about a particular customer. By
creating a collection of *Customer* objects, you would be able to access the objects,
iterate through them, add new objects as they became available, or remove objects
as they became irrelevant.

The ArrayList Class

The *System.Collections.ArrayList* class provides general collection functionality
suitable for most purposes. This class allows you to dynamically add and remove
items from a simple list. Items in the list are retrieved by accessing the item index.
You can create a new instance of the *ArrayList* class as shown in the following
example:

Visual Basic .NET

```
Dim myList As New System.Collections.ArrayList()
```

Visual C#

```
System.Collections.ArrayList myList = new System.Collections.ArrayList();
```

The Add Method

Once instantiated, you can add items to the *ArrayList* using the *Add* method, as
follows:

Visual Basic .NET

```
Dim myWidget As New Widget()
myList.Add(myWidget)
```

Visual C#

```
Widget myWidget = new Widget();
myList.Add(myWidget);
```

The list of objects managed by the *ArrayList* is a zero-based collection. Zero-based means that the first object added to the list is assigned the index zero and every subsequent object to be added is assigned to the next available index.

The Item Property Indexer

You can retrieve the item at a particular index by using the *Item* property. In Visual Basic .NET, the *Item* property is the default property for collections. Thus, you can access it without using the *Item* property name, allowing syntax similar to that of an array. In Visual C#, default properties are called *indexers*, and you must use the array-like syntax rather than specifically use the *Item* property name. Default properties and indexers are discussed in detail in the next lesson. The following example demonstrates how to retrieve a reference to an object in a collection. Both correct syntaxes for accessing the *Item* property are shown.

Visual Basic .NET

```
Dim myObject As Object
myObject = myList(0)
' The following line is equivalent to the preceding line
myObject = myList.Item(0)
```

Visual C#

```
object myObject;
myObject = myList[0];
```

All references contained in a collection are of type *Object*. Thus, the *Item* property returns a reference to an *Object* regardless of the actual type of the object contained therein. If you want to obtain a reference of the same type as the object contained in the list, you must explicitly cast the reference, as follows:

Visual Basic .NET

```
Dim myWidget As Widget
' Assumes a collection containing several Widget objects
myWidget = CType(widgetCollection(0), Widget)
```

Visual C#

```
Widget myWidget;
myWidget = (Widget)widgetCollection[0];
```

The Remove and RemoveAt Methods

You can remove an item from a collection by using the *Remove* and *RemoveAt* methods. The *Remove* method requires a reference to an object contained within th collection as a parameter and removes that object from the collection. For exampl

Visual Basic .NET

```
Dim myWidget As New Widget()
Dim myList As New System.Collections.ArrayList()
' Adds the Widget to the collection
myList.Add(myWidget)
' Remove the Widget from the collection
myList.Remove(myWidget)
```

Visual C#

```
Widget myWidget = new Widget();
System.Collections.ArrayList myList = new
    System.Collections.ArrayList();
// Adds the Widget to the collection
myList.Add(myWidget);
// Removes the Widget from the collection
myList.Remove(myWidget);
```

If you attempt to remove an object that is not contained by a collection, you will not receive an error, but the line will be ignored.

The *RemoveAt* method allows you to remove an object at a particular index. For example:

Visual Basic .NET

```
Dim myList As New System.Collections.ArrayList()
' Adds three widgets to the collection
Dim X As Integer
For X = 1 to 3
    Dim aWidget As New Widget()
    myList.Add(aWidget)
Next
' Removes the widget at index 1
myList.RemoveAt(1)
```

Visual C#

```
System.Collections.ArrayList myList = new
    System.Collections.ArrayList();
// Adds three widgets to the collection
for (int x = 0; x < 3; x++)
{
    Widget myWidget = new Widget();
```

```
    myList.Add(myWidget);
}
// Removes the Widget at index 1
myList.RemoveAt(1);
```

Note that as items are removed from a collection, the index numbers are reassigned to occupy any available spaces. Thus, index values are not static and might not always return the same reference.

The Count Property

The *Count* property returns the number of items in a collection. Because the collection index is zero-based, the *Count* property will always return one greater than the upper bound of the array.

Other Types of Collection Classes

The *System.Collections* namespace contains several other collection classes that you can use to organize groups of objects. These classes provide additional or specialized functionality that is unavailable in the *ArrayList* class. Some of these classes are briefly summarized in Table 3.6.

Table 3.6.   Members of *System.Collections*

Class	Description
BitArray	Manages a compact array of bits (1 and 0)
CollectionBase	Serves as a base for implementing your own collection class; provides much of the back-end functionality required for collections
Hashtable	Represents a collection of key-and-value pairs that are organized based on the hash code of the key
Queue	Manages a group of objects on a first-in, first-out basis
SortedList	Organizes a group of objects and allows you to access those objects either by index or by a key value
Stack	Manages a group of objects on a first-in, last-out basis

Enumerating the Members of an Array or a Collection

Visual Basic .NET and Visual C# provide a specialized syntax for looping through the members of an array or a collection. The *For Each (foreach)* statement allows you to examine each member of an array or collection in turn. The syntax is as follows:

Visual Basic .NET

```
Dim myArray() As Integer = {1,2,3,4,5}
Dim I As Integer
For Each I in myArray
    MessageBox.Show(I.ToString())
Next
```

Visual C#

```
int[] myArray = new int[] {1,2,3,4,5};
foreach (int I in myArray)
{
    MessageBox.Show(I.ToString());
}
```

When using this syntax with collections, you must ensure that all members of the collection are of the same type as the iteration variable. If you attempt to iterate through members of a collection that cannot be assigned to the iteration variable, an *InvalidCastException* will be thrown. To avoid this problem when working wi collections that contain different types of objects, declare the iteration variable a an *Object* and use the *typeof* operator (Visual Basic .NET) or the *GetType* metho (Visual C#) to determine if the object is the correct type. An example follows:

Visual Basic .NET

```
' Assumes that myList is an ArrayList that contains Strings and
' a variety of objects of other types
Dim o As Object
For Each o In myList
    If TypeOf o Is String Then
        MessageBox.Show(o.ToString())
    End If
Next
```

Visual C#

```
// Assumes that myList is an ArrayList that contains Strings and
// a variety of objects of other types
foreach (object o in myList)
{
    if (o.GetType() == typeof(string))
    {
        MessageBox.Show(o.ToString());
    }
}
```

It is important to note that when using the *For Each* (*foreach*) syntax, the referen that the iteration variable holds to the members of the collection is read-only. Thu you cannot use *For Each* (*foreach*) to make changes to items contained in an arr or collection. If you want to loop through the members of your array or collectio and make changes to those members, you should use a *For...Next* (*for*) loop, as demonstrated in the following example:

Visual Basic .NET

```
Dim myArray() As Integer = {1,2,3,4,5}
Dim x As Integer
For x = 0 to myArray.GetUpperBound(0)
   myArray(x) += 1
   MessageBox.Show(myArray(x).ToString())
Next
```

Visual C#

```
int[] myArray = new int[] {1,2,3,4,5};
for (int x = 0; x <= myArray.GetUpperBound(0); x++)
{
   myArray[x] ++;
   MessageBox.Show(myArray[x].ToString());
}
```

Lesson Summary

- Constants and enumerations make your code less error prone and easier to read and maintain. They do this by substituting friendly names for frequently used values. You define a constant with the *Const* (*const*) keyword. The *Enum* (*enum*) keyword is used to declare an enumeration. Constants can be of any data type. Enumerations must be of a numeric integral type.

- Arrays can be one-dimensional or multidimensional. Multidimensional arrays can be either rectangular or jagged. In rectangular arrays, every member of each dimension is extended into the other dimensions by the same length. In jagged arrays, individual members of one dimension can be extended into other dimensions by different lengths. In either case, the more dimensions, the more complex the array.

- Collections allow you to manage groups of objects, which can be of the same type or of different types. There are several types of collections, and all are available in the *System.Collections* namespace. *System.Collections.ArrayList* provides the basic functionality suitable for most applications.

- You can use the *For Each* (*foreach*) statement to iterate through the members of an array or a collection, but you cannot alter members using this statement. To loop through an array or a collection and alter the members, use the *For...Next* (*for*) statement.

Lesson 3: Implementing Properties

Properties are members of classes that expose member variables or objects. Proper ties have similarities to both fields and methods. Values are set and retrieved usin the same syntax as fields: getting a value from a property or setting a value with a property actually calls a specialized method that carries out these functions. Prop erties can contain code that validates values before setting them or carries out any other function required by the application.

After this lesson, you will be able to

- Explain how to implement properties
- Describe how to create a read-only or write-only property
- Explain what a default property or indexer is and how to create one
- Explain how to expose a collection of objects as a property

Estimated lesson time: 30 minutes

Implementing Properties

Properties allow you to expose member values and objects in a more robust way than simply using fields. A property is essentially a specialized method that looks like a field. Property values are set and retrieved in the same manner as fields, as shown in the following example:

Visual Basic .NET

```
' Sets the value of the TextBox1.Text property
TextBox1.Text = "Text Property"
Dim myString As String
' Returns the value of TextBox1.Text and assigns it to myString
myString = TextBox1.Text
```

Visual C#

```
// Sets the value of the TextBox1.Text property
textBox1.Text = "Text property";
string myString;
// Returns the value of TextBox1.Text and assigns it to myString
myString = textBox1.Text;
```

At this level, a property looks and acts exactly like a field. However, the code behind a property is actually a bit more complex. Properties are divided into two special methods, a *getter* and a *setter*, which get and set the value of the property, respectively. The following example demonstrates a property declaration for a property called *MyText*:

Visual Basic .NET

```vb
' Creates a private local variable to store the value
Private mText As String
' Implements the property
Public Property MyText() As String
   Get
      ' Returns the value stored in the local variable
      Return mText
   End Get
   Set(ByVal Value As String)
      ' Set the value of the local variable
      mText = Value
   End Set
End Property
```

Visual C#

```csharp
// Creates a private local variable to store the value
private string mText;
// Implements the property
public string MyText
{
   get
   {
      // Returns the value stored in the local variable
      return mText;
   }
   set
   {
      // Sets the value of the local variable
      mText = value;
   }
}
```

The *Value* (*value*) keyword is a special keyword used in the setter of a property. It always represents the value to which the property is being set. Properties can expose any kind of object, array, or collection. The value or object is usually stored in a private local variable (*mText* in the preceding example) and retrieved when the property is accessed.

Because it behaves in essentially the same manner as a field, the preceding example is a fairly trivial example of a property. A key advantage of properties is that you can provide additional code in the getter and setter of the property to perform calculations or validate the entry. The following example demonstrates how to create a property where the value is validated before being set:

Visual Basic .NET

```vb
Private mLength As Integer
Public Property Length() As Integer
   Get
```

```
          ' Returns the value stored in the local variable
          Return mLength
        End Get
        Set(ByVal Value As Integer)
          ' Validates that the value does not exceed the maximum value
          ' of 32
          If Value > 32 Then
              MessageBox.Show(Value.ToString & _
                  " is too large a value for this property!")
          Else
              mLength = Value
          End If
        End Set
End Property
```

Visual C#

```
private int mLength;
public int Length
{
    get
    {
      // Returns the value stored in the local variable
      return mLength;
    }
    set
    {
      // Validates that the value does not exceed the maximum value
      // of 32
      if (value > 32)
          MessageBox.Show(value.ToString() +
              " is too large a value for this property!");
      else
          mLength = value;
    }
}
```

To create a property

1. Create a private member field or object to hold the value or object that will be returned by the property.

2. Write the code for the property that will return the value.

3. Add any validation code in the getter or the setter that is required for the property.

Read-Only and Write-Only Properties

Sometimes, you will need to implement a property that can return a value to the client but cannot be changed once the class is initialized. Infrequently, you might need to create a property that can be changed but not read. These properties are called *read-only* and *write-only* properties, respectively.

Creating Read-Only Properties

Read-only properties are created in a manner similar to regular properties. In Visual Basic .NET, the property must be marked with the *ReadOnly* keyword and the setter is omitted. In Visual C#, creating a read-only property is as simple as providing only a getter and omitting the setter from a property. The private variable that holds the property value is also usually marked *ReadOnly* (*readonly*) although this is not required. The following example demonstrates a read-only property:

Visual Basic .NET

```
Private ReadOnly mInt As Integer
Public ReadOnly Property InstanceNumber() As Integer
    Get
        Return mInt
    End Get
End Property
```

Visual C#

```
private readonly int mInt;
public int InstanceNumber
{
    get
    {
        return mInt;
    }
}
```

Because the variable holding the data for the property is read-only, it cannot be set or changed in code. You must set an initial value for the variable in the constructor of the class or when the variable is initialized.

To create a read-only property

1. Create a private member variable to hold the property value. This variable must be marked *ReadOnly* in Visual Basic .NET and *readonly* in Visual C#.

2. Implement the property, supplying a getter but not a setter. In Visual Basic .NET, the property should also be marked *ReadOnly*.

3. Set the value of the private member variable in the constructor of the class for which it is a member.

Write-Only Properties

Although used infrequently, it is possible to create properties that can be written to but not read by the client. You might implement a write-only property that controls localization properties of a form. When a different locale is set, code in the property executes to make the appropriate changes to the form, and there is no need to access the value of the property.

A write-only property is created in a manner analogous to a read-only property. If the value of the write-only property is to be stored, you will need to create a private member variable to hold it. The property itself is implemented as a regular property, but only a setter is supplied. The getter is omitted. In Visual Basic .NET, the property must be marked with the *WriteOnly* keyword.

To create a write-only property

1. If needed, create a private member variable to hold the value of the write-only property.
2. Implement your property supplying only a setter. In the setter, write any code that you want to execute when the property is set. In Visual Basic .NET, you must also mark the property with the *WriteOnly* keyword.

Parameterized Properties

Most properties you create will return a single value or object. In Visual Basic .NET, you can create properties that accept parameters when accessed. These properties usually expose a range, or array, of values. For example, a single *Engine* object might have several *Cylinders*. Rather than expose each one individually, you could create a *Cylinder* property that returned or set each cylinder based on a supplied parameter.

You implement a parameterized property the same as a normal property except that you declare the parameter in the property declaration. Then, in the getter and setter of the property, you write appropriate code to retrieve the appropriate value or object. The following example exposes an array of objects through a parameterized property:

Visual Basic .NET

```
' Creates the array to hold the property values
Private mCylinders(7) As Cylinder
Public Property Cylinders(ByVal i As Integer) As Cylinder
    Get
        ' Validates the property value
        If I > 7 Then
            MessageBox.Show("Property value out of range!")
            Exit Property
        End If
        ' If the object doesn't exist, it creates a new one
        If mCylinders(i) Is Nothing Then
```

```
        mCylinders(i) = New Cylinder()
    End If
    Return mCylinders(i)
End Get
Set(ByVal Value As Cylinder)
    ' Validates the property value
    If i > 7 Then
        MessageBox.Show("Property value out of range!")
        Exit Property
    End If
    mCylinders(i) = Value
End Set
End Property
```

Visual C# does not allow you to create parameterized properties except for the indexer. (See the next section.)

Default Properties and Indexers

In Visual Basic .NET, you can designate a default property for your component. A default property is always a parameterized property and is usually used to expose a range, an array, or a collection of values. Enabling a default property only makes sense if the primary purpose of the object is to contain and expose other objects. If you mark a property as default, you can use the property name interchangeably with the object name. Thus, the following code functions interchangeably:

Visual Basic .NET

```
' This example assumes that the Item property is the default
' property of the myCollection object
myCollection.Item(2) = "Default properties!"
myCollection(2) = "Default properties!"
```

Because you can use the object name without further qualification to access the default property, you can have only one default property per class. You implement a default property by using the *Default* keyword in the property declaration as follows:

Visual Basic .NET

```
Public Default Property Item(I As Integer) As String
    ' Property Implementation omitted
End Property
```

In Visual C#, the indexer is the equivalent of a Visual Basic .NET default property. The indexer is a specialized property that allows you to expose a group of objects on the name of the object. The name used in the indexer code is always *this*, which indicates that the name of the object itself will be used to access the property. A sample implementation of a Visual C# indexer follows:

Visual C#

```
// Creates an array to store the values exposed by the indexer
private int[] IntArray;
// The index variable in brackets is used to retrieve the correct item
public int this[int index]
{
   get
   {
      return IntArray[index];
   }
   set
   {
      IntArray[index] = value;
   }
}
```

To create a default property in Visual Basic .NET

Create a parameterized property that returns an object based on the parameter. Use the *Default* keyword in the property declaration.

To create an indexer in Visual C#

Create a property named *this*, and designate an index variable for the property. Write code that returns the appropriate object based on the index.

Collection Properties

If your object exposes an undetermined number of objects of the same type, you can expose a collection of objects through a property. Exposing collections of objects as properties allows you to control access to your subordinate objects and validate assignments.

There are a few different ways to implement collection properties. How you choose to do so depends on the kind of functionality you need to implement. Simple collection properties can simply return the collection, allowing clients to add and remove members to the collection, as well as to use all of the collection's methods. Most likely, you would expose the collection as a read-only property to prevent the client from assigning the property to a new instance of the collection class itself. The objects in the collection still can be changed with the collection's own methods. An example of a simple collection property follows:

Visual Basic .NET

```
Private ReadOnly mWidgets As New System.Collections.ArrayList()
Public ReadOnly Property Widgets() As System.Collections.ArrayList
   Get
       Return mWidgets
   End Get
End Property
```

Visual C#

```
private readonly System.Collections.ArrayList mWidgets = new
    System.Collections.ArrayList();
public System.Collections.ArrayList Widgets
{
    get
    {
        return mWidgets;
    }
}
```

Although this approach is simple and allows you access to the collection's members, there is one significant problem. Most of the collection classes in the *System.Collections* namespace accept and return their members as objects, which means that any kind of type can be added or removed to the collection. Thus, there is no type checking when members are added to the collection, and retrieved members must be explicitly converted to the correct type. If you want to manage groups of differently typed objects in a single property, this approach will be adequate.

To create a simple collection property

Implement a read-only property that returns the collection.

For more robust collection properties, you should wrap your collection object in the property and provide explicit conversion and validation code within the property. Doing so allows you to access the collection members by index and control the types that are added to the collection. In Visual Basic .NET, you must implement a property of this type as a parameterized property. An example follows:

Visual Basic .NET

```
Private mWidgets As New System.Collections.ArrayList()
Public Property Widget(I As Integer) As Widget
    Get
        Return CType(mWidgets(I), Widget)
    End Get
    Set(ByVal Value As Widget)
        mWidgets(I) = Value
    End Set
End Property
```

Because Visual C# does not allow parameterized properties, you must implement a property of this type either as an indexer or as a pair of methods. An example of the latter follows:

Visual C#

```
private System.Collections.ArrayList mWidgets = new
    System.Collections.ArrayList();
public Widget GetWidget(int I)
```

```
{
    return (Widget)mWidgets[I];
}
public void SetWidget(int I, Widget Wid)
{
    mWidgets[I] = Wid;
}
```

This approach allows for properties that are strongly typed and exposes a collection of like-typed items. There are drawbacks, however. With this approach, you lose the ability to iterate through the collection using *For Each...Next* (*foreach*), and any other methods of the property that you want to expose to the client must be wrapped as well. Additionally, the syntax concessions required in Visual C# might be unsuitable.

To create a strongly typed collection property

- In Visual Basic .NET, create a parameterized property that returns a member of a private collection based on the index. Use the *CType* keyword to convert the object returned by the collection to the appropriate type.

- In Visual C#, create a pair of methods that get and set the object at the appropriate index in a private collection. In the *get* method, explicitly convert the object returned by the collection to the appropriate type.

For properties that require an even stronger implementation, you can implement your own strongly typed collection by inheriting from the *System.Collections.CollectionBase* class. This class provides most of the background functionality collections require and allows you to provide your own implementations of the *item* property. With a strongly typed collection, you can expose the collection directly in the property (as shown in the preceding example) and still have access to all the collection functionality. The collection will only accept members of the type you specify and will incorporate any other functionality you require. Inheritance is discussed in detail in Chapter 4, including an exercise demonstration on how to create a strongly typed collection.

Lesson Summary

- Properties allow you to expose member variables or objects and provide code to validate property values or perform other functions when the property is accessed. Read-only and write-only properties are useful for limiting the client's ability to read or write to your properties. Visual Basic .NET allows you to create properties that accept parameters and can expose a range of values.

- A default property allows access to values exposed by a property without using the property name for qualification. Default properties must be parameterized properties. An indexer is the Visual C# equivalent of a default property.

- Collection properties are used to expose groups of objects exposed by your classes. There are several ways to do this, but each method has advantages and drawbacks as follows:

  - A simple collection property can return a private member collection object, but this approach is the least robust.

  - A property can return an object and access a private member collection object by index. This approach is more robust, but presents some limitations in the usability of your class.

  - Implementing a strongly typed collection class is developmentally intensive, but provides the most robust method for exposing a strongly typed collection of classes.

Lesson 4: Implementing Delegates and Events

Events are messages that indicate a noteworthy occurrence in another part of the application. When an event is raised, other parts of your application are given an opportunity to respond by executing methods called event handlers. In Chapter 2, you learned how to use Visual Studio .NET to write handlers for events raised by forms and controls. In this lesson, you will learn how to declare and raise your own events, write event handlers for those events, and dynamically add and remove event handlers at run time.

After this lesson, you will be able to

- Explain what a delegate is and how to create one
- Describe how to declare and raise events from your application
- Explain how to implement event handlers and associate them with events
- Describe how to dynamically add and remove event handlers at run time

Estimated lesson time: 30 minutes

Events are members of your class. An event represents a message that is sent to other parts of the application. When a noteworthy activity occurs in the application, your application can *raise* the event, which sends out the message. The event can wrap any arguments that contain information about the event and send them along with the event. Other parts of the application *handle* the event, which means that a method is executed in response to the event. Any method that handles an event must have the same signature as the event itself; that is, it must take the same kinds of arguments as the event passes. An event can be handled by more than one method, and a single method can handle more than one event.

Delegates

Special classes called *delegates* are central to how events work. A delegate is essentially a type-safe function pointer. It allows you to pass a reference to the entry point for a method and invoke that method without making an explicit method call. When you declare a delegate, you specify the signature of the method that it can call and the return type. The following example demonstrates how to declare a delegate:

Visual Basic .NET

```
Public Delegate Function myDelegate(ByVal D As Double) As Integer
```

Visual C#

```
public delegate int myDelegate(double D);
```

This example declares a delegate called *myDelegate* that can be used to invoke methods that return an integer and take a double as a parameter. To make use of the delegate, you must create a new instance that specifies the method to be called. In Visual Basic .NET, you use the *AddressOf* operator to create a reference to the address of the method. In Visual C#, you specify the method by name. For example:

Visual Basic .NET

```
' This method is the target for the delegate
Public Function ReturnInt(ByVal d As Double) As Integer
' Method implementation omitted
End Function
' This line creates an instance of the myDelegate delegate that
' specifies ReturnInt
Dim aDelegate As New myDelegate(addressof ReturnInt)
```

Visual C#

```
// This method is the target for the delegate
public int ReturnInt(double D)
{
   // Method implementation omitted
}
// This line creates an instance of the myDelegate delegate that
// specifies ReturnInt
public void amethod()
{
    myDelegate aDelegate = new myDelegate(ReturnInt);
}
```

In Visual C#, if you create a delegate to an instance method, you must also initialize the delegate within a method. Delegates to static methods can be initialized outside a method.

Once declared and assigned, you can use the delegate to invoke the method in the same manner you would make a function call, which is shown as follows:

Visual Basic .NET

```
aDelegate(12345)
```

Visual C#

```
aDelegate(12345);
```

To create and invoke a delegate

1. Declare the delegate, and provide a signature identical to the signature of the methods you want to invoke.
2. Create an instance of the delegate that points to a method that has the appropriate signature.
3. Invoke the delegate by referencing its name.

Declaring and Raising Events

As you learned in Chapter 2, forms and controls have built-in member events that are raised when events occur. For example, the *Click* event is raised when a user clicks a button. You can declare member events for your classes that can be raised when appropriate.

Declaring events is directly tied to delegates. In Visual C#, you must explicitly des ignate the delegate type that your event will use. Visual Basic .NET provides much of this functionality behind the scenes—you only need to supply the name of the event and the signature of the method it requires. A default delegate matching this signature is created.

To declare an event with Visual Basic .NET

Use the *Event* keyword to declare an event. Supply a signature that represents the signature of the type of method that you would like to handle the event. You can use any access modifiers, such as *Public*, *Private*, or *Protected*. For example:

Visual Basic .NET

```
Public Event CalculationComplete(ByVal Total As Double)
```

To declare an event with Visual C#

Use the *Event* keyword to declare an event. Supply the type of delegate that the event will use. You can use any access modifiers, such as *public*, *private*, or *protected*. For example:

Visual C#

```
public delegate void calculationDelegate(double d);
public event calculationDelegate CalculationComplete;
```

Once an event is declared, you can raise it in code when the designated event occurs. For example, you might have a component that represents a bank account, which could raise an *Overdrawn* event whenever the balance falls below zero.

To raise an event in Visual Basic .NET

Use the *RaiseEvent* keyword to raise the event, calling the event by name. Enclose any required parameters in parentheses. An example of the appropriate syntax follows:

Visual Basic .NET

```
RaiseEvent CalculationComplete(66532)
```

To raise an event in Visual C#

Events in Visual C# are raised by calling them by name as you would a method. Any required parameters should be enclosed in parentheses. An example follows:

Visual C#

```
CalculationComplete(66532);
```

Implementing Event Handlers

Once an event is declared, it must be associated with one or more event handlers before it can be raised. An event handler is a method that is called through a delegate when an event is raised. You must create associations between events and event handlers to achieve your desired results. If you attempt to raise an event in Visual Basic .NET that has no event handlers associated with it, nothing will happen. If you raise an event that has no event handlers in Visual C#, an error will result.

Like other members, there are instance events and *Shared* (*static*) events. Creating an event handler for an instance event requires that an association be made between a method and an object event. The object must be declared to create the event handler association. *Shared* (*static*) events, however, belong to the class itself rather than to any one instance of a class. To create an event handler for those events, you do not need to declare an instance of the class beforehand.

Event Handlers in Visual Basic .NET

In Visual Basic .NET, event handlers must be *Sub*s and cannot return a value. You can associate a *Sub* with a given event by using the *AddHandler* keyword. *AddHandler* allows you to specify an event and designate a pointer to the method with which that event will be associated. The pointer is created using the *AddressOf* operator. An example follows:

Visual Basic .NET

```
Private Sub Form1_Load(ByVal sender As System.Object, ByVal e As _
    System.EventArgs)
    AddHandler myEvent, AddressOf myHandler
End Sub
```

The *AddHandler* keyword cannot be used declaratively; it must be used inside a method. Thus, the association between the event and the event handler does not exist before the application's execution; rather, it is added at run time. For event handler associations that exist for the lifetime of the object, the *AddHandler* keyword should be placed in the class's constructor.

Visual Basic .NET also allows you to create event handler associations at design time using the *Handles* clause. To use the *Handles* clause, the object must be declared with the *WithEvents* keyword. The *WithEvents* keyword informs the containing object that it will be receiving events from the contained object.

You use the *Handles* clause by adding it to the end of your method declaration and specifying object event that you are handling. For example:

Visual Basic .NET

```
Public Sub DisplayResults() Handles Account.CalculationComplete
' Implementation omitted
End Sub
```

Event Handlers in Visual C#

Unlike in Visual Basic .NET, event handlers in Visual C# can return a value, and that value can be assigned to a variable in the same manner as a function call. You associate a method with a given event by creating a new instance of the appropriate delegate, which specifies the appropriate method and uses the += operator to make the association. You also can use the += operator to associate an event with an instance of a delegate that already exists. For example:

Visual C#

```
// These examples assume the existence of a method called
// DisplayResults that has the appropriate signature for
// CalculationDelegate
// Creates a new delegate to create the association
Account.CalculationComplete += new calculationDelegate(DisplayResults);
// Creates an association with an existing delegate
calculationDelegate calc = new calculationDelegate(DisplayResults);
Account.CalculationComplete += calc;
```

Default delegates are provided for the events of the controls and classes of the .NET Framework base class library. If you want to manually add an event handler for one of these events, you do not need to declare a new delegate. Rather, you can create a new instance of the predefined default delegate. For example, the delegate class that is used for events for most of the controls in the *System.Windows.Forms* namespace is *System.EventHandler*. The following example demonstrates how to designate an event handler for the *Click* event of a control named *button1*:

Visual C#

```
button1.Click += new System.EventHandler(clickHandler);
```

Unlike Visual Basic .NET, Visual C# has no mechanism for creating event handler associations declaratively.

To handle an event in Visual Basic .NET

- Use the *AddHandler* keyword to create an association between an event and a method to handle that event. The *AddressOf* operator allows you to receive a pointer to the appropriate method. Event handlers must have the same signature as the event being handled.

- Alternatively, you can use the *Handles* keyword to associate a method with an event at design time. The method must be a member method of an object that was declared with the *WithEvents* keyword.

To handle an event in Visual C#

Create an instance of the appropriate delegate for the event that specified the method that will handle the event, and use the += operator to associate the event with the delegate.

Event Handlers That Handle Multiple Events

You can create event handlers that handle multiple events. For example, you might want to do this when you have more than one instance of a class or control that raises the same events. For example, you might have a group of buttons on a form that share a similar role in the application. You might create a single method to handle the *Click* event for all of these buttons and distinguish between them by using the *sender* parameter.

Associating multiple events with a single handler is simple. You use the *AddHandler* or += operator in exactly the same way in which you would add a single event handler. For example:

Visual Basic .NET

```
' Assumes the existence of a method called ClickHandler with the
' correct signature to receive button click events
AddHandler Button1.Click, AddressOf ClickHandler
AddHandler Button2.Click, AddressOf ClickHandler
```

Visual C#

```
// Assumes the existence of a method called ClickHandler with the
// correct signature to receive button click events
button1.Click += new System.EventHandler(ClickHandler);
button2.Click += new System.EventHandler(ClickHandler);
```

In Visual Basic .NET, you can also use the *Handles* clause to associate multiple events with a single event handler. To create multiple associations, create a *Handles* clause and add multiple events separated by commas. The following example demonstrates this approach:

Visual Basic .NET

```
Private Sub ClickHandler (ByVal sender As System.Object, e As _
   System.EventArgs) Handles Button1.Click, Button2.Click, _
   Button3.Click
   ' Implementation omitted
End Sub
```

Events with Multiple Handlers

An event can be handled by more than one event handler. When an event is handled by more than one handler, all the methods handling that event are executed. The order in which the methods execute is the same as the order in which the association was created. Thus, if event x is associated in code with handlers y, z, and q (in that order), when the event is raised, the order of handler execution will be y, z, and q. In Visual C#, if you return a value with your event, it will be the value of the last method executed.

To associate an event with multiple handlers, all you have to do is create an association between the event and each handler. In Visual Basic .NET, you can use the *Handles* clause to declaratively associate several methods with an event. If this approach is used, the order of method execution is less predictable and should be tested to learn whether it will have an effect on the dynamics of the application.

Removing Handlers at Run Time

You already learned how to dynamically add event handlers. The *AddHandler* keyword in Visual Basic .NET and the += operator in Visual C# can be used to dynamically create associations between events and methods. You also can remove event handler associations at run time. For example, suppose you have a class that models a bank account that raises a *NotSufficientFunds* event every time the account owner tries to submit a check for an amount greater than the account balance. You might associate this event with two methods: a *ChargeAccount* method, which assesses a fee for writing a Non-Sufficient Funds (NSF) check, and a *Notify* method, which notifies the account owner that the account is overdrawn. You would call the *ChargeAccount* method every time an NSF check was passed, but it would be redundant to call the *Notify* method more than once before the account balance became positive. In this case, you could remove the event handler for the *Notify* method and reinsert it when the account balance returned to the positive side.

The method by which you remove an event handler is similar to the method by which you add one. In Visual Basic. NET, you use the *RemoveHandler* method to disassociate an event from a delegate obtained with the *AddressOf* operator. In Visual C#, you use the -= operator to dynamically remove an association between an event and a method. This operator requires a reference to a delegate of the appropriate signature, and it must reference the method to be removed. The following code demonstrates how to remove the association between the *Account.CalculationComplete* event and the *DisplayResults* method:

Visual Basic .NET

```
RemoveHandler Account.CalculationComplete, AddressOf DisplayResults
```

Visual C#

```
Account.CalculationComplete -= new calculationDelegate(DisplayResults);
```

Lesson Summary

- Events are members of classes that are used to communicate interesting occurrences between classes. An instance of a class can raise a member event to send out the message. The event can be handled by methods that are designated as event handlers. These methods execute when the event is raised.

- Delegates provide the functionality behind events. A delegate is a strongly typed function pointer. It can be used to invoke a method without making an explicit call to that method. The creation of associations between events and event handlers requires the use of delegates. In Visual Basic .NET, the role of the delegate is largely behind the scenes, whereas in Visual C#, it is more explicit.

- Events are declared as members of the class. In Visual Basic .NET, only the event need be declared, but in Visual C#, the event must reference an appropriate delegate. A member event is raised by using the *RaiseEvent* statement in Visual Basic .NET or by calling the event by name in Visual C#. Events in Visual Basic .NET cannot return a value, but events in Visual C# can return a value.

- Methods that handle events are called event handlers. You can create associations between events and event handlers in code. In Visual Basic .NET, the *AddHandler* keyword creates an association between an event and a method represented by a delegate obtained with the *AddressOf* operator. In Visual C#, the event handler is created by using the += operator to associate a delegate with the event. In Visual Basic .NET, you can also use the *Handles* clause to create event handler associations declaratively.

- Events can have multiple event handlers associated with them, and multiple events can be handled by the same method. Event handlers can be removed dynamically.

Lab 3-1: Adding Components and Implementing Members

In this lab, you will create a *DoughnutMachine* class that represents a doughnut-making machine for your Virtual Doughnut Factory. This class will create instances of a *Doughnut* class on a regular schedule and update the display form through events. The solution to this lab is available on the Supplemental Course Materials CD-ROM in the \Labs\Ch03\Lab 3-1\Solution folder.

Before You Begin

Before you begin this lab, you must have completed and opened the Chapter 2 lab or loaded the Chapter 2 lab solution from the CD-ROM

Estimated lesson time: 45 minutes

Exercise 3.1: Creating the DoughnutMachine Component

In this exercise, you will create a component that represents a doughnut-making machine. This class will create and manage instances of a *Doughnut* class and expose a collection of doughnuts. In addition, it will implement member events tha inform the containing component when a doughnut is ready.

▶ **To create the DoughnutMachine component**

1. From the Project menu, choose Add Component. The Add New Item window appears. Name your component **DoughnutMachine**, and click OK. The component designer opens.

2. In the Toolbox, under the Windows Forms tab, double-click Timer. A *Timer* component is added to the designer.

3. In Solution Explorer, right-click DoughnutMachine and choose View Code.

4. Add an enum to your component that represents the different types of doughnuts. Your enum should look like this:

Visual Basic .NET

```
Public Enum DoughnutType
   Glazed
   Sugar
   Chocolate
   ChocolateCake
   Custard
   Grape
   Lemon
```

```
        PlainCake
        SugarCake
End Enum
```

Visual C#

```
public enum DoughnutType
{
    Glazed,
    Sugar,
    Chocolate,
    ChocolateCake,
    Custard,
    Grape,
    Lemon,
    PlainCake,
    SugarCake
}
```

5. Add a property to your class to indicate the flavor of doughnut it is currently making. Include a private variable to hold the property value. This property should return a *DoughnutTypes* enum value. The following code is a sample of what your property should look like:

Visual Basic .NET

```
Private mFlavor As DoughnutType
Public Property Flavor() As DoughnutType
    Get
        Return mFlavor
    End Get
    Set (ByVal Value As DoughnutType)
        mFlavor = Value
    End Set
End Property
```

Visual C#

```
private DoughnutType mFlavor;
public DoughnutType Flavor
{
    get
    {
        return mFlavor;
    }
    set
    {
        mFlavor = value;
    }
}
```

6. Within the bounds of the *DoughnutMachine* class, create a nested *Doughnut* class to represent a doughnut. It should have a *flavor* property, a *price* property and a read-only property, which represents the time it was made. Because read only variables can be set only in the constructor, you must also create a constructor for the class that sets the value of the time the doughnut instance was made. Your class should look something like this:

Visual Basic .NET

```
Public Class Doughnut
    ' These variables hold the property values
    Private mFlavor As DoughnutType
    ' A default value for price
    Private mPrice As Single = .50
    Private ReadOnly mTimeOfCreation As Date
    ' These are the properties of your class
    Public Property Flavor() As DoughnutType
        Get
            Return mFlavor
        End Get
        Set(ByVal Value As DoughnutType)
            mFlavor = Value
            End Set
    End Property
    Public Property Price() As Single
        Get
            Return mPrice
        End Get
        Set(ByVal Value As Single)
            mPrice = Value
            End Set
    End Property
    Public ReadOnly Property TimeOfCreation() As Date
    Get
            Return mTimeOfCreation
    End Get
    End Property
    ' This is the constructor. It sets the value of
    ' mTimeOfCreation
    Public Sub New(ByVal Flavor As DoughnutType)
        ' Date.Now is a property of Date that returns the
        ' current time.
        mTimeOfCreation = Date.Now
        mFlavor = Flavor
    End Sub
End Class
```

Visual C#

```csharp
public class Doughnut
{
    // These variables hold the property values
    private DoughnutType mFlavor;
    // A default value for price
    private float mPrice = .50F;
    private readonly System.DateTime mTimeOfCreation;
    // These are the properties of your class
    public DoughnutType Flavor
    {
        get
        {
            return mFlavor;
        }
        set
        {
            mFlavor = value;
        }
    }
    public float Price
    {
        get
        {
            return Price;
        }
        set
        {
            mPrice = value;
        }
    }
    public System.DateTime TimeOfCreation
    {
        get
        {
            return mTimeOfCreation;
        }
    }
    // This is the constructor. It sets the value of mTimeOfCreation
    public Doughnut(DoughnutType Flavor)
    {
        // System.DateTime.Now is a property of System.DateTime that
        // returns the current time
        mTimeOfCreation = System.DateTime.Now;
        mFlavor = Flavor;
    }
}
```

7. Create a private member collection and a default property (Visual Basic .NET) or an indexer (Visual C#) for the *DoughnutMachine* class that exposes the members of this collection. This collection will hold the instances of the *Doughnut* class that are created by the *DoughnutMachine*. An example follows

Visual Basic .NET

```
Private mDoughnuts As New System.Collections.ArrayList()
Public Default Property Doughnuts(Index As Integer) As Doughnut
   Get
      Return CType(mDoughnuts(Index), Doughnut)
   End Get
   Set (Value As Doughnut)
      mDoughnuts(Index) = Value
   End Set
End Property
```

Visual C#

```
private System.Collections.ArrayList mDoughnuts = new
   System.Collections.ArrayList();
public Doughnut this[int Index]
{
   get
   {
      return (Doughnut)mDoughnuts[Index];
   }
   set
   {
      mDoughnuts[Index] = value;
   }
}
```

8. Add a public event to be raised when a doughnut is created. In Visual C#, you should also declare a *public* delegate.

Visual Basic .NET

```
Public Event DoughnutComplete()
```

Visual C#

```
public delegate void DoughnutCompleteDelegate();
public event DoughnutCompleteDelegate DoughnutComplete;
```

9. Using the drop-down menus in the code editor (Visual Basic. NET) or the Events button in the designer (Visual C#), add an event handler for the *Timer1.Tick* event.

10. Add code to the event handler you created in the previous step that creates a new *Doughnut*, adds it to the *mDoughnuts* collection, and raises the *Doughnut-Complete* event. An example follows:

Visual Basic .NET

```
Private Sub Timer1_Tick(ByVal sender As Object, ByVal e As _
   System,EventArgs) Handles Timer1.Tick
   Dim aDoughnut As New Doughnut(Me.Flavor)
   mDoughnuts.Add(aDoughnut)
   RaiseEvent DoughnutComplete()
End Sub
```

Visual C#

```
private void timer1_Tick(object sender, System.EventArgs e)
{
   Doughnut aDoughnut = new Doughnut(this.Flavor);
   mDoughnuts.Add(aDoughnut);
   DoughnutComplete();
}
```

11. Add two write-only properties named *Enabled* and *Interval* as *Boolean* (*bool*) and *Integer* (*int*), respectively. These properties will serve to set the internal properties of the timer. An example follows:

Visual Basic .NET

```
Public WriteOnly Property Enabled() As Boolean
   Set(ByVal Value As Boolean)
      Timer1.Enabled = Value
   End Set
End Property
Public WriteOnly Property Interval() As Integer
   Set(ByVal Value As Integer)
      Timer1.Interval = Value
   End Set
End Property
```

Visual C#

```
public bool Enabled
{
   set
   {
      timer1.Enabled = value;
   }
}
public int Interval
{
   set
   {
      timer1.Interval = value;
   }
}
```

12. Add a method to the *DoughnutMachine* class that sets the machine to make the correct type of doughnuts, sets the appropriate interval, and turns the machine on. This method should take a *DoughnutType* as a parameter. An example follows:

Visual Basic .NET

```
Public Sub MakeDoughnuts(ByVal dFlavor As DoughnutType)
    Flavor = dFlavor
    Select Case dFlavor
        Case DoughnutType.Chocolate
            Interval = 15000
        Case DoughnutType.ChocolateCake
            Interval = 12000
        Case DoughnutType.Custard
            Interval = 10000
        Case DoughnutType.Glazed
            Interval = 10000
        Case DoughnutType.Grape
            Interval = 10000
        Case DoughnutType.Lemon
            Interval = 10000
        Case DoughnutType.PlainCake
            Interval = 5000
        Case DoughnutType.Sugar
            Interval = 8000
        Case DoughnutType.SugarCake
            Interval = 6000
    End Select
    Enabled = True
End Sub
```

Visual C#

```
public void MakeDoughnuts(DoughnutType dFlavor)
{
    Flavor = dFlavor;
    switch(dFlavor)
    {
        case DoughnutType.Chocolate:
            Interval = 15000;
            break;
        case DoughnutType.ChocolateCake:
            Interval = 12000;
            break;
        case DoughnutType.Custard:
            Interval = 10000;
            break;
        case DoughnutType.Glazed:
            Interval = 10000;
            break;
```

```
        case DoughnutType.Grape:
          Interval = 10000;
          break;
        case DoughnutType.Lemon:
          Interval = 5000;
          break;
        case DoughnutType.PlainCake:
          Interval = 5000;
          break;
        case DoughnutType.Sugar:
          Interval = 8000;
          break;
        case DoughnutType.SugarCake:
          Interval = 6000;
          break;
    }
    Enabled = true;
}
```

13. From the Build menu, choose Build Solution to build your solution.

Exercise 3.2: Adding the DoughnutMachine to the User Interface

In this exercise, you will create an instance of *DoughnutMachine* in *frmMain* to create doughnuts for your virtual storefront. You will add code to set the flavor of the doughnuts you are making and add a method to handle the *DoughnutComplete* event as it is raised by your *DoughnutMachine* component. You also will add a method to halt doughnut production.

1. Add a class-level variable to represent an instance of the *DoughnutMachine* component. For example:

Visual Basic .NET

```
Private myDoughnutMachine As DoughnutMachine
```

Visual C#

```
private DoughnutMachine myDoughnutMachine;
```

2. Create an event handler for *frmMain_Load*. In this method, create a new instance of *DoughnutMachine* and assign it to the *myDoughnutMachine* variable. For example:

Visual Basic .NET

```
Private Sub frmMain_Load(ByVal sender As System.Object, ByVal e As _
    System.EventArgs) Handles MyBase.Load
    myDoughnutMachine = New DoughnutMachine()
End Sub
```

Visual C#

```csharp
private void frmMain_Load(object sender, System.EventArgs e)
{
    myDoughnutMachine = new DoughnutMachine();
}
```

3. Create private variables to hold the values corresponding to the number of doughnuts currently in inventory. For example:

Visual Basic .NET

```vb
Private mRaisedGlazed As Integer
Private mRaisedSugar As Integer
Private mRaisedChocolate As Integer
Private mCakePlain As Integer
Private mCakeChocolate As Integer
Private mCakeSugar As Integer
Private mFilledLemon As Integer
Private mFilledGrape As Integer
Private mFilledCustard As Integer
```

Visual C#

```csharp
private int mRaisedGlazed;
private int mRaisedSugar;
private int mRaisedChocolate;
private int mCakePlain;
private int mCakeChocolate;
private int mCakeSugar;
private int mFilledLemon;
private int mFilledGrape;
private int mFilledCustard;
```

4. Add a submenu to the Make menu item of the Doughnuts Menu. Add the item Raised, Cake, and Filled. Set the names of these items to mnuRaised, mnuCake and mnuFilled, respectively. Add a submenu to the Raised menu item with the items Glazed, Sugar, and Chocolate. Set the names of these items to mnuRaisedGlazed, mnuRaisedSugar, and mnuRaisedChocolate. When complete, your menu should look like Figure 3.1 in the designer.

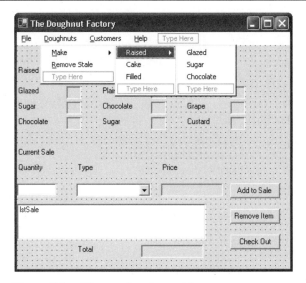

Figure 3.1.   The user interface with menus.

5. In the click handler for mnuRaisedGlazed, write code that calls the *Doughnut-Machine.MakeDoughnut* method, indicating the kind of doughnut to make. You should also set the *Checked* property of this menu item to true and the *Check* property of mnuRaisedSugar and mnuRaisedChocolate to false. A sample follows:

Visual Basic .NET

```
Private Sub mnuRaisedGlazed_Click(ByVal sender As System.Object, _
    ByVal e As System.EventArgs) Handles mnuRaisedGlazed.Click
    mnuRaisedGlazed.Checked = True
    mnuRaisedSugar.Checked = False
    mnuRaisedChocolate.Checked = False
    myDoughnutMachine.MakeDoughnuts( _
        DoughnutMachine.DoughnutType.Glazed)
End Sub
```

Visual C#

```
private void mnuRaisedGlazed_Click(object sender, System.EventArgs e)
{
    mnuRaisedGlazed.Checked = true;
    mnuRaisedSugar.Checked = false;
    mnuRaisedChocolate.Checked = false;
    myDoughnutMachine.MakeDoughnuts(
        DoughnutMachine.DoughnutType.Glazed);
}
```

Create similar methods for mnuRaisedSugar and mnuRaisedChocolate.

1. Create a method to handle the *DoughnutComplete* event of myDoughnutMachine. It should increment the appropriate variable and write the value to the appropriate text box. The following example demonstrates how it could be implemented:

Visual Basic .NET

```
Private Sub DoughnutCompleteHandler()
    Select Case myDoughnutMachine.Flavor
        Case DoughnutMachine.DoughnutType.Glazed
            mRaisedGlazed += 1
            txtGlazedRaised.Text = mRaisedGlazed.ToString
        Case DoughnutMachine.DoughnutType.Sugar
            mRaisedSugar += 1
            txtSugarRaised.Text = mRaisedSugar.ToString
        Case DoughnutMachine.DoughnutType.Chocolate
            mRaisedChocolate += 1
            txtChocolateRaised.Text = mRaisedChocolate.ToString
    End Select
    End Sub
```

Visual C#

```
private void DoughnutCompleteHandler()
{
    switch (myDoughnutMachine.Flavor)
    {
        case DoughnutMachine.DoughnutType.Glazed:
        mRaisedGlazed ++;
        txtGlazedRaised.Text = mRaisedGlazed.ToString();
        break;
    case DoughnutMachine.DoughnutType.Sugar:
        mRaisedSugar ++;
        txtSugarRaised.Text = mRaisedSugar.ToString();
        break;
    case DoughnutMachine.DoughnutType.Chocolate:
        mRaisedChocolate ++;
        txtChocolateRaised.Text = mRaisedChocolate.ToString();
        break;
    }
}
```

2. In the Form1_Load event handler, add code to "hook up" the *myDoughnut-Machine.DoughnutComplete* event with the doughnut complete event handler as follows:

Visual Basic .NET

```
AddHandler myDoughnutMachine.DoughnutComplete, AddressOf _
    DoughnutCompleteHandler
```

Visual C#

```
myDoughnutMachine.DoughnutComplete += new
DoughnutMachine.DoughnutCompleteDelegate(DoughnutCompleteHandler);
```

3. Add a menu item to the Doughnuts menu titled **&Stop**, and name it **mnuStop**. In the click event handler for this menu item, set the *Enabled* property of myDoughnutMachine to false. For example:

Visual Basic .NET

```
Private Sub mnuStop_Click(ByVal sender As System.Object, ByVal e _
    As System.EventArgs) Handles mnuStop.Click
    myDoughnutMachine.Enabled = False
End Sub
```

Visual C#

```
private void mnuStop_Click(object sender, System.EventArgs e)
{
    myDoughnutMachine.Enabled = false;
}
```

4. Build and save your solution.

5. To test your solution, press F5 to start the application.

6. From the Doughnuts menu, choose Raised, and then Sugar. Note that a check mark appears next to the sugar menu item. Every eight seconds, the value in the Raised Sugar text box should be incremented. Follow the same steps with the Glazed menu item. The appropriate box should be incremented every 10 seconds. Similarly, for Chocolate, the appropriate box should be incremented every 15 seconds.

7. From the Doughnuts menu, choose Stop to stop the production of doughnuts.

Lab 3-2: Creating a Class

In this lab, you will create a *Fraction* class that models a fractional number. You will implement properties that represent the numerator and the denominator. You will also implement methods to reduce the fraction and convert the instance of the fraction class to a *String* or a *Double*. Finally you will build a small Windows Forms application to test your class.

Before You Begin

There are no prerequisites to completing this lab.

Estimated lesson time: 30 minutes

Exercise 3.3: Creating the Fraction Class

In this exercise, you will create the *Fraction* class and implement its properties and members.

▶ **To Create the Fraction Project**

1. From the File menu, choose New and then Project. In the New Project dialog box, choose a Windows Forms project, name it Fraction and click OK. The new project opens to the Windows Forms designer.

2. From the Project menu, choose Add Class. Name the class **Fraction**, and click OK.

3. Just under the class declaration, add private variables to hold the values for the numerator and the denominator, as shown here:

Visual Basic .NET

```
Private mNumerator As Integer
Private mDenominator As Integer
```

Visual C#

```
private int mNumerator;
private int mDenominator;
```

4. In the body of the class, add properties to represent the numerator and the denominator, as shown in the following code. These properties should be read/write properties that set and return the values stored in the private fields you added in Step 2.

Visual Basic .NET

```
Public Property Numerator() As Integer
    Get
        Return mNumerator
    End Get
```

```
      Set(ByVal Value As Integer)
         mNumerator = Value
      End Set
   End Property

   Public Property Denominator() As Integer
      Get
         Return mDenominator
      End Get
      Set(ByVal Value As Integer)
         mDenominator = Value
      End Set
   End Property
```

Visual C#

```csharp
public int Numerator
{
   get
   {
      return mNumerator;
   }
   set
   {
      mNumerator = value;
   }
}

public int Denominator
{
   get
   {
      return mDenominator;
   }
   set
   {
      mDenominator = value;
   }
}
```

5. Next add a method to reduce fractions when necessary. This method should be
    Private because it will not be accessible outside the class.

Visual Basic .NET

```
Private Sub Reduce()
   Dim i As Integer
   For i = Denominator To 2 Step -1
      If Numerator Mod i = 0 And Denominator Mod i = 0 Then
         Numerator = Numerator / i
```

```
            Denominator = Denominator / i
            Exit For
        End If
    Next
End Sub
```

Visual C#

```
private void Reduce()
{
    int i;
    for(i = Denominator; i > 1; i--)
    {
        if (Numerator % i == 0 && Denominator % i == 0)
        {
            Numerator = Numerator / i;
            Denominator = Denominator / i;
            break;
        }
    }
}
```

6. Create a constructor that will initialize the values of the *Numerator* and *Denom inator* properties, and reduce the fraction if necessary. Note that Visual C# classes begin with a default constructor that takes no parameters. You will have to replace that constructor with the one shown in this example:

Visual Basic .NET

```
Public Sub New(ByVal Numerator As Integer, ByVal Denominator As Integer)
    mNumerator = Numerator
    mDenominator = Denominator
    'Calls reduce to reduce the fraction if necessary
    Reduce()
End Sub
```

Visual C#

```
public Fraction(int Numerator, int Denominator)
{
    mNumerator = Numerator;
    mDenominator = Denominator;
    // Calls reduce to reduce the fraction if necessary
    Reduce();
}
```

7. Finally add *ToString* and *ToDouble* methods to convert your class to a *String* (*string*) and *Double* (*double*), respectively. Note that since your class implicitly inherits from *System.Object*, you must use the *Overrides* (*override*) keyword to override the implementation of *ToString* inherited from the *Object* class. The *Overrides* (*override*) keyword is further discussed in Chapter 4.

Visual Basic .NET

```
Public Function ToDouble() As Double
    Return Numerator / Denominator
End Function
Public Overrides Function ToString() As String
    Return Numerator.ToString & "/" & Denominator.ToString
End Function
```

Visual C#

```
public double ToDouble()
{
    return (double)Numerator / (double)Denominator;
}
public override string ToString()
{
    return Numerator.ToString() + "/" + Denominator.ToString();
}
```

8. From the Build menu, choose Build All to build and save your project.

Exercise 3.4: Testing the Fraction Class

In this exercise, you will build a simple Windows Forms application that will accept values for the numerator and denominator of a fraction, create a new instance of the *Fraction* class, and display this class converted to a string and a double.

1. In Solution Explorer, right-click Form1 and choose View Designer. The Designer for Form1 opens.

2. Add the controls listed in Table 3.7 to the form, and set the text property as indicated.

Table 3-7.   Controls for Form1

Control	Text
Label1	Numerator
Label2	Denominator
Label3	Fraction as String
Label4	(no text)
Label5	Fraction as Double
Label6	(no text)
TextBox1	(no text)
TextBox2	(no text)
Button1	Simplify and Display Fraction

When you have added controls to your form, position them appropriately. Figure 3.2 demonstrates one example of how this could be done.

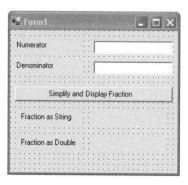

Figure 3.2. Testing the *Fraction* class.

The two text boxes will be used to enter values for the numerator and denominator of an instance of the *Fraction* class, which will be created and displayed when Button1 is pressed.

3. In the designer, double-click Button1 to open the code window to the click event handler. In the click event handler, add code to create a new instance of the *Fraction* class and display the value on the form, as shown below:

Visual Basic .NET

```
Private Sub Button1_Click(ByVal sender As System.Object, ByVal e As _
    System.EventArgs) Handles Button1.Click
    ' Try and Catch are statements used for handling errors.
    ' They will be discussed further in Chapter 5
    Try
        Dim numerator As Integer
        Dim denominator As Integer
        'Retrieves values from the two textboxes.
        numerator = Integer.Parse(TextBox1.Text)
        denominator = Integer.Parse(TextBox2.Text)
        ' Creates a new instance of the Fraction class
        Dim aFraction As New Fraction(numerator, denominator)
        ' Displays the Fraction as a fraction and as a string
        Label4.Text = aFraction.ToString
        Label6.Text = (aFraction.ToDouble).ToString
    Catch ex As Exception
        MessageBox.Show("Please check the values and try again!")
    End Try
End Sub
```

Visual C#

```csharp
private void button1_Click(object sender, System.EventArgs e)
{
    // Try and Catch are statements used for handling errors.
    // They will be discussed further in Chapter 5
    try
    {
        int numerator;
        int denominator;
        numerator = int.Parse(textBox1.Text);
        denominator = int.Parse(textBox2.Text);
        // Creates a new instance of the Fraction class
        Fraction aFraction = new Fraction(numerator, denominator);
        // Displays the Fraction as a fraction and as a string
        label4.Text = aFraction.ToString();
        label6.Text = (aFraction.ToDouble()).ToString();
    }
    catch
    {
        MessageBox.Show("Please check the values and try again!");
    }
}
```

4. Press F5 to build and test your application.

Review

The following review questions are intended to reinforce key concepts and information presented in this chapter. If you are unable to answer a question, return to the appropriate lesson and review, and then try the question again. Answers to the questions can be found in Appendix A.

1. Explain when a type conversion will undergo an implicit conversion and when you must perform an explicit conversion. What are the dangers associated with explicit casts?

2. Explain why you might use enums and constants instead of their associated literal values.

3. Briefly summarize the similarities and differences between arrays and collections.

4. Explain how properties differ from fields. Why would you expose public data through properties instead of fields?

5. Explain what a delegate is and how one works.

6. Briefly explain how to convert a string representation of a number to a numeric type, such as an *Integer* or a *Double*.

7. What are the two kinds of multidimensional arrays? Briefly describe each.

CHAPTER 4

Object-Oriented Programming and Polymorphism

About This Chapter

In this chapter, you will learn the fundamentals of object-oriented programming. You will learn how to create overloaded methods and how to implement polymorphic behavior with interfaces, and through inheritance.

Before You Begin

To complete the lessons in this chapter, you must have completed Chapter 2 and Chapter 3.

Lesson 1: Introduction to Object-Oriented Programming

Programming in the .NET Framework environment is done with objects. Objects are programmatic constructs that represent packages of related data and functionality. Objects are self-contained and expose specific functionality to the rest of the application environment without detailing the inner workings of the object itself. Objects are created from a template called a *class*. The .NET base class library provides a set of classes from which you can create objects in your applications. You also can use the Microsoft Visual Studio programming environment to create your own classes. This lesson introduces you to the concepts associated with object-oriented programming.

After this lesson, you will be able to

- Describe the members of an object
- Describe the difference between an object and a class
- Explain what is meant by "object model"
- Explain what is meant by "abstraction," "encapsulation," and "polymorphism"

Estimated lesson time: 20 minutes

Objects, Members, and Abstraction

An object is a programmatic construct that represents something. In the real world, objects are cars, bicycles, laptop computers, and so on. Each of these items exposes specific functionality and has specific properties. In your application, an object might be a form, a control such as a button, a database connection, or any of a number of other constructs. Each object is a complete functional unit, and contains all of the data and exposes all of the functionality required to fulfill its purpose. The ability of programmatic objects to represent real-world objects is called *abstraction*.

Classes Are Templates for Objects

Classes were discussed in Chapter 1 and represent user-defined reference types. Classes can be thought of as blueprints for objects: they define all of the members of an object, define the behavior of an object, and set initial values for data when appropriate. When a class is instantiated, an in-memory instance of that class is created. This instance is called an *object*. To review, a class is instantiated using the *New* (*new*) keyword as follows:

Visual Basic .NET

```
' Declares a variable of the Widget type
Dim myWidget As Widget
' Instantiates a new Widget object and assigns it to the myWidget
' variable
myWidget = New Widget()
```

Visual C#

```
// Declares a variable of the Widget type
Widget myWidget;
// Instantiates a new Widget object and assigns it to the myWidget
// variable
myWidget = new Widget();
```

When an instance of a class is created, a copy of the instance data defined by that class is created in memory and assigned to the reference variable. Individual instances of a class are independent of one another and represent separate programmatic constructs. There is generally no limit to how many copies of a single class can be instantiated at any time. To use a real-world analogy, if a car is an object, the plans for the car are the class. The plans can be used to make any number of cars, and changes to a single car do not, for the most part, affect any other cars.

Objects and Members

Objects are composed of members. Members are properties, fields, methods, and events, and they represent the data and functionality that comprise the object. Fields and properties represent data members of an object. Methods are actions the object can perform, and events are notifications an object receives from or sends to other objects when activity happens in the application.

To continue with the real-world example of a car, consider that a *Car* object has fields and properties, such as *Color*, *Make*, *Model*, *Age*, *GasLevel*, and so on. These are the data that describe the state of the object. A *Car* object might also expose several methods, such as *Accelerate*, *ShiftGears*, or *Turn*. The methods represent behaviors the object can execute. And events represent notifications. For example, a *Car* object might receive an *EngineOverheating* event from its *Engine* object, or it might raise a *Crash* event when interacting with a *Tree* object.

Object Models

Simple objects might consist of only a few properties, methods, and perhaps an event or two. More complex objects might require numerous properties and methods and possibly even subordinate objects. Objects can contain and expose other objects as members. For example, the *TextBox* control exposes a *Font* property, which consists of a *Font* object. Similarly, every instance of the *Form* class contains and exposes a *Controls* collection that comprises all of the controls contained by the form. The *object model* defines the hierarchy of contained objects that form the structure of an object.

An object model is a hierarchical organization of subordinate objects contained and exposed within a main object. To illustrate, let's revisit the example of a car as an object. A car is a single object, but it also consists of subordinate objects. A *Car* object might contain an *Engine* object, four *Wheel* objects, a *Transmission* object, and so on. The composition of these subordinate objects directly affects how the *Car* object functions as a whole. For example, if the *Cylinders* property of the *Engine* subordinate object is equal to 4, the *Car* will behave differently than a *Car* whose *Engine* has a *Cylinders* property value of 8. Contained objects can have subordinate objects of their own. For example, the contained *Engine* object might contain several *SparkPlug* objects.

Encapsulation

Encapsulation is the concept that implementation of an object is independent of its interface. Put another way, an application interacts with an object through its interface, which consists of its public properties and methods. As long as this interface remains constant, the application can continue to interact with the component, even if implementation of the interface was completely rewritten between versions.

Objects should only interact with other objects through their public methods and properties. Thus, objects should contain all of the data they require, as well as all of the functionality that works with that data. The internal data of an object should never be exposed in the interface; thus, fields rarely should be *Public* (*public*).

Returning to the *Car* example. If a *Car* object interacts with a *Driver* object, the *Car* interface might consist of a *GoForward* method, a *GoBackward* method, and a *Stop* method. This is all the information that the *Driver* needs to interact with the *Car*. The *Car* might contain an *Engine* object, for example, but the *Driver* doesn't need to know about the *Engine* object—all the *Driver* cares about is that the methods can be called and that they return the appropriate values. Thus, if one *Engine* object is exchanged for another, it makes no difference to the *Driver* as long as the interface continues to function correctly.

Polymorphism

Polymorphism is the ability of different classes to provide different implementations of the same public interfaces. In other words, polymorphism allows methods and properties of an object to be called without regard for the particular implementation of those members. For example, a *Driver* object can interact with a *Car* object through the *Car* public interface. If another object, such as a *Truck* object or a *SportsCar* object, exposes the same public interface, the *Driver* object can interact with them without regard to the specific implementation of that interface. There are two principal ways through which polymorphism can be provided: *interface polymorphism* and *inheritance polymorphism*.

Interface Polymorphism

An *interface* is a contract for behavior. Essentially, it defines the members a class should implement, but states nothing at all about the details of that implementation. An object can implement many different interfaces, and many diverse classes can implement the same interface. All objects implementing the same interface are capable of interacting with other objects through that interface. For example, the *Car* object in the previous examples might implement the *IDrivable* interface (by convention, interfaces usually begin with *I*), which specifies the *GoForward*, *GoBackward*, and *Halt* methods. Other classes, such as *Truck*, *Forklift*, or *Boat* might implement this interface and thus are able to interact with the *Driver* object. The *Driver* object is unaware of which interface implementation it is interacting with; it is only aware of the interface itself. Interface polymorphism is discussed in detail in Lesson 3.

Inheritance Polymorphism

Inheritance allows you to incorporate the functionality of a previously defined class into a new class and implement different members as needed. A class that inherits another class is said to derive from that class, or to inherit from that class. A class can directly inherit from only one class, which is called the *base class*. The new class has the same members as the base class, and additional members can be added as needed. Additionally, the implementation of base members can be changed in the new class by overriding the base class implementation. Inherited classes retain all the characteristics of the base class and can interact with other objects as though they were instances of the base class. For example, if the *Car* class is the base class, a derived class might be *SportsCar*. The *SportsCar* class might be the base class for another derived class, the *ConvertibleSportsCar*. Each newly derived class might implement additional members, but the functionality defined in the original *Car* class is retained. Inheritance polymorphism is discussed in detail in Lesson 4.

Lesson Summary

- Abstraction is the representation of real-world objects as programmatic constructs. Programmatic objects can represent real-world objects through their implementation of members.

- Classes are the blueprints for objects. When an object is created, a copy of the class is created in memory, and values for member variables are initialized. A class can act as a template for any number of distinct objects.

- Encapsulation is a principle of object-oriented programming. An object should contain all of the data it requires and all of the code necessary to manipulate that data. The data of an object should never be made available to other objects. Only properties and methods should be exposed in the interface.

- Polymorphism is the ability of different objects to expose different implementations of the same public interface. Two major types of polymorphism exist in Visual Basic .NET and Visual C#:

  - **Interface polymorphism.** An interface defines a contract for behavior. It specifies what members must be implemented, but provides no details as to their implementation. An object can implement many unrelated interfaces, and many diverse objects can implement the same interface.

  - **Inheritance polymorphism.** Objects can inherit functionality from one another. An inherited class retains the full implementation of its base class, and instances of inherited classes can be treated as instances of the base class. Inherited classes can implement additional functionality as required.

Lesson 2: Overloading Members

Overloading allows you to create multiple members with the same name. Each member that shares a name must have a different signature. Overloading is most commonly used in methods, but Visual C# allows you to overload operators as well. In this lesson, you will learn how to create overloaded members.

After this lesson, you will be able to

- Explain how to create an overloaded method
- Describe how to create an overloaded operator in Visual C#

Estimated lesson time: 15 minutes

You might want to create a member that can accept different sets of parameters. Take the following method as an example:

Visual Basic .NET
```
Public Sub Display(ByVal DisplayValue As Integer)
    ' Implementation Omitted
End Sub
```

Visual C#
```
public void Display(int DisplayValue)
{
    // Implementation omitted
}
```

This method is perfectly acceptable on its own. But suppose you want to allow the client to designate a *duration* parameter for the method if needed? Or perhaps you would like the method to be able to accept an integer or a string as the *Display-Value* parameter. Visual Basic .NET allows you to designate optional parameters, but this functionality is unavailable in Visual C#. Furthermore, optional parameters do not address the second situation where a method needs to accept arguments that could be of multiple types.

The solution is to provide overloads. Overloads are multiple methods with the same name. Overloaded methods must have different signatures, but need not have the same return type or access level. When an overloaded method is called, the common language runtime examines the types of the arguments supplied in a method call. It then matches the argument list with the available overload signatures and calls the one that fits. If no overload fits the types of arguments that are supplied, an error results.

Member methods are the most commonly overloaded member type. You can create overloaded methods in both Visual Basic .NET and Visual C#. Visual C# allows you to overload operators, thereby providing custom operator functionality for user-defined types.

Creating Overloading Methods

You can create an overloaded method in the same way you would create any other method: by declaring the method with a name, an access level, a return type, and an argument list. An overloaded method must have the same name as a preexisting method, but must have a different signature. Access level and return type can be the same or different. The following code sample demonstrates an overloaded method:

Visual Basic .NET

```
' This example demonstrates an overloaded method.
Public Sub DisplayMessage(ByVal I As Integer)
    MessageBox.Show(I.ToString())
End Sub
' This method has the same name as the previous method, but is
' distinguishable by signature
Public Sub DisplayMessage(ByVal S As String)
    MessageBox.Show(S)
End Sub
```

Visual C#

```
// This example demonstrates an overloaded method.
public void DisplayMessage(int I)
{
    MessageBox.Show(I.ToString());
}
// This method has the same name as the previous method, but is
// distinguishable by signature
public void DisplayMessage(string S)
{
    MessageBox.Show(S);
}
```

Two methods are defined, each with the same name but with different signatures and a separate implementation. When a method with the name *DisplayMessage* is called, the runtime examines the argument type supplied to it. If a *String* is provided, the method that takes a *String* is called. If an *Integer* is provided, the method that takes an *Integer* is called.

To create an overloaded method

1. Declare a method that has the same name as an existing method. This method must have a signature that differs from any preexisting methods of the same name. The access level and return type can be the same or different from other methods of the same name.

2. Provide an implementation for the newly declared method.

Overloading Operators with Visual C#

When working with user-defined types, it is sometimes convenient to define arithmetic, logical, or comparison operators that can operate with these types. Take for example the following *struct*:

Visual C#

```
public struct HoursWorked
{
    float RegularHours;
    float OvertimeHours;
}
```

This simple *struct* might be used in an accounting application to keep track of the number of regular hours and the number of overtime hours an employee works. But working with multiple instances of this *struct* can prove difficult. For instance, suppose you want to add two instances together. You would have to create a new method specifically to add the instances. If you want to add more than two instances, you would have to call this method multiple times. Visual C# allows you to define operator behaviors for user-defined types. To enable the use of the addition operator with your *struct*, for example, you would overload the + operator and implement the appropriate behavior.

To create an overloaded operator, use the *operator* keyword with the following basic syntax:

Visual C#

```
public static type operator op (Argument1[, Argument2])
{
    implementation
}
```

The *type* component of the syntax represents the type that this operator acts on and returns. *Argument1* and *Argument2* represent the arguments that the operator takes. For a unary operator, there will be only one argument, and it must be of the same type as *type*. For a binary operator, there will be two arguments, and at least one must be the same type as *type*. *Op* represents the operator itself, such as +, –, >, *!=*, and so on. An overloaded operator must be *public* so that clients working with your user-defined type can access it. An overloaded operator must also be *static*. The definition for an overloaded operator must occur within the user-defined type that it is to act upon. Although these examples use structs, you can define overloaded operators for both structs and classes—there is no difference in the way they are defined. The following example demonstrates creating an overloaded + operator for the previously defined *HoursWorked* struct:

Visual C#

```
public struct HoursWorked
{
  float RegularHours;
  float OvertimeHours;
  // The overloaded operator must occur within the class
  // it acts upon
  public static HoursWorked operator + (HoursWorked a,
    HoursWorked b)
  {
    HoursWorked Result = new HoursWorked();
    Result.RegularHours = a.RegularHours + b.RegularHours;
    Result.OvertimeHours = a.OvertimeHours + b.OvertimeHours;
    return Result;
  }
}
```

Once the overloaded operator is defined, you can use it in code just as you would any other operator. The following example demonstrates code that adds together two instances of the *HoursWorked* struct:

Visual C#

```
// This example assumes that the variables Sunday and Monday
// represent instances of the HoursWorked struct that have been
// created and had appropriate values set.
HoursWorked total = new HoursWorked();
total = Sunday + Monday;
```

As with overloaded methods, you can create several additional implementations of overloaded operators as long as they differ in signature. To extend the example of the *HoursWorked* struct, you might want to add an *Integer* to the *NormalHours* field using the + operator. You can create an additional overload of the + operator to carry out this task. An example follows:

Visual C#

```
public struct HoursWorked
{
  float RegularHours;
  float OvertimeHours;
  // This is the overloaded operator defined in the
  // previous example
  public static HoursWorked operator + (HoursWorked a,
    HoursWorked b)
  {
    HoursWorked Result = new HoursWorked();
    Result.RegularHours = a.RegularHours + b.RegularHours;
    Result.OvertimeHours = a.OvertimeHours + b.OvertimeHours;
    return Result;
  }
```

```
// An additional implementation of the + operator is
// defined below.
public static HoursWorked operator + (HoursWorked a, int b)
{
    HoursWorked Result = new HoursWorked();
    Result.RegularHours = a.RegularHours + b;
    return Result;
}
}
```

To create an overloaded operator with Visual C#

1. Declare the overloaded operator within the class or struct that it is to act upon. Use the *operator* keyword to signify that it is an operator, followed by the operator that you want to overload. Overloaded operators must be *public* and *static*. If the operator is a binary operator, at least one of the arguments must be of the same type that it returns.

2. Provide an appropriate implementation for the operator.

Lesson Summary

- Overloading allows you to create multiple methods with the same name but different implementations. Overloaded methods must differ in signature but can have the same or different return types and access levels. You declare overloaded methods just as you would declare a regular method.

- Visual C# allows you to define custom behaviors for operators when used with user-defined types. Overloaded operators must be *public* and *static*. You use the *operator* keyword to declare an overloaded operator.

Lesson 3: Interface Polymorphism

Interfaces allow you to define contracts for behavior. Different and diverse classes can implement the same interfaces and can thus interact with other objects in a polymorphic manner. In this lesson, you will learn how to define an interface, how to implement an interface, and how objects can interact through an interface.

After this lesson, you will be able to

- Describe how to define an interface
- Describe how to implement an interface
- Explain how interfaces enable polymorphism

Estimated lesson time: 30 minutes

An interface is a contract. Any object that implements a given interface guarantees to provide an implementation of the members defined in that interface. If an object requires interaction with a specific interface, any object that implements that interface can supply the requisite interaction.

An interface defines only the members that will be made available by an implementing object. The definition of the interface states nothing about the implementation of the members, only the parameters they take and the types of values they will return. Implementation of an interface is left entirely to the implementing class.

It is possible, therefore, for different objects to provide dramatically different implementations of the same members. Take, for example, an interface named *IShape*, which defines a single method *CalculateArea*. A *Circle* class implementing this interface will calculate its area differently than a *Square* class implementing the same interface. However, an object that needs to interact with an *IShape* can call the *CalculateArea* method in either a *Circle* or a *Square* and obtain a valid result.

Defining Interfaces

Interfaces are defined with the *Interface* (*interface*) keyword. For example:

Visual Basic .NET

```
Public Interface IDrivable
End Interface
```

Visual C#

```
public interface IDrivable
{
}
```

This declaration defines the *IDrivable* interface, but does not define any members. Member methods must be defined with the method signature, but without access modifiers such as *public*, *private*, and so on. The interface access modifier determines the access modifier of the interface members. Thus, if you have a *Public* interface, all members must be *Public* as well. The following example demonstrates how to add methods to an interface:

Visual Basic .NET

```
Public Interface IDrivable
    Sub GoForward(ByVal Speed As Integer)
    Sub Halt()
    Function DistanceTraveled() As Integer
End Interface
```

Visual C#

```
public interface IDrivable
{
    void GoForward(int Speed);
    void Halt();
    int DistanceTraveled();
}
```

You also can add properties to your interface definitions. A definition for a property must include *ReadOnly* or *WriteOnly* when appropriate (in Visual Basic) or define getters, setters, or both (in Visual C#), as well as specify the return type for the property. An example of a property definition follows:

Visual Basic .NET

```
Public Interface IDrivable
' Additional member definitions omitted
' This defines a read-only property.
    ReadOnly Property FuelLevel() As Integer
End Interface
```

Visual C#

```
public interface IDrivable
{
// Additional member definitions omitted
    int FuelLevel
    {
        get;
        // To define a read-write property, add a set statement here
    }
}
```

Although you can define properties in interfaces, you are not allowed to define fields. This restriction ensures that classes that interact through the interface do not have access to the internal data of an object.

Interfaces can also define events. Interface events represent events raised by objec implementing the interface. Although any class that implements an interface mus provide an implementation for any member events, objects that interact through that interface are not obliged to handle any raised events. A default delegate type provided for the event in Visual Basic .NET; in Visual C#, you must explicitly de ignate the delegate type for the event. The following example demonstrates an interface definition for a member event:

Visual Basic .NET

```
Public Interface IDrivable
    ' Additional member definitions omitted
    Event OutOfFuel(ByVal sender As Object, e As System.EventArgs)
End Interface
```

Visual C#

```
public interface IDrivable
{
    // Additional member definitions omitted
    event System.EventHandler OutOfFuel;
}
```

To define an interface

Declare the interface using the *Interface* keyword (Visual Basic) or the *interface* keyword (Visual C#). Within the interface definition, define the signatures for the member methods, properties, and events that the interface will expose.

Polymorphism with Interfaces

Any object that implements a particular interface can interact with any other objec that requires that interface. Take the following method, for example:

Visual Basic .NET

```
Public Sub GoSomewhere(ByVal V As IDrivable)
' Implementation omitted
End Sub
```

Visual C#

```
public void GoSomewhere(IDrivable v)
{
    // Implementation omitted
}
```

This method requires an implementation of the *IDrivable* interface. Any object tha implements this interface can be passed as a parameter to this method. The object will be implicitly cast to the appropriate interface. When an object is interacting through its interface, only the interface members are accessible.

You also can explicitly cast objects that implement specific interfaces. The following example demonstrates how to cast a *Truck* object as the *IDrivable* interface (note that for this to work, *Truck* must implement *IDrivable*):

Visual Basic .NET

```
Dim myTruck As New Truck()
Dim myVehicle As IDrivable
' Casts myTruck to the IDrivable interface
myVehicle = CType(myTruck, IDrivable)
```

Visual C#

```
Truck myTruck = new Truck();
IDrivable myVehicle;
// Casts myTruck to the IDrivable interface
myVehicle = (IDrivable)myTruck;
```

Implementing Interfaces

In Visual Basic, interfaces are implemented by classes or structures with the *Implements* keyword. In Visual C#, the colon (*:*) is used to designate that a class or struct implements a specific interface. The following example demonstrates how to indicate that a class implements a specific interface:

Visual Basic .NET

```
Public Class Truck
    Implements IDrivable
    ' Additional implementation code omitted
End Class
```

Visual C#

```
public class Truck : IDrivable
{
    // Additional implementation code omitted
}
```

Classes can implement multiple interfaces. If you want to declare a class to implement multiple interfaces, you can specify the interfaces to be implemented as a comma-separated list as shown in the following examples.

Visual Basic .NET

```
Public Class Truck
    Implements IDrivable, IFuelBurning, ICargoCarrying
    ' Additional implementation code omitted
End Class
```

Visual C#

```
public class Truck : IDrivable, IFuelBurning, ICargoCarrying
{
   // Additional implementation code omitted
}
```

When a class or structure implements an interface, you must provide a separate implementation for each member of that interface. If multiple interfaces are implemented, you must provide an implementation for every member of each interface.

Implementing Interface Members in Visual C#

In Visual C#, you implement interface members in your class or structure by providing a member that has the same name as the member defined in the interface. This member must have the same access level as the interface. The following example demonstrates how to implement an interface member method:

Visual C#

```
public interface IDrivable
{
   void GoForward(int Speed);
}
public class Truck : IDrivable
{
   public void GoForward(int Speed)
   {
      // Implementation omitted
   }
}
```

When members of an interface are implemented in this manner, they are available to both the interface and the class itself. Thus, they can be accessed whether the object is cast as its own class or as the interface that it implements.

It is also possible to explicitly implement the interface and make its members unavailable to the interface of the class that is implementing it. When a member is implemented in this manner, the member can be accessed only when the object is cast as the interface it implements. You explicitly implement an interface member by providing an implementation for the fully qualified interface name. The following example demonstrates how to explicitly implement the *GoForward* method of *IDrivable*:

Visual C#

```
public class Truck : IDrivable
{
    void IDrivable.GoForward(int Speed)
    {
        // Implementation omitted
    }
}
```

Note that this member has no access modifier. Because it is an explicit implementation of the interface member, it will have the same access level as the member defined by the interface.

To implement an interface with Visual C#

1. Define a class that implements the desired interface. Use the colon (:) to declare which interface is being implemented in the class declaration. A class can implement multiple interfaces.

2. Provide an implementation for each member of the interface:

   ■ If you want a member to be available to the class and the interface, create a member with the same name, access level, and signature as the member defined by the interface.

   ■ If you want a member to be available only to the interface, implement it using the fully qualified interface name. It is unnecessary to provide an access modifier.

Implementing Interface Members with Visual Basic .NET

In Visual Basic .NET, you specify that a class member implements an interface member by using the *Implements* keyword. The class member that implements the interface member must have the same signature as defined in the interface, but it does not need to have the same access level. The following example shows how to implement an interface member method:

Visual Basic .NET

```
Public Interface IDrivable
    Sub GoForward(ByVal Speed As Integer)
End Interface
Public Class Truck
    Implements IDrivable
    Public Sub GoForward(ByVal Speed As Integer)
        Implements IDrivable.GoForward
        ' Implementation omitted
    End Sub
End Class
```

The class member that implements an interface member need not have same nam‹ as the interface member. For example, the following is a perfectly legal implemen‹ tation of the *GoForward* method of the *IDrivable* interface:

Visual Basic .NET

```
Public Sub Move(ByVal Speed As Integer)
    Implements IDrivable.GoForward
    ' Implementation omitted
End Sub
```

Any calls to the *GoForward* method of the interface in the foregoing example will be mapped to the *Move* method of the implementing class.

You also can specify a different access level for a class method that implements an interface method. For example, you can implement a method of a *Public* interface‹ with a *Private* class method. If you take this approach, the method will be *Public* when accessed through the interface, but will remain *Private* when accessed as a member of the class.

To implement an interface with Visual Basic .NET

1. Define a class that implements the desired interface. Use the *Implements* key‑ word to declare which interface is being implemented in the class declaration. A class can implement multiple interfaces.

2. Use the *Implements* keyword to provide an implementation for each interface member.

Lesson Summary

- An interface defines a contract for behavior. It defines the members that will be‹ exposed through the interface, and the parameters and return types of those members. Any object that implements an interface can interact with any objec‹ that requires that interface. Both classes and structures can implement inter‑ faces, including multiple interfaces.

- Implementation of interface members is left to the class or structure that imple‹ ments the member.

- The *Implements* keyword in Visual Basic .NET and the colon (*:*) in Visual C# declare that a class or structure implements an interface. If a class or structure implements an interface, it also must provide an implementation for each mem‹ ber defined in that interface.

- In Visual C#, you can implement interface members in two ways:

  - By implementing a member with the same name, signature, and access leve‹ as the member defined in the interface. This member will be available to both the class that implements it and the interface.

- By explicitly implementing the interface member using the fully qualified member name. If implemented in this manner, the member will be available only to the interface.

- In Visual Basic .NET, you implement an interface member by creating a class or structure member with the same signature as the interface member, and use the *Implements* keyword to map the interface member to the class member. The name and access level of the class member can differ from that of the interface member.

Lesson 4: Inheritance Polymorphism

Inheritance allows you to declare a new class that retains all the members and fun⟨ tionality of a previously defined class. This enables you to create classes that implement basic, common functionality, and then create specialized subclasses tha serve different but related functions. In this lesson, you will learn how to use inhe⟨ itance to derive new classes from base classes, how to create new implementation of base class members, and how to create abstract base classes.

After this lesson, you will be able to

- Describe how to extend a base class
- Explain how to override and shadow base class members
- Describe an abstract class
- Explain how to create abstract members

Estimated lesson time: 60 minutes

Inheritance

Inheritance allows you to create several classes that are distinct but share a common functionality. Specialized classes, called *derived classes*, *inherit* from a common class called the *base class*. A derived class is also said to *extend* a base class. The base class encapsulates the common functionality that will be present in each derived class, while the derived classes provide additional functionality specific t⟨ each class. For example, let's consider a class named *Truck*. The *Truck* class provides all of the basic functionality that a car might need. It has the methods to make it go forward, backward, and turn, and it encapsulates all of the necessary objects to do so. You might create a derived class named *PickupTruck* that inherits *Truck*. Because it inherits *Truck*, it has all the basic functionality that *Truck* provides. You could then choose to implement additional functionality specific to the class, such as a *Cargo* property. *PickupTruck* could then serve as a base class for an additiona⟨ derived class—*FourWheelDrivePickupTruck*, for example.

Polymorphic Behavior in Inherited Classes

Inherited classes generally have an "is-a" relationship with the base class. A *FourWheelDrivePickupTruck* is a *PickupTruck*, and a *PickupTruck* is a *Truck*. Any instance of a derived class can behave polymorphically as an instance of its base class. Thus, if a method requires a *Truck* object, you can supply a *PickupTruck* object. Any derived class may be implicitly converted to its base class. When cast to its base class, any members implemented by the derived class will be inaccessible—only the members of the base class will be available.

Creating Inherited Classes

You can create an inherited class by using the *Inherits* keyword in Visual Basic .NET or the colon (*:*) in Visual C#. The following example declares a *PickupTruck* class that inherits the *Truck* class:

Visual Basic .NET

```
Public Class PickupTruck
    Inherits Truck
    ' Additional implementation omitted
End Class
```

Visual C#

```
public class PickupTruck : Truck
{
    // Additional implementation omitted
}
```

Classes can only inherit a single base class, but also can implement additional interfaces. If your class implements multiple interfaces in addition to inheriting a class, you must use the *Implements* keyword immediately after the *Inherits* keyword (Visual Basic .NET) or list the interfaces after the colon following the base class (Visual C#). For example:

Visual Basic .NET

```
Public Class FourWheelDrivePickupTruck
    Inherits PickupTruck
    Implements IFourWheelDrive
    ' Additional implementation omitted
End Class
```

Visual C#

```
public class FourWheelDrivePickupTruck :
    PickupTruck, IFourWheelDrive
{
    // Additional implementation omitted
}
```

Once an inherited class is declared, you can implement additional members to add custom functionality to a class.

To declare an inherited class

- In Visual Basic .NET, use the *Inherits* keyword to designate the base class.
- In Visual C#, specify the base class after the colon in the declaration line.

Creating Classes That Cannot Be Inherited

At times, you might want to create classes that cannot serve as a base for other classes. For example, you might create a specialized class for use in your components that would not be useful as a base of functionality for other programmers. In these instances, you can mark your class as *NotInheritable* (Visual Basic .NET) or *sealed* (Visual C#). The following example demonstrates how to apply the *NotInheritable* and *sealed* keyword:

Visual Basic .NET

```
Public NotInheritable Class AClass
    ' Implementation omitted
End Class
```

Visual C#

```
public sealed class AClass
{
    // Implementation omitted
}
```

Inherited Members

When you create an inherited class, the new class possesses all the functionality found in the base class. In addition to adding new members, you can change the implementation of inherited members to suit specialized purposes. *Overriding* base members allows you to substitute a new implementation of an existing member for the base class implementation. In Visual Basic .NET, you can also *shadow* base members. Shadowing base members allows you to obscure a base member and implement a new member with the same name but completely different characteristics including signature, access level, or even member type. Visual C# allows you to *hide* base class members, which allows you to obscure a base member and implement a new member with the same name and signature, but with different other characteristics. Overriding, shadowing, and hiding are discussed in the following sections.

Overriding Base Class Members

When inheriting from a base class, you can provide a different implementation for base class members by overriding them with your own implementation for a base class member of the same name. For example, a *Car* class might have a *GoForward* method. If a *SportsCar* class inherited from the *Car* class, you might want to provide a different implementation of the *GoForward* method. Only base class methods and properties can be overridden. Member variables and events cannot be overridden.

You can declare a different implementation of a member by using the *Overrides* keyword (Visual Basic .NET) or the *override* keyword (Visual C#). The new implementation must have an identical signature and return type as the member it is overriding, and must have the same access level. For example:

Visual Basic .NET

```
' This example assumes the existence of a GoForward method in the
' base class
Public Class SportsCar
   Inherits Car
   ' This line declares the overridden method
   Public Overrides Sub GoForward(ByVal Speed As Integer)
      ' Implementation omitted
   End Sub
End Class
```

Visual C#

```
// This example assumes the existence of a GoForward method in the
// base class
public class SportsCar : Car
{
   public override void GoForward(int Speed)
   {
      // implementation omitted
   }
}
```

When a member is overridden, the new member is called in place of the base class member. This is true regardless of the context in which the member is called. For example, if an instance of an inherited class is cast to its base class and an overridden method is called, the new implementation will be executed, even though the variable is of the base class type. The type of the object, not the variable, determines which member is called.

To override a base class member, that member must be marked as *Overridable* (Visual Basic .NET) or *virtual* (Visual C#). Members not so marked are considered fixed and are not overridable. The following example demonstrates how to declare an *Overridable* (*virtual*) method.

Visual Basic .NET

```
Public Overridable Sub OverrideMe()
   ' Implementation omitted
End Sub
```

Visual C#

```
public virtual void OverrideMe()
{
   // Implementation omitted
}
```

To override a base class member

1. Ascertain that the member you are attempting to override is *Overridable* (*virtual*). If the member you want to override is not overridable, you must hide it instead, as shown later in this lesson.

2. Provide a new implementation of the member using the *Overrides* (*override*) keyword.

Shadowing Base Class Members with Visual Basic .NET

In the previous section, you learned how to replace an implementation of a member in a base class with a different implementation of the same member. It is also possible to hide the implementation of a base class member and replace it with a completely new member that might have a different access level, signature, or even be different type of member. This is called shadowing. In Visual Basic .NET, you use the *Shadows* keyword to substitute a new implementation for a base class member.

Visual Basic .NET

```
' This is the base class
Public Class MyBaseClass
    Public Function MyMethod(ByVal I As Integer) As String
       ' Implementation omitted
    End Function
End Class
' This class inherits the base class
Public Class MyInheritedClass
    Inherits MyBaseClass
    ' This function shadows the MyMethod sub defined in the base class.
    ' Note that this member has a completely different signature, access
    ' level and returns a different type of value.
    Friend Shadows Function MyMethod(ByVal S As String) As Integer
        ' Implementation omitted
    End Function
End Class
```

Hiding Base Class Members with Visual C#

When working in Visual C#, you can obscure a base class member and replace it with a completely new implementation. This is called hiding. When you hide a member, you replace the base class implementation with a new implementation. The new implementation must have the same signature as the member that is being hidden and be the same kind of member, but it can have a different access level, return type, and completely different implementation. Any method that has the same name as a preexisting method but a different signature is treated as an overload of that method and will not hide the preexisting method. The *new* keyword is used to hide a base class member as shown in this example:

Visual C#

```
// This is the base class
public class MyBaseClass
{
   public string MyMethod(int I)
   {
      // Implementation omitted
   }
}
// This class inherits the base class
public class MyInheritedClass : MyBaseClass
{
   // This function shadows the MyMethod method defined in the base
   // class. Note that this member has the same signature but a
   // different access level, and now returns a different type of
   // value.
   internal new int MyMethod(int I)
   {
      // Implementation omitted
   }
}
```

Maintaining Compatibility with Shadowed or Hidden Members

When you shadow or hide a class member, you hide the base class implementation and create a new implementation that need not have the same characteristics as the base class member. This can have grave implications for interoperating with other objects. If an object calls the *MyMethod* function from the preceding example, it would expect a return type of *String*, and when an *Integer* was returned from the shadowed member instead, an error would result. You must therefore take great care when shadowing or hiding a member; it should be done only in cases where you are certain compatibility will not be broken.

Although obscured, the base class implementation of shadowed or hidden members is still accessed under certain circumstances. Whether the base class implementation or the new implementation is accessed depends on the type of the variable, rather than the type of the object, as in overridden members. For example, consider the following code sample:

Visual Basic .NET

```
' This example uses the MyBaseClass and MyInheritedClass classes
' defined in the previous code example.
Dim X As New MyInheritedClass()
Dim Y As MyBaseClass
' X and Y now refer to the same object, but the variables have
' different types.
Y = X
```

```
' Because the variable X is of the MyInheritedClass type, the new
' member will be called by this line.
X.MyMethod("A String")
' However, because the variable Y is of the MyBaseClass type, the
' original implementation of the member will be called by this line.
Y.MyMethod(42)
```

Visual C#

```
// This example uses the MyBaseClass and MyInheritedClass classes
// defined in the previous code example.
MyInheritedClass X = new MyInheritedClass();
MyBaseClass Y;
// X and Y now refer to the same object, but the variables have
// different types.
Y = X;
// Because the variable X is of the MyInheritedClass type, the new
// member will be called by this line.
X.MyMethod(42);
// However, because the variable Y is of the MyBaseClass type, the
// original implementation of the member will be called by this line.
Y.MyMethod(42);
```

As this example demonstrates, the type of the variable determines whether a *shadowed* (*hidden*) member or the original member is called. Thus, you can change the implementation of a member without destroying the ability of a class to behave polymorphically.

If a class with a shadowed or hidden member is inherited, the shadowed or hidden member is not inherited, and the new class will expose the base member.

To shadow or hide a member

- In Visual Basic .NET, use the *Shadows* keyword to shadow a member and provide a new implementation. The new implementation can have a different signature, access level, and return type, or it can be a different type of member.

- In Visual C#, use the *new* keyword to hide a member and provide a new implementation. The new implementation must have the same signature and be the same type of member, but it can have a different access level or return type.

Accessing Base Class Members

When creating overridden or hidden members, you might want to access implementation of the member in the base class. You can access base members by using the *MyBase* (Visual Basic .NET) or *base* (Visual C#) keyword. These keywords provide a reference to the base class implementation and allow you to invoke the members implemented in the base class. The following code sample demonstrates how to invoke a member of a base class:

Visual Basic .NET

```
' This example demonstrates calling the base class implementation of
' MyMethod from within an override of that method
Public Overrides Function MyMethod(ByVal I As Integer) As String
   MyBase.MyMethod(I)
   ' Additional implementation omitted
End Function
```

Visual C#

```
// This example demonstrates calling the base class implementation of
// MyMethod from within an override of that method
public override string MyMethod(int I)
{
   base.MyMethod(I);
   // Additional implementation omitted
}
```

Protected Members

In Chapter 1, you learned about class member access levels. To review, *Public* (*public*) members are accessible to all parts of an application, including external classes. *Friend* or *internal* members are accessible to members of the local assembly, but not to external callers. *Private* (*private*) members are available only within the class itself and cannot be accessed from any other callers including inherited classes. Two other access levels have not been fully discussed: *Protected* (*protected*) and *Protected Friend* (*protected internal*).

When the *Protected* (*protected*) keyword is used with a class member, the member has the same access visibility to external callers as when the *Private* (*private*) keyword is used. The difference, however, is that protected members are accessible by derived classes as well. Consider the following example:

Visual Basic .NET

```
' The base class defines two methods: a private method and a protected
' method.
Public Class BaseClass
   ' A private method cannot be called from derived classes
   Private Sub Method1()
      ' Implementation omitted
   End Sub
   ' A protected member can be called from derived classes
   Protected Sub Method2()
      ' Implementation omitted
   End Sub
End Class
' The inherited class inherits from BaseClass
Public Class InheritedClass
   Inherits BaseClass
   Public Sub Demo()
```

```
        ' This call is legal because the protected access level allows
        ' access to the member defined by the BaseClass
        Me.Method2()
        ' This call will not compile because it attempts to access a
        ' private member of the base class.
        Me.Method1()
    End Sub
End Class
```

Visual C#

```
// The base class defines two methods: a private method and a protected
// method.
public class BaseClass
{
    // A private method cannot be called from derived classes
    private void Method1()
    {
        // Implementation omitted
    }
    // A protected member can be called from derived classes
    protected void Method2()
    {
        // Implementation omitted
    }
}
// The inherited class inherits from BaseClass
public class InheritedClass : BaseClass
{
    public void Demo()
    {
        // This call is legal because the protected access level allows
        // access to the member defined by the BaseClass
        this.Method2();
        // This call will not compile because it attempts to access a
        // private member of the base class.
        this.Method1();
    }
}
```

The preceding example demonstrates the difference between private members and protected members. The method *Demo* attempts to use a reference to an instance of *InheritedClass* (*Me* or *this*) to call *Method1* and *Method2*. Because both of these methods are defined in the base class, their access level determines whether or not they can be called from the inherited class. The call to *Method2* succeeds because *Method2* has the *Protected* (*protected*) access modifier. But because *Method1* is *Private* (*private*), it is not accessible, even to inheriting classes.

A second access level is *Protected Friend* (*protected internal*). This access modifier provides the union of *Protected* (*protected*) access and *Friend* (*internal*) access.

Thus, a member that is *Protected Friend* or *protected internal* can be accessed by classes in the assembly or by classes that inherit its class, in addition to access from within the class itself.

Abstract Classes and Members

When creating components, you might want to create a base class that provides some invariant functionality but leaves implementation of other members to inheriting classes. You can accomplish this through the use of *abstract classes*, which are classes that must be inherited.

Abstract classes are similar to interfaces, but share many features with classes. An abstract class cannot be instantiated on its own; it must be inherited first. Abstract classes can provide all, some, or none of the actual implementation of a class. Like interfaces, they can specify members that must be implemented in inheriting classes. Unlike interfaces, a class can inherit only one abstract class. Like classes, abstract classes can provide fully implemented members, but unlike classes, abstract classes also can specify members that must be implemented by the inheriting classes.

Creating Abstract Classes

You specify a class as an abstract class by using the *MustInherit* keyword in Visual Basic .NET or the *abstract* keyword in Visual C#. For example:

Visual Basic .NET

```
Public MustInherit Class AbstractClass
    ' Implementation omitted
End Class
```

Visual C#

```
public abstract class AbstractClass
{
    // Implementation omitted
}
```

Creating Abstract Members

Like a regular class, an abstract class can implement any members. Regular members of an abstract class can be *Overridable* (*virtual*), in which case inheriting classes can create their own implementations of the members as needed, or they can be non-virtual, and thus have a fixed implementation that will be common to all inheriting members.

Abstract classes also can specify abstract members. An abstract member declaration is very similar to the declaration of an interface member. Only the member type, access level, required parameters, and return type are specified. No details regarding implementation of the member are defined in the method declaration. Thus, only the member interface is specified.

To declare an abstract member, you use the *MustOverride* keyword in Visual Basic .NET, and the *abstract* keyword in Visual C#. Abstract members must be declared in abstract classes. If you try to declare an abstract member in a nonabstract class, a compiler error will result. The following code example demonstrates an abstract class with three abstract members:

Visual Basic .NET

```
Public MustInherit Class Car
    Public MustOverride Sub GoForward(ByVal I As Integer)
    Public MustOverride Function CheckSpeed() As Integer
    Public MustOverride Property Color() As String
End Class
```

Visual C#

```
public abstract class Car
{
    public abstract void GoForward(int I);
    public abstract int CheckSpeed();
    public abstract string Color
    {
        get;
        set;
    }
}
```

Note that with Visual C#, you must specify a getter and/or a setter for abstract properties. If both a getter and a setter are specified, they both must be implemented in the derived class. In Visual Basic .NET, properties are assumed to be read/write unless *ReadOnly* or *WriteOnly* is specified.

Inheriting from an Abstract Class

When a nonabstract class inherits from an abstract class, it must provide an implementation for every abstract member defined by the abstract class. An implementation is provided by overriding the member in the same way you would override a member in any other class. The following example demonstrates an implementation of the abstract class shown in the previous example:

Visual Basic .NET

```
Public Class MyCar
    Inherits Car
    Public Overrides Sub GoForward(ByVal I As Integer)
    ' Specific implementation of this method would go here
    End Sub
    Public Overrides Function CheckSpeed() As Integer
    ' Implementation for this method goes here
    End Function
```

```
Public Overrides Property Color() As String
    Get
        ' Both the getter and the setter must be implemented
    End Get
    Set(ByVal Value As String)
        ' Setter implementation goes here
    End Set
End Property
End Class
```

Visual C#

```csharp
public class MyCar : Car
{
    public override void GoForward(int I)
    {
        // Specific implementation of this method would go here
    }
    public override int CheckSpeed()
    {
        // Implementation for this method goes here
    }
    public override string Color
    {
        get
        {
            // Both the getter and the setter must be implemented
        }
        set
        {
            // Setter implementation goes here
        }
    }
}
```

You also can create new abstract classes by inheriting from existing abstract classes. In this case, the derived abstract class is not required to provide an implementation for abstract members defined in the base class, but these members can be implemented at this time if desired.

To declare an abstract class

1. Use the *MustInherit* keyword with Visual Basic .NET or the *abstract* keyword with Visual C# in the class declaration to indicate an abstract class.

2. Use the *MustOverride* (Visual Basic .NET) or *abstract* (Visual C#) keyword with any abstract members that you want to define in your class.

3. Implement any nonabstract members required by your class.

Lesson Summary

- Through inheritance, you can create classes that combine the functionality of previously defined class with new specialized functionality. Inherited classes contain all the members of their base class, and instances of an inherited class can act polymorphically as instances of their base class.

- Adding members to your inherited class provides custom functionality. You also can provide new implementation for existing members. There are two ways to do this:

  - Overriding members
  - Shadowing (Visual Basic .NET) or hiding (Visual C#) members

- You can always access the base class implementation of a member by using th *MyBase* keyword (Visual Basic .NET) or the *base* keyword (Visual C#). You can use the *Protected* (*protected*) access modifier to make a member defined i a base class available to an inherited class.

- Abstract classes allow you to create a class that defines the interface of the clas yet provides part or none of the implementation. Abstract classes cannot be instantiated on their own; rather, they must be inherited. To provide an implementation for an abstract member in an inherited member, you must override the member.

Lab 4: Using Inherited Classes

In this lab, you will learn to create inherited classes. You will extend the *Fraction* class from Lab 3-2 and create a *CompoundFraction* class that allows the user to initialize the class with a fraction and a whole number, and displays the value of the fraction as a compound fraction. You will then create an overloaded operator (with Visual C#) or implement an Add method (with Visual Basic) to add two *Fraction* objects together. Finally, you will create a strongly typed collection class that manages a collection of Fraction instances. The solution to this lab is available on the Supplemental Course Materials CD-ROM in the \Labs\Ch04\Solution folder

Before You Begin

You should have completed Lab 3-2, or loaded the Lab 3-2 solution from the Supplemental Course Materials CD-ROM.

Estimated lesson time: 45 minutes

Exercise 4.1: Creating the CompoundFraction Class

In this exercise, you will create the *CompoundFraction* class by inheriting from the *Fraction* class and providing additional functionality. You will add an additional constructor that allows the user to specify a whole number in addition to a numerator and denominator when initializing. You will also implement an overridden *ToString* method that displays the value represented by the fraction as a whole number and fraction, rather than just as a fraction.

▶   **To create the CompoundFraction class**

1. In the designer, choose Add Class from the Project menu. The Add New Item dialog box opens. Name your class CompoundFraction and click ok. The new class is added to your project, and the code window opens.

2. In the code window, specify that your class inherits the *Fraction* class. This is done by using the Inherits keyword (in Visual Basic .NET), or by using the : operator in the class declaration (in Visual C#) as shown below:

Visual Basic .NET

```
Public Class CompoundFraction
    Inherits Fraction
End Class
```

Visual C#

```csharp
using System;
namespace Lab4CSharp
{
    /// <summary>
    /// Summary description for CompoundFraction.
    /// </summary>
    public class CompoundFraction : Fraction
    {
        public CompoundFraction()
        {
            //
            // TODO: Add constructor logic here
            //
        }
    }
}
```

3. Add a constructor (Visual Basic .NET) or modify the provided constructor (Visual C#) to initialize the class. This constructor should accept a value for the numerator and denominator, and pass those values to the base class constructor. An example is shown:

Visual Basic .NET

```vbnet
Public Sub New(ByVal Numerator As Integer, _
    ByVal Denominator As Integer)
    MyBase.New(Numerator, Denominator)
End Sub
```

Visual C#

```csharp
public CompoundFraction(int Numerator, int Denominator) :
    base(Numerator, Denominator)
{
}
```

4. Add an additional constructor that allows the user to specify a whole number in addition to the numerator and denominator. Since you must make a call to the constructor of the base class, you should convert the whole number parameter to the numerator equivalent before calling the base class constructor. Your finished constructor should look like the example:

Visual Basic .NET

```vbnet
Public Sub New(ByVal Numerator As Integer, ByVal Denominator As _
    Integer, ByVal WholeNumber As Integer)
    MyBase.New(Numerator + (WholeNumber * Denominator), Denominator)
End Sub
```

Visual C#

```
public CompoundFraction(int Numerator, int Denominator,
    int WholeNumber) :
    base(Numerator + (WholeNumber * Denominator), Denominator)
{
}
```

5. Add a third constructor that allows the user to create a new *CompoundFraction* instance from an existing *Fraction* instance. This constructor should pass the Numerator and Denominator of the supplied *Fraction* instance to the base constructor. An example follows.

Visual Basic .NET

```
Public Sub New(ByVal f As Fraction)
    MyBase.New(f.Numerator, f.Denominator)
End Sub
```

Visual C#

```
public CompoundFraction(Fraction f) :
    base(f.Numerator,f.Denominator)
{
}
```

6. Override the *ToString* method to provide a new implementation that returns a string that represents the value of the *CompoundFraction* class instance, but returns a whole number and a fraction when appropriate instead of simply the numerator over the denominator. When finished, your *ToString* method should look something like the example shown below:

Visual Basic .NET

```
Public Overrides Function ToString() As String
    Dim Result As String
    Dim tempNumerator As Integer = Numerator
    Dim wholenumber As Integer = 0
    ' This loop reduces the fraction to its compound representation
    Do While tempNumerator >= Denominator
        tempNumerator -= Denominator
        wholenumber += 1
    Loop
    ' Determines if there is a whole number component
    If Not wholenumber = 0 Then
        Result = wholenumber.ToString
    End If
    ' Determines if there is a fractional component
    If Not tempNumerator = 0 Then
        If Not wholenumber = 0 Then Result &= " "
        Result &= tempNumerator.ToString & "/" & Denominator.ToString
    End If
    Return Result
End Function
```

Visual C#

```csharp
public override string ToString()
{
    string Result = "";
    int tempNumerator = Numerator;
    int wholenumber = 0;
    // This loop reduces the fraction to its compound representation
    while (tempNumerator >= Denominator)
    {
        tempNumerator -= Denominator;
        wholenumber ++;
    }
    // Determines if there is a whole number component
    if (!(wholenumber == 0))
        Result = wholenumber.ToString();
    // Determines if there is a fractional component
    if (!(tempNumerator == 0))
    {
        if (!(wholenumber == 0))
            Result += " ";
        Result += tempNumerator.ToString() + "/"
            + Denominator.ToString();
    }
    return Result;
}
```

7. In Solution Explorer, right-click Form1 and choose View Designer. The designer for Form1 opens. From the Toolbox, add a new label and textbox control to the form (you may need to make Form1 larger) and set the text values as shown in Table 4.1.

Table 4.1.   Properties for the New Controls

Control	Text Value
Label7	Whole number
TextBox3	(blank)

8. In Solution Explorer, right-click Form1 and choose View Code. The code window for Form1 opens. Locate the *Button1_Click* method, and modify it to create a new *CompoundFraction* instance instead of a *Fraction* instance and to check *TextBox3* for any input and incorporate it appropriately. The following example demonstrates what your modified code should look like.

Visual Basic .NET

```vbnet
Private Sub Button1_Click(ByVal sender As System.Object, _
    ByVal e As System.EventArgs) Handles Button1.Click
    Try
        Dim numerator As Integer
        Dim denominator As Integer
```

```
        Dim wholenumber As Integer
        Dim afraction As CompoundFraction
        numerator = Integer.Parse(TextBox1.Text)
        denominator = Integer.Parse(TextBox2.Text)
        If Not TextBox3.Text = "" Then
            wholenumber = Integer.Parse(TextBox3.Text)
            afraction = New CompoundFraction(numerator, denominator, _
                wholenumber)
        Else
            afraction = New CompoundFraction(numerator, denominator)
        End If
        Label4.Text = afraction.ToString
        Label6.Text = afraction.ToDouble
    Catch ex As Exception
        MessageBox.Show("Please check the values and try again!")
    End Try
End Sub
```

Visual C#

```
private void button1_Click(object sender, System.EventArgs e)
{
    try
    {
        int numerator;
        int denominator;
        int wholenumber;
        CompoundFraction aFraction;
        numerator = int.Parse(textBox1.Text);
        denominator = int.Parse(textBox2.Text);
        if (!(textBox3.Text == ""))
        {
            wholenumber = int.Parse(textBox3.Text);
            aFraction = new CompoundFraction(numerator, denominator,
                wholenumber);
        }
        else
        {
            aFraction = new CompoundFraction(numerator, denominator);
        }
        label4.Text = aFraction.ToString();
        label6.Text = (aFraction.ToDouble()).ToString();
    }
    catch
    {
        MessageBox.Show("Please check the values and try again!");
    }
}
```

9. Press F5 to build and run your application. Test your new *CompoundFraction* class with a variety of values for each entry. Note that the *ToString* method now displays the value as a compound fraction instead of a simple fraction.

Exercise 4.2: Creating Overloaded Operators or Shared Methods

In this exercise, you will implement functionality that allows you to add two instances of the *CompoundFraction* class. For Visual C#, you will implement and overloaded + operator. For Visual Basic .NET. you will implement a *Shared Add* method.

▶ **To implement the Add functionality**

1. In Solution Explorer, right-click Fraction and choose View Code. The Code window opens.

   In the Code editor, add the following overloaded operator/method:

   ### Visual Basic .NET

   ```
   Public Shared Function Add(ByVal fraction1 As Fraction, _
       ByVal fraction2 As Fraction) As Fraction
       Dim tempDenominator As Integer
       Dim tempNumerator1 As Integer
       Dim tempNumerator2 As Integer
       Dim Result As Fraction
       tempDenominator = fraction1.Denominator * fraction2.Denominator
       tempNumerator1 = fraction1.Numerator * fraction2.Denominator
       tempNumerator2 = fraction2.Numerator * fraction1.Denominator
       Result = New Fraction(tempNumerator1 + tempNumerator2, _
           tempDenominator)
       Result.Reduce()
       Return Result
   End Function
   ```

   ### Visual C#

   ```
   public static Fraction operator +(Fraction fraction1,
       Fraction fraction2)
   {
       int tempDenominator;
       int tempNumerator1;
       int tempNumerator2;
       Fraction Result;
       tempDenominator = fraction1.Denominator * fraction2.Denominator;
       tempNumerator1 = fraction1.Numerator * fraction2.Denominator;
       tempNumerator2 = fraction2.Numerator * fraction1.Denominator;
   ```

```
    Result = new Fraction(tempNumerator1 + tempNumerator2,
        tempDenominator);
    return Result;
}
```

2. From the Build menu, choose Build Solution to build and save your work. You will test this functionality in the next exercise.

Exercise 4.3: Creating a Strongly Typed Collection Class

In this exercise, you will create a strongly typed collection class by inheriting from the *CollectionBase* class. Your new collection class will accept only *Fraction* objects, and will include methods to add and remove a *Fraction* to and from the collection, as well as functionality to access each member of the collection by its index. Finally, you will implement a method that returns the total of all *Fraction* objects contained in the collection.

▶ **To create the strongly typed collection**

1. From the Project menu, choose Add Class. The Add New Item dialog box opens. Name this new class *FractionCollection*.

2. Inherit from the *CollectionBase* class to provide a basic core of collection-type functionality to your new class. An example is shown below:

Visual Basic .NET

```
Public Class FractionCollection
    Inherits CollectionBase
End Class
```

Visual C#

```
public class FractionCollection : System.Collections.CollectionBase
```

3. Implement an *Add* method that allows the user to add a *Fraction* instance to the collection. You should do this by creating a method that can accept only a *Fraction* instance, and calls the *Add* method of the internal *List* object of *Collection-Base*. An example is shown:

Visual Basic .NET

```
Public Sub Add(ByVal f As Fraction)
    List.Add(f)
End Sub
```

Visual C#

```
public void Add(Fraction f)
{
    List.Add(f);
}
```

4. Implement a *Remove* method that removes a particular *Fraction* instance from the collection. You can implement this functionality by passing the method parameter to the *Remove* method of the internal *List* object, as shown below:

Visual Basic .NET

```
Public Sub Remove(ByVal f As Fraction)
    List.Remove(f)
End Sub
```

Visual C#

```
public void Remove(Fraction f)
{
    List.Remove(f);
}
```

5. Implement a default property (Visual Basic .NET) or indexer (Visual C#) that takes an integer parameter as an index and returns or sets the object that is located at that index. An example is shown below:

Visual Basic .NET

```
Default Public Property Item(ByVal I As Integer) As Fraction
    Get
        Return CType(List.Item(I), Fraction)
    End Get
    Set(ByVal Value As Fraction)
        List.Item(I) = Value
    End Set
End Property
```

Visual C#

```
public Fraction this[int i]
{
    get
    {
        return (Fraction)List[i];
    }
    set
    {
        List[i] = value;
    }
}
```

6. Implement a method that returns the total of all *Fraction* objects contained in the collection. This method should use the *Shared Fraction.Add* method (for Visual Basic .NET) or the overloaded + operator (for Visual C#). For example:

Visual Basic .NET

```
Public Function Total() As Fraction
    Dim Result as Fraction
    If Me.Count = 0 Then
        Result = New Fraction(0,1)
    Else If Me.Count = 1 Then
        Result = Me.Item(0)
    Else
        Result = Me.Item(0)
        Dim Counter As Integer
        For Counter = 1 to Me.Count -1
            Result = Fraction.Add(Result, Me.Item(Counter))
        Next
    End If
    Return Result
End Function
```

Visual C#

```
public Fraction Total()
{
    Fraction Result;
    if (this.Count == 0)
    {
        Result = new Fraction(0,1);
    }
    else if (this.Count == 1)
    {
        Result = this[0];
    }
    else
    {
        Result = this[0];
        int Counter;
        for(Counter = 1; Counter < this.Count; Counter ++)
        {
            Result = Result + this[Counter];
        }
    }
    return Result;
}
```

7. In Solution Explorer, right-click Form1 and choose View Designer. From the Toolbox, add three buttons to the form (you may need to make Form1 larger). When finished, your form should look similar to Figure 4.1. Set the Text property of the buttons as shown in Table 4.2.

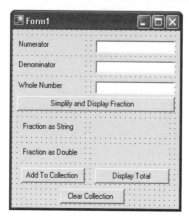

Figure 4.1. The Test form.

Table 4.2.   Text Property of New Buttons

Button	Text
Button2	Add To Collection
Button3	Display Total
Button4	Clear Collection

8. In Solution Explorer, right-click Form1 and choose View Code. The Code Editor opens. Add a line of code, within the class member declaration section, to declare and instantiate a new instance of the *FractionCollection* class, as shown below.

Visual Basic .NET

```
Private myFractions As New FractionCollection
```

Visual C#

```
private FractionCollection myFractions = new FractionCollection();
```

9. In Solution Explorer, right-click Form1 to return to the designer. Double-click Button2, the Add to Collection button, to create an event handler for that button's Click event. Add code to this method that creates a new fraction from the values in the textboxes and adds that fraction to the fraction collection, then clears the textboxes. An example is shown below. Note that the code is very similar to the code you provided for *Button1.Click*.

Visual Basic .NET

```
Private Sub Button2_Click(ByVal sender As Object, _
    ByVal e As System.EventArgs) Handles Button2.Click
    Try
    Dim numerator As Integer
    Dim denominator As Integer
    Dim wholenumber As Integer
```

```
        Dim afraction As Fraction
        numerator = Integer.Parse(TextBox1.Text)
        denominator = Integer.Parse(TextBox2.Text)
        If Not TextBox3.Text = "" Then
            wholenumber = Integer.Parse(TextBox3.Text)
            afraction = New Fraction(numerator, denominator, _
                wholenumber)
        Else
            afraction = New Fraction(numerator, denominator)
        End If
        myFractions.Add(afraction)
        TextBox1.Text = ""
        TextBox2.Text = ""
        TextBox3.Text = ""
    Catch ex As Exception
        MessageBox.Show("Please check the values and try again!")
    End Try
End Sub
```

Visual C#

```csharp
private void button2_Click(object sender, System.EventArgs e)
{
    try
    {
        int numerator;
        int denominator;
        int wholenumber;
        Fraction aFraction;
        numerator = int.Parse(textBox1.Text);
        denominator = int.Parse(textBox2.Text);
        if (!(textBox3.Text == ""))
        {
            wholenumber = int.Parse(textBox3.Text);
            aFraction = new Fraction(numerator, denominator,
                wholenumber);
        }
        else
        {
            aFraction = new Fraction(numerator, denominator);
        }
        myFractions.Add(aFraction);
        textBox1.Text = "";
        textBox2.Text = "";
        textBox3.Text = "";
    }
    catch
    {
        MessageBox.Show("Please check the values and try again!");
    }
}
```

10. Return to the Designer, and double-click Button3, the Display Total button, to generate an event handler for this button's click event. Add a line of code to this method to display the total of the *Fraction* objects in the collection in a *MessageBox*, as shown below.

Visual Basic .NET

```
Public Sub Button3_Click(ByVal sender As Object, _
    ByVal e As System.EventArgs) Handles Button3.Click
    Dim cf As New CompoundFraction(myFractions.Total)
    MessageBox.Show(cf.ToString)
End Sub
```

Visual C#

```
public void button3_Click(object sender, System.EventArgs e)
{
    CompoundFraction cf = new CompoundFraction(myFractions.Total());
    MessageBox.Show(cf.ToString());
}
```

11. Return to the Designer, and double-click Button4, the Clear Collection button, to generate an event handler for this button's click event. Add a line of code to this method to clear the *FractionCollection*, as shown below:

Visual Basic .NET

```
Public Sub Button4_Click(ByVal sender As Object, _
    ByVal e As System.EventArgs) Handles Button4.Click
    myFractions.Clear()
End Sub
```

Visual C#

```
public void button4_Click(object sender, System.EventArgs e)
{
    myFractions.Clear();
}
```

12. Press F5 to build and test your work. Add several different combinations of fractions to the new collection and view the totals. Note that even though you are creating *CompoundFraction* objects in the application, and the collection is designed to accept *Fraction* objects, everything works out fine. When a *CompoundFraction* instance is added to the collection, it behaves polymorphically as a *Fraction*.

Review

The following review questions are intended to reinforce key concepts and information presented in this chapter. If you are unable to answer a question, return to the appropriate lesson and review, then try the lesson again. Answers to the questions can be found in Appendix A.

1. Briefly explain encapsulation and why it is important in object-oriented programming.

2. What is method overloading, and when is it useful?

3. You need to create several unrelated classes where each class exposes a common set of methods. Briefly outline a strategy that will allow these classes to polymorphically expose that functionality to other classes.

4. You need to create several classes that provide a core set of functionality, but each class must be able to interact with a different set of objects. Outline a strategy for developing these classes with the least development time.

5. Describe an abstract class, and explain when one might be useful.

C H A P T E R 5

esting and Debugging Your Application

About This Chapter

In this chapter, you will learn to use the debugging tools, along with the *Trace* and *Debug* classes and how they can be used to diagnose problems with program execution. You will learn how to create an effective unit test plan. Throwing and handling exceptions are also covered.

Before You Begin

There are no prerequisites to complete the lessons in this chapter.

Lesson 1: Using the Debugging Tools

Programming errors are inevitable. Even very experienced programmers occasionally introduce errors, also known as bugs, while writing code. Debugging is the process of locating and fixing these errors. In this lesson, you will learn about the kinds of errors you are likely to encounter and the tools available to isolate and correct these errors.

After this lesson, you will be able to

- Describe the common types of errors
- Explain what Break mode is and how to set breakpoints
- Describe how to step through code
- Describe some of the debugging windows that are available and explain how to use them

Estimated lesson time: 45 minutes

Types of Errors

There are three basic types of errors you might encounter when writing code. *Syntax errors* represent code that cannot be understood by the compiler. *Run-time errors* are errors that occur when an attempt is made to perform an operation that is impossible to carry out. *Logical errors* are errors that result when code compiles and executes correctly, but returns an unexpected result. In this section, we will examine each error type in turn.

Syntax Errors

A syntax error occurs when the compiler cannot compile the code it is given. For example, a syntax error occurs when keywords are typed incorrectly, punctuation is omitted, or an incorrect construct is parsed. The following example demonstrates two syntax errors:

Visual Basic .NET

```
Public Sub SyntaxError()
    System.Windows.Forms.MessageBoxShow("Where's the error?")
```

Visual C#

```
public void SyntaxError()
{
    System.Windows.Forms.MessageBoxShow("Where's the error?");
```

First, a period is missing between *MessageBox* and *Show*, creating an unrecognizable command for the compiler. Second, the closing construct for the method is missing (*End Sub* in Microsoft Visual Basic .NET and *}* in Microsoft Visual C#). Both errors will create a condition that the compiler cannot interpret.

You can easily identify syntax errors with Visual Studio .NET. Whenever you build your project, syntax errors are detected automatically and underscored in the code. Detected errors are also added to the Task List window, shown in Figure 5.1.

Figure 5.1.   The Task List window

Double-click any error in the Task List window, and the cursor will highlight that error in the code window. Frequently, this action provides sufficient information to correct the error. However, if further information is required, you can obtain help on the highlighted item by pressing F1.

Visual Basic .NET performs syntax checking when code is typed. Syntax errors are immediately underlined and added to the Task List window. It is unnecessary to build the project to identify syntax errors.. Visual C# also performs automatic syntax checking when code is typed, but the level of error detection is less sophisticated.

To identify and correct syntax errors

1. Build the project. Syntax errors will be detected and added to the Task List window. If you are working in Visual Basic .NET, syntax errors will be added to the Task List window.

2. Double-click an error in the Task List window. The error will be highlighted in the code editor.

3. Correct the error. If necessary, you can obtain help by pressing F1.

Run-Time Errors

Run-time errors occur when the application attempts to perform an operation that is not allowed. This includes operations that are impossible to carry out, such as division by zero, and operations that are not allowed, as in the case of security exceptions. When a run-time error occurs, an exception describing the error is thrown. Exceptions are special classes that are used to communicate error states between different parts of the application. You can write code to handle exceptions so that they do not halt execution of your application. Handling exceptions is covered in greater detail in Lesson 4 of this chapter.

Logical Errors

Logical errors occur when the application compiles and executes correctly, but does not produce the expected results. These can be the most difficult type of errors to track down, because there might not be any indication as to the source of the error. Logical errors can result from something as innocuous as a misplaced decimal point. For example:

Visual Basic .NET

```
Public Function CalculateSalary(ByVal HourlyRate As Single) As Single
    Dim YearlySalary As Single
    YearlySalary = HourlyRate * 52 * 400
    Return YearlySalary
End Function
```

Visual C#

```
public float CalculateSalary(float HourlyRate)
{
    float YearlySalary;
    YearlySalary = HourlyRate * 52 * 400;
    return YearlySalary;
}
```

The method in the example takes a value for an hourly wage and calculates a yearly salary by multiplying the hourly wage by the number of weeks in the year and hours in a week. An error occurs because the value is multiplied by 400 instead of 40 hours per week. This method will compile and execute correctly, but inappropriate results will be reported. You can detect logical errors by feeding test data into your application and analyzing the results. Testing is covered in Lesson 3 of this chapter. To identify the source of logical errors in code, it is often necessary to examine the code line-by-line. This can be done in Break mode.

Break Mode

Break mode allows you to halt program execution and execute code one line at a time. While in Break mode, you can use the debugging tools to examine the values of application variables and properties. Visual Studio .NET enters Break mode under any of the following circumstances:

- You choose Step Into, Step Over, or Step Out from the Debug menu or toolbar.
- Execution reaches a line that contains an enabled breakpoint.
- Execution reaches a *Stop* statement.
- An unhandled exception is thrown.

Table 5.1 summarizes the features found on the Debug menu.

Table 5.1.   Debug Menu Items

Menu Item	Shortcut Key	Description
Windows		Opens a submenu of debugging windows. These windows are discussed in detail later in this lesson.
Start/Continue	F5	Runs the application in Debug mode. If the application is in Break mode, this option continues program execution.
Break All	Ctrl+Alt+Break	Causes program execution to halt and enter Break mode at the current program line. Choose Continue to resume execution.
Stop Debugging	Shift+F5	Stops the debugger and returns Visual Studio .NET to Design mode.
Detach All		Detaches the debugger from all processes it is debugging. This closes the debugger but does not halt program execution.
Restart	Ctrl+Shift+F5	Terminates and restarts application execution.
Apply Code Changes		Used only with C/C++ programming. Cannot be used with Visual Basic .NET or Visual C#.
Processes		Displays the Processes window.
Exceptions	Ctrl+Alt+E	Displays the Exceptions window.
Step Into	F11	Runs the next executable line of code. If the next line calls a method, Step Into stops at the beginning of that method.
Step Over	F10	Runs the next executable line of code. If the next line calls a method, Step Over executes that method and stops at the next line within the current method.
Step Out	Shift+F11	Executes the remainder of the current method and breaks at the next executable line of code in the calling method.
QuickWatch	Ctrl+Alt+Q	Displays the QuickWatch window.
New Breakpoint	Ctrl+B	Displays the New Breakpoint window.
Clear All Breakpoints	Ctrl+Shift+F9	Removes all breakpoints from the application.
Disable All Breakpoints		Disables all breakpoints, but does not delete them.

Additionally, some debugging functions can be accessed by right-clicking on an element in the code window and choosing a function from the pop-up menu. Some of these functions are summarized in Table 5.2.

Table 5.2.   Code Window Pop-Up Menu Debugging Functions

Menu Item	Description
Insert Breakpoint	Inserts a breakpoint at the selected line.
New Breakpoint	Displays the New Breakpoint window.
	This menu item is identical to the Debug menu item of the same name.
Add Watch	Adds the selected expression to the Watch window.
QuickWatch	Displays the QuickWatch window. This menu item is identical to the Debug menu item of the same name.
Show Next Statement	Highlights the next statement to be executed.
Run To Cursor	Runs program execution to the selected line.
Set Next Statement	Designates the selected line as the next line of code to be executed. The selected line must be in the current procedure.

Some of the more commonly used debugging features are discussed in the following sections.

Using Step Into

You can use Step Into to examine your program execution line-by-line. When you choose Step Into to step through your code, the application executes the current line, and then returns to Break mode. If the current line is a method call, the debugger advances to the first line of that method. After the line has been executed, you can examine the state of your application using the various debugging windows.

To use Step Into

Select Step Into from the Debug menu or from the Debug toolbar, or press F11.

Using Step Over

You can use Step Over in much the same way you use Step Into. Step Over behaves identically to Step Into, except when a function call is encountered; in this case, Step Over executes the entire function call and advances to the next line. You should use Step Over when you want to stay at the same level in your code and there is no need to analyze any nested method calls.

To use Step Over

Select Step Over from the Debug menu or from the Debug toolbar, or press F10.

Using Step Out

Step Out allows you to execute the remainder of code in the current procedure. If the current procedure was called from another method, execution advances to the statement following the line that called that procedure.

To use Step Out

Select Step Out from the Debug menu or from the Debug toolbar, or press Shift+F11.

Using Run To Cursor

The Run To Cursor option allows you to choose a line of code and execute all of the code in the application up to that line. You can use this option to skip over blocks of code that do not need to be executed line-by-line. For example, you might use Run To Cursor to step over a large loop.

To use Run To Cursor

In the code editor, place the cursor on the line you want to run to. This line must be an executable line of code. Right-click and choose Run To Cursor.

Using Set Next Statement

You can use Set Next Statement to skip over sections of code. Set Next Statement allows you to set the next statement within the current method to be executed, skipping over any intermediate code. Unlike Run To Cursor, the code that is skipped is not executed. You can use Set Next Statement to skip sections of code that contain known bugs. You also can use Set Next Statement to choose a line of code that has already been executed.

To use Set Next Statement

1. In the code editor, place the cursor on the line you want to designate as the next executed line. This line must be an executable line of code within the current procedure.

2. Right-click, and choose Set Next Statement. You can then use Step Into to execute the line.

Examining Variable Values

You can examine the value of program variables while in Break mode by hovering the mouse pointer over the variable in code. The current value of the variable will be displayed in a pop-up box. This technique provides a quick and easy way to determine the current value of a variable. For more detailed information about a variable's state, you should use the Watch, Autos, or Locals windows, which are further discussed in this lesson.

Setting Breakpoints

You can designate lines of code or conditions that will cause the application to break in the debugger. These are called breakpoints. You can use breakpoints to set lines of code or conditions that will halt program execution. There are four types of breakpoints:

- **Function breakpoints.** Cause the application to enter Break mode when a specified location within a function is reached.

- **File breakpoints.** Cause the application to enter Break mode when a specified location within a file is reached.

- **Address breakpoints.** Cause the application to enter Break mode when a specified memory address is accessed.

- **Data breakpoints.** Cause the application to enter Break mode when the value of a variable changes. This option is not available when programming in Visual Basic .NET and Visual C#.

To set a function breakpoint

Function breakpoints are the breakpoints that are most commonly used. You can set a function breakpoint in one of three different ways:

- By clicking the gray bar to the left of the code window at the desired line. This will insert a breakpoint at the specified line.

- By right-clicking the desired line of code and choosing Insert Breakpoint from the pop-up window.

- By choosing New Breakpoint from the Debug menu or by right-clicking in the code editor and choosing New Breakpoint from the pop-up menu. You can then add a new breakpoint by setting the appropriate parameters in the New Breakpoint window.

The Breakpoints Window

The Breakpoints window allows you to manage all of your breakpoints in a single window, as shown in Figure 5.2. You can display the Breakpoints window by choosing Windows from the Debug menu, then selecting Breakpoints.

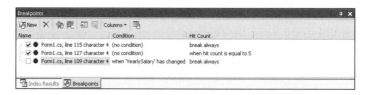

Figure 5.2. The Breakpoints window.

The Breakpoints window lists all of the breakpoints in your project, where the breakpoint is located, and any conditions attached to the breakpoint. You can choose additional columns of information about your breakpoints from the Columns drop-down menu. You can disable a breakpoint by clearing the check box next to it. Also, the button in the top-left corner of the window allows you to create a new breakpoint, delete a breakpoint, or clear or disable all breakpoints.

Clearing and Disabling Breakpoints

When a breakpoint is no longer needed, you can remove it. Or, if you want to retain a breakpoint, but do not need it at that moment, you can disable it. You can use the Breakpoints window to manage your breakpoints. You also can remove or disable a breakpoint in the code editor.

To remove a breakpoint in the code editor

Click the breakpoint in the gray bar to the left of the code editor. This will remove the breakpoint.

To disable a breakpoint in the code editor

Right-click the breakpoint in the code editor, and choose Disable Breakpoint. This will disable the breakpoint.

Breakpoint Properties and Setting Breakpoint Conditions

You can view a breakpoint's properties by right-clicking the breakpoint in either the code editor (Visual Basic .NET only) or the Breakpoints window and choosing Properties. This causes the Breakpoint Properties window to be displayed. The Breakpoint Properties window has three tabs: Function, File, and Address, and each tab shows the breakpoint expressed as that particular type. Thus, you might set a Function breakpoint in the code editor, but that breakpoint also can be expressed as a File breakpoint or an Address breakpoint, and that information can be found in the Breakpoint Properties window.

In addition to the three tabs, the Breakpoint Properties window has two buttons: the Conditions button and the Hit Count button. Pressing the Condition button displays the Breakpoint Condition window, which allows you to designate an expression that causes the breakpoint to be active only if the expression is *true* or if the expression changes. When testing whether an expression is *true*, the expression that you designate can be any valid expression that resolves to a Boolean value. For example, you could set a breakpoint in code, choose the Is True radio button, and designate the condition 'myBoolean = False' (Visual Basic .NET) or 'myBoolean == false' (Visual C#). This would cause the breakpoint to be active only when the variable named *myBoolean* is *false*. You also can use the negation operator to get the same effect, for example, 'Not myBoolean' (Visual Basic .NET) or !myBoolean (Visual C#).

Another method is to designate a variable or expression that when changed will cause execution to break. In this case, the expression you designate needs only to be a valid expression. For example you could choose the 'has changed' radio button and designate 'myVariable' or any other variable name. You can also designate more complex expressions, such as 'x + y', which causes the breakpoint to be enabled only when the value of x + y changes.

Pressing the Hit Count button in the New Breakpoint dialog box opens the Break-point Hit Count window, where you can set the breakpoint to be active only when it has been hit a predetermined number of times, a multiple of a predetermined number of times, or a number of times that is equal to or greater than a predetermined number. For example, if you set the hit count condition to break only when the hit count is a multiple of 10, program execution will break every tenth time the breakpoint is encountered.

Note   The breakpoint must be active to be counted. Thus, if you have a breakpoint that has conditions of 'x = true' and 'break when the hit count is a multiple of 10', program execution will break only when this breakpoint is encountered for the tenth time.

Using the Debugging Windows

Visual Studio provides several tools, or windows, to monitor program execution. Some, such as the Output window and the Command window, are available in Design mode. Others, such as the Locals window, are visible only while debugging.

The Output Window

The Output window displays all of the command-line output from the application as the application is compiled and executed. This output includes notifications from the application that assemblies have loaded, as well as output from *Debug* and *Trace* statements. When debugging your application, you primarily will use the Output window to receive *Debug* notifications. Using the *Debug* class is discussed in Lesson 2 of this chapter. The Output window is usually visible by default, but if it is not visible, you can display it by choosing View, then Other Windows, and selecting Output.

The Locals, Autos, and Watch Windows

The Locals, Autos, and Watch windows are windows that allow you to monitor the status of program variables while the application is being debugged. Additionally, these windows allow you to edit the values of variables while debugging. This can be useful when testing how procedures respond to different input.

The Locals Window

When the program is running in Debug mode, the Locals window allows you to monitor the values of all the variables in the current procedure. The Locals window contains three columns of information: a Name column that displays the name of the variable, a Value column that displays the variable's value, and a Type column that displays the variable's type. Complex types such as classes or structures are displayed in a tree view that can be expanded to reveal the values of their members. As program execution shifts from method to method, the variables displayed within the Locals window also shift so that only the local variables are displayed. You can alter the value of a variable in the Locals window by selecting its value under the Value column and typing a new value. Note that only strings and numeric values can be changed in this manner. You cannot set a class or structure variable to refer to another instance of that class or structure, although you can change variable values within the class or structure. When a value is changed, it appears as red in the Value column.

To display the Locals window

While debugging your application, choose Debug then Windows, and select Locals.

The Autos Window

The Autos window is like an abbreviated form of the Locals window. The Autos window displays the same data columns as the Locals window, but only displays the variables in the current line and the previous line (Visual C#) or the variables in the current line and three lines on either side of the current line (Visual Basic .NET). You can alter the variable value in the Autos window, just as you would in the Locals window.

To display the Autos window

While debugging your application, choose Debug, then Windows, and select Autos.

The Watch Window

The Watch window is where you designate a variable to track. Variables added to the Watch window remain in the window even when they are out of scope. Like the Locals and Autos windows, the Watch window displays the variable's Name, Value, and Type, and you can alter the running values of noncomplex variables by typing a new value into the Value column. Visual Studio .NET provides four separate Watch windows for designating multiple sets of watch variables.

You can quickly evaluate a variable by using the QuickWatch dialog box, which can be displayed by right-clicking a variable and choosing QuickWatch. The QuickWatch dialog box shows you the Name, Value, and Type of a single variable, and gives you the option of adding it to the Watch window. You also can use the QuickWatch dialog box to edit the variable value by typing a new value in the Value column.

To display the Watch window

While debugging your application, choose the Debug menu, then Windows, and select Watch1, Watch2, Watch3, or Watch4.

To display the QuickWatch dialog box

In the code editor, right-click a variable and choose QuickWatch from the pop-up menu.

To add a variable to the Watch window

You can add a variable to the Watch window in one of the following ways:

- Select an empty row in the Watch window and type the variable name.
- In the code editor, right-click on a variable and choose Add Watch from the pop-up menu.
- Using the mouse, highlight and drag a variable from the code editor, the Autos window, or the Locals window.
- In the QuickWatch dialog box, press the Add Watch button.

Immediate Mode in the Command Window

The Immediate mode of the Command window is used to execute procedures, eval uate expressions, or change variable values during debugging. You can display the Command window in Immediate mode by selecting Debug, then Windows, and then Immediate.

In Immediate mode, the command window can evaluate any valid statements or method calls but cannot accept data declarations. If the application is in Break mode, you can enter a statement or method call in the Command window, as you would in the code editor. When you press Enter, Visual Studio switches to run time and executes the statement. The application returns to Break mode after execution of the statement or method call is complete.

You can print variable values directly in the Command window when the application is in Break mode—the question mark (?) lets you print the value of an expression or variable in the Command window. The following example multiplies the current values of x and y and prints them to the Command window:

```
? X*Y
```

Note that the syntax is the same for both Visual Basic .NET and Visual C#. In the case of Visual C#, no semicolon is required to terminate the line. You can use the same syntax to print the value of any property currently in scope. For example, the code

```
? TextBox1.Text
```

prints the current value of the *Text* property of TextBox1.

The assignment operator can be used to assign a new value to an existing variable. The following code example sets the value of x to 5:

```
X = 5
```

Note that the variable must be already declared.

To display the Command window

From the View menu, choose Other Windows, then Command Window. You can also display the Command window in Immediate mode by selecting Debug, then Windows, and then Immediate.

Other Windows

Several additional windows allow you to obtain information on your program's execution or manage Break mode while you are debugging. Table 5.3 summarizes the other windows that are available from the Debug menu.

Table 5.3.   Other Windows Available from the Debug Menu

Window	Summary
Running Documents	Displays a list of documents currently loaded into the process you are running.
Me (Visual Basic .NET) / This (Visual C#)	Displays the data members of the object associated with the current method.
Call Stack	Displays the names of functions on the call stack, parameter types, and parameter values.
Threads	Allows for examination and control of threads in the program you are debugging.
Modules	Lists the modules (DLL or EXE files) used by your program.
Memory	Displays the raw values stored in memory. You can use a Memory window to view large buffers, strings, and other data that do not display well in the Locals, Autos, or Watch windows.
Disassembly	Shows assembly code corresponding to the instructions created by the compiler.
Registers	Displays register contents. You can keep the Registers window open as you step through your program to see register values change as code executes.

Lesson Summary

- The three types of errors you might encounter while writing your program are.
  - Syntax errors, which represent syntax the compiler cannot interpret.
  - Run-time errors, which occur when an impossible operation is attempted.
  - Logical errors, which compile and execute correctly, but return unexpected results.
- You can use Break mode to examine your code line-by-line to identify and correct errors. Visual Studio .NET provides several options for stepping through code, including:
  - **Step Into.** To step through each line of code as it executes, including calls to other functions
  - **Step Over.** To step through each line of code as it executes, but step over calls to other functions
  - **Step Out.** To execute the remainder of code in the current function and stop at the next line in the function that called it, if applicable
  - **Run To Cursor.** To designate a line with the cursor and execute all the code leading up to that line
  - **Set Next Statement.** To set the next statement to be executed, skipping and not executing any intermediate lines
- Breakpoints, used for debugging, are designated lines of code where execution halts and the application enters Break mode. Breakpoints can have conditions attached that determine whether the application will break or not. The Breakpoints window is where you manage, create, disable, or clear breakpoints.
- Visual Studio .NET provides several tools for evaluating your program. The Locals, Autos, and Watch windows allow you to observe program variables while the application is running. The Command window allows you to execute code and print variable and property values to the window. Additional windows allow you to observe a variety of data regarding your application.

Lesson 2: Using the Debug and Trace Classes

The *Debug* and *Trace* classes allow you to produce and log informative messages about your application's conditions without having to interrupt application execution. In this lesson, you will learn how to use the *Debug* and *Trace* classes, how to add Trace Listeners and Trace switches, and how to configure Trace switches in a program that is already compiled and released.

After this lesson, you will be able to

- Explain how to display error messages using the *Debug* and *Trace* classes
- Describe how to create Trace Listeners and log Trace output
- Describe how to create and use Trace switches
- Explain how to configure Trace switches in the application's .config file

Estimated lesson time: 45 minutes

When debugging simple applications, debugging tasks more complex than examining your code line-by-line, as described in the previous lesson, are usually unneeded. Complex applications are another matter, however. Large programs can have hundreds of thousands of lines of code. When an error occurs, it might be impossible to uncover logical errors by simply stepping through code and examining application variables. The *Debug* class is a way for you to create and log informative messages about program conditions while your application executes. The *Trace* class allows you to create diagnostic instrumentation that can deliver informative messages about program conditions even after your application is compiled and released.

How Tracing Works

Trace and *Debug* are classes in the *System.Diagnostics* namespace that contain *Shared* (*static*) methods that allow you to test conditions at run time and log the results. Output from these methods is displayed in the Output window and can be viewed while debugging. The output also is sent to the *Listeners* collection. The *Listeners* collection contains a group of classes that can receive output from the *Trace* and *Debug* classes. *Trace* and *Debug* share the same *Listeners* collection, and all the Listeners in the collection receive the input from *Trace* and *Debug*. There are different kinds of Listeners, including some that write to text files and Trace Listeners, which write to event logs. After program execution, you can examine the Listener traces to identify errors in your application. Tracing is also useful in program optimization, which is discussed in Chapter 9.

The *Trace* and *Debug* classes are identical. They expose the same methods and properties and write output to the same set of *Listeners*. The only difference between *Trace* and *Debug* is that *Trace* statements are included by default when the

program is compiled into a release build, whereas *Debug* statements are not. Thus
the *Debug* class is principally used for debugging in the development phase, while
Trace can be used for testing and optimization after an application is compiled and
released.

Writing Trace and Debug Output

You can write output to the *Listeners* collection by using the methods exposed by
the *Trace* and *Debug* classes. These classes expose six methods for writing output
which are:

- **Write.**   Writes text to the *Listeners* collection unconditionally.

- **WriteLine.**   Writes text to the *Listeners* collection and follows the text with a
  carriage return.

- **WriteIf.**   Writes text to the *Listeners* collection if the specified Boolean
  expression is true.

- **WriteLineIf.**   Writes text and a carriage return to the *Listeners* collection if the
  specified Boolean expression is true.

- **Assert.**   Writes an assertion message to the *Listeners* collection if the specified
  Boolean expression is false. It also causes a message box to be displayed with
  the assertion message.

- **Fail.**   Creates an assertion that automatically fails without testing a condition.
  An assertion message is written to the *Listeners* collection, and a message box
  is displayed with the message.

The following code example demonstrates how to invoke these methods:

Visual Basic .NET

```
' Since Trace and Debug expose only static methods and properties, you
' do not need to create an instance of either class.
' Writes text to the Listeners collection.
Trace.Write("Trace Message 1")
' Writes text and a carriage return to the Listeners collection.
Trace.WriteLine("Trace Message 2")
' Writes text if the supplied expression is true
Debug.WriteIf(X=Y, "X equals Y")
' Writes text and a carriage return if the supplied expression is true
Debug.WriteLineIf(X=Y, "X equals Y")
' Writes output and displays a message box if the condition is false
Trace.Assert(X=Y, "X does not equal Y!")
' Writes output and displays a message box unconditionally
Debug.Fail("Drive B is no longer valid.")
```

Visual C#

```
// Since Trace and Debug expose only static methods and properties, you
// do not need to create an instance of either class.
// Writes text to the Listeners collection.
```

```
Trace.Write("Trace Message 1");
// Writes text and a carriage return to the Listeners collection.
Trace.WriteLine("Trace Message 2");
// Writes text if the supplied expression is true
Debug.WriteIf(X==Y, "X equals Y");
// Writes text and a carriage return if the supplied expression is true
Debug.WriteLineIf(X==Y, "X equals Y");
// Writes output and displays a message box if the condition is false
Trace.Assert(X==Y, "X does not equal Y!");
// Writes output and displays a message box unconditionally
Debug.Fail("Drive B is no longer valid.");
```

You can alter the indentation level of *Trace* messages as they are written to the *Listeners* collection by calling the *Indent* and *Unindent* methods, and by setting the *IndentSize* and *IndentLevel* properties. These methods and properties are useful for creating hierarchical displays of error messages. The *IndentSize* property gets or sets the number of spaces in a single indent, and *IndentLevel* gets or sets the number of indents currently being applied. The *Indent* method increases the *IndentLevel* by one, while the *Unindent* method decreases the *IndentLevel* by one.

To write output using Trace or Debug

1. If necessary, set the indent level to the appropriate position by using the *Indent* and *Unindent* methods. For example:

   #### Visual Basic .NET

   ```
   ' Increases the IndentLevel by one
   Trace.Indent()
   ```

   #### Visual C#

   ```
   // Increases the IndentLevel by one
   Trace.Indent();
   ```

2. Call one of the following methods to write output to the *Listeners* collection:

   - Call *Write* or *WriteLine* to write *Trace* output unconditionally.
   - Call *WriteIf* or *WriteLineIf* to test a condition and write output if the condition is true.
   - Call *Fail* to write *Trace* output unconditionally and display a message box.
   - Call *Assert* to test a condition, write output, and display a message box if the condition proves false.

The Listeners Collection

All output from the *Trace* and *Debug* classes is directed to the *Listeners* collection. The *Listeners* collection is a collection that organizes and exposes classes that are capable of receiving *Trace* output. Each member of the *Listeners* collection receives any and all output from the *Trace* and *Debug* classes. How that output is handled is then up to the individual listener.

The *Listeners* collection is initialized with one member, which is an instance of the *DefaultTraceListener* class. As the name implies, the *DefaultTraceListener* is created automatically and will receive *Trace* and *Debug* output even if no other listeners are attached. *Trace* output received by the *DefaultTraceListener* is directed to the debugger. It is through the *DefaultTraceListener* that *Trace* output is displayed in the Visual Studio Output window. If you want to log *Trace* messages to refer to them separate from the debugger, you must add at least one more listener. The .NET Framework base class library provides two classes that can log *Trace* output the *EventLogTraceListener* class and the *TextWriterTraceListener* class. Both classes inherit from the *MustInherit* (*abstract*) class *TraceListener*.

Logging Trace Output to Text

The *TextWriterTraceListener* class writes its output as text, either to a *Stream* object or to a *TextWriter* object. For example, the *Console.Out* property is a *TextWriter*. Thus, you could create a *TextWriterTraceListener* that writes all its output to the Console window. Another use for *Stream* and *TextWriter* objects is writing to text files. To create a *TextWriterTraceListener* that writes *Trace* output to a text file you must first create or open the file that will be used to record the output. Next you need to create an instance of the *TextWriterTraceListener* that specifies that file as its target. In addition, you need to add the *TextWriterTraceListener* to the *Listeners* collection. The following example demonstrates how to create a listener that logs *Trace* output to a text file:

Visual Basic .NET

```
' This line opens the specified file or creates it if it does not exist
Dim myLog As New System.IO.FileStream("C:\myFile.txt", _
    IO.FileMode.OpenOrCreate)
' Creates the new Trace Listener that specifies myLog as the target for
' output.
Dim myListener As New TextWriterTraceListener(myLog)
' Adds myListener to the Listeners collection.
Trace.Listeners.Add(myListener)
```

Visual C#

```
// This line opens the specified file or creates it if it does not
// exist. Note that you must use a double slash in the string instead
// of a single because the slash is an escape character in C#
System.IO.FileStream myLog = new System.IO.FileStream("C:\\myFile.txt",
    System.IO.FileMode.OpenOrCreate);
// Creates the new TraceListener that specifies myLog as the target for
// output
TextWriterTraceListener myListener = new
    TextWriterTraceListener(myLog);
// Adds myListener to the Listeners collection
Trace.Listeners.Add(myListener);
```

Note   If a file by the specified name already exists, opening the file with *IO.FileMode.OpenOrCreate* will overwrite any content present. If you want to add content to an existing file, specify *IO.FileMode.Append* when declaring your *FileStream* object.

Another overload of the *TextWriterTraceListener* constructor allows you to simply name the text file to be written to. Using this constructor, the text file will be created if it does not exist, and appended to if it does. A code example is shown here:

Visual Basic .NET

```
Dim myListener As New TextWriterTraceListener("C:\myFile.txt")
```

Visual C#

```
TextWriterTraceListener myListener = new
    TextWriterTraceListener("C:\\myFile.txt");
```

When the code in either of these two samples executes, all output from the *Trace* and *Debug* classes is written to *myListener*. In order for them to be written to the file, however, you must flush the *Trace* buffer by calling the *Flush* method as follows:

Visual Basic .NET

```
Trace.Flush()
```

Visual C#

```
Trace.Flush();
```

Alternatively, you can set the *Trace.AutoFlush* property to *true*, as shown in the following example. This technique causes the buffer to be flushed after every write:

Visual Basic .NET

```
Trace.AutoFlush = True
```

Visual C#

```
Trace.AutoFlush = true;
```

To log Trace and Debug output to a text file

1. Create an instance of a *FileStream* object that specifies the appropriate text file.
2. Create an instance of a *TextWriterTraceListener* that specifies the new *FileStream* object as its target.
3. Add the new listener to the *Trace.Listeners* collection.
4. Set *Trace.AutoFlush* to *true*, or call *Trace.Flush* after making a write.

Logging Trace Output to an EventLog

You can use the *EventLogTraceListener* to log *Trace* output to an *EventLog* object
The method for doing this is essentially the same as logging to a text file. You cre
ate a new *EventLog* or specify an already existing log, create a new *Event-
LogTraceListener*, and add it to the *Listeners* collection. *Trace* output is then
logged to the specified *EventLog* as *EventLogEntry* objects.

To log Trace and Debug output to an EventLog

1. Declare an instance of an *EventLog* object and assign it to an existing event log
   or to a new event log.

   #### Visual Basic .NET

   ```
   ' Creates a new event log. "Debug Log" is the log's display name.
   Dim myLog As New EventLog("Debug Log")
   ```

   #### Visual C#

   ```
   // Creates a new event log. "Debug Log" is the log's display name.
   EventLog myLog = new EventLog("Debug Log");
   ```

2. Set the *Source* property for the *EventLog*. If the *Source* property is not set, an
   error will result.

   #### Visual Basic .NET

   ```
   myLog.Source = "Trace Output"
   ```

   #### Visual C#

   ```
   myLog.Source = "Trace Output";
   ```

3. Create a new instance of *EventLogTraceWriter* that specifies the new log as the
   target for *Trace* output.

   #### Visual Basic .NET

   ```
   Dim myListener As New EventLogTraceListener(myLog)
   ```

   #### Visual C#

   ```
   EventLogTraceListener myListener = new EventLogTraceListener(myLog);
   ```

4. If necessary, set the *Trace.AutoFlush* property to *true*, or call *Trace.Flush* after
   each write.

Using Trace Switches

When debugging, you usually will want to receive all output from your *Debug* and
Trace statements. After an application is compiled and released, however, it is
more typical to enable tracing only in special cases. Trace switches are configurable switches used to display *Trace* statements. Trace switches can be configured
within the application by altering the application configuration file after it has been
compiled and distributed.

The .NET Framework base class library contains two kinds of Trace switches. Instances of the *BooleanSwitch* class return a Boolean value. Thus, like a toggle switch, they are either on or off. The *TraceSwitch* class allows users to set the level represented by the switch to one of five settings, depending on the kind of output the user wants to receive.

You create an instance of a *BooleanSwitch* or a *TraceSwitch* the same way as any other class. Both switches require two parameters in their constructor: a *DisplayName*, which is the name of the switch in the user interface, and a *Description*, which contains a short description of the switch. For example:

Visual Basic .NET

```
Dim myBooleanSwitch As New BooleanSwitch("Switch1", _
    "Controls Data Tracing")
Dim myTraceSwitch As New TraceSwitch("Switch2", _
    "Controls Form1 Tracing")
```

Visual C#

```
BooleanSwitch myBooleanSwitch = new BooleanSwitch("Switch1",
    "Controls Data Tracing");
TraceSwitch myTraceSwitch = new TraceSwitch("Switch2",
    "Controls Form1 Tracing");
```

The *TraceSwitch* class has five settings that represent different levels of errors. These settings are exposed by the *TraceSwitch.Level* property. This property can be set to any of five values represented by the *TraceLevel* enumerator. The five values are as follows:

- **TraceLevel.Off.** Represents a *TraceSwitch* that is inactive. The integer value is 0.
- **TraceLevel.Error.** Represents brief error messages. The integer value is 1.
- **TraceLevel.Warning.** Represents error messages and warnings. The integer value is 2.
- **TraceLevel.Info.** Represents error messages, warnings, and short informative messages. The integer value is 3.
- **TraceLevel.Verbose.** Represents error messages, warnings, and detailed descriptions of program execution. The integer value is 4.

Additionally, the *TraceSwitch* class exposes four read-only Boolean properties that represent the *Trace* levels. The Boolean properties are:

- *TraceSwitch.TraceError*
- *TraceSwitch.TraceWarning*
- *TraceSwitch.TraceInfo*
- *TraceSwitch.TraceVerbose*

These read-only properties correspond to *Trace* levels of the same names. When the *TraceSwitch.Level* property is set, these four properties are also set to the appropriate level. For example, if the *TraceSwitch.Level* property is set to *TraceLevel.Info*, the *TraceSwitch.TraceInfo* property will return *true*. Additionally *TraceSwitch.TraceError* and *TraceSwitch.TraceWarning* also will return *true*. When a specified level is set, it and all lower levels return *true*.

Trace statements use Trace switches to test whether *Trace* output is needed. The *Trace.WriteIf* and *Trace.WriteLineIf* methods test a Trace switch to learn whether the switch is enabled or set to the appropriate *Trace* level. For example:

Visual Basic .NET

```
' This example assumes the existence of a BooleanSwitch object named
' myBooleanSwitch and a TraceSwitch object named myTraceSwitch
Trace.WriteIf(myBooleanSwitch.Enabled = True, "Error.")
Trace.WriteLineIf(myTraceSwitch.TraceInfo = True, _
    "Type Mismatch Error")
```

Visual C#

```
// This example assumes the existence of a BooleanSwitch object named
// myBooleanSwitch and a TraceSwitch object named myTraceSwitch
Trace.WriteIf(myBooleanSwitch.Enabled == true, "Error");
Trace.WriteLineIf(myTraceSwitch.TraceInfo == true,
    "Type Mismatch Error");
```

Note that there is no automatic "hookup" between Trace switches and *Trace* statements. It is up to you to create the connection by testing the switches in code. If you use the unconditional write methods, such as *Trace.Write* and *Trace.WriteLine* *Trace* output will be written regardless of the status of any switches.

To create and use Trace switches

1. Create an instance of either the *BooleanSwitch* class or the *TraceSwitch* class, as appropriate. You must supply the *DisplayName* parameter and the *Description* parameter.

2. Test the status of the switches in code by using the *Trace.WriteIf* and *Trace.WriteLineIf* methods.

Configuring Trace Switches

Trace switches can be turned on and off after your application has been compiled and distributed. Trace switches are configured by manipulating the application's .config file, which is an XML file that contains information for the application. The .config file must be located in the same folder as the executable and must have the name (application name).exe.config. Not all applications have a .config file, so if you want to use Trace switches, you might need to create a .config file for your program. When your application executes code that creates a Trace switch, it checks the .config file for information about that switch. This file is examined once per switch. If you want to change any settings after a particular Trace switch has been created, you must stop the application, make changes to the .config file, and then restart the application.

When you create an instance of a Trace switch, one of the parameters you must supply is the DisplayName. This is the name used to configure the Trace switch in the .config file. When editing the .config file, you must specify not only the name of the switch, but also the value to which it is to be set. The value must be an integer. For *BooleanSwitch* objects, zero represents off, and any nonzero value represents on. For *TraceSwitch* objects, the values zero, one, two, three, and four correspond to *TraceLevel.Off*, *TraceLevel.Error*, *TraceLevel.Warning*, *TraceLevel.Info*, and *TraceLevel.Verbose*, respectively. Any value greater than 4 is treated as *TraceLevel.Verbose*.

To enable the end user to configure tracing when necessary, you should include extensive inline documentation in the .config file.

To create the .config file and configure Trace switches

1. Create your Trace switches in code and give them appropriate DisplayName values.

2. If your application does not have a .config file, create a new one as follows:

   - In Visual Basic .NET, choose Add New Item from the Project menu. From the Add New Item dialog box, choose Application Configuration File. The .config file opens.

   - In Visual C#, choose Add New Item from the Project menu. From the Add New Item Dialog box, choose Text File. Name the file app.config. The text editor opens. Type the following XML into the text editor:

     ```
     <?xml version="1.0" encoding="utf-8" ?>
     <configuration>
     </configuration>
     ```

3. Between the *<configuration>* and *</configuration>* tags, add the appropriate XML to declare your Trace switches and set the values. The following code demonstrates how to add XML for switches named *myBooleanSwitch* and *myTraceSwitch*:

   ```
   <system.diagnostics>
      <switches>
         <add name="myBooleanSwitch" value="0" />
         <add name="myTraceSwitch" value="3" />
      </switches>
   </system.diagnostics>
   ```

   In this example, *myBooleanSwitch* is set to off, and *myTraceSwitch* is set to *TraceLevel.Info*.

4. If you need to activate or deactivate any of your Trace switches, change the switch value as appropriate. For example, to activate *myBooleanSwitch*, you would change the XML element to read:

```
<add name="myBooleanSwitch" value="1" />
```

The rest of the XML remains unchanged.

5. Add inline comments that document each switch and explain the different levels. Explicit documentation is crucial to helping your users understand how to use your application. The final file might look like this:

```
<system.diagnostics>
    <switches>
        <!-- This switch controls tracing globally. If you want to
             receive Trace messages, set the value to a non-zero
             integer. To disable tracing, set this switch to zero -->
        <add name="myBooleanSwitch" value="0" />
        <!-- This switch controls the level of information from
             Trace. For no information set the value to zero. Set
             the value to 1,2,3, or 4 for minimal, normal, detailed,
             or verbose messages respectively -->
        <add name="myTraceSwitch" value="3" />
    </switches>
</system.diagnostics>
```

Lesson Summary

- The *Debug* and *Trace* classes allow you to display and log messages about application conditions while the program is executing. The *Debug* and *Trace* classes are identical. Both classes expose methods used to create *Trace* output.

- Output from *Trace* and *Debug* statements is received by members of the *Trace.Listeners* collection, a collection of objects that are able to receive *Trace* output and process it. The three kinds of *TraceListeners* are

  - *DefaultTraceListener*
  - *TextWriterTraceListener*
  - *EventLogTraceListener*

- Trace switches are used to configure *Trace* statements. *BooleanSwitch* objects are either on or off. *TraceSwitch* objects expose a *TraceSwitch.Level* property that is used to determine the verbosity of *Trace* statements.

- You can configure Trace switches after the application is compiled by setting appropriate values in the application's .config file.

Lesson 3: Creating a Unit Test Plan

Once you complete the code for your application, you should test it to ensure that it functions according to specification. Although the compiler detects syntax errors, run-time errors and logical errors might not be revealed without thoroughly testing your program. In this lesson, you will learn how to design an efficient test plan for your component or application. Additionally, you will learn how to create a multicultural test environment and how to provide multicultural test data to your application.

After this lesson, you will be able to

- Describe how to create a test plan for your classes
- Explain how to create a multicultural test environment for your application
- Describe how to provide multicultural test data to your application

Estimated lesson time: 30 minutes

The Unit Test Plan

Most code contains errors when first written. Thus, you should expect your code to have bugs when first written. However, a *final* application that is full of bugs or does not function according to specification is useless. You create a final version from a bug-laden first draft through testing.

Testing and debugging are separate but related activities. Debugging refers to the actual finding and correcting of code errors, whereas testing is the process by which errors are found. Testing is usually broken down by method. Individual methods are tested with a variety of inputs and execution parameters. This approach is called unit testing. Most applications are too complex to allow every possible variation of input and run conditions to be tested. Indeed, consider the following method as an example:

Visual Basic .NET

```
Public Sub DisplayName(ByVal Name As String)
   System.Windows.Forms.MessageBox.Show(Name)
End Sub
```

Visual C#

```
public void DisplayName(string Name)
{
   System.Windows.Forms.MessageBox.Show(Name);
}
```

Assume that the method that calls *DisplayName* limits the size of the *Name* parameter to eight characters and allows only the letters of the standard U.S. English alphabet. This means that this method could receive 26^8, or approximately 200 billion possible strings as input. It is easy to see how testing every possible input value for an application is an impossible task.

It is equally obvious that such rigorous testing is unnecessary. In the preceding example, it is unlikely that any one string will produce errors that will not be produced by other strings. Thus, you can logically narrow down your input string to a few representative examples that test the method and provide assurance that the method functions properly. These examples are called *test cases*.

How you design your set of test cases is fundamental to your testing success. Too few test cases can lead to incomplete testing, which will likely allow errors to slip into your final product. On the other hand, too many test cases wastes time and money while yielding redundant results. You must decide on an appropriate test plan for your application with a goal of completeness and coverage of likely scenarios.

Designing Test Cases

As a minimal starting point when designing test cases, every line of code must be tested. Thus, if there are any decision structures in your method, you will need to define test cases that follow all possible branches of the code. Consider the following method:

Visual Basic .NET

```
Public Sub TestMethod(ByVal X As Boolean, ByVal Y As Boolean)
    If X = True Then
        MessageBox.Show("X is True")
    Else
        MessageBox.Show("X is False.")
    End If
    If Y = True Then
        MessageBox.Show("Y is True")
    Else
        MessageBox.Show("Y is False")
    End If
End Sub
```

Visual C#

```
public void TestMethod(bool X, bool Y)
{
    if (X == true)
        MessageBox.Show("X is true");
    else
        MessageBox.Show("X is false");
    if (Y == true)
        MessageBox.Show("Y is true");
    else
        MessageBox.Show("Y is false");
}
```

The number of test cases needed to run every line of code in this method is two: one case where X and Y are *true*, and one case where X and Y are *false*. It soon becomes clear, however, that this approach is an inadequate test. Although every line of code is executed, no provisions are made for the variance of data. Depending on the values of the parameters provided to the method in the previous example, the method execution could take paths not covered by the test case—for example, if X is *true* but Y is *false*, the method execution will follow a path that was not covered in the test plan. To test all possible paths in this method requires two additional test cases: one where X is *true* but Y is *false*, and one where X is *false* but Y is *true*. Therefore, at minimum your design for a unit test should include testing of all possible data paths.

Testing Data

Testing the functionality of all possible data points is a good plan, but to make your application robust, you also should test whether it can handle different kinds of data. You want your application to behave normally and give expected results when data within normal parameters is provided, and it should gracefully and appropriately handle data that is outside of the specified bounds as well. Thus, to be thorough, you must test your application with a variety of data inputs ranging from normal to extraordinary. Specific types of data conditions used to create test cases are described in the following sections.

Normal Data

It is important to test data that is within the normal bounds of program execution. Although it is usually impossible to test the entire range of normal data, your test cases should contain several examples of data that is normal for the program to process. This data should span the normal range of operation and should include the normal minimum and maximum values.

Boundary Conditions

Special consideration should be given to testing data on the boundaries of normal conditions. This includes the normal minimum and maximum values for program data, as well as values that are "off by one." For example, to test the maximum boundary, you would include the maximum value, the maximum value minus one, and the maximum value plus one. This approach allows you to correct simple mistakes, such as using a > operator where a >= is required.

Bad Data

Using a variety of bad data in your test cases evaluates whether your program will crash in response to bad data or, worse, function normally and return inappropriate results. You should test values that are well outside of the normal scope of operation, including zero for non-zero values, negative numbers for positive data, and so on.

Data Combinations

Your test design should include a variety of combinations of the types of data previously mentioned. Errors might not be revealed until the correct data combination is used. For example, you might have a method that functions fine when each of its parameters is at its normal maximum, but fails when *all* of its parameters are at normal maximum. Similarly, combinations of known bad data can yield normal looking results. Consider the following method:

Visual Basic .NET

```
Public Function CalculateMySalary(ByVal Hours As Short, ByVal Weeks _
    As Short) As Integer
    ' This method assumes a WageConstant that provides the hourly rate
    Dim mySalary As Integer
    mySalary = Hours * Weeks * WageConstant
    Return mySalary
End Function
```

Visual C#

```
public int CalculateMySalary(short Hours, short Weeks)
{
    // This method assumes a WageConstant that provides the hourly rate
    int mySalary;
    mySalary = Hours * Weeks * WageConstant;
    return mySalary;
}
```

Given that a normal range for *Hours* might be 0 to 40, and a normal range for weeks might be 0 to 52, this method functions normally with nominal input. However, consider the following method call:

Visual Basic .NET

```
Dim Hooray As Integer
Hooray = CalculateMySalary(-40, -52)
```

Visual C#

```
int Hooray;
Hooray = CalculateMySalary(-40, -52);
```

A combination of bad data returns a seemingly normal result. For this reason, your test cases should test a variety of possible data combinations.

To create a unit test plan

1. Begin by creating test cases that execute every line in the test unit.
2. Add additional test cases until every possible path of data flow through the unit has been tested.

3. Add further cases to test variance in the data the unit will process. In addition to testing nominal data, you should test boundary conditions, bad data, and different combinations of good and bad data.

4. Determine the expected result of each test case in advance of the actual test.

5. Execute the tests and compare observed results with expected results.

Lesson Summary

- Unit testing using test cases is the process by which units of an application are tested to ensure that the units exhibit appropriate behavior during actual use. A test case is a set of run-time conditions that tests a given path and execution parameters.

- Test cases should be designed to test a variety of conditions. At minimum, you should create test cases that test every possible data path through a unit. Your tests should include

    - Normal data

    - Boundary conditions

    - Bad data

    - Combinations of the preceding data conditions

Lesson 4: Handling and Throwing Exceptions

After you have completed testing and debugging your application, run-time errors still might occur. For example, an application that saves data to a floppy disk will encounter an error if it attempts to save to a disk that is not ready. Even though the application code might execute as designed, an error still results. Visual Basic .NET and Visual C# provide structured exception handling as a means of writing code that recovers gracefully from errors and allows program execution to continue. You also can create and throw exceptions that communicate to the main program that an error has occurred.

After this lesson, you will be able to

- Describe how exceptions are handled by the common language runtime
- Create a structured exception handler
- Throw exceptions from your code

Estimated lesson time: 30 minutes

How Exceptions Are Handled

When an application encounters a run-time error, it raises an *exception*. Exceptions are instances of specialized classes that derive from the base class *System.Exception*. Exceptions include features that facilitate diagnosis and management of the error, such as:

- The *Message* property, which can contain a human-readable description of the error, as well as any other relevant information about the error.
- The *StackTrace* property, which contains a stack *Trace* to allow tracing and pinpointing of where the error occurred in the code.

In addition to system-defined exceptions, you can create custom exceptions by extending *System.ApplicationException*. This is discussed in detail later in this lesson.

When a run-time error is encountered, an instance of the exception corresponding to the error is created and passed from the method that generated the error up the call stack to the method that called it. If an exception-handling structure is encountered in that method, it is handled there. If no exception-handling structure is found, the exception is passed up the call stack to the next method, and so on. If no exception-handling structure is found anywhere in the call stack, the default exception handler is engaged. The default handler causes a message box to display the type of exception and any additional information the exception provides, and then the application terminates, with no opportunity to save work or attempt to recover from the error.

With structured exception handling, you can provide a means for your application to recover from unexpected errors or at least to have the chance to save data before closing.

Creating an Exception Handler

Exception handlers are implemented for specific methods. Thus, each method you create can have its own exception handler, specifically tailored to the method and exceptions it is likely to throw. Methods that are likely to throw exceptions, such as methods that involve file access, should implement exception handling. Exception handlers use a *Try...Catch...Finally* syntax. The following three general steps are involved in creating an exception handler:

1. Wrap the code with which the handler will be associated in a *Try* (*try*) block.
2. Add one or more *Catch* (*catch*) blocks to handle the possible exceptions.
3. Add any code that always must be executed to a *Finally* (*finally*) block. Such code will execute regardless of whether or not an exception is thrown.

The first step in creating an exception handler is to wrap the code in a *Try* (*try*) block. The *Try* (*try*) block forms the exception handler—if any statement in the code throws an exception or if any unhandled exception is received through call stack "bubbling," the method will attempt to handle it within this exception handler. If the exception cannot be handled, it will bubble farther up the call stack. The following example demonstrates the *Try* (*try*) block:

Visual Basic .NET

```
Try
    ' Normal program code goes here
    ' Error handling code, such as Catch and Finally blocks, goes here.
    ' The End Try statement encloses all error-handling code
End Try
```

Visual C#

```
try
{
    // Normal program code goes here
}
    // Error handling code, such as catch and finally blocks, goes
    // here, outside of the curly braces that delimit the try block.
```

In Visual Basic .NET, you can exit a *Try* block by using the *Exit Try* statement.

A *Try* (*try*) block can be followed by one or more *Catch* (*catch*) blocks. A *Catch* (*catch*) block contains code to be executed when an exception is handled. *Catch* (*catch*) blocks can be generic, catching all possible exceptions, or specific, catching exceptions of a given class. The following example demonstrates a generic

Catch (*catch*) block that will catch all exceptions thrown within a given *Try* (*try*) block:

Visual Basic .NET

```
' A Try block goes here
Catch
' The Catch block is terminated by the End Try statement,
' another Catch block, or the Finally block. This code will execute
' if any run-time error is encountered during execution.
```

Visual C#

```
// A try block goes here
catch
{
    // The catch block is bounded by the curly braces. This code will
    // execute if any run-time error is encountered during execution.
}
```

You also can obtain a reference to the exception that was thrown in the *Catch* (*catch*) statement. This can be useful because it allows you to access information contained within the exception in your error-handling routine. It also allows you to screen errors by type and create multiple *Catch* (*catch*) blocks to handle specific errors. The following example demonstrates how to catch a specific exception:

Visual Basic .NET

```
' A Try block goes here
Catch e As System.NullReferenceException
    ' If a NullReferenceException is thrown, it will be caught in this
    ' block. The variable e contains a reference to the exception that
    ' you can use to examine the information contained therein.
Catch e As System.Exception
    ' Since all exceptions derive from System.Exception, this block
    ' will catch any other exceptions that are thrown.
```

Visual C#

```
// A try block goes here
catch (System.NullReferenceException e)
{
    // If a NullReferenceException is thrown, it will be caught in
    // this block. The variable e contains a reference to the
    // exception that you can use to examine the information contained
    // therein.
}
catch (System.Exception e)
{
    // Since all exceptions derive from System.Exception, this block
    // will catch any other exceptions that are thrown.
}
```

Finally (*finally*) blocks contain code that must be executed regardless of whether an exception is thrown. This could be code to save data or release resources, or other code that is crucial to the application. The following code example demonstrates a *Try…Catch…Finally* (*try…catch…finally*) block:

Visual Basic .NET

```vbnet
Public Sub Parse(ByVal aString As String)
   Try
      Dim aDouble As Double
      ' If aString = Nothing, an ArgumentNullException will be thrown
      aDouble = Double.Parse(aString)
   Catch e As System.ArgumentNullException
      ' In this block, you would place any code that should be
      ' executed if a System.ArgumentNullException is thrown.
   Catch e As System.Exception
      ' This block will catch any other exceptions that might be
      ' thrown.
   Finally
      ' Any code that must be executed goes here. This code will be
      ' executed whether an exception is thrown or not.
   End Try
End Sub
```

Visual C#

```csharp
public void Parse(string aString)
{
   try
   {
      double aDouble;
      aDouble = Double.Parse(aString);
   }
   catch (System.ArgumentNullException e)
   {
      // In this block, you would place any code that should be
      // executed if a System.ArgumentNullException is thrown.
   }
   catch (System.Exception e)
   {
      // This block will catch any other exceptions that might be
      // thrown.
   }
   finally
   {
      // Any code that must be executed goes here. This code will be
      // executed whether an exception is thrown or not.
   }
}
```

If an error is encountered within a *Try* (*try*) block, execution is immediately transferred to the *Catch* (*catch*) blocks. The *Catch* (*catch*) blocks are then examined for one that can catch the exception. In the preceding example, there are two *Catch* (*catch*) blocks—one that specifically catches an *ArgumentNullException* and one that catches any other exceptions. Only one *Catch* (*catch*) block will be executed per error. After the code in the *Catch* (*catch*) block has executed, the code in the *Finally* (*finally*) block is executed. Normal application execution then resumes at the next line after the line that called the error-containing routine.

Note   Because only one *Catch* (*catch*) block is executed per exception, you must write *Catch* (*catch*) blocks from the most specific to the least specific. Thus, place any *Catch* (*catch*) blocks for specific exceptions first in your code, and follow them with a generalized error-handling routine.

At times, you might not want to handle exceptions in the local routine but instead will bubble them up to the method that called your routine. Even so, you might have code that needs to run even in the event of an exception. In this case, you can omit the *Catch* (*catch*) block and use a *Try...Finally* (*try...finally*) structure as follows:

Visual Basic .NET

```
Try
    ' Method code goes here
Finally
    ' Cleanup code goes here
End Try
```

Visual C#

```
try
{
    // Method code goes here
}
finally
{
    // Cleanup code goes here
}
```

To create an exception handler

1. Wrap the code for which you want errors to be handled within a *Try* (*try*) block.

2. If you want to handle exceptions locally, create one or more *Catch* (*catch*) blocks with the appropriate code to handle the exception.

3. If you have code that must be executed even in the event of an exception, enclose it within the *Finally* (*finally*) block.

Throwing Exceptions

There might be times when you want to throw exceptions. Generally speaking, these occasions are divided into the following two situations:

- You cannot completely handle a run-time error, but you want to partially handle it, and then bubble the exception up the call stack.

- An unacceptable condition occurs in a component that cannot be handled locally and needs to be communicated to its parent. This might involve throwing either a standard .NET exception or a custom exception specific to your component.

In this section, we will examine these two situations in more detail.

Rethrowing Exceptions

At times, your exception-handling structure might be unable to fully handle an exception. For example, you might have a method that is performing an extensive series of complex calculations when suddenly a *NullReferenceException* is thrown. The method might or might not be able to handle the exception. Your code should test conditions and determine whether or not it can handle the exception. If the exception cannot be handled in the context of the *Catch* (*catch*) block, your code should *rethrow* the exception by using the *Throw* (*throw*) keyword. For example:

Visual Basic .NET

```
Try
    ' Insert code to be executed
Catch e As System.NullReferenceException
    ' Code here should test the exceptions and current conditions to
    ' determine if the exception can be handled by the structure or if it
    ' bubbled up the stack. If it cannot be handled locally, the next line
    ' throws the exception further up the stack.
    Throw e
End Try
```

Visual C#

```
try
{
    // Insert code to be executed
}
catch (System.NullReferenceException e)
{
    // Code here should test the exceptions and current conditions to
    // determine if the exception can be handled by the structure or if it
    // bubbled up the stack. If it cannot be handled locally, the next
    // line throws the exception further up the stack.
    throw e;
}
```

If you have a generic *Catch* (*catch*) block that doesn't provide a reference to the exception, you can still rethrow the exception it receives by using the *Throw* (*throw*) keyword without any arguments. For example:

Visual Basic .NET

```
' This line is the beginning of a Catch block
Catch
    Throw
```

Visual C#

```
// This line is the beginning of a catch block
catch
{
    throw;
}
```

Alternatively, you might want to provide additional information to the next application level. Instead of rethrowing the same exception, you can wrap it in a new exception. The *InnerException* property is set in the constructor of a new exceptio and can hold a reference to an existing exception. Thus, you can supplement the information contained within the system exception by setting the relevant properties of a new exception and wrapping the original exception in the *InnerException* property. The following example demonstrates how to create and throw a new exception that provides an informative string message and wraps the original exception:

Visual Basic .NET

```
' This is the first line of a Catch block
Catch e as NullReferenceException
    Throw New NullReferenceException("Widget A is not set", e)
```

Visual C#

```
// This is the first line of a catch block
catch (NullReferenceException e)
{
    throw new NullReferenceException("Widget A is not set", e);
}
```

To rethrow an exception

Choose the appropriate option from the following:

- Use the *Throw* (*throw*) keyword to throw the exception that was received by the *Catch* (*catch*) block.
- Wrap the exception in a new exception that provides additional information and use the *Throw* (*throw*) keyword to throw it.

Custom Exceptions

A second scenario in which you might throw a new exception is in component development. If a condition occurs in your component that cannot be resolved, it is proper to throw an exception to the client application. Exceptions of this type are usually custom exceptions, because the common language runtime throws an exception if any of the standard exception conditions occur.

Note   Exceptions are for exceptional circumstances. They should not be used for client–component communication—you should use events for that. Exceptions should only be thrown when conditions make it impossible for program execution to proceed without intervention.

You can create custom exceptions by inheriting from the *System.ApplicationException* class. The *ApplicationException* class encapsulates all the functionality that an exception requires, including the *Message*, *StackTrace*, and *InnerException* properties, and can serve as a base for custom functionality tailored to your component. The following example demonstrates how to create a custom exception by inheriting from *ApplicationException*. This new exception requires a fictitious object named *Widget* in the constructor and exposes that object through a read-only property.

Visual Basic .NET

```
Public Class WidgetException
    Inherits System.ApplicationException
    ' This variable holds the Widget
    Private mWidget As Widget
    ' This property exposes the Widget
    Public ReadOnly Property ErrorWidget() As Widget
        Get
            Return mWidget
        End Get
    End Property
    ' The constructor takes a Widget, and a String that can be used
    ' to describe program conditions at the time of the error. You can
    ' provide different overloads of the constructor to take different
    ' sets of parameters
    Public Sub New(ByVal W As Widget, ByVal Message As String)
        ' Calls the constructor of the base class, and sets the Message
        ' property inherited from ApplicationException
        MyBase.New(Message)
        ' sets the Widget property
        mWidget = W
    End Sub
End Class
```

Visual C#

```
public class WidgetException:System.ApplicationException
{
    // This variable holds the Widget
```

```
Widget mWidget;
public Widget ErrorWidget
{
   get
   {
      return mWidget;
   }
}
// The constructor takes a Widget, and a string that can be used
// to describe program conditions at the time of the error. You can
// provide different overloads of the constructor to take different
// sets of parameters
//
// Declares the constructor for the class and calls the base class
// constructor that sets the Message property inherited from
// ApplicationException
public WidgetException(Widget W, string S) : base(S)
{
   // Sets the Widget property
   mWidget = W;
}
}
```

After you create your exception class, you can throw a new instance of it when conditions become unacceptable. For example:

Visual Basic .NET

```
Dim Alpha As New Widget()
' Code that corrupts Widget Alpha omitted
Throw New WidgetException(Alpha, "Widget Alpha is corrupt!")
```

Visual C#

```
Widget Alpha = new Widget();
// Code that corrupts Widget Alpha omitted
throw new WidgetException(Alpha, "Widget Alpha is corrupt!");
```

To throw a custom exception

1. Define the custom exception class. It should inherit *System.ApplicationException* and expose any properties containing additional information for the clients that will handle the exception. The values of these properties should be assignable through the class's constructor.

2. When appropriate, use the *Throw* (*throw*) keyword to throw a new instance of the exception, setting any appropriate parameters in the constructor.

Lesson Summary

- Exceptions are how the common language run-time reports run-time errors. When an exception is thrown, it is passed up the call stack until it finds an exception-handling structure. If no such structure is found, an unhandled exception is handled by the runtime's default exception handler, which leads to program termination.

- You can design routines to handle exceptions. These routines allow an application to recover from an unexpected error, or at least terminate gracefully. An exception-handling structure can consist of up to three parts:

  - *Try* (*try*) block
  - *Catch* (*catch*) block
  - *Finally* (*finally*) block

- After an exception is handled, control returns to the method in which the exception-handling routine resides.

- You can use the *Throw* (*throw*) keyword inside a *Catch* (*catch*) block to rethrow the exception currently being handled. This passes the exception up the call stack. You also can wrap the current exception in a new exception by setting the new exception's *InnerException* property.

- You can create and throw custom exceptions by inheriting from the *System.ApplicationException* class. Exceptions should not be used for communication between components and clients; rather, they should be reserved for exceptional circumstances.

Lab 5-1: Debugging an Application

In this lab, you will open a small application that contains syntax, run-time, and logical errors. You will correct syntax errors, design a test plan to identify and correct run-time and logical errors in two methods, and use the Visual Studio debugging tools to monitor program execution. The solution to this lab is available on the Supplemental Course Materials CD-ROM in the \Labs\Ch05\Lab 5-1\Solution folder.

Before You Begin

There are no prerequisites to starting this lab.

Estimated lesson time: 30 minutes

Exercise 5-1.1: Identifying Syntax Errors

In this exercise, you will use Visual Studio .NET to identify and correct syntax errors in the sample project. To open the Lab 5-1 project:

1. Start Visual Studio.
2. From the File menu, choose Open, and then Project. The Open Project dialog box appears.
3. Browse to the \Labs\Ch05\Lab 5-1\Partial folder and choose either VB or C Sharp, as appropriate. Click Open to open the solution.

▶   **To identify and correct syntax errors**

1. From the Build menu, click Build Solution. Syntax errors appear in the Task List window, as shown in Figures 5.3 and 5.4.

Figure 5.3. The Task List window in Visual Basic .NET

Figure 5.4. The Task List window in Visual C#

2. For Visual Basic .NET, double-click the error that reads "Select Case must end with a matching End Select". You are taken to the end of the Select Case block. Examine the code and correct the error by correcting the syntax in the End Select line. Note that only two errors are displayed in the Task List window.

   For Visual C#, double-click the first error that reads "} expected". You are taken to the end of the operation handler. Carefully examine each pair of curly braces to determine which one is missing its partner. Correct the error by adding the appropriate brace to the end of the first *switch* statement.

3. For Visual C# only, from the Build menu, choose Build Solution to reassess your code for errors. Note that two additional errors are found.

4. Double-click the first error in the Task List. You are taken to an error that cannot find a member named CurretOperation. Change this statement to read CurrentOperation to correct the error.

5. Double-click the final error in the Task List. Correct the spelling of Regiter2 to correct the error.

6. From the Build menu, choose Build Solution. Note that no further errors are discovered.

Exercise 5-1.2: Identifying Run-Time Errors

Now that you have rid your code of syntax errors, you can tackle the run-time errors and logical errors. In the next two sections, you will test two methods, each of which contains one or more errors. You should examine each method to develop a test plan for that method. Every possible data path should be tested with a variety of normal and abnormal input. Continue your test plan until you feel confident that all errors have been found. Then, check your work against the solution in \Labs\Ch05\Lab 5-1\Solution.

▶ **To identify and correct a run-time error**

1. Locate the *NumberHandler* method. This is a fairly simple method with minimal data path branching. This method builds a string of numbers as buttons 1 through 9 are pressed on the calculator face.

2. Develop a test plan for this method. Your test plan should explore all possible data branches and test the method with a variety of input and application variable values. Determine the expected results of each test case in advance. Table 5.4 demonstrates some of the test cases you might use.

Table 5.4. Test Cases for the NumberHandler Method

Button Pressed	Value of *LabelDisplay.Text*	Value of *CurrentNumberString*	Value of *CurrentNumberString* expected
1	"0"	""	"1"
4	"44"	"44"	"444"
9	"1266345578456"	"1266345578456"	"12663455784569"
9	"-3446.222231"	"-3446.222231"	"-3446.2222319"
3	"6"	"6"	"63"

3. Execute your tests. Use the Locals, Autos, and Watch windows to observe the values of variables as the program executes. Use the Immediate window to assign values to variables. You can use Set Next Statement to rerun code multiple times.

4. Log your results and correct any run-time errors you find.

Exercise 5-1.3: Identifying Logical Errors

Logical errors are the most difficult types of errors to identify. It frequently takes repeated testing to observe a problem and additional testing to identify the source of the error. In the next section, you will identify a logical error in another method of this application.

▶ **To identify and correct a logical error**

1. Locate the method named *EqualsHandler*. This method handles operations for the calculator when the equals (=) button is pressed. The number contained by the variable *Register1* is added to, subtracted from, multiplied by, or divided into the number contained by *Register2*, and the value of that operation is assigned to Result. The user interface is then updated.

2. Execute the test plan shown in Table 5.5. Although incomplete, the plan does test every logical path through the method and should be sufficient to find a logical error. Note that boundary analysis and in-depth testing has been omitted for the purpose of brevity.

Table 5.5. **Test Cases for the EqualsHandler Method**

Current Operation	Register1	Register2	Expected Value of Result
Operation.Plus	442	5789	6231
Operation.Minus	400000	222222	177778
Operation.Multiply	23	12	276
Operation.Divide	3345	34	98.3823529411765

3. Diagnose and resolve any logical errors you encounter.

Lab 5-2: Creating, Throwing, and Handling Exceptions

In this lab, you will create a custom exception that represents an attempt to divide by zero. Since you will raise this exception from the application, you will use a custom exception rather than the built-in *DivideByZeroException*. You will create code to test whether division by zero is taking place, and throw the exception when division by zero takes place. Finally, you will add code to handle the exception and allow the application to continue gracefully. The solution to this lab is available on the Supplemental Course Materials CD-ROM in the \Labs\Ch05\Lab 5-2\Solution folder.

Before You Begin

You should have completed Lab 5-1 or loaded the Lab 5-1 solution from the Supplemental Course Materials CD-ROM.

Estimated lesson time: 30 minutes

Exercise 5-2.1: Creating the MyDivideByZeroException class

In this exercise, you will create a custom exception that represents an illegal attempt to divide by zero.

▶   **To create the MyDivideByZeroException class**

1. In Solution Explorer, right-click Form1 to open the code editor.
2. In the code editor locate the end of the *Form1* class definition. Add the following code after the *Form1* class definition to define a new exception class:

    Visual Basic .NET

    ```
    Public Class MyDivideByZeroException
         Inherits ApplicationException
    End Class
    ```

    Visual C#

    ```
    public class MyDivideByZeroException : ApplicationException
    {
    }
    ```

3. Create a constructor for your new class that calls the base class constructor and sets the message property to an informative string, as shown in the following example:

Visual Basic .NET

```
Public Sub New()
   MyBase.New("You have attempted to divide by zero!")
End Sub
```

Visual C#

```
public MyDivideByZeroException()
   : base("You have attempted to divide by zero!")
{

}
```

4. From the Build menu, choose Build Solution to build, and save your work.

Exercise 5-2.2: Raising Exceptions

In this exercise, you will create a method that tests if the value passed to it is zero, and raises an exception if it is. You will then add code to call this method to test the divisor of each division operation.

▶   **To add code to raise exceptions**

1. In the code editor, locate the *Form1 End Class* statement (Visual Basic .NET) or the *Form1* closing *}* statement (Visual C#). Immediately before the end of the class, add the following method:

Visual Basic .NET

```
Private Sub ValidateDivisor(ByVal Divisor As Double)
   If Divisor = 0 Then
      Dim anException As New MyDivideByZeroException()
      Throw anException
   End If
End Sub
```

Visual C#

```
private void ValidateDivisor(double Divisor)
{
   if(Divisor == 0)
   {
      MyDivideByZeroException anException = new MyDivideByZeroException();
      throw anException;
   }
}
```

2. Locate the *EqualsHandler* method. Locate the line that reads *Case Operation.Divide* (Visual Basic .NET) or *case Operation.Divide* (Visual C#). Beneath this line, add a call to *ValidateDivisor* as shown below. Make a similar modification to the *OperationHandler* method.

Visual Basic .NET

```
ValidateDivisor(Double.Parse(Register1))
```

Visual C#

```
ValidateDivisor(Double.Parse(Register1));
```

3. Press Ctrl+F5 to build your application and run without debugging. Attempt to divide a number by zero. Note that application execution halts while an exception-handling box is displayed. You have the option of attempting to proceed or quitting the application immediately.

Exercise 5-2.3: Handling Exceptions

In this exercise you will add *Try...Catch...Finally* blocks to your application to handle the new exceptions. In the *Catch* block you will catch any *MyDivideByZero* exceptions and display a message that admonishes the user not to divide by zero but does not crash the program. You will leave the *Finally* block blank—it will be used in the next lab.

▶   **To add Try...Catch...Finally blocks to your application**

1. Locate the *Case Operation.Divide* (Visual Basic .NET) and *case Operation.Divide:* (Visual C#) clauses of the *EqualsHandler* and *OperationHandler* methods and modify them to resemble the following:

Visual Basic .NET

```
Case Operation.Divide
   Try
      ValidateDivisor(Double.Parse(Register1))
      Result = Double.Parse(Register2) / Double.Parse(Register1)
      ' In the EqualsHandler method, this block should also contain
      ' the line CurrentOperation = Operation.Divide
   Catch ex As MyDivideByZeroException
   Finally
   End Try
```

Visual C#

```
case Operation.Divide:
   try
   {
      ValidateDivisor(Double.Parse(Register1));
      Result = Double.Parse(Register2) / Double.Parse(Register1);
      // In the EqualsHandler method, this block should also contain
      // the line CurrentOperation = Operation.Divide;
   }
   catch (MyDivideByZeroException ex)
   {
   }
```

```
finally
{

}
```

2. In the *Catch* block, add code to inform the user that an attempt was made to divide by zero and then continue with the program, as shown below:

Visual Basic .NET

```
MessageBox.Show("An Exception was thrown. The message was: " & _
    ex.Message & "Please check your figures.")
```

Visual C#

```
MessageBox.Show("An Exception was thrown. The message was: " +
    ex.Message + "Please check your figures.");
```

3. Press Ctrl+F5 to build and run your application. Notice that now when you attempt to divide by zero your code in the catch block runs instead of the default exception handler.

Lab 5-3: Implementing Tracing

In this lab, you will add tracing functionality to your application. You will add a Trace switch and *Trace* statements to your application that log usage of division and the number of times the user attempts to divide by zero. You will log *Trace* out put to a text file, and enable and disable tracing from the application's configuration file. The solution to this lab is available on the Supplemental Course Materials CD-ROM in the \Labs\Ch05\Lab 5-3\Solution folder.

Before You Begin

You should have completed Lab 5-2 or loaded the Lab 5-2 solution from the Supplemental Course Materials CD-ROM.

Estimated lesson time: 20 minutes

Exercise 5-3.1: Adding Trace Functionality

In this exercise, you will add code statements to implement *Trace* functionality in your application. You will create a new Trace Listener that records *Trace* output to a text file. You will add a *BooleanSwitch* to your application that determines whether *Trace* output is produced, and you will add *Trace* statements to write output to the *Listeners* collection.

▶ **To add Trace functionality**

1. In the designer, double-click Form1 to open the code editor to the *Form.Load* event handler.

2. For Visual C# only, add the following line at the top of the code editor with the other *using* statements:

Visual C#

```
using System.Diagnostics;
```

3. In the *Form.Load* event handler, add code to declare a new *TextWriterTraceListener* and add it to the *Listeners* collection. An example is shown below:

Visual Basic .NET

```
Dim myListener As New TextWriterTraceListener("C:\myTraceLog.txt")
Trace.Listeners.Add(myListener)
```

Visual C#

```
TextWriterTraceListener myListener = new
    TextWriterTraceListener("C:\\myTraceLog.txt");
Trace.Listeners.Add(myListener);
```

4. Outside of any method and near the top of your class definition, declare a global *BooleanSwitch* as shown below:

Visual Basic .NET

```
Public myBooleanSwitch As New BooleanSwitch("myBooleanSwitch", _
    "This switch controls tracing in this application")
```

Visual C#

```
public BooleanSwitch myBooleanSwitch =
    new BooleanSwitch("myBooleanSwitch",
    "This switch controls tracing in this application");
```

5. In the *OperationHandler* and *EqualsHandler* methods, locate the *Catch* block that you added in the previous lab. Add the following lines to these *Catch* blocks beneath the *MessageBox.Show* statement:

Visual Basic .NET

```
Trace.WriteLineIf(myBooleanSwitch.Enabled, _
    "User attempted to Divide by Zero")
Trace.Flush()
```

Visual C#

```
Trace.WriteLineIf(myBooleanSwitch.Enabled,
    "User attempted to Divide by Zero");
Trace.Flush();
```

6. In the *Finally* blocks that you created in the previous lab, add the following lines:

Visual Basic .NET

```
Trace.WriteLineIf(myBooleanSwitch.Enabled, _
    "Division operation attempted")
Trace.Flush()
```

Visual C#

```
Trace.WriteLineIf(myBooleanSwitch.Enabled,
    "Division operation attempted");
Trace.Flush();
```

7. From the Build menu, choose Build All to save your work.

Exercise 5-3.2: Creating a .config file and testing tracing

In this exercise you will create a .config file for your application and add XML code to enable *myBooleanSwitch* in your application. You will then test the race functionality in your application.

1. Create a configuration file for your application by the method appropriate to the language you are using.

- For Visual Basic .NET and Visual C# 2003: From the Project menu, choose Add New Item. In the Add New Item Dialog Box, choose Application Con figuration File.

- For Visual C# 2002: From the Project menu, choose Add New Item. In the Add New Item Dialog Box, choose Text File. Rename the new text file App.config and add the following XML code:

```xml
<?xml version="1.0" encoding="utf-8" ?>
<configuration>
```

2. In between the *<configuration>* and *<\configuration>* tags, add the following XML code to activate *myBooleanSwitch*:

```xml
<system.diagnostics>
  <switches>
    <add name="myBooleanSwitch" value="1" />
  </switches>
</system.diagnostics>
```

3. Press F5 to run your application. Try a few division operations with the calcula tor application, including a few attempts to divide by zero.

4. From the Debug menu, choose Stop Debugging to stop the application. Examine the Output window. Note that *Trace* output has been directed to the Output window, which is the default Trace listener.

5. Open C:\myTraceLog.txt with Notepad. Note that *Trace* output has been logged to this file also.

Review

The following review questions are intended to reinforce key concepts and information presented in this chapter. If you are unable to answer a question, return to the appropriate lesson and review, then try the lesson again. Answers to the questions can be found in Appendix A.

1. Describe Break mode and some of the available methods for navigating in Break mode.

2. When would you use the Watch window?

3. You are deploying a beta version of a large application and want to collect performance data in text files while the application is in use. Briefly describe a strategy for enabling this scenario.

4. When testing a method, should you test data that is known to be outside the bounds of normal operation? Why or why not?

5. Briefly explain what each segment of a *Try…Catch…Finally* (*try…catch…finally*) block does.

C H A P T E R   6

Data Access Using ADO.NET

About This Chapter

This chapter describes how to access data with Microsoft ADO.NET. You will learn how to create a data-access architecture for your application, connect to Microsoft SQL Server and other databases, bind data to the user interface, and handle data errors.

Before You Begin

To complete the lessons in this chapter, you must first complete Chapters 1 through 5.

Lesson 1: Overview of ADO.NET

Most applications require some kind of data access. Desktop applications need to integrate with central databases, Extensible Markup Language (XML) data stores, or local desktop databases. ADO.NET data-access technology allows simple, powerful data access while maximizing system resource usage.

After this lesson, you will be able to

- Describe the major components of ADO.NET data access
- Explain the role of each data-access component
- Describe in general terms how ADO.NET data access is facilitated

Estimated lesson time: 30 minutes

Different applications have different requirements for data access. Whether your application simply displays the contents of a table, or processes and updates data to a central SQL server, ADO.NET provides the tools to implement data access easily and efficiently.

Disconnected Database Access

Previous data-access technologies provided continuously connected data access by default. In such a model, an application creates a connection to a database and keeps the connection open for the life of the application, or at least for the amount of time that data is required. However, as applications become more complex and databases serve more and more clients, connected data access is impractical for a variety of reasons, including the following:

- Open database connections are expensive in terms of system resources. The more open connections there are, the less efficient system performance becomes.
- Applications with connected data access are difficult to scale. An application that can comfortably maintain connections with two clients might do poorly with 10 and be completely unusable with 100.
- Open database connections can quickly consume all available database licenses, which can be a significant expense. In order to work within a limited set of client licenses, connections must be reused whenever possible.

ADO.NET addresses these issues by implementing a *disconnected* data access model by default. In this model, data connections are established and left open only long enough to perform the requisite action. For example, if an application requests data from a database, the connection opens just long enough to load the data into the application, and then it closes. Likewise, if a database is updated, the connection opens to execute the UPDATE command, and then closes again. By keeping connections open only for the minimum required time, ADO.NET conserves system resources and allows data access to scale up with a minimal impact on performance.

ADO.NET Data Architecture

Data access in ADO.NET relies on two entities: the *DataSet*, which stores data on the local machine, and the *Data Provider*, a set of components that mediates interaction between the program and the database.

The DataSet

The *DataSet* is a disconnected, in-memory representation of data. It can be thought of as a local copy of the relevant portions of a database. Data can be loaded into a *DataSet* from any valid data source, such as a SQL Server database, a Microsoft Access database, or an XML file. The *DataSet* persists in memory, and the data therein can be manipulated and updated independent of the database. When appropriate, the *DataSet* can then act as a template for updating the central database.

The *DataSet* object contains a collection of zero or more *DataTable* objects, each of which is an in-memory representation of a single table. The structure of a particular *DataTable* is defined by the *DataColumns* collection, which enumerates the columns in a particular table, and the *Constraint* collection, which enumerates any constraints on the table. Together, these two collections make up the table *schema*. A *DataTable* also contains a *DataRows* collection, which contains the actual data in the *DataSet*.

The *DataSet* contains a *DataRelations* collection. A *DataRelation* object allows you to create associations between rows in one table and rows in another table. The *DataRelations* collection enumerates a set of *DataRelation* objects that define the relationships between tables in the *DataSet*. For example, consider a *DataSet* that contains two related tables: an Employees table and a Projects table. In the Employees table, each employee is represented only once and is identified by a unique EmployeeID field. In the Projects table, an employee in charge of a project is identified by the EmployeeID field, but can appear more than once if that employee is in charge of multiple projects. This is an example of a *one-to-many* relationship; you would use a *DataRelation* object to define this relationship.

Additionally, a *DataSet* contains an *ExtendedProperties* collection, which is used to store custom information about the *DataSet*.

The Data Provider

The link to the database is created and maintained by a data provider. A data provider is not a single component, rather it is a set of related components that work together to provide data in an efficient, performance-driven manner. The first version of the Microsoft .NET Framework shipped with two data providers: the SQL

Server .NET Data Provider, designed specifically to work with SQL Server 7 or later, and the OleDb .NET Data Provider, which connects with other types of data bases. Microsoft Visual Studio .NET 2003 added two more data providers: the ODBC Data Provider and the Oracle Data Provider. Each data provider consists o versions of the following generic component classes:

- The *Connection* object provides the connection to the database.

- The *Command* object executes a command against a data source. It can execut non-query commands, such as INSERT, UPDATE, or DELETE, or return a *DataReader* with the results of a SELECT command.

- The *DataReader* object provides a forward-only, read-only, connected recordse

- The *DataAdapter* object populates a disconnected *DataSet* or *DataTable* with data and performs updates.

Note   Throughout this chapter, whenever information is applicable to member classes of any data provider, the classes are referred to by the generic name. For example, *Command* can mean *OleDbCommand* or *SqlCommand*.

Data access in ADO.NET is facilitated as follows: a *Connection* object establishes a connection between the application and the database. This connection can be accessed directly by a *Command* object or by a *DataAdapter* object. The *Command* object provides direct execution of a command to the database. If the command returns more than a single value, the *Command* object returns a *DataReader* to pro vide the data. This data can be directly processed by application logic. Alternatively, you can use the *DataAdapter* to fill a *DataSet* object. Updates to the database can be achieved through the *Command* object or through the *DataAdapter*.

The generic classes that make up the data providers are summarized in the following sections.

The Connection Object

The *Connection* object represents the actual connection to the database. Visual Studio .NET 2003 supplies two types of *Connection* classes: the *SqlConnection* object, which is designed specifically to connect to SQL Server 7 or later, and the *OleDb-Connection* object, which can provide connections to a wide range of database types. Visual Studio .NET 2003 further provides a multipurpose *ODBCConnection* class, as well as an *OracleConnection* class optimized for connecting to Oracle databases. The *Connection* object contains all of the information required to open a channel to the database in the *ConnectionString* property. The *Connection* object also incorporates methods that facilitate data transactions.

The Command Object

The *Command* object is represented by two corresponding classes, *SqlCommand* and *OleDbCommand*. You can use *Command* objects to execute commands to a database across a data connection. *Command* objects can be used to execute stored procedures on the database and SQL commands, or return complete tables. *Command* objects provide three methods that are used to execute commands on the database:

- **ExecuteNonQuery.**   Executes commands that return no records, such as INSERT, UPDATE, or DELETE
- **ExecuteScalar.**   Returns a single value from a database query
- **ExecuteReader.**   Returns a result set by way of a *DataReader* object

The DataReader Object

The *DataReader* object provides a forward-only, read-only, connected stream recordset from a database. Unlike other components of a data provider, *DataReader* objects cannot be directly instantiated. Rather, the *DataReader* is returned as the result of a *Command* object's *ExecuteReader* method. The *SqlCommand.ExecuteReader* method returns a *SqlDataReader* object, and the *OleDbCommand.ExecuteReader* method returns an *OleDbDataReader* object. Likewise, the ODBC and Oracle *Command.ExecuteReader* methods return a *DataReader* specific to the ODBC and Oracle Data Providers respectively. The *DataReader* can supply rows of data directly to application logic when you do not need to keep the data cached in memory. Because only one row is in memory at a time, the *DataReader* provides the lowest overhead in terms of system performance, but it requires exclusive use of an open *Connection* object for the lifetime of the *DataReader*.

The DataAdapter Object

The *DataAdapter* is the class at the core of ADO.NET disconnected data access. It is essentially the middleman, facilitating all communication between the database and a *DataSet*. The *DataAdapter* fills a *DataTable* or *DataSet* with data from the database whenever the *Fill* method is called. After the memory-resident data has been manipulated, the *DataAdapter* can transmit changes to the database by calling the *Update* method. The *DataAdapter* provides four properties that represent database commands. The four properties are:

- **SelectCommand.**   Contains the command text or object that selects the data from the database. This command is executed when the *Fill* method is called and fills a *DataTable* or a *DataSet*.
- **InsertCommand.**   Contains the command text or object that inserts a row into a table.
- **DeleteCommand.**   Contains the command text or object that deletes a row from a table.

- *UpdateCommand.*   Contains the command text or object that updates the values of a database.

When the *Update* method is called, changes in the *DataSet* are copied back to the database, and the appropriate *InsertCommand*, *DeleteCommand*, or *UpdateCommand* is executed.

Lesson Summary

- ADO.NET is a data-access technology that is primarily disconnected and designed to provide efficient, scalable data access.
- Data is represented within a *DataSet* object, which is a disconnected, in-memory copy of part or all of a database.
- A data provider is a set of classes that provide access to databases. The main components of data providers are:
  - *Connection*
  - *Command*
  - *DataReader*
  - *DataAdapter*
- Visual Studio .NET includes two data providers:
  - The SQL Data Provider, which contains classes optimized for accessing SQL Server 7 or later
  - The OleDb Data Provider, which contains classes that provide access to a broad range of database formats
- Two additional data providers are included in Visual Studio .NET 2003:
  - The ODBC Data Provider, which facilitates access to many different database formats
  - The Oracle Data Provider, which contains classes optimized for accessing Oracle databases

Lesson 2: Overview of Structured Query Language

Structured Query Language (SQL) is the universal language of relational databases. SQL can be used to retrieve and filter records from databases, to add records to databases, to delete records from a database, and to change the values of an existing record.

Using SQL statements behind the scenes, ADO .NET handles most of the actual database interaction for you through the classes contained in a data provider. In some cases, though, it is important to be able to generate SQL statements to interact directly with a database. For example, you might want to dynamically build SQL statements in response to user input to retrieve a custom set of rows. In this lesson, you will learn the basics of SQL syntax.

After this lesson, you will be able to

- Describe basic SQL syntax
- Construct simple SELECT, UPDATE, INSERT, and DELETE commands
- Use the WHERE clause to filter the results returned by a SQL query and use the ORDER BY clause to specify a sort order

Estimated lesson time: 30 minutes

Structured Query Language uses four basic statements to interact with a database. The SELECT statement is used to retrieve records from a database; the UPDATE statement is used to update data in a database; the INSERT statement is used to insert a new row into a table; and the DELETE statement is used to delete a record.

Note   The information provided in this section covers only the basics of Structured Query Language—it should not be considered comprehensive. You are encouraged to supplement your reading with additional texts if you find the subject interesting.

The SELECT Statement

The SELECT statement is the command used to retrieve records from a database. A SELECT statement can be divided into four segments:

- **SELECT.**   This segment allows you to specify which fields will be retrieved.
- **FROM.**   This segment allows you to specify which table or tables will be used to get the fields specified in the SELECT segment.

- **WHERE.**   (Optional) This segment allows you to apply filter conditions to the rows retrieved.

- **ORDER BY.**   (Optional) This segment allows you to specify a field by which to order the returned records.

The minimum syntax for an SQL SELECT statement is as follows:

```
SELECT fields
FROM tables;
```

fields represents the field or fields to be retrieved, and *tables* represents the table or tables where those fields will be found. For example, to retrieve the EmployeeID and StartDate fields from the Employees table, you use the following statement:

```
SELECT EmployeeID, StartDate FROM Employees;
```

Note   In SQL Server, SQL statements are terminated with a semicolon (;).

You can use the * character to represent all fields in a table or tables. Thus, if you wanted to retrieve all fields from the Employees table, your query would look like this:

```
SELECT * FROM Employees;
```

Note   If specific fields are required for a query, you should select the specific fields instead of using the * character. This ensures that the correct fields are always returned in the same order regardless of any data-table changes that might have occurred.

The WHERE clause

You might want to limit or filter the records that you retrieve from the database, such as only the records with a particular value in one field—the optional WHERE clause gives you this choice. To illustrate, the following statement selects all records from the Employees table if the value of the FirstName field is 'Bob':

```
SELECT *
FROM Employees
WHERE FirstName = 'Bob';
```

Note   To specify a string literal in an SQL statement, you must enclose the literal in single quotes (' ').

You can use logical operators such as AND or OR to specify multiple conditions. The following code example retrieves all records from the Employees table where the LastName field is 'Jones' and the FirstName field is 'Joe':

```
SELECT *
FROM Employees
WHERE FirstName = 'Joe' AND LastName = 'Jones';
```

You can use the IN operator to retrieve records by matching the value of a field to values specified in a list. The following SQL statement shows an example of WHERE...IN. This statement will retrieve the FirstName and LastName fields from the Employees table if the Country field is 'US' or 'UK':

```
SELECT FirstName, LastName
FROM Employees
WHERE Country IN ('UK', 'US');
```

You also can use the BETWEEN operator to specify that a value lies within a specified range. This example retrieves all records from the Sales table if the FinalPrice field is between 100 and 200:

```
SELECT *
FROM Sales
WHERE FinalPrice BETWEEN 100 AND 200;
```

The WHERE clause also allows you to search string fields for similar, but not exact, matches using the LIKE operator. The LIKE operator allows you to use wildcard characters to specify a pattern to match. In an SQL query, the underscore (_) character represents any single character, and the percent (%) character represents any number of characters. The following SQL statement is an example:

```
SELECT *
FROM Employees
WHERE FirstName LIKE 'Wil_';
```

This statement matches 'Will' but not 'Willy' or 'William'. The scenario changes in the following code example:

```
SELECT *
FROM Employees
WHERE FirstName LIKE 'Wil%';
```

In this case, the statement matches 'Will', 'William', 'Wilhelmina', and any other FirstName values that begin with 'Wil'.

The ORDER BY Clause

The ORDER BY clause, which is also optional, allows you to specify the order in which records are returned. You can use the ASC option to specify ascending order, or the DESC option to specify descending order. The default order is ascending (A to Z, 0 to 9). The following code example selects all fields from the Employees table and returns them in descending order by salary:

```
SELECT *
FROM Employees
ORDER BY Salary DESC;
```

The DELETE Statement

A DELETE statement is used to delete records from the database. You can use a delete statement to delete single records or groups of data based on criteria.

Warning   The DELETE statement is irreversible. Once data is deleted, it cannot be recovered unless the database was previously archived. Take great care when using DELETE statements.

In general, the DELETE statement follows the same syntax as the SELECT statement. The difference is that you do not specify fields to delete, as you can only delete entire rows. You can use the WHERE clause to specify the record or records to be deleted. The following statement deletes any records from the Employees table where the FirstName is 'Joe' and the LastName is 'Jones':

```
DELETE FROM Employees
WHERE FirstName = 'Joe' AND LastName = 'Jones';
```

Note that you can use the same operators in the WHERE clause of the DELETE statement that you can use in the SELECT statement, such as logical operators IN, LIKE, and BETWEEN.

The UPDATE statement

You might need to change the values of existing records to reflect changes in real-world situations. For example, customers move, their addresses change, and the records that represent them must be changed to take the new information into account. Database records can be updated using the UPDATE statement.

The general syntax for an UPDATE statement is as follows:

```
UPDATE tablename
SET column1 = value1, … ,columnN = valueN
[WHERE predicates];
```

In this syntax, tablename represents the name of the table in which the updated records exist; column1 represents the first column to be updated; and value1 represents the value to be updated in that column. As many column-value pairs as necessary can be specified this way, separated by commas. The WHERE clause of an UPDATE statement is optional, as it is with the SELECT and DELETE statements. Also, like the DELETE statement, an UPDATE statement cannot be rolled back. To reverse an UPDATE statement, you must perform another UPDATE statement to reset the data or restore the database from an existing backup.

The following code example shows how to update the LastName field of the Employees table if the FirstName is 'Mary' and the LastName is 'Smith':

```
UPDATE Employees
SET LastName = 'Jones'
WHERE FirstName = 'Mary' AND LastName = 'Smith';
```

Note that you can use IN, BETWEEN, LIKE, and other operators in the WHERE clause, just as you would with a SELECT statement.

The INSERT INTO Statement

When it is necessary to add new records to a database, you can use the INSERT INTO statement. This statement causes the insertion of a new record into the specified table. The general syntax for the INSERT INTO statement is as follows:

```
INSERT INTO table [(column1, … , columnN)]
VALUES (value1, … , valuen);
```

In this example, table represents the table that will receive the new record. column1 through columnN are optional. If particular columns are not specified, records will be inserted in the default order specified by the table. Note that this can be hazardous, as the structure of the table might change without the knowledge of the developer. Whenever possible, you should specify the affected columns in an INSERT INTO statement. Values for the new record are represented by value1 through valuen. If a value is not specified for a column, it will remain a null value. The following code example demonstrates adding a new record to the Employees table:

```
INSERT INTO Employees (FirstName, LastName, Title, Salary)
VALUES ('Joe', 'Jones', 'Boss', 100000);
```

Lesson Summary

Structured Query Language (SQL) is a language used for communicating with databases. Although ADO.NET handles most of the database interaction, you can manually retrieve, update, insert, or delete records using well-formed SQL statements. The SELECT statement is used to retrieve records, and is divided into four major sections: SELECT, FROM, WHERE, and ORDER BY. Each section allows you to specify different aspects of the records to be retrieved. You can use the DELETE statement to remove records from a database. The UPDATE statement is used to update values in existing records, and the INSERT INTO statement is used to add new records to an existing tables.

Lesson 3: Accessing Data

Visual Studio .NET has many built-in wizards and designers to help you shape your data-access architecture rapidly and efficiently. With minimal actual coding, you can implement robust data access for your application. However, the ADO.NET object model is fully available through code to implement customized features or to fine-tune your program. In this lesson, you will learn how to connect to a database with ADO.NET and retrieve data to your application. You will learn to use the visual designers provided by Visual Studio .NET and direct code access.

After this lesson, you will be able to

- Establish a connection to a database
- Create and configure a *DataAdapter*
- Create a *Command* object that uses SQL strings
- Create a *Command* object that accesses stored procedures on the database
- Create a typed *DataSet*
- Fill a *DataSet* with a *DataAdapter*
- Use a *DataReader* to programmatically access data

Estimated lesson time: 60 minutes

Connecting to a Database

You can implement a database connection in many different ways. The easiest way is to create a connection at design time using the graphical tools in Visual Studio .NET.

Current data connections are managed in the Server Explorer window. This window is normally docked to the left pane of the integrated development environment (IDE) and shares the same space as the Toolbox. If the Toolbox is visible, you can view the Server Explorer by clicking the Server Explorer tab at the bottom of the Toolbox, or by choosing Server Explorer from the View menu. The Server Explorer is shown in Figure 6.1.

Server Explorer displays data connections currently available to Visual Studio .NET as child nodes of the Data Connections node. If you want to add one of these child nodes to your project, all you need to do is drag the connection from the Server Explorer window to the designer. A new *Connection* object of the appropriate type is created and automatically configured to connect to your database.

Figure 6.1. The Server Explorer.

To add a connection from Server Explorer

Drag the node that represents a database from the Server Explorer window to the designer.

You can also create a new connection in the Server Explorer by right-clicking the Data Connections node and choosing Add Connection. This launches the Data Link Properties dialog box, as shown in Figure 6.2.

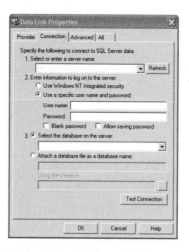

Figure 6.2. The Data Link Properties dialog box.

The Data Link Properties dialog box is a visual way to configure your data connection. The Providers tab allows you to choose the database provider that you will use in your connection. The Connection tab allows you to configure the specific properties of your connections, and the Advanced tab configures properties not normally needed for every connection. The All tab allows you to view and edit settings for all the properties. Once you have configured your new connection, click OK to close the Data Link Properties window. The new connection appears in the Server Explorer window and can be dragged to your designer.

To create a new connection in Server Explorer

1. In the Server Explorer, right-click Data Connections and choose Add Connection to open the Data Link Properties window.
2. On the Provider tab, choose the appropriate provider for your data connection.
3. On the Connection tab, choose the database you want to connect. Depending on the provider, you also might have to set properties such as the server name or password settings.
4. After you have entered the appropriate information, click the Test Connection button to verify that the connection is functional.
5. Drag the new connection from the Server Explorer, and drop it on the designer surface. A new connection object of the appropriate type is created and correctly configured.

You also can create a database connection manually by dragging a *Connection* object from the Toolbox to the designer or by declaring and instantiating the object in your code. If you create a connection in code, you will have to manually set the *ConnectionString* property. The following code example demonstrates how to create a *Connection* object in code and set the *ConnectionString* property:

Visual Basic .NET

```
' Declares and instantiates a new OleDbConnection object
Dim myConnection As New OleDbConnection()
' Sets the connection string to indicate a Microsoft Access
' database at the specified path
myConnection.ConnectionString = _
    "Provider=Microsoft.Jet.OLEDB.4.0;" & _
    "DataSource=C:\Northwind\Northwind.mdb"
```

Visual C#

```
// Declares and instantiates a new OleDbConnection object
OleDbConnection myConnection = new OleDbConnection();
// Sets the connection string to indicate a Microsoft Access
// database at the specified path
myConnection.ConnectionString =
    "Provider=Microsoft.Jet.OLEDB.4.0;DataSource=" +
    "C:\\Northwind\\Northwind.mdb";
```

Note Depending on your database provider and configuration, you might have to supply additional parameters in the connection string. Whenever possible, it is rec ommended that you implement connections using the visual tools supplied by Visual Studio .NET.

To create a new connection in code

1. Declare and instantiate the appropriate type of *Connection* object.

2. Set the *ConnectionString* property.

To create a new connection in the designer

1. Drag the appropriate type of *Connection* object from the Data tab of the Tool-box to the designer.

2. In the Properties window, set the *ConnectionString* property.

Using Data Commands

A *Command* object contains a reference to a database stored procedure or SQL statement and can execute that statement across an active data connection. A *Com mand* object contains all the information it requires to execute the command, including a reference to the active connection, the specification for the command itself, and any parameters required by the command.

As with other classes in data providers, there are two types of *Command* classes. The *OleDbCommand* class is designed to interact with a wide variety of database types. The *SqlCommand* class is designed to interact specifically with SQL Server 7 or later.

Because they only require an active connection and do not need to interact with a *DataAdapter*, *Command* objects provide a fast and efficient way to interact with a database. *Command* objects can be used to perform the following actions:

- Execute commands that do not return records such as INSERT, UPDATE, and DELETE.

- Execute commands that return a single value.

- Execute Database Definition Language (DDL) commands, such as CREATE TABLE, or ALTER.

- Work with a *DataAdapter* to return a *DataSet*.

- Return a result set directly through an instance of a *DataReader* object. This provides the fastest way to access data and is useful when read-only data is required.

- Return a result set as an XML stream. This method is only available with the *SqlCommand* class.

- Return a result set from multiple tables or command statements.

Creating and Configuring a Data Command

You can create a data command in three ways:

- By dragging a stored procedure (a query that is stored on the database server itself) from the Server Explorer window to the designer.
- By dragging an appropriate *Command* from the Toolbox Data tab to the designer and configuring it in the Properties window.
- By declaring and instantiating the appropriate type of *Command* object in code and configuring it manually.

Dragging a stored procedure to the designer is the most straightforward way to create a data command. Any stored procedure on a database can be used to create a *Command* object. When a stored procedure is dragged onto the designer, a *Command* object of the appropriate type is created automatically. The new command references the stored procedure and can be used immediately to execute the stored procedure as is—no additional configuration is necessary.

To create a Command object that references an existing stored procedure

Drag the stored procedure from the Server Explorer to the designer. An appropriately configured instance of a *Command* object is created.

Creating a *Command* object in the designer is almost as easy as dragging a stored procedure. You can create a *Command* object by dragging either an *SqlCommand* or an *OleDbCommand* from the Toolbox Data tab to the designer. This creates an instance of the *Command* object you selected. Once created, the *Command* object must be configured by setting the *Connection*, *CommandType*, and *CommandText* properties.

The *CommandType* property determines what kind of command is contained by the *CommandText* property. There are three possible values for the *CommandType* property, which are:

- **Text.**   A value of *Text* indicates that the value contained in the *CommandText* property will be parsed as an SQL text command. When this is the case, the *CommandText* property must be set to a valid SQL expression. A *Command* object can contain multiple SQL statements separated by semicolons (;) if batched SQL commands are supported by the target database. If a *Command* object contains more than one SQL statement, the statements execute sequentially when the command executes.
- **StoredProcedure.**   If the *CommandType* property is set to *StoredProcedure*, the value contained in the *CommandText* property must contain the name of an existing stored procedure on the database. Executing this command causes the stored procedure of the same name to execute.

- ***TableDirect.***   A *CommandType* of *TableDirect* indicates that the name of a table or tables must be indicated by the *CommandText* property. Executing this command returns all of the columns and all of the rows of the table or tables named in the *CommandText* property.

The *Connection* property must be set to an active connection of the appropriate type (that is, a *SqlCommand* must have a *SqlConnection* as its connection, and an *OleDbCommand* must have an *OleDbConnection*).

Executing Commands

Each type of *Command* object has three methods to execute the command it represents:

- *ExecuteNonQuery*
- *ExecuteScalar*
- *ExecuteReader*

The *SqlCommand* class exposes an additional method, *ExecuteXmlReader*, for executing the command it represents.

Each of these methods executes the data command represented by the *Command* object. The difference between these methods lies in the values they return. *ExecuteNonQuery* is the simplest method, as it executes the data command, but returns no value. Thus, *ExecuteNonQuery* is the method typically used to call SQL commands or stored procedures of the INSERT, UPDATE, or DELETE types. Additionally, this is the only way in ADO.NET to execute DDL commands such as CREATE or ALTER. The *ExecuteScalar* method returns the first column of the first row of data returned by the command, no matter how many rows the command actually selects. *ExecuteReader* returns a *DataReader* object that can iterate through a result set in a forward-only, read-only manner without involving a *DataAdapter*. This is the fastest and often the most efficient way to retrieve data when you do not need to update or otherwise manipulate the database itself. The *SqlCommand* class exposes one additional method, which is *ExecuteXmlReader*. This class returns an *XmlReader* object that iterates through the result set and provides data in a forward-only, read-only manner, formatted as XML.

Parameters

Data commands frequently make use of parameters. Often, the values of some elements of a data command are unknown until run time. Consider an application that tracks inventory for a bookstore. It might contain a function that looks up books by title. This functionality can be implemented by querying the database with a SQL statement similar to the following code example:

```
SELECT * FROM Books WHERE (Title LIKE [value])
```

At design time, you know that you want the application to find all the books with a title similar to a value supplied by the user at run time. Because you do not know in advance what value the user will supply, you must employ a mechanism for supplying the value to the statement at run time.

Parameters are values that fill placeholders left in the command text. Each parameter is an instance of the *OleDbParameter* or *SqlParameter* class, as appropriate. Parameters are stored in the *Command* object's *Parameters* property, and at run time the values are read from the property and placed into the SQL statement or supplied to the stored procedure.

Command objects provide a *Parameters* collection that exposes a collection of *Parameter* objects of the appropriate type. Some of the properties exposed by the *Parameter* objects are as follows:

- *DbType* (This property is not visible in the designer.)
- *Direction*
- *OleDbType* (*OleDbParameters* only)
- *ParameterName*
- *Precision*
- *Scale*
- *Size*
- *SourceColumn*
- *SourceVersion*
- *SQLType* (*SQLParameters* only)
- *Value*

In *OleDbParameters*, the *DbType* and *OleDbType* properties are related. The *DbType* property represents the type of parameter, as represented in the common type system (CTS). However, because not all databases are CTS compliant, the *OleDbType* property represents the type of parameter as it exists in the database. The *Parameter* object performs all necessary conversions of the application type to the database type. Because the two properties are related, changing the value of one changes the value of the other to a supporting type. In *SqlParameter* objects, the *DbType* property and the *SqlType* property share a similar relationship, wherein the *SqlType* property specifies the SQL database type represented by the parameter.

The *Direction* property specifies whether the parameter is for input or output. The possible values for this property are *Input*, *Output*, *InputOutput*, or *ReturnValue*, which indicates the parameter is to contain a return value from a stored procedure or function.

In code, you can refer to members of the *Parameters* collection by their index or by their name. The *ParameterName* property specifies the name that can be used as a key to specify the parameter in code. The following code example demonstrates two different ways to set the value of the first parameter in the collection, which is named *myParameter*:

Visual Basic .NET

```
' This line sets the value by referring to the index of the parameter
OleDbCommand1.Parameters(0).Value = "Hello World"
' This line sets the value by referring to the name of the parameter
OleDbCommand1.Parameters("myParameter").Value = "Goodbye for now"
```

Visual C#

```
// This line sets the value by referring to the index of the parameter
OleDbCommand1.Parameters[0].Value = "Hello World";
// This line sets the value by referring to the name of the parameter
OleDbCommand1.Parameters["myParameter"].Value = "Goodbye for now";
```

The *Precision*, *Scale*, and *Size* properties all affect the size and accuracy of the parameters. *Precision* and *Scale* are used with numeric and decimal parameters. Respectively, they represent the maximum number of digits of the *Value* property and the number of decimal places that *Value* resolves to. *Size* is used with binary and string parameters and represents the maximum size of data in the column.

SourceColumn and *SourceVersion* are used when the parameter is bound to a column in a *DataTable*. The *SourceColumn* property specifies the column used to look up or map values, and the *SourceVersion* property specifies which version of the column to use when it is being edited.

The *Value* property contains the value represented by the parameter.

When the *CommandType* property of the *Command* object is set to *Text*, you must specify a placeholder for any parameters that will be inserted into the SQL statement. With *OleDbCommand* objects, this placeholder takes the form of a question mark (?). For example:

```
SELECT EmpId, Title, FirstName, LastName
FROM Employees
WHERE (Title = ?)
```

In this example, the question mark indicates where the parameter will be inserted. You also can specify multiple parameters, as follows:

```
SELECT EmpId, Title, FirstName, LastName
FROM Employees
WHERE (FirstName = ?) AND (LastName = ?)
```

When the command text requires multiple parameters, the parameters are inserted in the order that they appear in the Parameters collection.

When using a *SqlCommand* object, you must use named parameters. Placeholders for a named parameter are created by preceding the name of your parameter (as specified by the *ParameterName* property) with an @ symbol. For example, the following SQL statement specifies a named parameter named *Title*:

```
SELECT EmpId, Title, FirstName, LastName
FROM Employees
WHERE (Title = @Title)
```

The following procedures describe how to use a *Command* object to execute different kinds of commands.

To use a Command object to execute a nonquery command

This procedure is used to execute INSERT, UPDATE, and DELETE commands as well as DDL commands such as CREATE TABLE and ALTER.

1. Set the *CommandType* property to *StoredProcedure* if specifying a stored procedure or *Text* if specifying a SQL string.
2. Set the *CommandText* property to the name of the stored procedure or the desired SQL string, as appropriate.
3. Specify any parameters and their appropriate values.
4. Call the *Command.ExecuteNonQuery* method. An example of this method follows:

Visual Basic .NET

```
' This command is identical whether you are using the OleDbCommand
' class or the SqlCommand class
myCommand.ExecuteNonQuery()
```

Visual C#

```
// This command is identical whether you are using the OleDbCommand
// class or the SqlCommand class
myCommand.ExecuteNonQuery();
```

To use a Command object to return a single value

1. Set the *CommandType* property to *StoredProcedure* if specifying a stored procedure or *Text* if specifying a SQL string.
2. Set the *CommandText* property to the name of the stored procedure or the desired SQL string, as appropriate.
3. Specify any parameters and their appropriate values.
4. Call the *Command.ExecuteScalar* method. An example of this method follows:

Visual Basic .NET

```
' This command is identical whether you are using the OleDbCommand
' class or the SqlCommand class
Dim O As Object
O = myCommand.ExecuteScalar()
```

Visual C#

```
// This command is identical whether you are using the OleDbCommand
// class or the SqlCommand class
Object O;
O = myCommand.ExecuteNonScalar();
```

Using DataReaders

Executing nonquery or scalar-returning commands with a *Command* object is straightforward. To use a *Command* object with queries that return more than one value, however, you must use the *ExecuteReader* method to return a *DataReader*.

A *DataReader* is a lightweight object that provides read-only, forward-only data in a fast and efficient manner. To expose the values directly to program logic, you can use the *DataReader* to iterate through the records returned in a result set. Using a *DataReader* rather than a *DataAdapter* to fill a *DataSet* is more efficient, but it is also more limited. This is because the data provided is read-only; no updates can be performed with a *DataReader*. Also, the data access is forward-only; once a record has been read, it cannot be returned to. Additionally, a *DataReader* is a connected data-access structure requiring exclusive use of an active connection for the entire time it is in existence.

Creating a DataReader

A *DataReader* cannot be created explicitly. Rather, you must instantiate a *DataReader* by making a call to a *Command* object's *ExecuteReader* command. Like other members of the different data providers, each *DataProvider* has its own class of *DataReader*. An *OleDbCommand* object returns an *OleDbDataReader*, while a *SqlCommand* object returns a *SqlDataReader*. For example:

Visual Basic .NET

```
' This example assumes the existence of an OleDbCommand object
' and a SqlCommand object named myOleDbCommand and mySqlCommand
' respectively
Dim myOleDbReader As System.Data.OleDb.OleDbDataReader
Dim mySqlReader As System.Data.SqlClient.SqlDataReader
' This call creates a new OleDbReader and assigns it to the variable
myOleDbReader = myOleDbCommand.ExecuteReader()
' This call creates a new SqlReader and assigns it to the variable
mySqlReader = mySqlCommand.ExecuteReader()
```

Visual C#

```
// This example assumes the existence of an OleDbCommand object
// and a SqlCommand object named myOleDbCommand and mySqlCommand
// respectively
System.Data.OleDb.OleDbDataReader myOleDbReader;
System.Data.SqlClient.SqlDataReader mySqlReader;
// This call creates a new OleDbReader and assigns it to the variable
myOleDbReader = myOleDbCommand.ExecuteReader();
// This call creates a new SqlReader and assigns it to the variable
mySqlReader = mySqlCommand.ExecuteReader();
```

When a *Command* object's *ExecuteReader* method is called, the *Command* object executes the command it represents and builds a *DataReader* of the appropriate type, which can be assigned to a reference variable.

Simple Data Access with the DataReader

Once you have a reference to a *DataReader*, you can iterate through the records and read them into memory as needed. When the *DataReader* is first returned, it is positioned before the first record of the result set. To make the first record available, you must call the *Read* method. If a record is available, the *Read* method advances the *DataReader* to the next record and returns *True* (*true*). If a record is not available, the *Read* method returns *False* (*false*). Thus, it is possible to use the *Read* method to iterate through the records with a *While* (*while*) loop, as shown in the following code example:

Visual Basic .NET

```
While myDataReader.Read()
    ' Code here will be executed once for each record returned in
    ' the result set
End While
```

Visual C#

```
while (myDataReader.Read())
{
    // Code here will be executed once for each record returned in
    // the result set
}
```

When a record is being read by the *DataReader*, the values in the individual columns are exposed through the indexer or default property as an array of objects that can be accessed by their ordinal values or by the column name. For example:

Visual Basic .NET

```
While myDataReader.Read()
    Dim myObject As Object = myDataReader(3)
    Dim myOtherObject As Object = myDataReader("CustomerID")
End While
```

Visual C#

```
while (myDataReader.Read())
{
    object myObject = myDataReader[3];
    object myOtherObject = myDataReader["CustomerID"];
}
```

All of the values exposed by the *DataReader* in this manner are exposed as objects although you can retrieve strongly typed data from the *DataReader* as well. This process is discussed later in this lesson.

After you have finished reading data with the *DataReader*, you must call the *Close* method to close the *DataReader*. If *Close* is not called, the *DataReader* will main tain exclusive access to the active connection and no other object can use it. You also can set the *CommandBehavior* property to *CloseConnection* when you call *ExecuteReader*. This causes the connection to close automatically, eliminating the need to explicitly call *Close*.

Visual Basic .NET

```
myDataReader.Close()
```

Visual C#

```
myDataReader.Close();
```

Accessing Columns of Data with a DataReader

The following sample code demonstrates how to iterate through the records returned in a result set and write one column of data to the console window. This example assumes the existence of an *OleDbCommand* object named *myOleDbCom mand* with its *Connection* property set to a connection named *myConnection*.

Visual Basic .NET

```
' Opens the active connection
myConnection.Open()
' Creates a DataReader and assigns it to myReader
Dim myReader As System.Data.OleDb.OleDbDataReader = _
    myOleDbCommand.ExecuteReader()
' Calls Read before attempting to read data
While myReader.Read()
    ' You can access the columns either by column name or by ordinal
    ' number
    Console.WriteLine(myReader("Customers").ToString())
End While
' Always close the DataReader when you are done with it
myReader.Close()
' And close the connection if not being used further
myConnection.Close()
```

Visual C#

```csharp
// Opens the active connection
myConnection.Open();
// Creates a DataReader and assigns it to myReader
System.Data.OleDb.OleDbDataReader myReader =
    myOleDbCommand.ExecuteReader();
// Calls Read before attempting to read data
while (myReader.Read())
{
    // You can access the columns either by column name or by ordinal
    // number
    Console.WriteLine(myReader["Customers"].ToString());
}
// Always close the DataReader when you are done with it
myReader.Close();
// And close the connection if not being used further
myConnection.Close() ;
```

To access data with a DataReader

1. Call your *Command* object's *ExecuteReader* method and assign the returned *DataReader* to an appropriately typed variable.

2. Iterate through the result set within a *While* (*while*) loop. You should perform any operations with the data while inside this loop. You must call the *DataReader* object's *Read* method before using the data.

3. When finished, call the *DataReader* object's *Close* method to release the connection.

Retrieving Typed Data Using a DataReader

Although the data exposed by a *DataReader* is typed as objects, the *DataReader* also exposes methods to retrieve data contained in a result set. These methods are named *Get*, along with the name of the type to be retrieved. For example, the method to retrieve a Boolean value is *GetBoolean*. If you know the type of data in a given column, you can use *Get* methods to return strongly typed data from that column. For example:

Visual Basic .NET

```vbnet
Dim myBoolean As Boolean
myBoolean = myDataReader.GetBoolean(3)
```

Visual C#

```csharp
bool myBoolean;
myBoolean = myDataReader.GetBoolean(3);
```

When using these methods, you must use the column's ordinal number; you canne use the column name. If you only know the column name, you can look up the ordinal number with the *GetOrdinal* method, as follows:

Visual Basic .NET

```
Dim CustomerID As Integer
Dim Customer As String
' Looks up the ordinal number for the column named 'CustomerID'
CustomerID = myDataReader.GetOrdinal("CustomerID")
' Retrieves a string from that field and assigns it to Customer
Customer = myDataReader.GetString(CustomerID)
```

Visual C#

```
int CustomerID;
string Customer;
// Looks up the ordinal number for the column named 'CustomerID'
CustomerID = myDataReader.GetOrdinal("CustomerID");
// Retrieves a string from that field and assigns it to Customer
Customer = myDataReader.GetString(CustomerID);
```

To retrieve typed data using a DataReader

1. If necessary, look up the column's ordinal number by calling the *GetOrdinal* method on the column name.

2. Call the appropriate *Get* method of the *DataReader*, specifying the ordinal number of the column to return.

Using Multiple Result Sets

If the *CommandType* property of your *Command* object is set to *Text*, and if this feature is supported by your database, you can return multiple result sets with a sit gle command by providing multiple SQL commands in the *CommandText* property To indicate multiple commands, separate each command with a semicolon (;). Fo example:

```
SELECT *
FROM Accounts;
SELECT *
FROM Creditors
```

When multiple SQL statements are specified in the *CommandText* property of a *Command* object, the statements are executed sequentially. If more than one state ment returns a result set, multiple result sets are returned by the *DataReader*, also sequentially.

The *DataReader* returns the first result set automatically. To access the next result set, you must call the *NextResult* method. Like the *Read* method, the *NextResult* method returns *False* (*false*) when there are no more result sets to be read. Unlike the *Read* method, however, the *DataReader* comes into existence positioned at the first result set. If the *NextResult* method is called before the first result set is read, the first result set is discarded, and the next result set is read. The following code example demonstrates how to use the *NextResult* method to loop through result sets:

Visual Basic .NET

```
Do
    While myReader.Read()
    ' Add code here to loop through the records of the current
    ' result set
    End While
    ' Switches to the next result set, or returns False if all result
    ' sets have been read
Loop While myReader.NextResult()
```

Visual C#

```
do
{
    while (myReader.Read())
    {
        // Add code here to loop through the records of the current
        // result set
    }
} while (myReader.NextResult());
```

To read multiple result sets with a DataReader

1. Set the *CommandType* property of your *Command* object to *Text*.
2. Specify multiple SQL statements in the *CommandText* property of your *Command* object. These should be separated by a semicolon.
3. Call the *ExecuteReader* method of your *Command* object and assign the *DataReader* to a variable.
4. Use the *DataReader* object's *NextResult* method to iterate through the result sets.

Executing Ad Hoc SQL Queries

At times, you might not know until run time which SQL query you want to execute. You might want to receive a search string through user input, programmatically determine columns to be returned, or even determine the appropriate table at run time. You can create, configure, and execute commands all at run time.

The first step in executing an ad hoc SQL query is to build the command string. When building the command string, you should start by creating the outline of the command string. Where required, add string variables that represent the values to be inserted at run time. Use the concatenation operator to connect the strings. For example:

Visual Basic .NET

```
' Assumes that aString has been declared and the value set previously
' in code
Dim Cmd As String
Cmd = "SELECT * FROM Employees WHERE Name = '" & aString & "'"
```

Visual C#

```
// Assumes that aString has been declared and the value set previously
// in code
string Cmd;
Cmd = "SELECT * FROM Employees WHERE Name = '" + aString + "'";
```

Caution   In the WHERE clause of a SQL statement, string values to be passed to the database must be enclosed in single quotes (' '). If the variable includes any additional single quotes, they should be replaced by two single quotes (' '). Otherwise, the query will fail.

The *Command* classes of each data provider expose constructors that allow you to set the *CommandText* and *Connection* properties at instantiation. After setting these properties, all you need to do is open the connection and execute the command. The following code example demonstrates how a method might receive a search string, build an ad hoc SQL command, and execute it against the database:

Visual Basic .NET

```
' This example assumes an OleDb connection named myConnection.
' It also assumes Imports System.Data.OleDb
Public Sub DeleteRecord(aString As String)
   Dim Cmd As String
   Cmd = "DELETE * FROM Employees WHERE Name = '" & aString & "'"
   ' Specifies Cmd as the command string and myConnection as the
   ' connection
   Dim myCommand As New OleDbCommand(Cmd, myConnection)
   ' Opens the Connection and executes the command
   myConnection.Open()
   myCommand.ExecuteNonQuery()
   ' Always close the connection
   myConnection.Close()
End Sub
```

Visual C#

```csharp
// This example assumes an OleDB connection named myConnection.
// It also assumes using System.Data.OleDb
public void DeleteRecord(string aString)
{
    string Cmd;
     Cmd = "DELETE * FROM Employees WHERE Name = '" + aString + "'";
    // Specifies Cmd as the command string and myConnection as the
    // connection
    OleDbCommand myCommand = new OleDbCommand(Cmd, myConnection);
    // Opens the Connection and executes the command
    myConnection.Open();
    myCommand.ExecuteNonQuery();
    // Always close the connection
    myConnection.Close();
}
```

Caution   When creating and executing ad hoc SQL statements, you must perform validation on any values that come from user input. Failure to validate user input can leave your application vulnerable to SQL injection attacks, which occur when a malicious user passes a damaging SQL statement as a string through unvalidated user input, resulting in the SQL statement being executed against the database. SQL injection attacks can be extremely damaging, costly, and difficult to repair. Always validate user input that is used to generate ad hoc SQL statements.

Creating and Configuring DataAdapters

DataAdapter objects provide the link between a data source and a *DataSet* by managing the data exchange. A *DataAdapter* is responsible for moving data between a data source and a *DataSet*. In some applications, this movement is strictly one-way. Other applications, however, might require continued querying and updating of the data source. The *DataAdapter* incorporates the functionality required to retrieve data, populate a *DataSet*, and perform updates as required.

Two primary *DataAdapter* objects are included with Visual Studio .NET. The *Sql-DataAdapter* is designed to provide optimal communication with SQL Server 7 or later. *TheOleDbDataAdapter* provides access to any data source that is exposed by an *OleDb Provider*. Visual Studio .NET 2003 includes two additional *DataAdapter* objects: the *ODBCDataAdapter* and the *OracleDataAdapter*.

A single *DataAdapter* is generally used to manage data exchange between a single *DataTable* object in a *DataSet* and a single-source database table. Because *DataSet* objects can contain multiple tables, you should create a single *DataAdapter* for each table you want to add to the *DataSet*.

There are three ways to create a *DataAdapter*: You can drag database elements from the Server Explorer; you can use the new Data Adapter Configuration Wizard; or you can manually create and configure the *DataAdapter* in code. The following sections describe each of these approaches.

Creating a DataAdapter Using Server Explorer

The easiest way to create a *DataAdapter* is by using the Server Explorer window. The Data Connections node of the Server Explorer window lists each installed data connection. Each Data Connection node expands in turn to provide detail about the database it represents, including a list of available tables, views, and stored procedures. You can create a *DataAdapter* that represents a table by dragging a table from the Server Explorer window onto the designer. The resulting *DataAdapter* is of the correct type and has *SelectCommand*, *UpdateCommand*, *InsertCommand*, and *DeleteCommand* properties that are correctly configured.

Note   Although you can create a *DataAdapter* from a Data view, it is not recommended for read-write data operations because the designer frequently encounters difficulties generating the UPDATE, INSERT, and DELETE commands for operations that involve multiple tables.

You also can configure your *DataAdapter* to return a subset of the available columns in a table. To do this, expand the node that represents the table that contains the columns you want to select. You can then select individual columns by clicking the column entries while holding down the Ctrl key. When you have selected the columns you want to add, drag them to the designer. This creates a *DataAdapter* that is configured to manage only these columns.

Note   To automatically generate the INSERT, DELETE, and UPDATE statements, you must include the column that defines the primary key.

To create a DataAdapter in Server Explorer

1. In the Server Explorer window, expand the node that represents the connection to the database you are using in your application.

2. Expand the Tables node to display the tables present in the database.

3. Select your table. If you do not want to use the entire table, expand the node represented by the table to display the individual columns. Select columns with the mouse while holding down the Ctrl key.

4. Drag your selection to the designer. A new instance of the appropriate type of *DataAdapter* is created and configured.

Creating a DataAdapter with the Data Adapter Configuration Wizard

You can create a new *DataAdapter* by dragging the appropriate *DataAdapter* class from the Toolbox to the designer. This launches the Data Adapter Configuration Wizard.

To create a DataAdapter with the Data Adapter Configuration Wizard

1. From the Data tab of the Toolbox, drag the appropriate type of *DataAdapter* onto the designer. This launches the Data Adapter Configuration Wizard. Click Next to begin configuring your *DataAdapter*.

2. In the Choose Your Data Connection page, select the appropriate Data Connection from the drop-down menu. Click Next to continue.

Note   If your database is not listed in the drop-down menu, you can create a new connection by clicking the New Connection button. This opens the Data Link Properties window.

---

3. In the Choose a Query Type page, you are given three options to choose how you want your *DataAdapter* to communicate with your database. These choices are summarized in Table 6.1.

Table 6.1.   DataAdapter Database Communication Options

Option	Description
Use SQL statements.	This option allows you to specify a SQL SELECT statement to select the data that will be retrieved by the *DataAdapter*. The wizard then generates the appropriate INSERT, UPDATE, and DELETE commands.
Create new stored procedures.	This option allows you to specify a SQL SELECT statement to create a new stored procedure. The wizard then generates new stored procedures for the INSERT, UPDATE, and DELETE commands.
Use existing stored procedures.	This option allows you to specify existing stored procedures for the SELECT, INSERT, UPDATE, and DELETE commands.

Depending on your data provider, some of these options might be unavailable. If an option is unavailable, it appears grayed out in this page.

Choose the appropriate option, and click Next to continue.

4. Depending on the choice you made in Step 3, you will see one of two panes.

- If you chose Use SQL Statements or Create New Stored Procedures, you will see the SQL Statement Generation pane. Type the appropriate SELECT command into the pane, or click the Query Builder button to build your statement with the SQL Query Builder. Appropriate INSERT, DELETE, and UPDATE commands or stored procedures will be generated.

- If you select Use Existing Stored Procedures, you will see the Bind Commands To Existing Stored Procedures page. From each of the four drop-down menus, choose the appropriate stored procedure to perform the SELECT, UPDATE, INSERT, and DELETE commands.

Note   The SQL Query Builder is a graphical tool that can assist you in building SQL statements. If you are unfamiliar with SQL syntax, this tool can be a great benefit. See Lesson 2 of this chapter for an overview of SQL syntax.

---

5. Click Finish. Your *DataAdapter* is now configured and ready to use.

Retrieving Data Using DataAdapters

A *DataSet* is an in-memory representation of data that is inherently disconnected from the database. A *DataSet* can represent a complete set of data including multiple tables, data relationships, and constraints. Because a *DataSet* is a disconnected representation of data, it can include data from multiple data sources. *DataAdapter* objects manage all interactions between *DataSet* objects and databases.

The *DataAdapter* encapsulates the functionality required to fill a *DataSet* with data and to update the database. It acts as a bridge between the connection and the *DataSet*. The *DataAdapter* maintains a reference to a database connection in its *Connection* property, which represents the database that any data actions are executed against. The *DataAdapter* also exposes a *SelectCommand* property that contains instructions for selecting data from a data source as a *Command* object. Like other data provider members, there is a *DataAdapter* implementation for each data provider.

You can fill a *DataSet* with data by calling the *Fill* method of the *DataAdapter*. The *Fill* method executes the instructions contained within the *SelectCommand* property across the connection specified by the *Connection* property, and fills a specified *DataSet* with the resultant data. You must specify either a *DataSet* or a *DataTable* as the target of a *Fill* method. For example:

Visual Basic .NET

```
' This example assumes the existence of a Data Adapter named
' myDataAdapter
Dim myDataSet As New DataSet()
' Executes the SelectCommand and fills myDataSet with the resultant
' data
myDataAdapter.Fill(myDataSet)
```

Visual C#

```
// This example assumes the existence of a Data Adapter named
// myDataAdapter
DataSet myDataSet = new DataSet();
// Executes the SelectCommand and fills myDataSet with the resultant
// data
myDataAdapter.Fill(myDataSet);
```

Note that no interactions with the *Connection* object take place. When the *Fill* command is executed, the connection opens just long enough to retrieve the selected data, and then it closes again. Once the data is retrieved, it becomes disconnected from the database. It then can be manipulated by program logic independent of the database and updated as necessary.

To retrieve data with a DataAdapter

1. Create an instance of the appropriate type of *DataAdapter* that specifies the data you want to select.
2. Create an instance of a *DataSet* or *DataTable* object.
3. Call the *Fill* method of the *DataAdapter*, specifying the *DataTable* or *DataSet* as the target.

When working with *DataAdapter* objects, a single *DataAdapter* is generally used to manage a single table of data. If you want to load multiple tables into a single *DataSet*, you should use multiple *DataAdapter* objects. A single *DataSet* can be the target of multiple *Fill* commands. When each *DataAdapter* calls its *Fill* method, a new *DataTable* is created, filled with data, and added to the *DataSet*.

To fill a DataSet with multiple tables

1. Create an instance of a *DataSet*.
2. Create a *DataAdapter* of the appropriate type for each table you want to have represented in your *DataSet*.
3. Sequentially call the *Fill* method of each *DataAdapter*, specifying your *DataSet* as the target.

Note If you add related tables to your *DataSet*, these relationships are not carrie‹ over by the *DataAdapter*. You must manually re-create the relationships in your *DataSet* by creating new *DataRelation* objects. This is discussed in Lesson 3 of thi chapter.

Previewing Data

You can preview the data that will be returned by your *DataAdapter* objects by choosing Preview Data from the Data menu. This launches the Data Adapter Preview window shown in Figure 6.3.

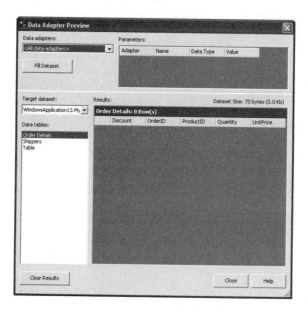

Figure 6.3. The Data Adapter Preview window.

This window allows you to verify that your *DataAdapter* objects are correctly con‹ figured and returning the correct data. Available *DataAdapter* objects are shown in the Data Adapter drop-down menu. You can choose to examine any or all of them. Available *DataSet* objects are shown in the Target Dataset drop-down menu, where you can choose the *DataSet* to fill. Clicking the Fill Dataset button executes the *Fill* method of the *DataAdapter* objects you chose and displays the results in the Results grid. Parameters are displayed in the Parameters grid.

Typed DataSet Objects

Standard *DataSet* objects are inherently weakly typed. Every data point is exposed as an object and must be converted to the appropriate type to perform any type-specific manipulations. Working with weakly typed variables can cause type-mismatch errors, which can be difficult to debug. As an alternative to working with weakly typed variables, ADO.NET provides a typed *DataSet*.

As the name implies, a typed *DataSet* is a *DataSet* that implements strong typing for each member. Tables and columns of a typed *DataSet* are accessible through user-friendly names for the tables and columns you are working with, and data is exposed as typed instead of as objects. This provides many advantages, such as increasing the readability and maintainability of your code. Type-mismatch errors are discovered at compile time instead of at run time, saving valuable testing cycles. You can use friendly name syntax instead of collection syntax, and your typed data members can be displayed at design time in the Intellisense window. To illustrate, the code example to follow contrasts equivalent lines of code written using untyped *DataSet* objects and typed *DataSet* objects. Each example returns the OrderID column from the first record of the Orders table of the *dsorders DataSet*. The first example is written using untyped *DataSet* objects.

Visual Basic .NET

```
Dim myOrder As String
myOrder = CType(dsOrders.Tables("Orders").Rows(0).Item("OrderID"), _
    String)
```

Visual C#

```
string myOrder;
myOrder = (string)dsOrders.Tables["Orders"].Rows[0]["OrderID"];
```

The following code example is written with a typed *DataSet*. Note how much easier the code is to read. Note also that explicit casts are unnecessary.

Visual Basic .NET

```
Dim myOrder As String
myOrder = dsOrders.Orders(0).OrderID
```

Visual C#

```
string myOrder;
myOrder = dsOrders.Orders[0].OrderID;
```

A typed *DataSet* is actually an instance of a new class derived from the *DataSet* class. The structure of the new class is based on an XML schema file (XSD file, which stands for XML Schema Definition) that defines the structure of the *DataSet*, including the names of the tables and columns. Because a schema file is required to create the new *DataSet*, you can only create a typed *DataSet* when you know the structure of the data with which you will be working.

You choose Generate Dataset from the Data menu to generate a typed *DataSet*. This displays the Generate Dataset dialog box shown in Figure 6.4.

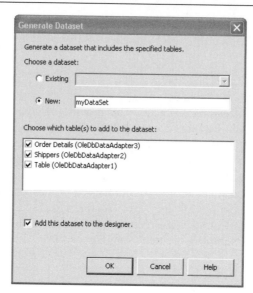

Figure 6.4. The Generate Dataset dialog box.

The window prompts you to choose a new *DataSet* or to regenerate an existing *DataSet*. The available tables and their *DataAdapter* objects are listed in the box. Selecting a check box at the bottom of the dialog box allows you to add an instance of your new *DataSet* class to the designer.

Clicking OK in this dialog box generates an XSD file with the correct schema for your *DataSet* and adds it to your project. If the check box was selected, an instance of a *DataSet* based on this schema is added to the designer. When you fill the new *DataSet*, the table and column names will match the names specified in the schema, and the data will be typed to match the type of data returned by the *Data-Adapter* objects.

To generate a new strongly typed DataSet

1. Create and configure *DataAdapter* objects of the appropriate type to return the data tables you want.

2. From the Data menu, choose Generate Dataset.

Tip   You can also right-click a *DataAdapter* in the designer and choose Generate Dataset, or click Generate Dataset in the Properties window.

1. In the Generate Dataset dialog box, choose New and give your *DataSet* an appropriate name.
2. From the list of available tables, select the tables to be included in your schema. If you want to add an instance of the *DataSet* to the designer, select that check box as well.
3. Click OK. An XSD file is generated and added to the project. If you have chosen to do so, an instance of your new class is also added to the designer.

To populate a strongly typed DataSet with data

Call the *Fill* method of each *DataAdapter* with data you want to add to the *DataSet*, specifying your *DataSet* as the target.

Lesson Summary

- The *Connection* object connects to a database. You can create a *Connection* object by dragging a connection from the Server Explorer to the designer or by creating a new *Connection* object.
- The *Command* object represents a SQL command or a reference to a stored procedure in the database. Three methods for executing database commands are shared by the *OleDbCommand* object and the *SqlCommand* object. They are:
  - *ExecuteNonQuery*
  - *ExecuteScalar*
  - *ExecuteReader*
- Parameters represent values required for the execution of commands represented by *Command* objects. The *OleDbCommand* object uses a question mark (?) as a placeholder for parameters in SQL statements, whereas the *SqlCommand* object uses named parameters.
- *DataReader* objects provide forward-only, read-only, connected data access and require the exclusive use of a data connection.
- *DataReader* objects expose methods that allow retrieval of strongly typed data.
- *DataAdapter* objects facilitate interaction between a database and a *DataSet* by managing the commands required to fill the *DataSet* from the database and update the database from the *DataSet*.
- Typed *DataSet* objects are instances of classes derived from the *DataSet* class that are based on an XML schema and expose strongly typed data and member tables, and columns with friendly names.

Lesson 4: Using DataSet Objects and Updating Data

The *DataSet* is the central component in disconnected data-access architecture. The ADO.NET data architecture uses *DataSet* objects for the in-memory representation of data. *DataSet* objects can be filled by *DataAdapter* objects, or you can create new *DataSet* objects by reading data from XML or a flat-text file. You also can create new *DataSet* objects programmatically by adding new rows. The data held in *DataSet* objects can be bound to and displayed in the user interface, updated, and used to update a database through a *DataAdapter*. In this lesson, you will learn how to create *DataSet* objects programmatically, how to add *DataRelation* objects to your *DataSet* objects, and how to update databases from a *DataSet*.

After this lesson, you will be able to

- Describe how to create a *DataSet* programmatically or by reading a flat file
- Explain how to add *Constraints* and *DataRelation* objects to a *DataSet*
- Explain how to update a database through a *DataAdapter*
- Explain how to execute database transactions
- Design a scheme for handling database update errors

Estimated lesson time: 60 minutes

A *DataSet* is an in-memory representation of data. It is, in essence, a copy of part or all of a database, stored locally on the client machine. Accessing the data contained in a *DataSet* does not require interaction with the database, and changes to the data stored in the *DataSet* have no effect on the database until such time as the database is updated.

In the previous lesson, you learned how to fill a *DataSet* from a *DataAdapter*. Although this is the primary way to create *DataSet* objects, you might need to access data that is stored in some other way, such as in an array of values or in a comma-delimited text file. In this section, you will learn alternative ways of creating and filling *DataSet* objects.

Creating and Filling DataSet Objects Without a DataAdapter

You can create *DataSet* objects programmatically, just as you would create any other object. For example:

Visual Basic .NET

```
Dim myDataSet As New DataSet()
```

Visual C#

```csharp
DataSet myDataSet = new DataSet();
```

The previous code example creates an empty *DataSet*. To populate a *DataSet*, you must first create a new *DataTable* and add it to the Tables collection, as follows:

Visual Basic .NET

```vb
Dim myTable As New DataTable()
myDataSet.Tables.Add(myTable)
```

Visual C#

```csharp
DataTable myTable = new DataTable();
myDataSet.Tables.Add(myTable);
```

Your new *DataSet* now has a single, empty table in its Tables collection. You can add multiple *DataTable* objects to the Tables collection of your *DataSet* programmatically.

Before you add actual data to the *DataSet*, you must create some kind of structure in each of the tables. You can add new columns programmatically by creating the columns and adding them to the Columns collection of the *DataTable*. When creating a new *DataColumn*, you can specify the column name. For example:

Visual Basic .NET

```vb
Dim AccountsColumn As New DataColumn("Accounts")
myDataSet.Tables(0).Columns.Add(AccountsColumn)
```

Visual C#

```csharp
DataColumn AccountsColumn = new DataColumn("Accounts");
myDataSet.Tables[0].Columns.Add(AccountsColumn);
```

You should create a column for each column of data you want to represent. Once all of your columns have been added to the *DataTable*, you can add *DataRows*. A *DataRow* is a collection of members that represents a row of a table in a database. You cannot directly instantiate a *DataRow*. Rather, you must call the *NewRow* method of the *DataTable* to which you are adding the *DataRow*. An example follows:

Visual Basic .NET

```vb
Dim myRow As DataRow
myRow = myDataSet.Tables(0).NewRow()
```

Visual C#

```csharp
DataRow myRow;
myRow = myDataSet.Tables[0].NewRow();
```

Once the new *DataRow* has been created, you can fill it with members from what ever source you desire, be it a collection, an array, or user input. In the following code example, the *DataRow* is populated with the members of a collection of strings:

Visual Basic .NET

```
' This example assumes the existence of an ArrayList object named
' StringCollection
Dim Counter As Integer
For Counter = 0 to StringCollection.Count -1
    myRow.Item(Counter) = StringCollection(Counter)
Next
```

Visual C#

```
// This example assumes the existence of an ArrayList object named
// StringCollection
for (int i = 0; i < StringCollection.Count; i ++)
{
    myRow[i] = StringCollection[i];
}
```

After the *DataRow* has been populated, you can add it to the *Rows* collection of the *DataTable*:

Visual Basic .NET

```
myDataSet.Tables(0).Rows.Add(myRow)
```

Visual C#

```
myDataSet.Tables[0].Rows.Add(myRow);
```

This process is repeated until all the members of the *DataSet* have been created and populated with data.

To create a DataSet programmatically

1. Declare and instantiate the *DataSet*.
2. Declare and instantiate one or more *DataTable* objects and add them to the *Tables* collection of the *DataSet*.
3. In each *DataTable*, declare and instantiate *DataColumn* objects to represent the columns of data in the table and add them to the *Columns* collection of the *DataSet*.
4. Create a new row of data using the *DataTable.NewRow* method.
5. Fill the new row with data.
6. Add the new row to the *Rows* collection of the *DataTable*.
7. Repeat Steps 4 through 6 until all of the data has been added.

Accessing Flat Files

In many legacy applications, data is stored in text files, sometimes called flat files. It might be necessary to read data from these files into an ADO.NET *DataSet*. Using the general scheme described in the previous section, you can read data from text files into a *DataSet* at run time. The *System.IO* namespace facilitates file access, and the methods exposed by the *System.String* class enable parsing the data contained in text files.

When reading data from a text file, you must first determine how the data is stored. Data stored in text files is usually separated by a common character called a delimiter. A delimiter can be a comma (,), a colon (:), a semicolon (;), or any other character. Rows of data are often stored as lines of text with a carriage return signifying the beginning of a new row. The number of entries in each row should correspond to the number of columns in the table.

Once the basic structure of the stored data has been determined, you can begin to construct your *DataSet* around it. You can use the techniques described in the previous section to programmatically construct your *DataSet*. You must create a single *DataTable* for each table of data you want to represent. Next, you should add the appropriate number of columns to your *DataSet*. Sometimes, the data in the file's first row is used for the column names. If this is the case, you should read the first line of the text file and name the columns programmatically.

A text file can be read with the *System.IO.StreamReader* class. This class can open a file and return the characters represented within it. Once the file has been opened, you can use the method of the *System.String* class to separate the data entries and add them to new data rows.

Because every flat file conceivably could have a different format, you must determine the correct procedure for accessing the data on an individual basis. The following code example demonstrates how to access data from a simple, common scenario: data stored in a text file where the rows are represented by lines and the entries are delimited by commas, a common format known as comma-separated values (CSV).

Visual Basic .NET

```
' This example assumes the existence of a text file named myFile.txt
' that contains an undetermined number of rows with seven entries
' in each row. Creates a new DataSet
Dim myDataSet As New DataSet()
' Creates a new DataTable and adds it to the Tables collection
Dim aTable As New DataTable("Table 1")
myDataSet.Tables.Add("Table 1")
' Creates and names seven columns and adds them to Table 1
Dim Counter As Integer
Dim aColumn As DataColumn
For Counter = 0 to 6
```

```
    aColumn = New DataColumn("Column " & Counter.ToString())
    myDataSet.Tables("Table 1").Columns.Add(aColumn)
Next
' Creates the StreamReader to read the file and a string variable to
' hold the output of the StreamReader
Dim myReader As New System.IO.StreamReader("C:\myFile.txt")
Dim mystring As String
' Checks to see if the Reader has reached the end of the stream
While myReader.Peek <> -1
    ' Reads a line of data from the text file
    mystring = myReader.ReadLine
    ' Uses the String.Split method to create an array of strings that
    ' represents each entry in the line. That array is then added as a
    ' new DataRow to Table 1
    myDataSet.Tables("Table 1").Rows.Add(mystring.Split(","c))
End While
```

Visual C#

```csharp
// This example assumes the existence of a text file named myFile.txt
// that contains an undetermined number of rows with seven entries
// in each row. Creates a new DataSet
DataSet myDataSet = new DataSet();
// Creates a new DataTable and adds it to the Tables collection
DataTable aTable = new DataTable("Table 1");
myDataSet.Tables.Add("Table 1");
// Creates and names seven columns and adds them to Table 1
DataColumn aColumn;
for (int counter = 0; counter < 7; counter ++)
{
    aColumn = new DataColumn("Column " + counter.ToString());
    myDataSet.Tables["Table 1"].Columns.Add(aColumn);
}
// Creates the StreamReader to read the file and a string variable to
// hold the output of the StreamReader
System.IO.StreamReader myReader = new
    System.IO.StreamReader("C:\\myFile.txt");
string myString;
// Checks to see if the Reader has reached the end of the stream
while (myReader.Peek() != -1)
{
    // Reads a line of data from the text file
    myString = myReader.ReadLine();
    // Uses the String.Split method to create an array of strings that
    // represents each entry in the line. That array is then added as
    // a new DataRow to Table 1
    myDataSet.Tables["Table 1"].
        Rows.Add(myString.Split(char.Parse(",")));
}
```

DataRelation Objects

A *DataRelation* object represents a relationship between two columns of data in different tables. For example, you might have a Customers table and an Orders table, each of which contains a CustomerID column. Each customer would be listed only once in the Customers table, but might be listed multiple times in the Orders table. The CustomerID in the Orders table specifies which customer in the Customers table placed the order. Thus, the CustomerID field of the Orders table directly refers to a particular row of data in the Customers field and can be used as a key to retrieve that row. Likewise, the CustomerID column in the Customers table can be used to retrieve any relevant rows in the Orders table. This is an example of a *one-to-many* relationship, where a unique identifier in one table might indicate multiple rows in another table. One-to-many is the most common type of data relationship. *DataRelation* objects are used to define these kinds of relationships.

You can use a *DataRelation* object to create this kind of relationship between two tables in a *DataSet*. The *DataRelation* objects of a particular *DataSet* are contained in the *Relations* property of the *DataSet*. A *DataRelation* is created by specifying the name of the *DataRelation*, the parent column, and the child column. In a typed *DataSet*, both columns must contain the same type. An example follows:

Visual Basic .NET

```
' Assumes the existence of two DataColumns, column1 and column2
Dim myRelation As New _
   DataRelation("Data Relation 1", column1, column2)
```

Visual C#

```
// Assumes the existence of two DataColumns, column1 and column2
DataRelation myRelation =
   new DataRelation("Data Relation 1", column1,
   column2);
```

Once you have created the *DataRelation*, you must add it to the *Relations* collection of the *DataSet* before it becomes active. For example:

Visual Basic .NET

```
myDataSet.Relations.Add(myRelation)
```

Visual C#

```
myDataSet.Relations.Add(myRelation);
```

To create a new DataRelation

1. Declare and instantiate a new *DataRelation* object that specifies a parent column and a child column within the same *DataSet*. If you are using a typed *DataSet*, the two columns must contain the same type.

2. Add the new *DataRelation* to the *Relations* collection of the *DataSet*.

Retrieving Related Records

You can use a *DataRelation* to retrieve parent and child rows. Related rows are retrieved by calling the *GetChildRows* or *GetParentRow* method of a *DataRow*. These methods require a valid *DataRelation* object as a parameter. The *GetChild-Rows* method returns an array of rows that have a child relationship as defined by the *DataRelation* object. The *GetParentRow* method is similar, but it returns only a single row that has a parent relationship as defined by the *DataRelation* object. The following code example demonstrates how to call these methods. It assumes two tables called Customers and Orders that are related through a *DataRelation* named *CustomersOrders*. Both tables are contained within a *DataSet* called *myDataSet*.

Visual Basic .NET

```
Dim ChildRows() As DataRow
Dim ParentRow As DataRow
' This returns all rows that have a child relationship to Row 1 of
' the Customers table as defined by the CustomersOrders DataRelation
ChildRows = _
    myDataSet.Tables("Customers").Rows(1).GetChildRows(CustomersOrders)
' This returns the row that has a parent relationship to row 5 of
' the Orders table as defined by the CustomersOrders DataRelation
ParentRow = _
    myDataSet.Tables("Orders").Rows(5).GetParentRow(CustomersOrders)
```

Visual C#

```
DataRow[] ChildRows;
DataRow ParentRow;
// This returns all rows that have a child relationship to Row 1 of
// the Customers table as defined by the CustomersOrders DataRelation
ChildRows =
    myDataSet.Tables["Customers"].Rows[1].GetChildRows(CustomersOrders);
// This returns the row that has a parent relationship to row 5 of
// the Orders table as defined by the CustomersOrders DataRelation
ParentRow =
    myDataSet.Tables["Orders"].Rows[5].GetParentRow(CustomersOrders);
```

Constraints

DataRelation objects work closely with constraints. Constraints define the rules by which data is added to and manipulated in *DataTables*. There are two kinds of constraints: the *UniqueConstraint* and the *ForeignKeyConstraint*.

The *UniqueConstraint* specifies that a column or columns should have no duplicate entries. It is usually used to define a primary key for a table. The *ForeignKeyConstraint* defines the rules used to update child rows when a parent row is edited.

Constraints are created in the following general manner: a constraint of the appropriate type is instantiated and then added to the *Constraints* collection of the table that contains the constrained column.

Constraints are enforced only when the *EnforceConstraints* property of the *DataSet* is set to *true*.

Unique Constraints

Creating a *UniqueConstraint* is relatively easy. The easiest way to create *UniqueConstraint* is to set the *Unique* property of a *DataColumn* to *True* (*true*), like this:

Visual Basic .NET

```
myDataColumn.Unique = True
```

Visual C#

```
myDataColumn.Unique = true;
```

This creates a *UniqueConstraint* behind the scenes and adds it to the *Constraints* collection. You can also explicitly create a new *UniqueConstraint* that specifies a column to be unique and add it to the *Constraints* collection manually, as follows:

Visual Basic .NET

```
Dim myConstraint As New UniqueConstraint(myDataColumn)
myDataTable.Constraints.Add(myConstraint)
```

Visual C#

```
UniqueConstraint myConstraint = new UniqueConstraint(myDataColumn);
myDataTable.Constraints.Add(myConstraint);
```

Unique constraints also can be used to specify a multicolumn key. For example, you might have an Employees table where a FirstName column could contain duplicate entries and a LastName column could contain duplicate entries, but the combination of values in the FirstName and LastName columns must be unique. You can specify an array of columns that must contain a unique combined value with a *UniqueConstraint*. For example:

Visual Basic .NET

```
Dim myColumns(1) As DataColumn
myColumns(0) = EmployeesTable.Columns("FirstName")
myColumns(1) = EmployeesTable.Columns("LastName")
Dim myConstraint As New UniqueConstraint(myColumns)
EmployeesTable.Constraints.Add(myConstraint)
```

Visual C#

```
DataColumn[] myColumns = new DataColumn[2];
myColumns[0] = EmployeesTable.Columns["FirstName"];
myColumns[1] = EmployeesTable.Columns["LastName"];
UniqueConstraint myConstraint = new UniqueConstraint(myColumns);
EmployeesTable.Constraints.Add(myConstraint);
```

Foreign Key Constraints

A *ForeignKeyConstraint* controls how child rows are affected when a parent row i
updated or deleted. You can create a *ForeignKeyConstraint* by specifying a parent
column and a child column. For example:

Visual Basic .NET

```
Dim myConstraint As New _
   ForeignKeyConstraint(CustomersTbl.Columns("CustomerID"), _
   OrdersTbl.Columns("CustomerID"))
```

Visual C#

```
ForeignKeyConstraint myConstraint = new
   ForeignKeyConstraint(CustomersTbl.Columns["CustomerID"],
   OrdersTbl.Columns["CustomerID"]);
```

Like *UniqueConstraints*, *ForeignKeyConstraints* are not active until added to the
Constraints collection of the appropriate table. You should add a *ForeignKeyConstraint* to the *Constraints* collection of the parent table as follows:

Visual Basic .NET

```
CustomersTbl.Constraints.Add(myConstraint)
```

Visual C#

```
CustomersTbl.Constraints.Add(myConstraint);
```

A *ForeignKeyConstraint* contains three rules that can be enforced in regard to a
parent-child relationship:

- *UpdateRule.*   Is enforced whenever a parent row is updated
- *DeleteRule.*   Is enforced whenever a parent row is deleted
- *AcceptRejectRule.*   Is enforced whenever the *AcceptChanges* method of the
  DataTable to which the constraint belongs is called

Each rule is exposed as a property of the constraint and can be set to the values in
Table 6.2.

Table 6.2.   Constraint Property Value Settings

Value	Result
Cascade	Changes in the parent row are cascaded to the child rows.
None	When changes are made to the parent row, there is no effect on the child rows. This can result in child records containing references to invalid parent records.

Table 6.2.   Constraint Property Value Settings

Value	Result
SetDefault	The foreign key in the related child records is set to its default value (as established by the column's *DefaultValue* property).
SetNull	The foreign key in the child table is set to *DBNull*. This setting can result in invalid data in the child table.

Note   The *AcceptRejectRule* can be set only to values of *Cascade* or *None*. *Cascade* is the default value for each of these rules.

Editing and Updating Data

Data contained within a *DataSet* can be manipulated and edited in the client. Values in *DataRow* objects can be changed, new *DataRow* objects can be added to a *DataSet*, and *DataRow* objects can be deleted from a *DataSet*. No changes, however, are reflected in the database until the database is updated through the *DataAdapter*.

Every *DataSet* maintains two versions of itself. The current version, which holds the client copy of the *DataSet* and any changes that have occurred, and the original version, which holds the state the data was in when the *DataSet* was first filled. When the *Update* method of the *DataAdapter* is called, the original values are used to generate the UPDATE, INSERT, and DELETE commands that are used to perform the database update.

Editing Data

Data contained in a *DataSet* can be edited two ways: through data-bound controls in the user interface or programmatically. Changes made through data-bound controls are reflected in the relevant row. Data binding is discussed in greater detail in Lesson 5 of this chapter.

It is also possible to add values to a *DataRow* programmatically by setting the value of the appropriate *DataRow* item. The values represented by the *Item* property (in Visual Basic .NET) or the *indexer* (in Visual C#) correspond to each column of the row. An example follows:

Visual Basic .NET

```
' Because the item is the indexer for the DataRow object,
' you can access the item either by index or by column name
myDataRow(2) = "Splunge"
myDataRow("Customers") = "Winthrop"
```

Visual C#

```
// Because the item is the indexer for the DataRow object, you
// can access the item either by index or by column name
myDataRow[2] = "Splunge";
myDataRow["Customers"] = "Winthrop";
```

Each *DataRow* maintains two distinct states: an unedited version that contains the original values of the *DataRow* and an edited version. You can roll back changes made to the *DataRow* by calling the *RejectChanges* method at any time, as illustrated here:

Visual Basic .NET

```
myDataRow.RejectChanges()
```

Visual C#

```
myDataRow.RejectChanges();
```

If you want to commit any changes to the *DataRow*, you can call the *AcceptChanges* method. This has the effect of overwriting the original version of the *DataRow* with the edited version.

Visual Basic .NET

```
myDataRow.AcceptChanges()
```

Visual C#

```
myDataRow.AcceptChanges();
```

Caution   If you are managing your data access through a *DataAdapter* and intend to update your data source with your edits, you must not accept changes until you have called the *DataAdapter.Update* method. If you call the *AcceptChanges* method before calling the *Update* method, the *DataAdapter* will be unable to refer to the original version of the data and will fail to generate meaningful UPDATE commands.

You can determine the state of your *DataRow* by retrieving the *RowState* property. The *RowState* property can have one of five values, which are shown in Table 6.3.

Table 6.3.   RowState Property Values

RowState Value	Meaning
Unchanged	The row is either in its original form or has not been modified since *AcceptChanges* was called.
Modified	The row has been edited since the last time *AcceptChanges* was called.

Table 6.3.   RowState Property Values

RowState Value	Meaning
Added	The row is newly created and added to a *DataRowCollection*, and *AcceptChanges* has not been called.
Deleted	The row was deleted using the *DataRow.Delete* method.
Detached	The row was created but is not a part of any *DataRowCollection*.

DataTable and *DataSet* objects also expose *RejectChanges* and *AcceptChanges* methods, which reject or accept all of the changes in the *DataTable* or *DataSet*, respectively.

Updating the Database

Once the client copy of the data is ready to be copied back to the database, you can do so by calling the *Update* method of each *DataAdapter*. For example:

Visual Basic .NET

```
myDataAdapter.Update()
myOtherDataAdapter.Update()
```

Visual C#

```
myDataAdapter.Update();
myOtherDataAdapter.Update();
```

This copies the changes in the client copy of the data to the database. You can also specify a particular *DataSet*, *DataTable*, or array of *DataRows* to act as the basis for the update. For example:

Visual Basic .NET

```
myDataAdapter.Update(myDataSet)
myDataAdapter.Update(myDataTable)
myDataAdapter.Update(myDataRows)
```

Visual C#

```
myDataAdapter.Update(myDataSet);
myDataAdapter.Update(myDataTable);
myDataAdapter.Update(myDataRows);
```

Transactions

At times, you might want to execute several updates in such a way that either all succeed or none succeed. A banking program is a common example. Consider a method that debits an account in one table and credits an account in a second table. If the debit operation is successful, but the credit operation fails, the results would be disastrous. Transactions can solve problems of this nature. A transaction is a set of related operations that execute as a unit. Either all are successful or none are.

You initiate a transaction by calling the *BeginTransaction* method of any open *Con nection* object. This method returns a reference to the transaction. You must then assign this transaction to the *Transaction* property of each command involved in the transaction. Next you must execute each command in the transaction. If the result of each command is satisfactory, you can call *Transaction.Commit* to commi the changes to the database. If an error occurs, you can call *Transaction.Rollback* t roll back changes and address the error. The following code example demonstrates executing a transaction with an *OleDbConnection* named *myConnection* and two *OleDbCommand* objects named *Update1* and *Update2*.

Note To use data transactions, your underlying data source must support transac- tions.

Visual Basic .NET

```
' Transactions should be enclosed in a Try...Catch...Finally
' block to catch any exceptions that might occur
Dim myTransaction As System.Data.OleDb.OleDbTransaction
Try
    myConnection.Open()
    ' This creates a new transaction object and assigns it to
    ' myTransaction
    myTransaction = myConnection.BeginTransaction
    ' Adds Update1 and Update2 to the transaction.
    Update1.Transaction = myTransaction
    Update2.Transaction = myTransaction
    ' Executes Update1 and Update2
    Update1.ExecuteNonQuery()
    Update2.ExecuteNonQuery()
    ' If no exceptions occur, commits the transaction
    myTransaction.Commit()
Catch ex As Exception
    ' The transaction is not executed if an exception occurs
    myTransaction.Rollback()
Finally
    ' Whether an exception occurs or not, the connection is then closed
    myConnection.Close()
End Try
```

Visual C#

```
// Transactions should be enclosed in a Try...Catch...Finally
// block to catch any exceptions that might occur
System.Data.OleDb.OleDbTransaction myTransaction = null;
try
{
    myConnection.Open();
    // This creates a new transaction object and assigns it to
    // myTransaction
```

```
    myTransaction = myConnection.BeginTransaction();
    // Adds Update1 and Update2 to the transaction.
    Update1.Transaction = myTransaction;
    Update2.Transaction = myTransaction;
    // Executes Update1 and Update2
    Update1.ExecuteNonQuery();
    Update2.ExecuteNonQuery();
    // If no exceptions occur, commits the transaction
    myTransaction.Commit();
}
catch (Exception ex)
{
    // The transaction is not executed if an exception occurs
    myTransaction.Rollback();
}
finally
{
    // Whether an exception occurs or not, the connection is then
    // closed
    myConnection.Close();
}
```

To execute multiple commands transactionally

1. Open the database connection.
2. Obtain a reference to a transaction by calling the *Connection.BeginTransaction* method.
3. Assign this transaction to the *Transaction* property of each command you want to execute in the transaction.
4. Execute each transaction.
5. Call the *Transaction.Commit* method to commit the transaction.

If you are using *DataAdapter* objects to facilitate interaction with the database, you still can use transactions, although the process is more complicated. To begin, you must create a transaction with the *BeginTransaction* method of an open connection. You must then assign that transaction to the *Transaction* property of the *InsertCommand*, *UpdateCommand*, and *DeleteCommand* of each *DataAdapter* that will be involved in the database update. You can then call the *Update* method of each *DataAdapter* and call the *Commit* or *Rollback* method of the transaction as necessary.

Handling Update Errors

When updating data, errors can occur from a variety of causes. For example, attempting to duplicate a primary key causes an error, as does attempting to update a database that has been modified by another user. Regardless of the source of the error, you must anticipate and plan for possible errors when updating rows.

Both *SqlDataAdapters* and *OledbDataAdapters* provide a *RowUpdated* event that fire after a row update has been attempted but before any exception has been thrown. You can write code in this event to handle any update errors that might occur without going through resource-intensive exception handling blocks.

The *RowUpdated* event provides an instance of *SqlRowUpdatedEventArgs* or *Ole DbRowUpdatedEventArgs*, depending on the type of *DataAdapter* you are using. These event arguments provide information that can be used to determine the erro that occurred and how to proceed. Table 6.4 summarizes some of the properties found in the *SqlRowUpdatedEventArgs* and *OleDbRowUpdatedEventArgs* classes

Table 6.4.   RowUpdatedEventArgs Properties

Property	Description
Command	Represents the command to execute when performing the update
Errors	Returns any errors generated by the data provider when the comman executes
RecordsAffected	Returns the number of records affected by execution of the comman represented by the *Command* property
Row	Returns the row that was updated
Status	Returns the *UpdateStatus* of the command

You can determine if an error occurred by examining the *Status* property of the event arguments in the *RowUpdated* event handler. The *Status* property has four possible settings:

- **Continue.**   Means that the *DataAdapter* is to continue processing rows. If no errors have occurred, the *Status* property has this setting.
- **ErrorsOccurred.**   Indicates that one or more errors occurred while attempting to update this row.
- **SkipAllRemainingRows.**   Indicates that updates for the current row and any remaining rows should be skipped.
- **SkipCurrentRow.**   Indicates that the update for the current row should be skipped, but the rest of the updates should proceed normally.

If an error occurs, the *Status* property will have a value of *ErrorsOccurred*. You can choose to handle the error in the *RowUpdated* event handler by setting the *Status* property to another value. If the *Status* property is set to *SkipCurrentRow*, the *DataAdapter* will skip the update for the row that caused the error and proceed nor mally with the rest of the updates. If the *Status* property is set to *SkipAllRemaining Rows*, the *DataAdapter* will abort the rest of the update. If the *Status* property is set to *Continue*, the *DataAdapter* will ignore the error and continue. Note that this can cause unpredictable results depending on the data source. If the *Status* property remains *ErrorsOccurred*, the exception will be thrown and forwarded to the application's exception handling procedure.

You can use the *Errors* property to obtain information about the error that occurred. The *Errors* property returns the exception that represents the error that occurred.

How you choose to handle database update errors depends largely upon the individual circumstances of your application. In some cases, you might want exceptions to move up to the application exception handling code, and in other cases you might want to handle errors in the *RowUpdated* event handler. The following code example demonstrates a simple scheme for handling update errors in the *RowUpdated* event handler of a *SqlDataAdapter*:

Visual Basic .NET

```
Private Sub myDataAdapter_RowUpdated(ByVal sender As Object, _
   ByVal e As System.Data.SqlClient.SqlRowUpdatedEventArgs) _
   Handles myDataAdapter.RowUpdated
   ' Checks the event arguments Status property to see if an
   ' error occurred
   If e.Status = UpdateStatus.ErrorsOccurred then
      ' Informs the user that an error occurred and gives some
      ' information about it
      MessageBox.Show("An error of type " & e.Errors.ToString() & _
         "occurred. Here is some additional information: " & _
         e.Errors.Message)
      ' Skips the update for this row but proceeds with the rest
      e.Status = UpdateStatus.SkipCurrentRow
   End If
End Sub
```

Visual C#

```
private void myDataAdapter_RowUpdated(object sender,
   System.Data.SqlClient.SqlRowUpdatedEventArgs e)
{
   // Checks the event arguments Status property to see if an
   // error occurred
   if (e.Status == UpdateStatus.ErrorsOccurred)
   {
      // Informs the user that an error occurred and gives some
      // information about it
      MessageBox.Show("An error of type " + e.Errors.ToString() +
         "occurred. Here is some additional information: " +
         e.Errors.Message);
      // Skips the update for this row but proceeds with the rest
      e.Status = UpdateStatus.SkipCurrentRow;
   }
}
```

Lesson Summary

- You can create *DataSet* objects and *DataTable* objects independent of *Data-Adapter* objects and fill them programmatically.

- You can read and access text files using the *System.IO.StreamReader* class and parse them with methods of the *String* class.

- *DataRelation* objects represent parent-child relationships between columns of different tables. You can use *DataRelation* objects to enforce constraints and retrieve related rows of data.

- Constraints are rules that represent how data can be added to particular columns. There are two kinds of constraints: the *UniqueConstraint* and the *ForeignKeyConstraint*.

- A *DataSet* maintains two versions of data: the original version and a version that includes any modifications. When the *Update* method of the *DataAdapter* is called, the original version of the data is compared to the updated version and used to generate the commands needed for the update.

- You can execute multiple commands transactionally by obtaining a *Transaction* object from an open connection and assigning the *Transaction* property of the *Command* objects to that reference. After the commands have executed, all commands included in the transaction can be committed or rolled back.

- You can handle update errors in the *RowUpdated* event handler. You can determine if an error occurred by examining the event argument's *Status* property and you can handle errors by setting the *Status* property to an appropriate value.

Lesson 5: Binding, Viewing, and Filtering Data

Viewing data is a vital part of many applications. Data binding allows you to associate records in a data source with controls on a form, allowing them to be browsed and updated. In this lesson, you will learn how to use ADO.NET to bind data to controls in your application and how to manage the currency of records in your application. You also will learn how to use the *DataView* class to create filterable and sortable views of *DataTables* and how to manage multiple *DataViews* with the *DataViewManager* class.

After this lesson, you will be able to

- Describe the role of a data provider
- Describe the role of a data consumer
- Explain how to bind a property of a data consumer to a data provider
- Describe how currency is managed in Windows Forms
- Explain how to filter and sort data with the *DataView* component
- Describe the role of a *DataViewManager* and how to use one

Estimated lesson time: 45 minutes

Data Binding

Data binding refers to a relationship between a data provider and a data consumer. A data provider is a source for data and is linked to a data consumer, which receives data and processes or displays it. A traditional example of data binding is the relationship between a data-bound control, such as a *TextBox*, and a data source. The control displays the value of the column in the data source to which it is bound at the current row. As the current row changes, the value displayed by the control also changes.

Data Providers

In a data-binding relationship, the data provider is the object that provides data to bound properties and controls.

Note   In this context, the term *data provider* refers to any object that data consumers can be bound to, and does not refer to the data provider suite of components that facilitate disconnected database access.

In the .NET Framework, any object that implements the *IList* interface can be a data provider. This not only includes ADO.NET objects, such as *DataSets*, *Data-Tables*, and *DataColumns*, but also more mundane objects such as arrays or collections. *DataViews*, which are discussed later in this lesson, are a customizable view of data that can act as a data provider.

Data providers also manage the currency of data. In previous data access technologies, a cursor was used to manage data currency. As the cursor moved, the current record changed and bound controls were updated. Because data access in ADO.NET is fundamentally disconnected, there is no concept of a database cursor. Rather, each data source has an associated *CurrencyManager* object that keeps track of the current record. *CurrencyManager* objects are managed through a form's *BindingContext* object. Data currency is discussed in detail later in this lesson.

Data Consumers

The data consumer represents the control with bound properties. In the .NET Framework, you can bind any property of any control to a data source, provided that the property is accessible at run time. For example, you could bind the *Size* property of a control to a database record, or the location, or any other run-time–accessible property of the control.

Data binding has a wide variety of uses. A typical scenario that involves data binding is a data entry form. Several controls, such as *TextBox*, *CheckBox*, *ListBox*, and so on are bound to relevant columns of a *DataSet*. New records are entered manually by typing values for each column into the appropriate controls displayed on the form. When a record is complete, it is added to the *DataSet*, which then can be used to update the database.

There are two types of data binding: simple binding and complex binding. A simple-bound control binds one record at a time to a control. For example, a *Label* control can be simply bound to a column in a *DataTable*. In such a case, it would display the member of that column for the current record. Complex binding, on the other hand, allows multiple records to be bound to a single control. Controls such as *ListBox* or *ComboBox* can be complex bound to a single column in a *DataTable* or *DataView*. At run time, these controls display all members of that column rather than only the current row. Complex-bound controls are usually involved in displaying choices and allowing specific rows of data to be chosen. Controls such as the *DataGrid* are capable of even more complex binding and can be bound to all columns and rows of a particular *DataTable* or *DataView*, or even to a *DataSet*.

Creating a Simple-Bound Control

You can create a simple-bound control through the *DataBindings* property. The *DataBindings* property is an instance of the *ControlBindingsCollection* class that keeps track of and organizes which controls are bound to what data sources. At design time, the *DataBindings* property is displayed as a node in the Properties window. This node expands to list the properties that are most commonly data bound, as shown in Figure 6.5.

Figure 6.5.   Commonly data-bound properties.

To bind one of these properties to a data source, click the box next to it in the DataBindings node and open the resulting drop-down menu. A list of available data providers is displayed. Available *DataSet* objects are displayed as expandable nodes that reveal the available *DataTable* objects. Any *DataView* objects are also listed. Each of these can be expanded to reveal a list of columns provided by the data source. Browse through the list to the appropriate column and select it. This creates the binding for your control.

You can bind any property of your control to a data source. If you want to bind a property that is not listed beneath the DataBindings node, you can click the (Advanced) box under the DataBindings node and click the ellipses (...) in the box to view the Advanced Data Binding dialog box, as shown in Figure 6.6.

Figure 6.6.   The Advanced Data Binding dialog box.

The Advanced Data Binding dialog box lists all of the run-time–available properties of the control and allows you to choose the column to bind to the property.

To bind a property to a data source at design time

1. In the Properties window, expand the DataBindings node.

2. If the property you want to bind to a data source is listed beneath the node,
    choose the appropriate column of data from the drop-down menu.

    If the property you want to bind is not listed, click the ellipses (...) next to the
    (Advanced) box to open the Advanced Data Binding dialog box. Choose the
    property you want to bind, and in the adjacent box, choose the column of data
    to bind to it.

Data Binding at Run Time

At run time, you might want to change the data source a control is bound to. Or, a
design time, you might not know what data source a particular control might be
bound to. In a third scenario, you might want to bind your control to an array or
collection that is not instantiated until run time, in which case you must set the
binding in code. Data binding for a control is managed through the control's *Data
Bindings* property, which is an instance of a *ControlBindingsCollection* object. At
run time, you can add, remove, or clear data binding information by setting the
appropriate member of the *DataBindings* collection.

You can bind a property to a data source by using the *DataBindings.Add* method. This creates a new binding association and adds it to the *DataBindings* collection. The *Add* method takes three parameters: the property name you want to bind, as a string; the data source you want to bind to, as an object; and the data member of the data source to which you want to bind the property. The following code example demonstrates how to bind the *Text* property of a *TextBox* control to the CustomerID column of a table named Customers in a *DataSet* named *DataSet1*:

Visual Basic .NET

```
TextBox1.DataBindings.Add("Text", DataSet1.Customers, "CustomerID")
```

Visual C#

```
TextBox1.DataBindings.Add("Text", DataSet1.Customers, "CustomerID");
```

In some cases, you might be binding to an object that doesn't have multiple data members, such as a collection or array. In this case, you should supply an empty string as the third parameter. The following code example demonstrates how to bind a property of a control to an array:

Visual Basic .NET

```
Dim myStrings(3) As String
myStrings(0) = "A"
myStrings(1) = "String"
myStrings(2) = "Array"
TextBox1.DataBindings.Add("Text", myStrings, "")
```

Visual C#

```
String[] myStrings = new String[3];
myStrings[0] = "A";
myStrings[1] = "String";
myStrings[2] = "Array";
TextBox1.DataBindings.Add("Text", myStrings, "");
```

Similarly, to remove a data binding association from a control, you can call the *DataBindings.Remove* method. This method requires a *Binding* object as a parameter, which you also can access through the *DataBindings* property. The following code example demonstrates how to remove data binding from the *Text* property of a *Label* object:

Visual Basic .NET

```
Label1.DataBindings.Remove(Label1.DataBindings("Text"))
```

Visual C#

```
Label1.DataBindings.Remove(Label1.DataBindings["Text"]);
```

Additionally, you can remove all data bindings from a control by calling the *Data Bindings.Clear* method, as follows:

Visual Basic .NET

```
Label1.DataBindings.Clear()
```

Visual C#

```
Label1.DataBindings.Clear();
```

Data Currency

Navigation of records and updating of data-bound controls is managed in the data layer. Every data source manages navigation with a *CurrencyManager* object.

Note   In this instance, a data source refers to a one- or two-dimensional store of data, such as a *DataTable*, a *DataView*, an array, or a collection. A *DataSet*, which can contain many *DataTables*, can thus expose multiple data sources.

The *CurrencyManager* object keeps track of the current record for a particular data source. There can be multiple data sources in an application at one time, and each data source maintains its own *CurrencyManager*. Because multiple data sources can be represented on a single form at any given time, each form manages the *CurrencyManager* objects associated with those data sources through a central object called the *BindingContext*. The *BindingContext* organizes and exposes the *CurrencyManager* objects associated with each data source. Thus, you can use the *BindingContext* property of each form to manage the position of the current record for each data source. You access a particular currency manager by supplying the *BindingContext* property with the data source object of the *CurrencyManager* you want to retrieve. For example:

Visual Basic .NET

```
Me.BindingContext(DataSet1.Customers)
```

Visual C#

```
this.BindingContext[DataSet1.Customers]
```

When navigating records, the current record can be set by setting the *Position* property for a particular *BindingContext*, as shown in the following code examples:

Visual Basic .NET

```
' The following examples assume a Customers table of a DataSet named
' DataSet1 that is resident on the current Windows form
' Sets the current record to the first record of the data source
Me.BindingContext(DataSet1.Customers).Position = 0
' Advances the current record by one
Me.BindingContext(DataSet1.Customers).Position += 1
' Moves the current record back one
```

```
Me.BindingContext(DataSet1.Customers).Position -= 1
' Sets the current record to the fifth record in the data source
Me.BindingContext(DataSet1.Customers).Position = 4
' Advances to the last record
Me.BindingContext(DataSet1.Customers).Position = _
 DataSet1.Tables("Customers").Rows.Count - 1
```

Visual C#

```
// The following examples assume a Customers table of a DataSet named
// DataSet1 that is resident on the current Windows form
// Sets the current record to the first record of the data source
this.BindingContext[DataSet1.Customers].Position = 0;
// Advances the current record by one
this.BindingContext[DataSet1.Customers].Position ++;
// Moves the current record back one
this.BindingContext[DataSet1.Customers].Position --;
 // Sets the current record to the fifth record in the data source
this.BindingContext[DataSet1.Customers].Position = 4;
// Advances to the last record
this.BindingContext[DataSet1.Customers].Position =
   DataSet1.Tables["Customers"].Rows.Count - 1;
```

To navigate bound data in a Windows Form

Set the *Position* property for the appropriate *BindingContext* member.

Because the .NET Framework will not allow you to set the *Position* property to a value less than zero or greater than the upper bound of the collection, there is no possibility of an error occurring if you attempt to move before or after the end of the records. You might, however, want to incorporate program logic to provide visual cues to users to let them know when the end or beginning of a group of records is reached. The following code example demonstrates how to use the *PositionChanged* event of the *CurrencyManager* to disable back and forward buttons when the end of the record list is reached. As in the previous example, the *CurrencyManager* is accessed through the form's *BindingContext* property.

Visual Basic .NET

```
' This adds a method to handle the PositionChanged event
Public Sub OnPositionChanged(ByVal sender As Object, ByVal e As _
   System.EventArgs)
   ' Checks to see if the CurrencyManager is at the start of the
   ' records
   If Me.BindingContext(DataSet1, "Customers").Position = 0 Then
      ' Disables the back button
      BackButton.Enabled = False
   Else
      ' Enables the back button
      BackButton.Enabled = True
   End If
```

```
' Checks to see if the CurrencyManager is at the end of the records
If Me.BindingContext(DataSet1.Customers).Position = _
   DataSet1.Tables("Customers").Rows.Count -1 Then
   ' Disables the forward button
   ForwardButton.Enabled = False
Else
   ' Enables the forward button
   ForwardButton.Enabled = True
End If
End Sub


' You must also hook up the event to the method that is to handle
' it by adding the following line to the Form's constructor.
AddHandler Me.BindingContext(DataSet1.Customers).PositionChanged, _
   AddressOf Me.OnPositionChanged
```

Visual C#

```
// This adds a method to handle the PositionChanged event
public void OnPositionChanged(object sender, System.EventArgs e)
{
   // Checks to see if the CurrencyManager is at the start of the
   // records
   if (this.BindingContext[DataSet1.Customers].Position == 0)
      // Disables the back button
      BackButton.Enabled = false;
   else
      // Enables the back button
      BackButton.Enabled = true;
   // Checks to see if the CurrencyManager is at the end of the
   // records
   if (this.BindingContext[DataSet1.Customers].Position ==
      DataSet1.Tables["Customers"].Rows.Count -1)
      // Disables the forward button
      ForwardButton.Enabled = false;
   else
      // Enables the forward button
      ForwardButton.Enabled = true;
}


// You must also hook up the event to the method that is to handle
// it by adding the following line to the Form's constructor
this.BindingContext[DataSet1.Customers].PositionChanged += new
   EventHandler(this.OnPositionChanged);
```

Complex Binding

Some controls, such as *ListBox*, *ComboBox*, or *DataGrid* can be bound to more than one record at a time. This is called complex binding. Controls such as these are frequently involved in displaying choices and allow the user to select one of many displayed records. You can create a complex-bound control by setting the *DataSource* property of a control that supports complex binding. For example:

Visual Basic .NET

```
DataGrid1.DataSource = DataSet1.Customers
```

Visual C#

```
DataGrid1.DataSource = DataSet1.Customers;
```

You can also can create this association at design time by setting the *DataSource* property in the Properties window.

Controls such as *ListBox*, *CheckedListBox*, and *ComboBox* can display several records at once, but they can be bound to a single column only. For these controls, it is necessary to set the *DisplayMember* property, which is a string that represents the name of the column to bind to. For example:

Visual Basic .NET

```
ComboBox1.DataSource = DataSet1.Customers
ComboBox1.DisplayMember = "CustomerID"
```

Visual C#

```
ComboBox1.DataSource = DataSet1.Customers;
ComboBox1.DisplayMember = "CustomerID";
```

Filtering and Sorting Data

After you have filled a *DataSet*, you might find it useful to work with a subset of the data in memory. A *DataView* allows you to work with a subset of the data contained in a *DataTable*. You can think of a *DataView* as a filter that sits on top of a *DataTable*. It screens the data in a *DataTable* and presents it to the controls that are bound to it. It provides methods for sorting and filtering the data, and allows you to update the *DataTable* it represents.

Creating a DataView

You can create a new *DataView* by specifying the *DataTable* that it will filter. For example:

Visual Basic .NET

```
Dim myDataView As New DataView(myDataTable)
```

Visual C#

```
DataView myDataView = new DataView(myDataTable);
```

The code in the previous example creates a *DataView* object that represents the data in *myDataTable*. The data in this *DataView* can then be filtered and sorted by setting the *DataView* properties. You also can create a *DataView* that is not associated with any *DataTable*. You will be unable to bind to the *DataView* until you set the *Table* property, which is demonstrated as follows:

Visual Basic .NET

```
Dim myDataView As New DataView()
myDataView.Table = myDataTable
```

Visual C#

```
DataView myDataView = new DataView();
myDataView.Table = myDataTable;
```

You can also create a *DataView* and bind controls to it at design time. To create a *DataView* object at design time, drag a *DataView* object from the Toolbox Data tab to the designer and set the *Table* property in the Properties window. You can then bind controls to this *DataView* by setting the *DataBindings* properties in the Properties window.

Filtering and Sorting in a DataSet

DataView objects allow filtering and sorting of the data they expose. Filter and sort conditions can be changed at run time. When the filter or sort criteria for the *DataView* are changed, any controls bound to the *DataView* are updated with the new data subset.

Data sorting is accomplished by setting the *Sort* property. The *Sort* property takes a string that can be parsed to an expression that describes how to sort the data. Typically, this is the name of a column to sort by. For example:

Visual Basic .NET

```
myDataView.Sort = "CustomerID"
```

Visual C#

```
myDataView.Sort = "CustomerID";
```

You can sort by more than one column. If more than one column is specified, the column names should be separated by a comma. For example:

Visual Basic .NET

```
myDataView.Sort = "State, City"
```

Visual C#

```
myDataView.Sort = "State, City";
```

By default, rows are sorted in ascending order. To sort in descending order, append DESC to each column you want to sort in descending order. An example follows:

Visual Basic .NET

```
' In this example the rows will be sorted by descending state, but
' ascending city, as sorting is ascending unless otherwise marked
myDataView.Sort = "State DESC, City"
```

Visual C#

```
// In this example the rows will be sorted by descending state, but
// ascending city, as sorting is ascending unless otherwise marked
myDataView.Sort = "State DESC, City";
```

You filter data by setting the *RowFilter* property. The *RowFilter* property takes a string that can evaluate to an expression to be used for selecting records. For example, you can select only rows that contain a specific value in one column:

Visual Basic .NET

```
myDataView.RowFilter = "City = 'Seattle'"
```

Visual C#

```
myDataView.RowFilter = "City = 'Seattle'";
```

In general, *RowFilter* expressions must follow SQL WHERE clause syntax. An overview of this syntax is presented in Lesson 2 of this chapter. String literals within the *RowFilter* expression must be enclosed in single quotes ("). If a date is specified, it must be surrounded by the pound (#) symbol.

You can use the logical operators AND, OR, and NOT to build more complex expressions. For instance:

Visual Basic .NET

```
myDataView.RowFilter = "City = 'Seattle' AND State = 'WA'"
myDataView.RowFilter = "City = 'Seattle' OR State = 'WA'"
myDataView.RowFilter = "City = 'Des Moines' AND (NOT State = 'IA')"
```

Visual C#

```
myDataView.RowFilter = "City = 'Seattle' AND State = 'WA'";
myDataView.RowFilter = "City = 'Seattle' OR State = 'WA'";
myDataView.RowFilter = "City = 'Des Moines' AND (NOT State = 'IA')";
```

Arithmetic, concatenation, and relational operators can be used to form *RowFilter* expressions.

Visual Basic .NET

```
myDataView.RowFilter = "Length >= 10 AND Height < 4"
myDataView.RowFilter = "CityState = City + 'WA'"
myDataView.RowFilter = "Price * 1.086 <= 500"
```

Visual C#

```
myDataView.RowFilter = "Length >= 10 AND Height < 4";
myDataView.RowFilter = "CityState = City + 'WA'";
myDataView.RowFilter = "Price * 1.086 <= 500";
```

The IN and LIKE operators allow you to search for specific strings as demonstrated:

Visual Basic .NET

```
myDataView.RowFilter = "City IN ('Seattle', 'Tacoma', 'Blaine')"
' For string comparisons, * is a wildcard that stands for any single
' character, % stands for any number of any characters.
myDataView.RowFilter = "City LIKE 'Seatt%'"
```

Visual C#

```
myDataView.RowFilter = "City IN('Seattle', 'Tacoma', 'Blaine')";
// For string comparisons, * is a wildcard that stands for any single
// character, % stands for any number of any characters.
myDataView.RowFilter = "City LIKE 'Seatt%'";
```

In addition, the *DataView.RowState* property allows you to filter *DataRow* objects based on their state. Table 6.5 summarizes the possible settings for this property.

Table 6.5.   RowState Property Settings

Setting	Description
Unchanged	Displays rows that have not been changed
Added	Displays rows added since the last *DataSet* update
Deleted	Displays rows that have been deleted since the last *DataSet* update
OriginalRows	Original rows, including unchanged and deleted rows
CurrentRows	Current rows, including added, modified, and unchanged rows
ModifiedCurrent	A current version, which is a modified version of original data
ModifiedOriginal	The original version (although it has been modified and is available as *ModifiedCurrent*)

You can set this property to more than one of these values at once. For example, a *RowState* setting of *Added, Deleted* would display only rows that have been either newly added or recently deleted.

Editing Data with a DataView

DataView objects expose three properties that determine whether or not the underlying data represented by the *DataView* can be edited. These properties are summarized in Table 6.6.

Table 6.6.   Data Editing–Related Properties of the DataView Class

Property	Description
AllowDelete	When this property is set to *True* (*true*), the *DataView* allows deletion of rows from the underlying *DataTable*.
AllowEdit	When this property is set to *True* (*true*), the *DataView* allows rows of the underlying *DataTable* to be edited.
AllowNew	When this property is set to *True* (*true*), the *DataView* allows new rows to be added to the underlying *DataTable*.

By default, *DataView* objects are fully editable. If you want to make a read-only *DataView* or a *DataView* that does not allow adding or deleting rows, you can set any or all of the appropriate properties to *False* (*false*).

The DataViewManager class

The *DataViewManager* class is to the *DataSet* what the *DataView* is to the *Data-Table*. An instance of *DataViewManager* is associated with a *DataSet* and creates and manages *DataView* objects for the various tables in that *DataSet* on demand. You create a new *DataViewManager* by specifying a *DataSet* object as a parameter or by setting the *DataSet* property after the *DataViewManager* has been created. For example:

Visual Basic .NET

```
Dim myDataViewManager As New DataViewManager(myDataSet)
Dim myOtherDataViewManager As New DataViewManager
myOtherDataViewManager.DataSet = myOtherDataSet
```

Visual C#

```
DataViewManager myDataViewManager = new DataViewManager(myDataSet);
DataViewManager myOtherDataViewManager = new DataViewManager();
myOtherDataViewManager.DataSet = myOtherDataSet;
```

Once connected to a *DataSet*, *RowFilter*, *Sort*, and other properties can be managed through the *DataViewSettings* collection. The *DataViewSettings* property exposes a collection of *DataView* property values, one for each table in the *DataSet*. These values are set by specifying which table to set *DataView* properties for and then specifying the property itself. For example, the following code sample sets the *RowFilter* property for the *DataView* associated with the Customers table:

Visual Basic .NET

```
myDataViewManager.DataViewSettings("Customers").RowFilter = _
    "State = 'WA'"
```

Visual C#

```
myDataViewManager.DataViewSettings["Customers"].RowFilter =
    "State = 'WA'";
```

When needed, *DataViews* can be retrieved from the *DataViewManager* by using the *CreateDataView* method, which requires a reference to a *DataTable*. An exan ple follows:

Visual Basic .NET

```
Dim myDataView As DataView
myDataView = myDataViewManager.CreateDataView(DataSet1.Tables(0))
```

Visual C#

```
DataView myDataView;
myDataView = myDataViewManager.CreateDataView(DataSet1.Tables[0]);
```

Lesson Summary

- Data binding refers to the relationship between a data provider and a data con sumer. Data providers make data available, and data consumers receive data and display or otherwise process it.

- There are two kinds of data binding: simple binding and complex binding. A simple-bound control binds a single record at a time, whereas a complex-boun control binds all available records at once.

- Data binding for controls is managed through the *DataBindings* property. Any run-time–available property of a control can be bound to a data source.

- *CurrencyManager* objects manage data currency. Every data source has an associated *CurrencyManager* that keeps track of the current record. *Currency-Manager* objects are in turn managed by the *Form.BindingContext* property.

- A *DataView* is an object that is associated with a *DataTable* and provides a fil terable, sortable subset of the data contained by the underlying table.

- The *RowFilter* and *Sort* properties of *DataView* objects are used to specify sort ing and filtering conditions for a particular *DataView* object.

- A *DataViewManager* manages *DataView* objects for an entire *DataSet*. Individ ual *DataView* object properties can be set through the *DataViewSettings* prop erty, and individual *DataView* objects can be retrieved with the *CreateDataView* method.

Lesson 6: Using XML in ADO.NET

XML is the behind-the-scenes foundation of ADO.NET. Data is described in the XML format, and XML representations of *DataSet* objects, *DataTable* objects, and schemas can be written from in-memory representations of data and persisted as XML text files or streams. The *XmlDataDocument* class allows you to work directly with in-memory representations of XML and synchronize them with a *DataSet*. In this lesson, you will learn techniques for using the XML-based methods provided by ADO.NET.

After this lesson, you will be able to

- Explain how to retrieve an *XmlReader* from a *SqlCommand* object
- Describe how to fill a *DataSet* from an XML text file
- Describe how to write the contents of a *DataSet* to an XML stream
- Explain how to write the schema of a *DataSet* to an XML stream
- Describe how to read an XML schema onto a *DataSet*
- Explain how to create an *XmlDataDocument* and synchronize it with a *DataSet*
- Describe how to execute an Extensible Stylesheet Lanaguage Transformation (XSLT) transform on an *XmlDataDocument*

Estimated lesson time: 45 minutes

Retrieving XML from a SQL Server 2000 Database

Microsoft SQL Server 2000 contains built-in support for XML-based data access. Data can be retrieved from the database and read into memory in the XML format. The ADO.NET SQL Data Provider provides built-in support for retrieving XML from the database.

Retrieving an XmlReader with a SqlCommand

The *SqlCommand* class provides a method for retrieving data as XML. The *ExecuteXmlReader* returns an *XmlReader* object that exposes the data returned by the *SqlCommand* as a set of XML rows. The SQL SELECT query executed by the *ExecuteXmlReader* method must contain a *FOR XML* clause. This method is only available with the *SqlCommand* class and can be used only when connecting to SQL Server 2000 or later.

The *XmlReader* class is analogous to the *DataReader* class. It provides read-only, forward-only access to the XML returned by the query. Like the *DataReader*, the *XmlReader* requires the exclusive use of a connection.

The *XmlReader* exposes a *Read* method, similar to the *Read* method of a *Data-Reader*, which allows you to iterate through the nodes that are returned. Like a *DataReader*, the *Read* method advances the *XmlReader* to the next node of the XML stream and returns *false* when the last node is reached. Also like the *Data-Reader*, you must call the *Read* method before the first node is accessible. The following example demonstrates how to retrieve an *XmlReader* and read the XML stream it returns:

Visual Basic .NET

```
' This example assumes the existence of a valid SqlConnection named
' SqlConnection1.
Dim myReader As Xml.XmlReader
Dim mySQLCommand As New SqlClient.SqlCommand( _
    "SELECT * FROM Customers FOR XML AUTO, XMLDATA", SqlConnection1)
SqlConnection1.Open
myReader = mySQLCommand.ExecuteXmlReader()
While myReader.Read()
    ' Writes the content, including markup, of this node and any child
    ' nodes to the Console
    Console.WriteLine(myReader.ReadOuterXml())
End While
myReader.Close
SqlConnection1.Close
```

Visual C#

```
// This example assumes the existence of a valid SqlConnection named
// SqlConnection1.
System.Xml.XmlReader myReader;
SqlCommand mySQLCommand = new SqlCommand(
    "SELECT * FROM Customers FOR XML AUTO, XMLDATA", SqlConnection1);
SqlConnection1.Open();
myReader = mySQLCommand.ExecuteXmlReader();
while (myReader.Read())
{
    // Writes the content, including markup, of this node and any
    // child nodes to the Console
    Console.WriteLine(myReader.ReadOuterXml());
}
myReader.Close();
SqlConnection1.Close();
```

Using XML with DataSets

DataSets provide methods for interacting with data stored as XML. You can load data stored as an XML file or stream into a *DataSet*, or you can write the data represented in a *DataSet* to an XML file or stream. You can create typed *DataSet* objects of a known structure by reading an XML schema into the *DataSet*, and you can create a template for other typed *DataSet*s by writing the structure of the *DataSet* to an XML schema.

Reading XML into a DataSet

You can access XML data stores by using the *DataSet.ReadXml* method. This method allows you to specify an existing XML file or stream, or an existing *XmlReader* or *TextReader* object, and read the schema and data represented therein into a *DataSet*. The following code example demonstrates how to read XML from a file called myData.xml into a new *DataSet*:

Visual Basic .NET

```
Dim myDataSet As New DataSet()
myDataSet.ReadXml("C:\myData.XML")
```

Visual C#

```
DataSet myDataSet = new DataSet();
myDataSet.ReadXml("C:\\myData.XML");
```

If you want to create a *DataSet* with a specified structure but not load any data, you can read an XML schema with the *DataSet.ReadXmlSchema* method. Like the *ReadXml* method, the *ReadXmlSchema* method allows you to specify an existing XML file or stream, or an existing *XmlReader* or *TextReader* object, but *ReadXmlSchema* only reads the structure of the data into the *DataSet*, not the data itself. The following code example demonstrates how to read an XML schema from a file called mySchema.xml:

Visual Basic .NET

```
Dim myDataSet As New DataSet()
myDataSet.ReadXmlSchema("C:\mySchema.XML")
```

Visual C#

```
DataSet myDataSet = new DataSet();
myDataSet.ReadXmlSchema("C:\\mySchema.XML");
```

To read XML into a DataSet

Call the *DataSet.ReadXml* method.

To read an XML schema into a DataSet

Call the *DataSet.ReadXmlSchema* method.

Writing XML from a DataSet

DataSet objects can write the data they contain and the schema that describes the data as XML files. The *DataSet* object provides the *WriteXml* method to facilitate exporting data to an XML format. The *WriteXml* method allows you to specify a file, a stream, or an *XmlWriter* or *TextWriter* object to receive the XML output from the *DataSet*. The following code example demonstrates how to write the contents of a *DataSet* to an XML file called myXml.xml. If the specified file is not present, it is created automatically.

Visual Basic .NET

```
myDataSet.WriteXml("C:\myData.XML")
```

Visual C#

```
myDataSet.WriteXml("C:\\myData.XML");
```

Similarly, you can use the *WriteXmlSchema* method to write the structure of the *DataSet* without writing any of the data. The following code example writes a *DataSet* schema to a file called mySchema.xml:

Visual Basic .NET

```
myDataSet.WriteXmlSchema("C:\mySchema.XML")
```

Visual C#

```
myDataSet.WriteXmlSchema("C:\\mySchema.XML");
```

To write the contents of a DataSet to XML

Call the *DataSet.WriteXml* method.

To write the schema of a DataSet to XML

Call the *DataSet.WriteXmlSchema* method.

Using the XmlDataDocument Class

The *XmlDataDocument* class is designed to work closely with a *DataSet*. An *XmlDataDocument* is an in-memory representation of XML data, just as a *DataSet* is an in-memory representation of relational data. Data loaded into an *XmlDataDocument* can be manipulated using the W3C Document Object Model (DOM), and an *XmlDataDocument* can serve as a source for XSLT.

Note   A comprehensive discussion of XML document manipulation is beyond the scope of this text and would fill several chapters. This section touches upon the basics of working with the *XmlDataDocument* class.

Every *XmlDataDocument* has an associated *DataSet*. You can specify a preexisting *DataSet* when the *XmlDataDocument* is created by supplying a reference to the *DataSet* as a parameter in the constructor. An example follows:

Visual Basic .NET

```
Dim myDocument As New Xml.XmlDataDocument(myDataSet)
```

Visual C#

```
XmlDataDocument myDocument = new XmlDataDocument(myDataSet);
```

This synchronizes the *XmlDataDocument* with the *DataSet*. The data and schema contained in the *DataSet* are read into the *XmlDataDocument* automatically. When changes are made to one, the other is updated.

To create an XmlDataDocument from a preexisting DataSet

Supply a reference to the existing *DataSet* to the *XmlDataDocument* constructor. The data and schema of the *DataSet* will be loaded into the *XmlDataDocument*.

You can also create an *XmlDataDocument* without specifying an existing *DataSet*, as follows:

Visual Basic .NET

```
Dim myDocument As New Xml.XmlDataDocument()
```

Visual C#

```
XmlDataDocument myDocument = new XmlDataDocument();
```

In this case, a new, empty *DataSet* is created and associated with the *XmlDataDocument*. In either case, the *DataSet* associated with a particular *XmlDataDocument* can be retrieved through the *XmlDataDocument.DataSet* property.

You can load XML data into an *XmlDataDocument* from an XML file, an XML stream, an *XmlReader* object, or a *TextReader* that is reading an XML document. To load XML data into the *XmlDataDocument* and synchronize it with its *DataSet*, you must first call the *ReadXmlSchema* method of the *DataSet*, supplying the appropriate XML source for the schema. To be loaded into the *XmlDataDocument*, this schema must match the schema for the XML source, and usually the same XML source is used. Next the *Load* method of the *XmlDataDocument* is used to load the XML data into memory. The following code example demonstrates how to load XML data contained in a file named myXml.xml into an *XmlDataDocument*:

Visual Basic .NET

```
Dim myDocument As New Xml.XmlDataDocument()
myDocument.DataSet.ReadXmlSchema("C:\myXml.xml")
myDocument.Load("C:\myXml.xml")
```

Visual C#

```
XmlDataDocument myDocument = new XmlDataDocument();
myDocument.DataSet.ReadXmlSchema("C:\\myXml.xml");
myDocument.Load("C:\\myXml.xml");
```

To fill an XmlDataDocument from an XML data source

1. Create an instance of an *XmlDataDocument* using the parameterless constructor, as follows:

Visual Basic .NET

```
Dim myDocument As New Xml.XmlDataDocument()
```

Visual C#

```
XmlDataDocument myDocument = new XmlDataDocument();
```

2. Call the *ReadXmlSchema* method of the associated *DataSet* to load the XML schema into the *DataSet*, as follows:

Visual Basic .NET

```
myDocument.DataSet.ReadXmlSchema("C:\myXml.xml")
```

Visual C#

```
myDocument.DataSet.ReadXmlSchema("C:\\myXml.xml");
```

3. Call the *XmlDataDocument.Load* method to load the XML data. For example:

Visual Basic .NET

```
myDocument.Load("C:\myXml.xml")
```

Visual C#

```
myDocument.Load("C:\\myXml.xml");
```

Executing XSLT Transformations

XSLT is designed to facilitate transforming XML data into different formats. For example, an XML document might be converted to HTML for display on a Web page or it might be converted to a different XML format for a specialized application.

The .NET Framework provides the *XslTransform* class to execute XSLT transformations. To execute a transformation, the *XslTransform* class first needs to load a style sheet. This is a file that contains the formatting instructions for the XML data. You use the *XslTransform.Load* method to load the style sheet. The style sheet can be specified as either a URL that points to an XSL file that contains the style definitions or as any of a number of classes that contain an in-memory representation of the style sheet. The following code example declares a new *XslTransform* object and loads a style sheet file called myStyle.xsl:

Visual Basic .NET

```
Dim myTransform as New System.Xml.Xsl.XslTransform()
myTransform.Load("C:\myStyle.xsl")
```

Visual C#

```
Xml.Xsl.XslTransform myTransform = new System.Xml.Xsl.XslTransform();
myTransform.Load("C:\\myStyle.xsl");
```

After the style sheet is loaded, you can execute the transformation on an *XmlData-Document*. The *XslTransform.Transform* method requires three parameters; the first parameter is the object to transform. This can be an *XmlDataDocument* or any object that implements the *IXPathNavigable* interface. The second parameter is an instance of the *System.Xml.Xsl.XsltArgumentList* and is used to contain any parameters required by the style sheet. If the style sheet requires no parameters, you can pass *Nothing* (*null*) to this parameter. The third parameter is the object to which the output must be written. This can be an instance of a *Stream*, a *TextWriter*, or an *XmlWriter*. The following code example demonstrates how to apply a transform to an *XmlDataDocument* named *myDocument* and write the resulting transform to a text file. In this example, no parameters are used, so the second parameter will be *Nothing* (*null*).

Visual Basic .NET

```
' The StreamWriter will receive the output from the transform and
' write it to a text file
Dim myWriter As New System.IO.StreamWriter("myTextFile.txt")
myTransform.Transform(myDocument, Nothing, myWriter)
```

Visual C#

```
// The StreamWriter will receive the output from the transform and
// write it to a text file
System.IO.StreamWriter myWriter = new
    System.IO.StreamWriter("myTextFile.txt");
myTransform.Transform(myDocument, null, myWriter);
```

To execute an XSLT transformation

1. Declare an instance of *System.Xml.Xsl.XslTransform*.
2. Load the XSL style sheet with the *XslTransform.Load* method.
3. Call the *XslTransform.Transform* method to execute the transformation on an *XmlDataDocument*. You must supply any parameters required by the style sheet in the form of an *XsltArgumentList* object.

Lesson Summary

- XML is the behind-the-scenes foundation of ADO.NET. Data can be represented in memory or in a file as XML.

- An instance of an *XmlReader* can be obtained by executing a *SqlCommand* that contains a SELECT command that includes a valid *FOR XML* clause. The *XmlReader* provides connected, read-only, forward-only access to a database in XML format.

- The *DataSet* object can read and write data formatted as XML. The *ReadXml* and *WriteXml* methods are used to load XML into a *DataSet* and write data in XML format, respectively. *DataSets* can also read and write XML schemas with the *ReadSchema* and *WriteSchema* methods.

- The *XmlDataDocument* is an in-memory representation of an XML document that is synchronized with a *DataSet*. Any changes made to the *DataSet* are directly transmitted to the *XmlDataDocument* and vice versa.

- XSLT transforms are used to transform XML from one format to another. Transforms can be executed on an *XmlDataDocument* and require an XSLT style sheet that contains the definition for the transformation.

Lab 6-1: Connecting with a Database

In this lab, you will learn to incorporate different kinds of data access into your application. You will learn to read data from a database with a *DataReader*. You will then learn to use a *DataAdapter* to fill a *DataSet* and use that *DataSet* to update your database. Finally, you will learn to use the XML Designer to create a typed *DataSet*, and use the Data Form Wizard to create a master-detail data form. The solution to this lab is available on the Supplemental Course Materials CD-ROM in the \Labs\Ch06\Lab 6-1\Solution folder.

Before You Begin

Before you begin this lab, you must have the Microsoft Access 2000 data engine or a more recent engine installed on your computer.

Estimated lesson time: 60 minutes

Exercise 6-1.1: Adding Data Access and Using the DataReader

In this exercise, you will learn to use a *DataCommand* to return a *DataReader*, which will allow you to read data directly into your application. You will first create a connection to your database in the Server Explorer.

▶ **To add a new connection to an application**

1. Open Visual Studio .NET. From the File menu, choose New, Project. Choose a Windows Application project in the language of your choice, and click OK.

2. In the Server Explorer, right-click Data Connections and choose Add Connection. The Data Link Properties dialog box appears.

3. On the Provider tab, choose Microsoft Jet 4 OLE DB Provider. This is the data provider for Microsoft Access 2000. Choose Next to proceed to the Connection tab.

4. Under Select or Enter a Database Name, click the ellipses (...) to open the Select Access Database dialog box.

5. Browse to The Virtual Doughnut Shop.mdb, and select it. This file is located in the \Labs\Lab 6-1\Ch06 folder. Click Open to select the database.

6. Click Test Connection to verify that your connection is valid. A message box should appear indicating that the connection succeeded.

Note If you are not notified that your connection succeeded, go back to Step 5 to verify that you selected the correct database.

---

7. Click OK. A new connection is added to the Server Explorer.

▶ **To add and configure a DataCommand**

1. In the Server Explorer, drag the icon representing the database to the form. A new *OleDbConnection* object representing a connection to your database is added to your application.

2. From the Toolbox Data tab, drag an instance of *OleDbCommand* to your form. A new *OleDbCommand* named *OleDbCommand1* (*oleDbCommand1*) is added to your application.

3. Set the properties of *OleDbCommand1* (*oleDbCommand1*) as follows in Table 6.7.

Table 6.7.   Properties of OleDbCommand1 (oleDbCommand1)

Property	Value
Connection	oleDbConnection1
CommandText	SELECT * FROM Customers

Note   If you are asked whether you want to regenerate parameters, choose Yes.

4. From the Windows Forms tab of the Toolbox, drag a button and a ListBox over to your form. Change the *Button1.Text* (*button1.Text*) property to "Click to Execute DataReader". You might have to make the button larger for all the text to be visible.

5. In the designer, double-click Button1 (button1) to open the code editor to the default event handler for the *Button1.Click* (*button1.Click*) event. Add the following code to retrieve a *DataReader* and populate the ListBox:

Visual Basic .NET

```
Dim myReader As Data.OleDb.OleDbDataReader
Dim CustomerString As String
OleDbConnection1.Open()
myReader = OleDbCommand1.ExecuteReader()
While myReader.Read() = True
    ' Retrieves the first and last names from Customers and
    ' concatenates them into a single string
    CustomerString = myReader(1).ToString() & " " & _
        myReader(2).ToString()
    ' adds the string to the ListBox
    ListBox1.Items.Add(CustomerString)
End While
myReader.Close()
OleDbConnection1.Close()
```

Visual C#

```
System.Data.OleDb.OleDbDataReader myReader;
string CustomerString;
oleDbConnection1.Open();
 myReader = oleDbCommand1.ExecuteReader();
while (myReader.Read())
{
    // Retrieves the first and last names from Customers and
    // concatenates them into a single string
    CustomerString = myReader[1].ToString() + " " +
        myReader[2].ToString();
    // adds the string to the ListBox
    listBox1.Items.Add(CustomerString);
}
myReader.Close();
oleDbConnection1.Close();
```

6. Save and test your application. When you click the button, the ListBox should fill with the first and last names of the customers from the Customers table.

Exercise 6-1.2: Retrieving and Updating Data Using DataAdapter Objects and a DataSet

DataReader objects provide rapid database access, but they are read-only and do not allow you to update your data. In this exercise, you will implement two-way data access with a *DataAdapter* and a *DataSet*. You will fill the *DataSet* from the *DataAdapter* objects, bind the *DataSet* to a *DataGrid* control, and perform updates to the database.

▶ **To implement two-way data access**

1. From the Windows Forms tab of the Toolbox, drag a button to the surface of the form. Change the button's *Text* property to **Click here for Exercise 2**. Again, you might need to enlarge the button to make all of the text visible.

2. In the designer, double-click Button2 (button2) to open the default event handler for the *Button2.Click* (*Button2.Click*) event. Add the following code to the method:

Visual Basic .NET

```
Dim Exercise2 As New Form2()
Exercise2.Show()
```

Visual C#

```
Form2 Exercise2 = new Form2();
Exercise2.Show();
```

3. From the File Menu, choose Add New Item. Select Windows Form, and click Open to add a new Windows Form.

4. In the Server Explorer, click the node to the left of your new data connection. The node expands to display its child nodes. Click the node next to the Tables node to display the tables in your database.

5. From the Server Explorer, drag the icons representing the Customers, Items, and Orders tables to the form. An *OleDbDataAdapter* is created for each table, and an *OleDbConnection* is added as well, representing a connection to the database.

6. From the Data tab of the Toolbox, drag a DataSet onto the form. The Add Dataset dialog box opens. Choose Untyped Dataset, and click OK.

7. From the Windows Forms tab of the Toolbox, drag two buttons and a DataGrid to the form. Enlarge the datagrid in the designer so that it is readable and set the properties as shown in Table 6.8.

Table 6.8.   Form2 Control Properties

Property	Value
Button1.Text (button1.Text)	Get Data
Button2.Text (button2.Text)	Update Data
DataGrid1.DataSource (DataGrid1.DataSource)	DataSet1 (dataSet1)

8. In the designer view for Form2, double-click Button1 (button1) to open the code editor to the default event handler for the *Button1.Click (button1.Click)* event. Add the following code to this method:

Visual Basic .NET

```
' Calls the Fill method of each DataAdapter in turn and adds the
' resultant data to the dataset
OleDbDataAdapter1.Fill(DataSet1)
OleDbDataAdapter2.Fill(DataSet1)
OleDbDataAdapter3.Fill(DataSet1)
```

Visual C#

```
// Calls the Fill method of each DataAdapter in turn and adds the
// resultant data to the dataset
oleDbDataAdapter1.Fill(dataSet1);
oleDbDataAdapter2.Fill(dataSet1);
oleDbDataAdapter3.Fill(dataSet1);
```

9. In the designer view for Form2, double-click Button2 (button2) to open the code editor to the default event handler for the *Button2.Click (button2.Click)* event. Add the following code to this method:

Visual Basic .NET

```
' Calls the Update method of each DataAdapter in turn and updates
' any changes
OleDbDataAdapter1.Update(DataSet1)
OleDbDataAdapter2.Update(DataSet1)
OleDbDataAdapter3.Update(DataSet1)
```

Visual C#

```
// Calls the Update method of each DataAdapter in turn and updates
// any changes
oleDbDataAdapter1.Update(dataSet1);
oleDbDataAdapter2.Update(dataSet1);
oleDbDataAdapter3.Update(dataSet1);
```

10. Save and test your application. When the first form opens, click the button labeled Click here for Exercise 2 to open your work from this exercise. When you click the button labeled Get Data, the data will be loaded into the DataGrid.

    You can navigate the DataGrid by expanding the node in the upper-left corner of the DataGrid to display a list of tables. Click on each one to view the contents represented in these tables. You can then make changes in the DataGrid and update the database by clicking the button labeled UpdateDate. Note that changing some values might cause your program to function incorrectly. For example, changing an entry in a primary key field to a value that already exists in that column will cause a runtime exception.

    Note   Although these three tables are related in the database, no relations exist between them in the *DataSet*, so care must be taken when updating with new values. You will add Data Relations to a typed *DataSet* in the next exercise.

Exercise 6-1.3: Creating a Typed DataSet Using the XML Designer

In the preceding exercises, you used *DataReaders* and *DataAdapters* to retrieve untyped data. In this exercise, you will use the XML Designer to create a typed *DataSet* that will serve as a template for data in your application.

▶ **To add a typed DataSet to your application with the XML Designer**

1. From the Project menu, chose Add New Item. The Add New Item dialog opens.

2. In the Add New Item window, choose DataSet, and name your file **dsDough-nut.xsd**. Click Open, and the XML Designer opens.

3. Drag the Customers table from the Server Explorer onto the XML Designer. A new schema element representing the Customers table is added.

4. Drag the Items table and the Orders table to the designer. Note that a new schema element is created for each table.

You can then add *DataRelation* objects to your *DataSet*. You can do this at run tim in your code or at design time using the XML Designer. In the next section, you will use the XML Designer to add *DataRelation* objects to a *DataSet* schema.

▶ **To add DataRelation objects to your schema using the XML Designer**

1. From the Toolbox, drag a Relation object to the XML Designer and drop it on the Orders table schema. This opens the Edit Relation dialog box, as shown in Figure 6.7.

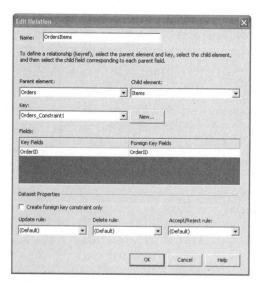

Figure 6.7. The Edit Relation dialog box.

2. In the Edit Relation dialog box, set the properties to the values shown in Table 6.9.

Table 6.9.   Relation Properties

Property	Value
Parent element	Orders
Child element	Items
Key Fields	OrderID
Foreign Key Fields	OrderID

Leave the other boxes at their preset values. Click OK to proceed.

A new *Relation* object is added to the *DataSet* schema.

3. Drag another Relation object onto the Orders table schema, and set the properties shown in Table 6.10 in the Edit Relation dialog box.

Table 6.10.   Data Relation Properties

Property	Value
Parent element	Customers
Child element	Orders
Key Fields	CustomerID
Foreign Key Fields	CustomerID

Leave the other boxes at their preset values. Click OK to proceed.

Another new *Relation* object is added to the *DataSet* schema.

4. From the File menu, choose Save All to save your work.

Exercise 6-1.4: Using the Data Form Wizard

Visual Studio .NET provides a Data Form Wizard that simplifies the task of creating forms to view and update data. In this exercise, you will use the Data Form
Wizard to create two master-detail forms that will be used to view and update data
in the database.

▶ **To create the master-detail data forms**

1. From the Project menu, choose Add New Item. The Add New Item dialog box
   appears.

2. Select the Data Form Wizard, and name the new form **CustomersOrders**.
   Click Open to continue. The Data Form Wizard begins.

3. Click Next to proceed.

4. Choose the *DataSet* you want to use as the basis for your form. You have the
   option of creating a new *DataSet* or using the *DataSet* you created in the previous exercise. Choose *dsDoughnut*, and click Next to continue.

5. The wizard automatically creates the methods necessary to fill and update the
   form unless you specify otherwise. Make sure the Include an Update Button
   check box is selected and leave the other two drop-down boxes at their default
   settings. Click Next to continue.

6. Choose the tables and fields you want to display on this form. From the Master
   or Single table drop-down menu, choose Customers. In the Detail table drop-
   down menu, choose Orders. Note that the fields represented in these tables
   appear in the list beneath the drop-down menu, allowing you to edit the fields
   included on the form. Verify that all fields are selected in each list, and click
   Next to continue.

7. The final page allows you to choose your display style. You can choose to dis
   play the master records in a DataGrid or in individual controls. If you choose t
   display your records in individual controls, you can add additional navigation
   controls through the Data Form Wizard as well. Choose Single record in individual controls for the display style, verify that all additional controls are
   selected, and click Finish to complete the CustomersOrders data form.

8. Repeat Steps 1 through 7, specifying Orders as the Master table and Items as
   the detail table. Name this form **OrdersItems**.

9. In the Solution Explorer, right-click Form2 and choose View Designer. The
   designer for Form2 opens.

10. From the Toolbox, drag two buttons onto the form. Name the buttons **btnView**
    Customers and **btnViewOrders**, and change their text properties to View Cu
    tomers and View Orders, respectively. You might need to rescale Form2 or the
    other components to make everything fit and be easily readable.

11. Double-click btnViewCustomers to open the *btnViewCustomers.Click* event
    handler. Add the following lines of code to this method:

Visual Basic .NET

```
Dim myCustomersOrders As New CustomersOrders()
myCustomersOrders.Show()
```

Visual C#

```
CustomersOrders myCustomersOrders = new CustomersOrders();
myCustomersOrders.Show();
```

12. Create a similar method to display the OrdersItems form when btnViewOrders
    is clicked.

13. Save and build your project.

▶ **Connecting the data form to the database**

The Data Form Wizard creates a skeleton data access form for your application and
adds logic to facilitate navigation of records, but you must still fill your *DataSet*
with data to be able to browse your database. In this section, you will add data
adapters to your forms that will manage filling the *DataSet* and updating the database.

1. In the Solution Explorer, right-click CustomersOrders and choose View
   Designer. The designer opens.

2. From the Server Explorer, drag the Customers table onto the designer. A new
   OleDbDataConnection and *OleDbDataAdapter* are added to your form.

3. From the Server Explorer, drag the Orders table and the Items table onto the
   designer. Note that a new *OleDbDataAdapter* is added for each table, but a new
   connection is not added.

4. Rename the controls as in Table 6.11.

Table 6.11.   Data Object Names

Old Name	New Name
OleDbDataConnection1 (oleDbDataConnection1)	dcDoughnut
OleDbDataAdapter1 (oleDbDataAdapter1)	daCustomers
OleDbDataAdapter2 (oleDbDataAdapter2)	daOrders
OleDbDataAdapter3 (oleDbDataAdapter3)	daItems

5. In the designer, double-click the Load button to open the *btnLoad.Click* event handler. Insert the following code to fill the *DataSet*:

Visual Basic .NET

```
' The data adapters fill the instance of the dsDoughnut dataset that
' was added by the data form wizard
daCustomers.Fill(objdsDoughnut)
daOrders.Fill(objdsDoughnut)
daItems.Fill(objdsDoughnut)
```

Visual C#

```
// The data adapters fill the instance of the dsDoughnut dataset that
// was added by the data form wizard
daCustomers.Fill(objdsDoughnut);
daOrders.Fill(objdsDoughnut);
daItems.Fill(objdsDoughnut);
```

6. In the Solution Explorer, right-click CustomersOrders and choose View Designer. The designer opens. Double-click the Update button to open the *btn-Update.Click* event handler. Insert the following code:

Visual Basic .NET

```
' The data adapters update the database with the current records
daCustomers.Update(objdsDoughnut)
daOrders.Update(objdsDoughnut)
daItems.Update(objdsDoughnut)
```

Visual C#

```
// The data adapters update the database with the current records
daCustomers.Update(objdsDoughnut);
daOrders.Update(objdsDoughnut);
daItems.Update(objdsDoughnut);
```

7. Repeat Steps 1 through 6 for the OrdersItems pages.

8. Save and test your work.

Lab 6-2: Connecting with an XML Data Store

The ADO .NET data adapters provide you with the tools necessary to interact with all kinds of relational databases. Sometimes, however, you might find it necessary to work with data stored in other formats. In this lab, you will connect to and interact with data stored in an XML file. You will create a typed dataset from a preexisting schema, and then load data from an XML file into that dataset and browse the data.

Before You Begin

There are no prerequisites to completing this lab.

Estimated lesson time: 45 minutes

Exercise 6-2.1: Accessing the XML Data Store

In this exercise, you will access data stores in an XML file. You will create a typed *DataSet* from a pre-existing schema definition, build a simple interface to view the data, and load the data from the XML file into the dataset.

▶ **To access an XML Data Store**

1. If you haven't already done so, copy the Northwind.xml and Dataset1.xsd files from the Supplemental Course Materials CD-ROM to your hard drive. The Northwind.xml file is an XML representation of the Microsoft Northwind sample database, a sample database included with Microsoft Access and Microsoft SQL Server. The Dataset1.xsd file is a representation of the schema of this database, including the relationships between the data.

2. With Visual Studio .NET, create a new Windows Forms.

3. From the Project menu, choose Add Existing Item. In the Add Existing Item dialog box, browse to Dataset1.xsd on your hard drive, and select it to add it to your project.

   Note Visual C# users must set the file type to All Files in the Type of File dropdown list box.

4. In Solution Explorer, double-click Dataset1.xsd to open the schema in Schema View. Examine the tables and relations represented by the schema. Note that the schema contains no actual data. Rather, it describes the types and relations of the data contained by the dataset.

5. In the Schema View, right-click the background and choose Generate Dataset to generate the typed dataset for your application.

6. In Solution Explorer, right-click Form1 and choose View Designer. The designer for Form1 opens.

7. From the Toolbox, drag a DataGrid control and two Button controls to the designer surface. Set the properties for the Button controls as shown in Table 6.12.

Table 6.12.   Button Properties

Button	Text Property	Name Property
Button1	Load Records	btnLoad
Button2	Save Records	btnSave

8. In the designer, double-click Form1 to open the *Form1.Load* event handler. Outside of the method declaration, add the following line of code:

Visual Basic .NET

```
Dim myDataset As New DataSet1()
```

Visual C#

```
DataSet1 myDataset = new DataSet1();
```

9. Within the *Form1.Load* event handler, add the following line of code:

Visual Basic .NET

```
DataGrid1.DataSource = myDataset
```

Visual C#

```
dataGrid1.DataSource = myDataset;
```

10. In Solution Explorer, right-click Form1 and choose View Designer to return to the designer. Double-click btnLoad to open the *btnLoad.Click* event handler and add the following code:

Visual Basic .NET

```
' In this example, <path> is a string representing the physical path
' to the Northwind.XML file on your hard drive.
myDataset.ReadXml(<path>)
```

Visual C#

```
// In this example, <path> is a string representing the physical path
// to the Northwind.XML file on your hard drive.
myDataset.ReadXml(<path>);
```

Note   In this example, *<path>* stands for a string that represents the physical path to the Northwind.xml file. Thus, if the Northwind.xml file were located in your root directory, you would replace *<path>* with *C:\Northwind.xml* for Visual Basic .NET and *C:\\Northwind.xml* for Visual C#.

---

11. In Solution Explorer, right-click Form1 and choose view designer to return to the designer. Double-click btnSave to open the *btnSave.Click* event handler and add the following code:

Visual Basic .NET

```
' In this example, <path> is a string representing the physical path
' to the Northwind.XML file on your hard drive.
myDataset.WriteXml(<path>)
```

Visual C#

```
// In this example, <path> is a string representing the physical path
// to the Northwind.XML file on your hard drive.
myDataset.WriteXml(<path>);
```

Note As in the previous example, *<path>* stands for a string that represents the physical path to the Northwind.xml file. Thus, if the Northwind.xml file were located in your root directory, you would replace *<path>* with *C:\North-wind.xml* for Visual Basic .NET and *C:\\Northwind.xml* for Visual C#.

12. Press F5 to build and test your application. Use the DataGrid to browse the data in the XML file and make changes. Save any changes you make and close the application. Press F5 to restart the application. Note that changes you made have been written to the XML file.

Review

The following questions are intended to reinforce key concepts and information presented in this chapter. If you are unable to answer a question, return to the appropriate lesson and review, then try the question again. Answers to the questions can be found in Appendix A.

1. What are the major components of a data provider, and what function does each fulfill?

2. Briefly contrast connected and disconnected data access in ADO.NET.

3. What are the four major parts of a SQL SELECT statement? Briefly describe each one.

4. In Visual Basic .NET or Visual C# programming, when would you use Structured Query Language (SQL)? How are SQL statements executed?

5. What are the three possible settings for the *CommandType* property of a *SqlCommand* object or an *OleDbCommand* object, and what does each mean?

6. How could you execute DDL commands, such as ALTER or CREATE TABLE, against a database using ADO.NET?

7. Briefly discuss the advantages and disadvantages of using typed *DataSet* objects.

8. How can you manage data currency on a form with several bound controls?

9. Describe how to use a *DataView* to filter or sort data.

10. Briefly describe an *XmlDataDocument* and how it relates to a *DataSet*.

11. What is meant by a SQL injection attack? How can you prevent one from occurring in your application?

12. How can you read XML data into a Dataset? How would you write data in a Dataset to an XML file? How would you retrieve a string representation of the XML contained within a Dataset? Describe each in general terms.

C H A P T E R   7

Creating Controls Using the .NET Framework

About This Chapter

This chapter describes how to create controls in the Microsoft .NET Framework. You will learn how to create a user control, a custom control, and an inherited control. Additionally, you will learn how to use the GDI+ graphics interface, as exposed through the *System.Drawing* namespace, and handle common tasks associated with controls.

Before You Begin

To complete the lessons in this chapter, you must have completed Chapters 1 through 5.

Lesson 1: Using GDI+

Microsoft Windows is a graphical interface. Users interact with applications through windows, which are graphical representations of application data and options. To take advantage of the rich user experience that Windows offers, you should design applications so that they expose their functionality to the user graph ically. Although the .NET Framework provides a wide array of graphical controls and methods that allow you to create fully visual applications, you might want to render your own graphic content or create a custom appearance for a control. To do so, and also to take full advantage of the features afforded by the Windows operat ing system, you must learn to use the Graphic Device Interface (GDI). In the .NET Framework, this interface is fully managed and is referred to as GDI+. Classes in the .NET Framework that expose the GDI+ functionality are found in the *System.Drawing* namespace and associated namespaces.

After this lesson, you will be able to

- Describe how to create and use a *Graphics* object
- Explain how to use pens, brushes, and colors
- Describe how to draw an outlined shape and a filled shape
- Describe how to render text
- Describe how to create a *GraphicsPath* and a *Region*

Estimated lesson time: 40 minutes

GDI+ is the name given to the .NET Framework managed implementation of the GDI, which is used to display graphical information on the computer screen. This interface is wrapped into six namespaces, broken down by functionality.

The System.Drawing Namespaces

The *System.Drawing* namespaces expose vast functionality. Although an exhaus tive dissection of these namespaces is beyond the scope of this book, this lesson will familiarize you with the techniques for accessing the classes and methods they contain. The general functions of the classes contained in the namespaces are sum marized in Table 7.1.

Table 7.1.   The System.Drawing Namespaces

Namespace	Contains
System.Drawing	Most of the classes involved in rendering graphical content to the screen. This is the primary namespace used for graphics programming.
System.Drawing.Design	Classes that provide additional functionality for design-time graphics operations.
System.Drawing.Drawing2D	Classes that render advanced visual effects.
System.Drawing.Imaging	Classes that allow advanced manipulation of image files.
System.Drawing.Printing	Classes that facilitate printing content.
System.Drawing.Text	Classes that facilitate advanced manipulation of fonts.

Almost all the classes that you need to render graphics are provided in the *System.Drawing* namespace. For advanced rendering, you also might need classes in the *System.Drawing.2D* namespace, and to enable printing, you will need classes in the *System.Drawing.Printing* namespace.

The Graphics Object

The *Graphics* object, located in the *System.Drawing* namespace, is the principal object used to render graphics. A *Graphics* object represents the drawing surface of a visual element, such as a form, a control, or an *Image* object. Thus, a form has an associated *Graphics* object that is used to draw inside the form; a control has an associated *Graphics* object that is used to draw inside the control, and so on. The *Graphics* object does the actual rendering of visual elements.

Because each *Graphics* object must be associated with a visual element, you cannot directly instantiate one with a call to the constructor. Instead, you must create a *Graphics* object directly from the visual element. Classes that inherit from *Control* (including *Form*) expose a *CreateGraphics* method that allows you to get a reference to the *Graphics* object associated with that control. The following code example demonstrates how to access the *Graphics* object of a *Form* named *myForm*:

Visual Basic .NET

```
Dim myGraphics As System.Drawing.Graphics
myGraphics = myForm.CreateGraphics()
```

Visual C#

```
System.Drawing.Graphics myGraphics;
myGraphics = myForm.CreateGraphics();
```

The *Graphics* object thus created can then be used to render graphics on that form

If you are working with images, you can use the *Graphics.FromImage* method to create a *Graphics* object associated with a particular *Image*. This method is a static method, so you do not need an active reference to a *Graphics* object to call it. The *Image* object can be any object that inherits from the *Image* class, such as an instance of *Bitmap*. The following code example demonstrates how to create a *Bitmap* object from a file and then create an associated *Graphics* object:

Visual Basic .NET

```
Dim myImage As New Bitmap("C:\myImage.bmp")
Dim myGraphics As System.Drawing.Graphics
myGraphics = Graphics.FromImage(myImage)
```

Visual C#

```
Bitmap myImage = new Bitmap("C:\\myImage.bmp");
System.Drawing.Graphics myGraphics;
myGraphics = Graphics.FromImage(myImage);
```

Note that the *Image* does not have to be visible to create a *Graphics* object or perform manipulations with it.

Coordinates

Rendering takes place on the screen in the region set by the bounds of the control. This region is measured in two-dimensional coordinates consisting of x and y values. By default, the origin of the coordinate system for each control is the upper-left corner, which has coordinates of (0,0). The coordinates are measured in screen pixels. The *System.Drawing* namespace contains a variety of structures used to describe locations or regions within the coordinate system. These structures are summarized in Table 7.2.

Table 7.2.   Coordinate and Shape Structures

Structure	Description
Point	Represents a single point with *Integer* (*int*) values of x and y
PointF	Represents a single point with *Single* (*float*) values of x and y
Size	Represents a rectangular size consisting of paired *Height* and *Width* values as integers
SizeF	A rectangular size consisting of a pair of *Single* (*float*) values, representing *Height* and *Width*
Rectangle	A representation of a rectangular region of the drawing surface with *Top*, *Bottom*, *Left*, and *Right* edges specified by *Integer* (*int*) values
RectangleF	A representation of a rectangular region of the drawing surface with *Top*, *Bottom*, *Left*, and *Right* edges specified by *Single* (*float*) values

As Table 7.2 suggests, there are two flavors of structure. Some structures take *Integer* values while others take floating-point values. *Integer* types, such as *Point*, *Size*, and *Rectangle*, can be implicitly converted to their floating-point counterparts. To convert a floating-point type to an integer type, however, you must explicitly convert each coordinate from the floating-point type to the integer type. For example:

Visual Basic .NET

```
Dim myPoint As Point
Dim myPointF As New PointF(13.5,33.21)
myPoint = New Point(CInt(myPointF.X), CInt(myPointF.Y))
```

Visual C#

```
Point myPoint;
PointF myPointF = new PointF(13.5F,33.21F);
myPoint = new Point((int)myPointF.X, (int)myPointF.Y);
```

It is important to note the relationship between the *Size* structures and the *Rectangle* structures. Although both denote a rectangular region of the drawing surface, *Size* structures indicate only the size of a rectangle and do not specify position. *Rectangle* structures, on the other hand, indicate the actual position of a specific rectangle on the drawing surface. You can create a *Rectangle* by supplying a *Size* plus a *Point* that serves as the upper-left corner of the *Rectangle* on the drawing surface. For example:

Visual Basic .NET

```
Dim myOrigin As New Point(10, 10)
Dim mySize As New Size(20, 20)
' Creates a 20 by 20 Rectangle with Point(10,10) as the upper
' left corner
Dim myRectangle As New Rectangle(myOrigin, mySize)
```

Visual C#

```
Point myOrigin = new Point(10, 10);
Size mySize = new Size(20, 20);
// Creates a 20 by 20 Rectangle with Point(10,10) as the upper
// left corner
Rectangle myRectangle = new Rectangle(myOrigin, mySize);
```

Drawing Shapes

The *Graphics* object encapsulates a variety of methods for rendering simple and complex shapes to the screen. These methods come in two general varieties. Those that begin with *Draw* are used to draw line structures, such as lines, arcs, and outlines of shapes; those that begin with *Fill* are used to render solid shapes, such as filled rectangles, ellipses, or polygons. These methods are summarized in Tables 7.3 and 7.4.

Table 7.3.   Methods for Drawing Line Structures

Method	Description
DrawArc	Draws an arc representing a portion of an ellipse
DrawBezier	Draws a Bezier spline
DrawBeziers	Draws a series of Bezier splines
DrawClosedCurve	Draws a closed curve through a series of points
DrawCurve	Draws an open curve through a series of points
DrawEllipse	Draws an ellipse defined by a bounding rectangle
DrawLine	Draws a line connecting two points
DrawLines	Draws a series of lines connecting an array of points
DrawPath	Draws a specified GraphicsPath object representing a complex shape
DrawPie	Draws a pie shape representing a slice of an ellipse
DrawPolygon	Draws a polygon created from a specified series of points
DrawRectangle	Draws a rectangle
DrawRectangles	Draws a series of rectangles

Table 7.4.   Methods for Rendering Filled Shapes

Method	Description
FillClosedCurve	Renders a filled closed curve specified by an array of points
FillEllipse	Renders a filled ellipse
FillPath	Renders a filled GraphicsPath object representing a complex shape
FillPie	Renders a filled pie shape representing a slice of an ellipse
FillPolygon	Renders a filled polygon specified by an array of points
FillRectangle	Renders a filled rectangle
FillRectangles	Renders a series of filled rectangles
FillRegion	Renders a filled Region object that usually corresponds to a complex shape

Each of these methods takes a different set of parameters that specify the coordinate points and location of the shapes to be drawn. Each method also requires an object to actually perform the rendering. For line structures, this object is a *Pen*. For filled shapes, the required object is a *Brush*.

Color, Brushes, and Pens

Color, brushes, and pens are used to determine how a graphical image will render. Pens render lines and arcs, brushes render filled shapes, and color specifies the color to display.

Color

The *Color* structure, which represents a single color, is found in the *System.Drawing* namespace. Individual colors are derived from four values: Alpha, which represents transparency, plus Red, Green, and Blue. Each of these parameters can have a range from 0 to 255. You can create new colors by specifying values with the *Color.FromArgb* method, like this:

Visual Basic .NET

```
Dim myColor As Color
myColor = Color.FromArgb(128, 255, 12, 43)
```

Visual C#

```
Color myColor;
myColor = Color.FromArgb(128, 255, 12, 43);
```

If you are working solely with opaque colors, you can omit the Alpha parameter and specify only Red, Green, and Blue values, as follows:

Visual Basic .NET

```
Dim myColor As Color
myColor = Color.FromArgb(255, 12, 43)
```

Visual C#

```
Color myColor;
myColor = Color.FromArgb(255, 12, 43);
```

You can also specify one of the named colors in the .NET Framework. These colors are provided to allow easy reference to known colors. The following code demonstrates an example:

Visual Basic .NET

```
Dim myColor As Color
myColor = Color.Tomato
```

Visual C#

```
Color myColor;
myColor = Color.Tomato;
```

Brushes

Brushes are used to render filled shapes. All brushes derive from the abstract base class *Brush* and provide different implementations of objects used to render filled objects in different styles. The different types of brushes and the namespaces in which they can be found are summarized in Table 7.5.

Table 7.5.   Types of Brushes

Type	Namespace	Description
SolidBrush	*System.Drawing*	A brush that uses a single, solid color
TextureBrush	*System.Drawing*	A brush that fills closed objects with an image
HatchBrush	*System.Drawing.Drawing2D*	A brush that paints using a hatched pattern
LinearGradientBrush	*System.Drawing.Drawing2D*	A brush that blends two colors along a gradient
PathGradientBrush	*System.Drawing.Drawing2D*	A brush that renders complex gradient effects

Creating a *SolidBrush* is as simple as specifying the color, as shown here:

Visual Basic .NET

```
Dim myBrush As New SolidBrush(Color.PapayaWhip)
```

Visual C#

```
SolidBrush myBrush = new SolidBrush(Color.PapayaWhip);
```

Other brushes have more complex constructors and require additional parameters. For example, a *TextureBrush* requires an *Image* object. A *LinearGradientBrush* requires two colors and a variety of other parameters, depending on which constructor is used.

Pens

Pens are used to draw lines and arcs, and they can be used to apply a variety of special effects to line structures. There is only one *Pen* class, and it cannot be inherited. Creating a pen can be as easy as specifying the color, for example:

Visual Basic .NET

```
Dim myPen As New Pen(Color.BlanchedAlmond)
```

Visual C#

```
Pen myPen = new Pen(Color.BlanchedAlmond);
```

This creates a pen with a color of blanched almond and a default width of one. You can also specify other widths in the constructor, as in this example:

Visual Basic .NET

```
Dim myPen As New Pen(Color.Lime, 4)
```

Visual C#

```
Pen myPen = new Pen(Color.Lime, 4);
```

This example creates a pen with a width of four. You can also create a pen from an existing brush. This allows you to create a pen that matches the visual scheme you are using in your interface and is a particularly useful technique if you want to use complex shading or other effects. The following code example demonstrates how to create a pen from a preexisting brush named *myBrush*:

Visual Basic .NET

```
Dim myPen As New Pen(myBrush)
```

Visual C#

```
Pen myPen = new Pen(myBrush);
```

You can also specify a width when creating a pen from a brush.

System Colors, Brushes, and Pens

When designing the user interface for your application, you might want any custom UI components to have the same look and feel as the system that the application will run on. The .NET Framework exposes colors used by the system through the *SystemColors* class. This class contains a set of static members that expose the colors currently used by the system. Thus, you can design custom UI elements with system colors so that at run time they will render using the current system palette. The following code example shows how to access one of the system colors:

Visual Basic .NET

```
Dim myColor As Color = SystemColors.HighlightText
```

Visual C#

```
Color myColor = SystemColors.HighlightText;
```

In addition to the *SystemColors* class, the .NET Framework provides a *SystemPens* class and a *SystemBrushes* class that provide access to default pens and brushes. You can use the members of these classes just as you would use any other *Pen* or *SolidBrush*.

Rendering Simple Shapes

You can use the methods provided by the *Graphics* class to draw a variety of simple shapes. The methods that can be used for these procedures were summarized in Table 7.3.

All of the methods that render line structures require a valid *Pen* object. Likewise, methods for rendering filled shapes require a valid *Brush* object. You also must supply whatever other objects the appropriate method requires. For example, the following code example demonstrates how to render an outlined rectangle with the *DrawRectangle* method:

Visual Basic .NET

```
' Creates the Rectangle object
Dim myRectangle As New Rectangle(0, 0, 30, 20)
' Creates the Graphics object that corresponds to the form
Dim g As Graphics = Me.CreateGraphics()
' Uses a system pen to draw the rectangle
g.DrawRectangle(SystemPens.ControlDark, myRectangle)
' Disposes the Graphics object
g.Dispose()
```

Visual C#

```
// Creates the Rectangle object
Rectangle myRectangle = new Rectangle(0, 0, 30, 20);
// Creates the Graphics object that corresponds to the form
Graphics g = this.CreateGraphics();
// Uses a system pen to draw the rectangle
g.DrawRectangle(SystemPens.ControlDark, myRectangle);
// Disposes the Graphics object
g.Dispose();
```

Because they hold a lot of system resources, you should always call *Dispose* on your *Graphics* objects when you are finished with them. Failure to call *Dispose* can degrade application performance. You also should call *Dispose* on any *Pen* or *Brush* objects you create. The following code example demonstrates how to render a filled ellipse and then properly dispose of the *Brush* and *Graphics* objects:

Visual Basic .NET

```
Dim myBrush As New SolidBrush(Color.MintCream)
Dim g As Graphics = Me.CreateGraphics()
' The ellipse will be inscribed within the rectangle
Dim myRectangle As New Rectangle(0, 0, 30, 20)
g.FillEllipse(myBrush, myRectangle)
' Dispose the Graphics object and the Brush
g.Dispose()
myBrush.Dispose()
```

Visual C#

```
SolidBrush myBrush = new SolidBrush(Color.MintCream);
Graphics g = this.CreateGraphics();
// The ellipse will be inscribed within the rectangle
Rectangle myRectangle = new Rectangle(0, 0, 30, 20);
g.FillEllipse(myBrush, myRectangle);
// Dispose the Graphics object and the Brush
g.Dispose();
myBrush.Dispose();
```

To render a simple shape

1. Create a *Graphics* object that represents the drawing surface on which you want to render.

2. Create any additional objects you might need, such as *Point*, *Rectangle*, *Pen* (for line structures), or *Brush* (for filled shapes).

3. Call the appropriate method of the *Graphics* object.

4. Dispose any *Pen* or *Brush* objects that you created by calling the *Dispose* method of that object.

5. Dispose the *Graphics* object.

Rendering Text

You can use the *Graphics* object to render text by using the *DrawString* method, which renders a string of text on the screen. The text is displayed in a specified font and is rendered using a specified *Brush* object. The method also requires some kind of location in the coordinate system of the drawing surface, such as a *PointF* to designate the upper-left corner. The following code example demonstrates how to render a string with the *Graphics.DrawString* method:

Visual Basic .NET

```
' This example uses the SystemBrush class to supply one of the
' system brushes
Dim g As Graphics = me.CreateGraphics()
Dim myString As String = "Hello World"
Dim myFont As New Font("Times New Roman", 36, FontStyle.Regular)
' The final two parameters are X and Y coordinates
g.DrawString(myString, myFont, SystemBrushes.Highlight, 0, 0)
' Always dispose your Graphics object
g.Dispose()
```

Visual C#

```
// This example uses the SystemBrush class to supply one of the
// system brushes
Graphics g = this.CreateGraphics();
String myString = "Hello World";
Font myFont = new Font("Times New Roman", 36, FontStyle.Regular);
```

```
// The final two parameters are X and Y coordinates
g.DrawString(myString, myFont, SystemBrushes.Highlight, 0, 0);
// Always dispose your Graphics object
g.Dispose();
```

To render text

1. If necessary, create *Font* and *Brush* objects appropriate to the style in which you want to render the string.

2. Obtain a reference to the *Graphics* object associated with the drawing surface on which you want to render the text.

3. Call the *Graphics.DrawString* method, specifying the appropriate *String*, *Font*, *Brush*, and location.

4. Dispose the *Graphics* object by calling *Graphics.Dispose*.

Rendering Complex Shapes

At times, you will find it necessary to render complex shapes. Although simple shapes such as rectangles, ellipses, and polygons have built-in methods to facilitate their rendering, complex shapes require a little more planning. The primary object used for rendering complex shapes is the *GraphicsPath* object. A member of the *System.Drawing.Drawing2D* namespace, the *GraphicsPath* object can describe any kind of closed shape or set of shapes. Thus, you could have a *GraphicsPath* that consists of ellipses, rectangles, and other regular objects, combined with irregular or amorphous shapes.

Creating a GraphicsPath

You create a *GraphicsPath* object by making a call to one of the *GraphicsPath* constructors. The simplest *GraphicsPath* constructor takes no parameters.

Visual Basic .NET

```
Dim myPath As New Drawing2D.GraphicsPath()
```

Visual C#

```
GraphicsPath myPath = new Drawing2D.GraphicsPath();
```

Additionally, you can specify arrays of points and bytes that describe the *Graphics-Path*. The array of points provides coordinates to map the path to, and the array of bytes describes what kind of line passes through the points. To create more readable and maintainable code, you can convert the array of bytes from the *System.Drawing.Drawing2D.PathPointType* enum. The following code example creates a very simple *GraphicsPath*:

Visual Basic .NET

```
' This example assumes Imports System.Drawing.Drawing2D
Dim myPath As New GraphicsPath(New Point() {New Point(1, 1), _
    New Point(32, 54), New Point(33, 5)}, New Byte() _
    {CType(PathPointType.Start, Byte), CType(PathPointType.Line, _
    Byte), CType(PathPointType.Bezier, Byte)})
```

Visual C#

```
// This example assumes using System.Drawing.Drawing2D
GraphicsPath myPath = new GraphicsPath(new Point[] {new Point(1, 1),
    new Point(32, 54), new Point(33, 5)}, new byte[] {
    (byte)PathPointType.Start, (byte)PathPointType.Line,
    (byte)PathPointType.Bezier});
```

Once it is created, you can add figures to the *GraphicsPath*. A figure represents a closed shape including simple shapes, such as ellipses and rectangles, and more complex shapes, such as irregular curves and font characters.

The *GraphicsPath* class contains several methods that allow you to add figures to the path. These are summarized in Table 7.6.

Table 7.6.   Methods for Adding Figures

Method	Description
AddClosedCurve	Adds a closed curve described by an array of points to the *Graphics-Path*
AddEllipse	Adds an ellipse to the *GraphicsPath*
AddPath	Adds a specified instance of *GraphicsPath* to the current path
AddPie	Adds a pie shape to the *GraphicsPath*
AddPolygon	Adds a polygon described by an array of points to the *GraphicsPath*
AddRectangle	Adds a rectangle to the *GraphicsPath*
AddRectangles	Adds an array of rectangles to the *GraphicsPath*
AddString	Adds a graphical representation of a string to the *GraphicsPath*, in the specified font

In addition to directly adding figures to the *GraphicsPath*, you can create figures by adding lines, arcs, and curves. You can begin a figure by calling *Graphics-Path.StartFigure*. After calling this method, you can use methods supplied by the *GraphicsPath* class to add line elements to the figure. Once you have completed your figure, you can call *GraphicsPath.CloseFigure* to close the figure. Doing so causes the last point to be created in a figure to connect automatically with the first one, as the following code example demonstrates:

Visual Basic .NET

```
' This example assumes Imports System.Drawing.Drawing2D
Dim myPath As New GraphicsPath()
myPath.StartFigure()
' Insert code to add line elements to the figure here
myPath.CloseFigure()
```

Visual C#

```
// This example assumes using System.Drawing.Drawing2D
GraphicsPath myPath = new GraphicsPath();
myPath.StartFigure();
// Insert code to add line elements to the figure here
myPath.CloseFigure();
```

If you call *StartFigure* and then call *StartFigure* again without calling *CloseFigure*, the first figure is left open.

Note   When rendered at run time, any open figures close by adding a line between the first and last points to be created in the figure.

Table 7.7 summarizes the *GraphicsPath* methods that add line elements to a figure

Table 7.7. Methods for Adding Line Elements

Method	Description
AddArc	Adds an arc to the current figure
AddBezier	Adds a Bezier curve to the current figure
AddBeziers	Adds a series of connected Bezier curves to the current figure
AddCurve	Adds a curve described by an array of points to the current figure
AddLine	Adds a line to the current figure
AddLines	Adds a series of connected lines to the current figure

To render a complex shape

1. Obtain a reference to the *Graphics* object associated with the drawing surface you want to render on.
2. Create a new instance of the *GraphicsPath* class.
3. Add figures to the *GraphicsPath* using the methods the *GraphicsPath* class provides.
4. Call *Graphics.DrawPath* to draw the outline of the path or *Graphics.FillPath* to draw a filled *GraphicsPath*.
5. Dispose the *Graphics* object.

Lesson Summary

- The *Graphics* object is the principal object used to render graphics. It represents a drawing surface and provides methods for rendering to that drawing surface.

- Pens, brushes, and colors are objects that are used to control how a graphic is rendered to a drawing surface. Pens draw lines, brushes fill shapes, and colors represent colors. You can use *SystemPens*, *SystemBrushes*, and *SystemColors* to maintain a coherent appearance with the rest of the application.

- Simple shapes and text can be rendered using the methods provided by the *Graphics* object.

- Complex shapes should be defined in terms of a *GraphicsPath* object, which exposes a variety of methods to facilitate defining complex shapes. When complete, a *GraphicsPath* object can be rendered by the *Graphics* object.

Lesson 2: Authoring Controls

Windows Forms programming is based on controls. Controls allow you to encapsulate discrete units of functionality and provide a graphical representation of that functionality to the user. The .NET Framework provides a variety of tools and techniques to help you create custom controls for your applications. In this lesson, you will learn about the different types of controls you can create and the tools available to help you create them.

After this lesson, you will be able to

- Describe the different types of user-authored controls
- Explain how each type of user-authored control is created
- Describe how to add properties, methods, and events to your controls
- Describe how to create an inherited control
- Describe how to create a user control
- Describe how to create a custom control

Estimated lesson time: 45 minutes

In the .NET Framework, controls are specialized classes that include code for rendering a graphical interface. There are several possible sources for the controls you use in your applications. The controls included with Microsoft Visual Studio .NET provide a broad range of functionality and allow development of client applications with a rich array of features. You can also purchase controls from third-party developers to use in your applications, or you can use existing ActiveX controls. Third-party controls can provide functionality not found in the .NET Framework set of controls. Additionally, if you need a control with a set of features unavailable in the .NET Framework controls or in the third-party controls, you can create your own controls.

Overview of Control Authoring

All controls in the .NET Framework inherit either directly or indirectly from the base class *Control*. This class provides all the basic, low-level functionality that a control needs. For example, the *Control* class provides logic for handling user input through keyboard and mouse interaction. It provides logic for interacting with Windows. And it further provides a set of properties, methods, and events that are common to all controls. It does not include logic that creates the unique functionality of the control, nor does it contain code for graphically rendering the control.

There are three basic techniques for creating a control. You can

- Inherit from an existing control.
- Inherit from *UserControl*.
- Inherit from *Control*.

Inheriting from an Existing Control

Inheriting from an existing control is the easiest and least time-consuming way to develop a new control. The new control contains all the functionality represented by the base control but can also serve as a base for new functionality. An inherited control also inherits the visual representation of the base control.

You should choose this technique if you need to replicate most or all of the functionality of an existing Windows Forms control but want to add custom functionality as well. You should also use this technique if you want to retain the functionality of an existing Windows Forms control but want to provide a new look and feel.

Most Windows Forms controls can be used as a base class for inheritance unless they are specified as *NotInheritable* (*sealed*). For example, you could create a *TextBox* control with built-in validation or a *PictureBox* control that allows the user to select filters to apply to the images.

You can also use inheritance to create controls that have the same functionality as the base control but have a different appearance, such as a *Button* that is round instead of square. Thus, a control that extends *Button* will look just like a regular *Button*—no additional code is needed to render the new control—but you can implement code to alter its appearance if you want.

You should not inherit from an existing Windows control if you need radically different functionality.

Inheriting from UserControl

Sometimes, a single control does not contain all the functionality you need. For example, you might want a control that you can bind to a data source to display a first name, a last name, and a phone number, each in a separate *TextBox*. Although it is possible to implement this logic on the form itself, it might be more efficient to create a single control that contains multiple text boxes, especially if this configuration is needed in several different applications. Controls that contain multiple Windows Forms controls bound together as a single unit are called *user controls*.

You can create a user control (sometimes called a *composite control*) by inheriting from the *UserControl* class. The *UserControl* class provides a base of functionality that you can build on by adding properties, methods, events, and other controls. The UserControl designer allows you to add other Windows Forms controls to the design surface and create code to implement custom functionality. The result is a user-designed control made up of multiple Windows Forms controls that act as a single coherent unit.

Limited design of the user control visual interface is possible, but most of the visual modifications you can make consist of simply configuring and positioning the constituent controls.

Creating a user control can be relatively simple task or complex, depending on the level of functionality the control must expose. You should consider creating a user control if you need to combine the functionality of multiple existing controls and add custom logic to the unit.

Inheriting from Control

If you require a richer visual interface or functionality that is not achievable with a user control or an inherited control, you can create a custom control. Custom controls derive from *Control*, the base class for all controls. The *Control* class provides a lot of the functionality common to all controls, such as interacting with the mouse and common events, such as *Click*. The *Control* class also provides a set of properties that are useful for controls, such as *Font*, *ForeColor*, *BackColor*, *Visible*, and so on. The *Control* class does not, however, provide any specific control functionality. All control logic specific to the control functionality must be programmed. Additionally, although the *Control* class provides many properties that support a visual depiction, the developer must program all the code for creating the control's visual representation. These steps can be time-consuming. You should consider creating a custom control only when you need a richness of form or functionality that cannot be supplied by an inherited control or a user control.

Adding Members to Controls

You can add properties, methods, fields, and events to your controls in the same manner as you add members to a class. You can create member declarations with any appropriate access level, and the form that hosts the control will be able to call any public members of that control.

Public properties that are added to controls are automatically displayed in the Properties window at design time. Thus they can be edited and configured by any user of your application. If you do not want a property to be displayed in the Properties window, you must mark the property with the *Browsable* attribute and specify *false*. The following code example shows how to mark a property so that it will not be displayed in the Properties window at design time:

Visual Basic .NET

```
<System.ComponentModel.Browsable(False)> _
    Public Property StockNumber() As Integer
' Property Code omitted
End Property
```

Visual C#

```
[System.ComponentModel.Browsable(false)]
public int StockNumber
{
    // Property code omitted
}
```

Creating an Inherited Control

An inherited control contains all the functionality provided by its base class and can serve as a base for new functionality as well. You create an inherited control by specifying a Windows Forms control as the base class for your control. The new control retains the same look and feel as the base control. The following code example demonstrates how to create a control that inherits from *Button*:

Visual Basic .NET

```
Public Class myButton
    Inherits System.Windows.Forms.Button
    ' Additional code omitted
End Class
```

Visual C#

```
public class myButton : System.Windows.Forms.Button
{
    // Additional code omitted
}
```

Adding New Functionality to an Inherited Control

One reason to create an inherited control is to add functionality to an existing Windows Forms control. You can either add new functionality to your control or you can override members exposed by the base class. For example, suppose you wanted to create a text box that only accepts numbers as user input. You might implement this control by overriding the *OnKeyPress* method, as shown in the following code example:

Visual Basic .NET

```
Public Class NumberBox
    Inherits System.Windows.Forms.TextBox
    Protected Overrides Sub OnKeyPress(ByVal e As KeyPressEventArgs)
        If Char.IsNumber(e.KeyChar) = False Then
```

```
        e.Handled = True
      End If
   End Sub
End Class
```

Visual C#

```
public class NumberBox : System.Windows.Forms.TextBox
{
   protected override void OnKeyPress(KeyPressEventArgs e)
   {
      if (char.IsNumber(e.KeyChar) == false)
         e.Handled = true;
   }
}
```

Creating a New Appearance for an Existing Control

Another reason you might create an inherited control is to alter the appearance of an existing Windows Forms class. You can create a new look and feel for an existing control by overriding the *OnPaint* method and providing your own rendering code. If you want to change the shape of the control, you must set the control's *Region* property in the *OnPaint* method. A *Region* is a class that describes a regular or irregular region of the screen—similar to a *GraphicsPath*. A *Region* can be created from a *GraphicsPath*. You can thus create a *GraphicsPath* to represent the shape of your control and then assign the control to a new *Region* based on the *GraphicsPath*. The following code example demonstrates how to create a button that renders as a string of text:

Visual Basic .NET

```
Public Class WowButton
   Inherits System.Windows.Forms.Button
   Protected Overrides Sub OnPaint(ByVal pe As PaintEventArgs)
      Dim myPath As New Drawing2D.GraphicsPath()
      ' This line sets the GraphicsPath to render a 72 point string
      ' in the FontFamily and the FontStyle of the control.
      myPath.AddString("Wow!", Font.FontFamily, Font.Style, 72, New _
         PointF(0, 0), StringFormat.GenericDefault)
      ' Creates a new Region from the GraphicsPath
      Dim myRegion As New Region(myPath)
      ' Assigns the new Region to the Region property of the control
      Me.Region = myRegion
   End Sub
End Class
```

Visual C#

```
public class WowButton : System.Windows.Forms.Button
{
    protected override void OnPaint(PaintEventArgs pe)
    {
        System.Drawing.Drawing2D.GraphicsPath myPath = new
            System.Drawing.Drawing2D.GraphicsPath();
        // This line sets the GraphicsPath to render a 72 point string
        // in the FontFamily and the FontStyle of the control. In C#,
        // you must explicitly convert Font.Style to an int.
        myPath.AddString("Wow!", Font.FontFamily, (int)Font.Style, 72,
            new PointF(0, 0), StringFormat.GenericDefault);
        // Creates a new Region from the GraphicsPath
        Region myRegion = new Region(myPath);
        // Assigns the new Region to the Region property of the control
        this.Region = myRegion;
    }
}
```

Note that the *WowButton* is not just a rectangular button with a transparent background and large text. It is a *Button* shaped like the letters in the word "Wow!" If you want to click it, you must click within the region bounded by those letters. Thus, you can change the shape of common controls to provide custom UI elements.

Note   Some controls, such as *TextBox*, are drawn by the form they exist on, not by the controls themselves. For these controls, the *Paint* event is never raised; thus, custom-rendering code is never called.

To create an inherited control

1. Create a class that inherits the control on which you want to base your control.

2. Add any custom functionality or code to render visual elements.

Creating a User Control

User controls represent a way to combine custom functionality, standard Windows Forms controls, and rapid development. A user control consists of one or more Windows Forms controls bound together in a single unit. The subordinate controls that make up a user control, called *constituent controls*, can be added to the user control designer at design time. You can add a user control to your project by choosing Add User Control from the Project menu. Figure 7.1 shows the UserControl designer with two constituent buttons and a *TextBox*.

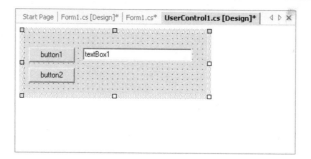

Figure 7.1.   The UserControl designer.

You can write custom functionality to respond to events raised by the constituent controls. For example, suppose you want to create a user control consisting of two constituent *TextBox* controls and a constituent *Label* control, and you want the label to automatically display the sum of the numeric values in each *TextBox* as the values are changed. You could implement this functionality by overriding the *OnKeyPress* method in each constituent *TextBox*, as shown in this example:

Visual Basic .NET

```
' You would also add a similar method for the KeyPress event of
' TextBox2
Private Sub TextBox1_KeyPress(ByVal Sender As Object, ByVal e As _
   KeyPressEventArgs) Handles TextBox1.KeyPress
   ' Verifies that a number was pressed
   If Char.IsNumber(e.KeyChar) = False Then
      e.Handled = True
   End If
   Label1.Text = (Integer.Parse(TextBox1.Text) + _
      Integer.Parse(TextBox2.Text)).ToString()
End Sub
```

Visual C#

```
// You would also add a similar method for the KeyPress event of
// TextBox2
protected override void OnKeyPress(object sender, KeyPressEventArgs e)
   {
   // Verifies that a number was pressed
   if (char.IsNumber(e.KeyChar) == false)
      e.Handled = true;
   Label1.Text = (int.Parse(TextBox1.Text) +
      int.Parse(TextBox2.Text)).ToString();
}
```

When you build and use a user control with Visual Studio .NET 2002, the constituent controls are treated as *Private* (*private*) by default. Thus, there is no way for future developers who might use your constituent controls to alter their properties, such as color, shape, or size. If you want to allow other developers to change the properties of constituent controls, you must selectively expose them through the properties of the user control. For example, consider a user control that contains a *Button* named *Button1*. If you want to expose the *BackColor* property of *Button1*, you do so by wrapping it in a property declaration for your user control, as shown in the following code example:

Visual Basic .NET

```
' This property declaration is in the user control class
Public Property ButtonColor() As Color
    Get
        Return Button1.BackColor
    End Get
    Set(ByVal Value As Color)
        Button1.BackColor = Value
    End Set
End Property
```

Visual C#

```
public Color ButtonColor
{
    get
    {
        return Button1.BackColor;
    }
    set
    {
        Button1.BackColor = value;
    }
}
```

You can also expose a constituent control entirely by changing the *Modifiers* property. This property is only available in the Properties window at design time—it does not exist at run time. The *Modifiers* property can be set to any access level and has the effect of setting the constituent control to that access level.

Note   In Visual Basic .NET 2003, constituent controls are declared by default with *Friend* access, and thus can be accessed by the owning form. In Visual C# 2003, the access level remains *private*.

To create a user control

1. Create a class that derives from the *UserControl* base class.
2. Add Windows Forms controls to the UserControl designer, and configure them appropriately.
3. Expose any constituent control properties.
4. Write any custom functionality for your user control.

Creating a Custom Control

As noted earlier, custom controls provide the highest level of configurability and customization, but they are also the most time-consuming to develop. Because the *Control* class provides no base visual representation, you are obliged to write the code to render the control's visual representation. In cases where a particularly complex visual representation is desired, this can be the most time-intensive part c the control development process.

The process of rendering a control to the drawing surface is called *painting*. Whe the control receives instruction that it needs to be rendered, it raises the *Paint* even This causes any handlers for the *Paint* event to be executed. In the *Control* class, the default handler for the *Paint* event is the *OnPaint* method.

The *OnPaint* method receives a single argument: an instance of *PaintEventArgs*. The *PaintEventArgs* class contains information about the drawing surface availabl to the control. Two notable members of *PaintEventArgs* are *Graphics* and *Clip-Rectangle*.

The *Graphics* member of *PaintEventArgs* is a *Graphics* object that represents the control's drawing surface. This reference to a *Graphics* object is used to render th visual representation of the control. The *ClipRectangle* member is a rectangle tha represents the area available for the control to draw in. When the control is first drawn, the *ClipRectangle* represents the bounds of the entire control. At times, regions of the control might be covered by other controls and portions of the visua representation might be obscured. When the control is redrawn, the *ClipRectangl* only represents the region that needs to be redrawn. Thus, the *ClipRectangle* should not be used to determine the size of the control. Instead, you should use th *Size* property to access the size of a custom control.

By default, coordinates are measured relative to the upper-left corner of the control which is assumed to be point (0,0). Coordinate points are measured in pixels by default. The following code example shows a very simple *OnPaint* method that renders the custom control as a single red ellipse:

Visual Basic .NET

```
' This example assumes Imports System.Drawing
Protected Overrides Sub OnPaint(ByVal pe As PaintEventArgs)
    Dim aBrush As New SolidBrush(Color.Red)
    Dim clientRectangle As New Rectangle(New Point(0,0), Me.Size)
    pe.Graphics.FillEllipse(aBrush, clientRectangle)
End Sub
```

Visual C#

```
// This example assumes using System.Drawing
protected override void OnPaint(PaintEventArgs e)
```

```
{
    Brush aBrush = new SolidBrush(Color.Red);
    Rectangle clientRectangle = new
        Rectangle(new Point(0,0), this.Size);
    e.Graphics.FillEllipse(aBrush, clientRectangle);
}
```

When a control is resized, the *ClipRectangle* is automatically resized but the control is not necessarily redrawn. If you want the control to be redrawn whenever it is resized, you must use the *Control.SetStyle* method to set the *ResizeRedraw* flag to *true*. The call to the *SetStyle* method should be placed in the constructor. The following code example demonstrates how to use the *SetStyle* method:

Visual Basic .NET

```
SetStyle(ControlStyles.ResizeRedraw, True)
```

Visual C#

```
SetStyle(ControlStyles.ResizeRedraw, true);
```

You can manually cause the control to redraw at any time by calling the *Refresh* method, as follows:

Visual Basic .NET

```
Refresh()
```

Visual C#

```
Refresh();
```

To create a custom control

1. Create a class that derives from the *Control* base class.
2. Add code to render the control in the *OnPaint* method.
3. Add any custom functionality to your control.

Lesson Summary

- All controls inherit either directly or indirectly from the base class *Control*. The *Control* class provides keyboard and pointer functionality as well as a set of common control properties.

- There are three primary approaches to control authoring: inheriting from an existing control, creating a user control, and creating a custom control.

- You can create an inherited control by inheriting from an existing Windows Forms control. The new control has the same visual representation and functionality as the base control.

- A user control encapsulates one or more Windows Forms controls and inherit from the *UserControl* class. Constituent controls are private by default and can not be accessed at run time unless specifically exposed by changing the *Modi| ers* property.

- A custom control is the most time-consuming approach to control developmen Custom controls inherit from the *Control* class without graphic representation In addition to writing code that represents the functionality of the control, you must provide code to paint the control.

esson 3: Common Tasks Using Controls

There are a variety of tasks common to each type of control you develop. In this lesson, you will learn about some of these tasks, such as adding your control to the toolbox, displaying it in Microsoft Internet Explorer, debugging it, providing a Toolbox bitmap for your control, and managing licensing.

After this lesson, you will be able to

- Add your control to the Toolbox
- Provide a Toolbox bitmap for your control
- Debug your control
- Manage control licensing
- View your control in Internet Explorer

Estimated lesson time: 20 minutes

Adding Your Control to the Toolbox

Once you have created a control, you will want to be able to work with it in your development projects. Adding your control to the Toolbox makes it accessible and easy to work with and allows you to add it to your projects at design time.

You can add a new control to the Toolbox by using the Customize Toolbox option. To access this option, right-click the Toolbox and choose Customize Toolbox, which launches the Customize Toolbox dialog box. From there, you can browse to the file that contains your control.

To add your control to the Toolbox

1. Right-click the Toolbox, and choose Customize Toolbox. The Customize Toolbox dialog box opens.
2. Choose the .NET Framework Components tab, and click the Browse button to open the File dialog box.
3. Browse to the folder with the DLL or EXE file that contains your control. Select the file, and click Open.
4. Verify that your control has been added to the list displayed in the Customize Toolbox dialog box, and click OK. Your control is added to the Toolbox.

Note   In Visual Studio .NET 2003, user controls built as a part of your project are automatically added to the Toolbox under the My UserControls tab. You can still add inherited controls and custom controls using the aforementioned procedure.

Providing a Toolbox Bitmap for Your Control

Visual Studio .NET provides a default icon that appears next to your controls in the Toolbox. You might, however, want to specify your own icon in the form of a bitmap. The following procedure details how to specify a bitmap to be used in the Toolbox with your control.

You specify a Toolbox bitmap by using the *ToolboxBitmapAttribute* class. This class is an attribute—a specialized class that provides metadata about your control. Using the *ToolboxBitmapAttribute*, you can specify either a 16-by-16-pixel bitmap file to be used as your Toolbox bitmap or you can specify a *Type* (*type*). If you specify a *Type* (*type*), your control will have the same Toolbox bitmap as that of the *Type* (*type*) you specified.

The *ToolboxBitmapAttribute* is attached to the class declaration of the control. In Visual Basic .NET, it appears in angle brackets (<>) before the class declaration on the same line. In Microsoft Visual C#, it should go within braces (*[]*) on the line immediately preceding the class declaration for the control.

To provide a Toolbox bitmap for your control by specifying a file

Use the *ToolboxBitmapAttribute* to specify the file that contains the bitmap, as follows:

Visual Basic .NET

```
<ToolboxBitmap("C:\Pasta.bmp")> Public Class PastaMaker
    ' Implementation omitted
End Class
```

Visual C#

```
[ToolboxBitmap(@"C:\Pasta.bmp")]
public class PastaMaker : Control
{
    // Implementation omitted
}
```

To provide a Toolbox bitmap by specifying a type

Use the *ToolboxBitmapAttribute* to specify the type whose bitmap you want to provide, as follows:

Visual Basic .NET

```
<ToolboxBitmap(GetType(Button))> Public Class myButton
    ' Implementation omitted
End Class
```

Visual C#

```
[ToolboxBitmap(typeof(Button))]
public class myButton : Button
{
    // Implementation omitted
}
```

Debugging Your Control

As with any development project, eventually you will have to debug your controls. Because controls are not stand-alone projects, they must be hosted within a Windows Forms project while debugging.

You must build your control before you can test it. Once the project containing your control has been built, you can place it on a form and debug as you would any other project.

If your control is part of an executable project, such as a Windows Forms project, you can add a new form to your project to host your control. If your control is part of a nonexecutable project, such as a class library or a Windows control library project, you must add an additional project to your solution to test your control.

To debug a control in a Windows Forms project

1. From the Build menu, choose Build Solution to build your solution.
2. If necessary, add a new form to your project. Set this form as the start-up form.
3. Add your control to the form, either in code or at design time. Adding your control to the Toolbox in code facilitates adding it at design time.
4. Press F5 to start your application. Your control is now available for debugging. You can set breakpoints in your control, step through code, and use the other debugging tools to find and correct bugs in your program.
5. You must rebuild the control before any changes will be apparent in the form. You can rebuild your solution by choosing Rebuild Solution from the Build menu.

To debug a control in a class library or Windows control library project

1. From the Build menu, choose Build Solution to build your solution.
2. From the File menu, choose Add Project and then choose New Project to add an additional project to your solution. The Add New Project dialog box opens.
3. In the Add New Project dialog box, choose Windows Application. Name the project, and click OK.
4. In Solution Explorer, right-click the References node of the new project and choose Add Reference. The Add Reference dialog box opens.

5. Choose the Projects tab. If the project containing your control is listed, select it and click OK. If it is not listed, click the Browse button and browse to the folder with the DLL file that contains your control. Select it, and click OK to continue

6. Add your control to the form in the new project, either in code or at design time. You might want to add your control to the Toolbox first to facilitate adding it at design time, as discussed earlier in this lesson.

7. Press F5 to start your application. Your control is now available for debugging You can set breakpoints in your control, step through code, and use the other debugging tools to find and correct bugs in your program.

Managing Control Licensing

Control licensing allows control developers to protect their intellectual property by ensuring that only authorized users can develop applications with their controls. The .NET Framework has a built-in control-licensing model. By default, it requires that a *LicenseProviderAttribute* be applied to any control that is to be licensed. This attribute specifies the *LicenseProvider* to use for validating the license. *LicenseProvider* is an abstract class that provides a standard interface for validation. In the constructor of the control, you call *LicenseManager.Validate* to return a reference to a valid license. The control will fail to load if it is not licensed.

The *LicenseManager.Validate* method validates the license by calling the *GetLicense* method of the indicated *LicenseProvider*, which retrieves the license and checks its validity by calling the *IsKeyValid* method. If the result is *true*, the license is granted. If the result is *false*, the control will not load. The particular validation scheme depends on the implementation of *LicenseProvider*. The .NET Framework includes an implementation of *LicenseProvider* named *LicFileLicenseProvider*. When this class is specified as the *LicenseProvider*, its implementation is used to determine if the license is valid. The *GetLicense* method of this provider examines the directory that contains the DLL file for this control for a text file named *FullName.LIC*, where *FullName* is the fully qualified name of the control. *IsKeyValid* then examines the first line of this text file for the line "*myClassName* is a licensed component." where *myClassName* is the fully qualified name of the component. You can override this functionality to provide your own validation logic. You should implement *Dispose* for every licensed control and include a line in the *Dispose* method to dispose of the license.

The following code example shows a control named *Widget* that implements licensing with the *LicFileLicenseProvider*:

Visual Basic .NET

```
' This example assumes Imports System.ComponentModel
' The LicenseProvider attribute specifies the kind of
' LicenseProvider to use.
<LicenseProvider(GetType(LicFileLicenseProvider))> Public Class _
    Widget
```

```
Inherits Control
Private myLicense As License
Public Sub New()
   ' Validates and retrieves a reference to the license
   myLicense = LicenseManager.Validate(GetType(Widget), Me)
   ' Additional constructor implementation omitted
End Sub
' Implements Dispose to dispose the license
Protected Overloads Overrides Sub _
   Dispose(ByVal Disposing As Boolean)
   If Not (myLicense Is Nothing) then
      myLicense.Dispose()
      myLicense = Nothing
   End If
End Sub
End Class
```

Visual C#

```csharp
// This example assumes using System.ComponentModel
// The LicenseProvider attribute specifies the kind of
// LicenseProvider to use.
[LicenseProvider(typeof(LicFileLicenseProvider))]
public class Widget : System.Windows.Forms.Control
{
    private License myLicense;
    public Widget()
    {
        // Validates and retrieves a reference to the license
        myLicense = LicenseManager.Validate(typeof(Widget), this);
        // Additional constructor implementation omitted
    }
    // Implements Dispose to dispose the license
    protected override void Dispose(bool Disposing)
    {
        if (myLicense != null)
        {
            myLicense.Dispose();
            myLicense = null;
        }
    }
}
```

To implement licensing management for your control

1. Specify the *LicenseProvider* to use by applying a *LicenseProviderAttribute* to your control class.

2. Create the license file in accordance with the implementation of the *LicenseProvider* that you are using.

3. In the constructor of your control, call *LicenseManager.Validate* to validate your license.

4. Dispose of your license in the control's *Dispose* method.

Hosting Your Control in Internet Explorer

Every Windows Forms control can be hosted in Internet Explorer. You can take advantage of this feature to create HTML pages with rich Windows Forms contro content. In this section, you will learn how to host your control in Internet Explorer.

For a control to be hosted in Internet Explorer, it must be installed to the Global Assembly Cache or it must reside in the same virtual directory as the HTML pag in which it is declared.

Note   Installing classes to the Global Assembly Cache is discussed in Chapter 9

You can add a Windows Forms control to an HTML page by using the *<OBJECT* tag. The *<OBJECT>* tag specifies that a compiled code object is to be inserted int the page. The *<OBJECT>* tag examines its *classid* property to identify what type of object to load. Thus, you specify your Windows Forms control in the *classid* property.

The *classid* for a Windows Forms control consists of two parts. The first part is th path to the file that contains the control. The second part is the fully qualified nam of the control. These are separated in the *classid* by the hash (#). The following code example demonstrates an *<OBJECT>* tag for a control in the ControlLibrary1.dll file (located in the same virtual directory as the HTML page with the fully qualified name *ControlLibrary1.myControl*:

```
<OBJECT id="myControl"
classid="http:ControlLibrary1.dll#ControlLibrary1.myControl
VIEWASTEXT>
</OBJECT>
```

To host your control in Internet Explorer

1. Save the DLL file that includes your control to the same virtual directory when the HTML page hosting it will reside, or install it to the Global Assembly Cache.

2. Create an *<OBJECT>* tag in the HTML page with the appropriate *classid* pro erty. The *classid* for a particular control consists of the path to the DLL file tha contains the control, followed by the pound sign (#), followed by the control' fully qualified name.

Lesson Summary

- You can add your controls to the Toolbox by right-clicking the Toolbox and choosing Customize Toolbox. Your controls will appear in the Toolbox with a default icon. If you want to specify a Toolbox bitmap for your control, use the *ToolboxBitmapAttribute*.

- To debug controls, they first must be built and hosted in a form. If your control is in an executable project, you can add a form to the project to serve as a test form. If your control is in a nonexecutable project, you must add a test project to host the form. Once hosted, you can use the regular Visual Studio debugging tools to debug your control. You must rebuild the control before changes will be incorporated.

- The .NET Framework provides a licensing model for licensing your controls. Specify a *LicenseProvider* by applying the *LicFileLicenseProvider* attribute to the control. Call *LicenseManager.Validate* to retrieve a reference to the license. When finished, dispose of the license.

- You can host your control in Internet Explorer by creating an *<OBJECT>* tag. The *<OBJECT>* tag specifies which control to load in the *classid* property.

Lab 7: Creating a Custom Control

In this lab, you will create a custom control named *PrettyClock*. This control will display the current time on the form in a graphically rich format. You will write code to render the control, add logic to implement the functionality, add code to the constructor to set the initial properties, and test your control. The solution to this lab is available on the Supplemental Course Materials CD-ROM in the \Labs\Ch07\Solution folder.

Before You Begin

There are no prerequisites to completing this lab.

Estimated lesson time: 30 minutes

Exercise 7.1: Creating the Control

In this exercise, you will create a custom control named *PrettyClock*. You will inherit from the *Control* class and add logic to paint the control and provide proper ties that control its appearance. Finally you will add a timer component to provide the timekeeping functionality.

▶   **To create the project**

1. From the File menu, choose New and then choose Project. The New Project dialog box opens.

2. In the New Project dialog box, choose Windows Application. Name your project **ControlTest**, and click OK.

3. From the Project menu, choose Add New Item. The Add New Item dialog box opens.

4. In the Add New Item dialog box, choose Custom Control and name your new item **PrettyClock**. Click Open to continue. A new custom control is added to your project.

5. In Solution Explorer, right-click *PrettyClock* and choose View Code. The Code window opens. Note that an override of the *OnPaint* method is stubbed out, and comments have been added to indicate that you need to add rendering code here.

You will now add code to create the control. Your control will render the current time to the screen, surrounded by a rectangle. You will use a *LinearGradientBrush* to paint the control to the screen and produce interesting graphic effects. You also will add properties to your control to allow developers to set the control's visual properties at run time.

1. At the top of the code editor, add the following lines to import the *System.Drawing* and *System.Drawing.Drawing2D* namespaces into your code:

Visual Basic .NET

```
Imports System.Drawing
Imports System.Drawing.Drawing2D
```

Visual C#

```
// In C#, 'using System.Drawing;' is added by default
using System.Drawing.Drawing2D;
```

2. Add a property to hold a color value. This property, along with the *ForeColor* property that was inherited from control, will be used to create the *LinearGradientBrush* that will paint the control. Your property should look something like the following code example:

Visual Basic .NET

```
' Adds the private variable to hold the Color value
Private mForeColorTwo As Color
' Adds the property itself
Public Property ForeColorTwo() As Color
    Get
        Return mForeColorTwo
    End Get
    Set(ByVal Value As Color)
        mForeColorTwo = Value
    End Set
End Property
```

Visual C#

```
// Adds the private variable to hold the Color value
private Color mForeColorTwo;
// Adds the property itself
public Color ForeColorTwo
{
    get
    {
        return mForeColorTwo;
    }
    set
    {
        mForeColorTwo = value;
    }
}
```

3. Add a *Single* (*float*) property named *Angle* to hold the angle for the *LinearGra dientBrush* to use. Because this will represent an angular value in degrees, include validation in the property to ensure that the property cannot be set less than 0 or greater than 360. An example of such a property follows:

Visual Basic .NET

```
Private mAngle As Single
Public Property Angle() As Single
    Get
        Return mAngle
    End Get
    Set(ByVal Value As Single)
        ' This scheme causes the value to be set low if an attempt is
        ' made to set it high, and vice versa. This allows one to
        ' circle through the angle path by incrementing the property
        If Value > 360 then
            mAngle = 0
        ElseIf Value < 0 then
            mAngle = 360
        Else
            mAngle = Value
        End If
    End Set
End Property
```

Visual C#

```
private float mAngle;
public float Angle
{
    get
    {
        return mAngle;
    }
    set
    {
        // This scheme causes the value to be set low if an attempt is
        // made to set it high, and vice versa. This allows one to
        // circle through the angle path by incrementing the property
        if (value > 360)
            mAngle = 0;
        else if (value < 0)
            mAngle = 360;
        else
            mAngle = value;
    }
}
```

4. In the *OnPaint* method, add code to create a *LinearGradientBrush* and render the current time using the control's *Font* object. You will use the control's *Size*, *ForeColor*, and *ForeColorTwo* properties to create the *LinearGradientBrush*. This code should all be added after the call to *MyBase.OnPaint* (Visual Basic .NET) or *base.onPaint* (Visual C#). For example:

Visual Basic .NET

```
' This line creates a new rectangle that represents the control
' created from the origin point and the control's Size property
Dim ControlRectangle As New Rectangle(New Point(0, 0), Me.Size)
' This line creates a new LinearGradientBrush that blends
' ForeColor and ForeColorTwo along the angle specified in angle.
Dim myBrush As New LinearGradientBrush(ControlRectangle, _
    ForeColor, ForeColorTwo, Angle)
' Creates a GraphicsPath object that will hold the text to be
' rendered
Dim myPath As New GraphicsPath()
' Adds a string representing the current time to the GraphicsPath
myPath.AddString(Now.ToLongTimeString(), Font.FontFamily, _
    Font.Style, Font.Size, New Point(0, 0), _
    StringFormat.GenericDefault)
' Renders the Graphics path
pe.Graphics.FillPath(myBrush, myPath)
```

Visual C#

```
// This line creates a new rectangle that represents the control
// created from the origin point and the control's Size property
Rectangle ControlRectangle = new
    Rectangle(new Point(0, 0), this.Size);
// This line creates a new LinearGradientBrush that blends
// ForeColor and ForeColorTwo along the angle specified in angle.
LinearGradientBrush myBrush = new
    LinearGradientBrush(ControlRectangle,
    ForeColor, ForeColorTwo, Angle);
// Creates a GraphicsPath object that will hold the text to be
// rendered
GraphicsPath myPath = new GraphicsPath();
// Adds a string representing the current time to the
// GraphicsPath
myPath.AddString(System.DateTime.Now.ToLongTimeString(),
    Font.FontFamily,
    (int)Font.Style, Font.Size, new Point(0, 0),
    StringFormat.GenericDefault);
// Renders the Graphics path
pe.Graphics.FillPath(myBrush, myPath);
```

5. Beneath the code you added in Step 4, add code to create a new *Pen* from the *LinearGradientBrush* and use it to draw a rectangle along the border of the con trol. Your code should be similar to the following:

Visual Basic .NET

```
' Creates a pen from myBrush with a thickness of 8 pixels
Dim myPen As New Pen(myBrush, 8)
' Renders a rectangle around the control
pe.Graphics.DrawRectangle(myPen, ControlRectangle)
```

Visual C#

```
// Creates a pen from myBrush with a thickness of 8 pixels
Pen myPen = new Pen(myBrush, 8);
// Renders a rectangle around the control
pe.Graphics.DrawRectangle(myPen, ControlRectangle);
```

6. From the File menu, choose Save All to save your work.

You will now set start-up properties in the designer. You also will add a *Timer* com ponent and add code to redraw the clock every second as well as add an interesting visual effect.

▶ **To add and configure a Timer**

1. In Solution Explorer, right-click *PrettyClock* and choose View Designer. The designer opens.

2. From the Windows Forms tab of the Toolbox, drag a *Timer* to the designer surface.

3. In the Properties window, set the *Interval* property to 1000 and the *Enabled* property to *true*.

4. In the designer, double-click the *Timer* to open the *Timer.Tick* event handler. Add the following code:

Visual Basic .NET

```
' This will cause the visual effect to change with each Tick
Angle += 10
' Causes the control to redraw
Me.Refresh()
```

Visual C#

```
// This will cause the visual effect to change with each Tick
Angle += 10;
// Causes the control to redraw
this.Refresh();
```

5. In Visual C#, you must add a call to *InitializeComponent* to the constructor of the control to initialize your component. For example:

Visual C#

```
public PrettyClock()
    {
        InitializeComponent();
    }
```

6. From the File menu, choose Save All to save your work.

Exercise 7.2: Testing Your Control

Once you have created your control, you must verify that it functions as planned. In this exercise, you will add your control to the Toolbox and then add it to your form. You will configure the control in the Toolbox and observe its functionality at run time.

▶ **To add your control to the Toolbox**

1. From the Build menu, choose Build Solution to build your solution.

2. Right-click an open space within the Toolbox, and choose Customize Toolbox. The Customize Toolbox dialog box opens.

3. Choose the .NET Framework Components tab, and click Browse to open the Open File dialog box.

4. Browse to the folder containing your project. In the \bin folder (Visual Basic .NET) or \bin\Debug folder (Visual C#), select ControlTest.exe, which is the compiled file that contains your control. Click OK to continue.

5. Verify that *PrettyClock* is listed in the Customize Toolbox dialog box list and that the check box next to it is selected. Click OK to continue.

▶ **To test your control**

1. In Solution Explorer, right-click Form1 and choose View Designer. The designer for Form1 opens.

2. From the General tab of the Toolbox, select *PrettyClock* and drag it to the form. A new instance of *PrettyClock* is added to the form.

3. Set the properties of this instance of *PrettyClock* to the values in Table 7.8.

Table 7.8.   PrettyClock Instance Properties

Property	Value
ForeColor	Red
ForeColorTwo	Yellow

Table 7.8. PrettyClock Instance Properties

Property	Value
Font.Size	40
Size	225, 50

Note that as you change the property values, the changes are immediately updated in the control instance in the form.

4. In the form, verify that the time is updated every second and that the graphics blend changes every second. Press F5 to run your application. Note that the behavior at run time is the same.

Review

These questions are intended to reinforce key concepts presented in the chapter. If you are unable to answer a question, review the relevant section and try again. Answers can be found in Appendix A.

1. Briefly describe the three types of user-developed controls and how they differ.

2. Describe the roles of *Graphics*, *Brush*, *Pen*, and *GraphicsPath* objects in graphics rendering.

3. Describe the general procedure for rendering text to a drawing surface.

4. Describe the role of the *LicenseProvider* in control licensing.

5. Describe how to create a form or a control with a non-rectangular shape.

C H A P T E R   8

Advanced .NET Framework Topics

About This Chapter

In this chapter, you will explore assorted topics in Microsoft .NET Framework programming. You will learn to implement print support, access external components, implement accessibility, provide help in your application, and implement globalization.

Before You Begin

To complete the lessons in this chapter, you must have completed chapters 1 through 7.

Lesson 1: Implementing Print Functionality

Printing data and documents is a common task in any business setting. The .NET Framework provides the *PrintDocument* component to facilitate printing and a host of other classes to support and configure your printer settings. In this lesson, you will learn how to create and configure a *PrintDocument* object, and how to use it to print text, text files, and graphics.

After this lesson, you will be able to

- Describe how to create and configure a *PrintDocument* object
- Explain how to print text
- Describe how to print graphics
- Describe how to use the *PrintPreview* control and the Print Preview dialog box
- Explain how to configure page settings with the *PageSetupDialog* control
- Describe how to implement printer selection with the *PrintDialog* control

Estimated lesson time: 45 minutes

Printing will undoubtedly play a major part in your business applications. Although electronic file and document storage is increasingly popular, printed material will not be replaced in the near future. Thus, you must be able to implement print capability in your applications. The .NET Framework provides classes and components that allow you to quickly and easily implement print support for your programs.

The PrintDocument Component

A printed document is represented by the *PrintDocument* component in the .NET Framework. Although it is not a control with a visual component, the *PrintDocument* component can be found on the Windows Forms tab of the Toolbox, from where it can be added to your application in the designer.

The *PrintDocument* object encapsulates all of the information necessary to print a page. It exposes a *PrinterSettings* property that contains information about the capabilities and settings of the printers; a *DefaultPageSettings* property that encapsulates the configuration for printing each printed page; and a *PrintController* property that describes how each page is guided through the printing process. Through these properties, it is possible to attain an exacting level of control over the print process.

Creating a PrintDocument Object

You can create a *PrintDocument* object either in the designer at design time or in code at run time. You can drag an instance of the *PrintDocument* object directly from the Toolbox to the designer. The new instance appears in the component tray and is automatically configured to work with the system's default printer.

You can also create an instance in code, as follows:

Visual Basic .NET

```
' Assumes Imports System.Drawing.Printing
Dim myPrintDocument As New PrintDocument()
```

Visual C#

```
// Assumes using System.Drawing.Printing;
PrintDocument myPrintDocument = new PrintDocument();
```

An instance created in code is also automatically configured to work with the default system printer.

How Printing Works

In the .NET Framework printing model, printed content is provided directly by the application logic. A print job is initiated by the *PrintDocument.Print* method. This starts the print job and then raises one or more *PrintPage* events. If there is no client method to handle this event, printing does not take place. By providing a method to handle this event, you can specify the content to be printed.

If the print job contains multiple pages, one *PrintPage* event is raised for each page in the job. This, in turn, causes the method handling the *PrintPage* event to execute multiple times. Thus, that method must implement some functionality to track the print job and ensure that successive pages of a multipage document are printed. Otherwise, the first page of the document will print multiple times.

The PrintPage Event

The *PrintPage* event is the main event involved in printing documents. To actually send content to the printer, you must handle this event and provide code to render the content in the *PrintPage* event handler. All of the objects and information needed to send content to the printer is wrapped in the *PrintPageEventArgs* object, which is received by this event handler. The *PrintPageEventArgs* object contains the properties listed in Table 8.1.

Table 8.1.   Properties of the PrintPageEventArgs Object

Property	Description
Cancel	Indicates whether or not a print job should be canceled
Graphics	The *Graphics* object used to render content to the printed page
HasMorePages	Gets or sets a value indicating whether additional pages should be printed

Table 8.1.   Properties of the PrintPageEventArgs Object

Property	Description
MarginBounds	Gets the *Rectangle* object that represents the portion of the page within the margins
PageBounds	Gets the *Rectangle* object that represents the total page area
PageSettings	Gets or sets the *PageSettings* object for the current page

Content is rendered to the printed page by the *Graphics* object provided in the *PrintPageEventArgs* object. The printed page in this case behaves just like a form, control or any other drawing surface that can be represented by a *Graphics* object. To render content, you use the same methods used to render content to a form. The following code example, where the content inscribes an ellipse inside the bounds of the margin, demonstrates a simple method to print a page:

Visual Basic .NET

```
' This method must handle the PrintPage event in order to be executed
Public Sub PrintEllipse(ByVal sender As System.Object, ByVal e As _
    System.Drawing.Printing.PrintPageEventArgs)
    e.Graphics.DrawEllipse(Pens.Black, e.MarginBounds)
End Sub
```

Visual C#

```
// This method must handle the PrintPage event in order to be executed
public void PrintEllipse(object sender,
    System.Drawing.Printing.PrintPageEventArgs e)
{
    e.Graphics.DrawEllipse(Pens.Black, e.MarginBounds);
}
```

The *MarginBounds* and *PageBounds* properties represent areas of the page surface. You can specify printing to occur inside the margin bounds of the page by calculating printing coordinates based on the *MarginBounds* rectangle. Printing that is to take place outside the margin bounds, such as headers or footers, can be specified by calculating the printing coordinates based on the *PageBounds* rectangle. As with painting to the screen, print coordinates are in pixels by default.

You can specify that a print job has multiple pages by using the *HasMorePages* property. By default, this property is set to *false*. When your program logic determines that multiple pages are required to print a job, you should set this property to *true*. When the last page is printed, the property should be reset to *false*.

Note   The method handling the *PrintPage* event must keep track of the number of pages in the job. Failure to do so can cause unexpected results while printing. For example, if you fail to set the *HasMorePages* property to *false* after the last page is printed, the application will continue to raise *PrintPage* events.

You can also cancel a print job without finishing the current page by setting the *Cancel* property to *true*.

You can create an event handler for the *PrintPage* event by double-clicking the *PrintDocument* instance in the designer to create a default event handler or by declaring the event handler in code as described in Chapter 3.

Printing Content

Initiating a print job is as easy as calling the *PrintDocument.Print* method. In this section, you will learn how to create the code that determines what content is sent to the printer.

Printing Graphics

Printing graphics is as easy as rendering them to the screen. You use the *Graphics* object supplied by *PrintPageEventArgs* to render graphics to the screen. Simple shapes can be printed, or complex shapes can be created and printed, using the *GraphicsPath* object. The following code example shows how to print a complex shape with a *GraphicsPath* object:

Visual Basic .NET

```vb
' This method must handle the PrintPage event
Public Sub PrintGraphics(ByVal Sender As System.Object, _
    ByVal e As System.Drawing.Printing.PrintPageEventArgs)
    Dim myPath As New System.Drawing.Drawing2D.GraphicsPath()
    myPath.AddPolygon(New Point() {New Point(1, 1), _
        New Point(12, 55), New Point(34, 8), New Point(52, 53), _
        New Point(99, 5)})
    myPath.AddRectangle(New Rectangle(33, 43, 20, 20))
    e.Graphics.DrawPath(Pens.Black, myPath)
End Sub
```

Visual C#

```csharp
// This method must handle the PrintPage event
public void PrintGraphics(object sender,
    System.Drawing.Printing.PrintPageEventArgs e)
{
    System.Drawing.Drawing2D.GraphicsPath myPath = new
        System.Drawing.Drawing2D.GraphicsPath();
    myPath.AddPolygon(new Point[] {new Point(1, 1),
        new Point(12, 55), new Point(34, 8), new Point(52, 53),
        new Point(99, 5)});
    myPath.AddRectangle(new Rectangle(33, 43, 20, 20));
    e.Graphics.DrawPath(Pens.Black, myPath);
}
```

To print a graphics job that has multiple pages, you must manually divide the job among pages and implement the appropriate logic. For example, the following method uses two pages to draw an ellipse that is twice as long as the page length:

Visual Basic .NET

```
Dim FirstPagePrinted As Boolean = False
' This method must handle the PrintPage event
Public Sub PrintBigEllipse(ByVal Sender As System.Object, ByVal _
    e As System.Drawing.Printing.PrintPageEventArgs)
    If FirstPagePrinted = False Then
        FirstPagePrinted = True
        e.HasMorePages = True
        e.Graphics.DrawEllipse(Pens.Black, New Rectangle(0, 0, _
            e.PageBounds.Width, e.PageBounds.Height * 2))
    Else
        e.HasMorePages = False
        FirstPagePrinted = False
        e.Graphics.DrawEllipse(Pens.Black, New Rectangle(0, _
            -(e.PageBounds.Height), e.PageBounds.Width, _
            e.PageBounds.Height * 2))
    End If
End Sub
```

Visual C#

```
bool FirstPagePrinted = false;
// This method must handle the PrintPage event
public void PrintBigEllipse(object sender,
    System.Drawing.Printing.PrintPageEventArgs e)
{
    if (FirstPagePrinted == false)
    {
        FirstPagePrinted = true;
        e.HasMorePages = true;
        e.Graphics.DrawEllipse(Pens.Black, new Rectangle(0, 0,
            e.PageBounds.Width, e.PageBounds.Height * 2));
    }
    else
    {
        e.HasMorePages = false;
        FirstPagePrinted = false;
        e.Graphics.DrawEllipse(Pens.Black, new Rectangle(0,
            -(e.PageBounds.Height), e.PageBounds.Width,
            e.PageBounds.Height * 2));
    }
}
```

This example uses the *FirstPagePrinted* variable to keep track of whether the first page or the second page is printing. Note that this variable is declared outside the method. If this variable were declared inside the method, it would reinitialize every time the method executed, and thus always return *false*. As the program prints each page, it redraws the image each time, changing the position of the ellipse's rectangle so as to orient the ellipse correctly across both pages.

Printing Text

Text is printed in the same way it is rendered to the screen. The *Graphics.Draw-String* method is used to output text to the printer. As with rendering text to the screen, to print you must specify a font for rendering the text, text to render, a *Brush* object, and coordinates at which to print. For example:

Visual Basic .NET

```
Dim myfont As New Font("Batang", 36, FontStyle.Regular, _
    GraphicsUnit.Pixel)
Dim Hello As String = "Hello World!"
e.Graphics.DrawString(Hello, myfont, Brushes.Black, 30, 30)
```

Visual C#

```
Font myfont = new Font("Batang", 36, FontStyle.Regular,
    GraphicsUnit.Pixel);
string Hello = "Hello World!";
e.Graphics.DrawString(Hello, myfont, Brushes.Black, 30, 30);
```

Note   When printing text, you must take steps in your code to ensure that you do not attempt to print outside the bounds of the page. If you do attempt to print outside the bounds of the page, any content that falls outside the page bounds will not be printed.

Printing Multiple Lines

When printing multiple lines of text, such as an array of strings or lines read from a text file, you must include logic to calculate the line spacing. You can calculate the number of lines per page by dividing the height of the margin bounds by the height of the font. Similarly, you can calculate the position of each line by multiplying the line number by the height of the font. The following code example demonstrates how to print an array of strings called *myStrings*:

Visual Basic .NET

```
' This variable keeps track of the current position in the array.
' It must be declared outside the method that handles the
' PrintPage event in order to keep from being reinitialized with
' each page
Dim ArrayCounter As Integer = 0
```

```vb
' This method handles a PrintDocument.PrintPage event. It assumes
' an array of strings called myStrings() has been declared and
' populated elsewhere in the application. It also assumes a font
' for printing has been initialized and called myFont
Private Sub PrintStrings(sender As Object, e As _
    PrintPageEventArgs)
    ' Declares the variables that will be used to keep track of
    ' spacing and paging
    Dim LeftMargin As Single = e.MarginBounds.Left
    Dim TopMargin As Single = e.MarginBounds.Top
    Dim MyLines As Single = 0
    Dim YPosition As Single = 0
    Dim Counter As Integer = 0
    Dim CurrentLine As String
    ' Calculate the number of lines per page.
    MyLines = e.MarginBounds.Height / _
        myFont.GetHeight(e.Graphics)
    ' Prints each line of the file, but stops at the end of a page
    While Counter < MyLines And ArrayCounter <= _
        myStrings.GetUpperBound(0)
        CurrentLine = myStrings(ArrayCounter)
        YPosition = TopMargin + Counter * _
            myFont.GetHeight(e.Graphics)
        e.Graphics.DrawString(CurrentLine, myFont, Brushes.Black, _
            LeftMargin, YPosition, New StringFormat())
        Counter += 1
        ArrayCounter += 1
    End While

    ' If more lines exist, print another page.
    If Not (ArrayCounter = myStrings.GetUpperBound(0)) Then
        e.HasMorePages = True
    Else
        e.HasMorePages = False
    End If
End Sub
```

Visual C#

```csharp
// This variable keeps track of the current position in the
// array. It must be declared outside the method that handles the
// PrintPage event in order to keep from being reinitialized with
// each page
int ArrayCounter = 0;
// This method handles a PrintDocument.PrintPage event. It
// assumes an array of strings called myStrings() has been
// declared and populated elsewhere in the application. It also
// assumes a font for printing has been initialized and called
// myFont
private void PrintStrings(object sender, PrintPageEventArgs e)
{
```

```
// Declares the variables that will be used to keep track of
// spacing and paging
float LeftMargin = e.MarginBounds.Left;
float TopMargin = e.MarginBounds.Top;
float MyLines = 0;
float YPosition = 0;
int Counter = 0;
string CurrentLine;
// Calculate the number of lines per page.
MyLines = e.MarginBounds.Height /
    myFont.GetHeight(e.Graphics);
// Prints each line of the file, but stops at the end of a
// page
while (Counter < MyLines && ArrayCounter <=
    myStrings.GetUpperBound(0))
{
    CurrentLine = myStrings[ArrayCounter];
    YPosition = TopMargin + Counter *
        myFont.GetHeight(e.Graphics);
    e.Graphics.DrawString(CurrentLine, myFont, Brushes.Black,
        LeftMargin, YPosition, new StringFormat());
    Counter ++;
    ArrayCounter ++;
}

// If more lines exist, print another page.
if (!(ArrayCounter == myStrings.GetUpperBound(0)))
    e.HasMorePages = true;
else
    e.HasMorePages = false;
}
```

Using Color

If your printer supports color printing, you will want to use a different set of printing options than when you are printing to a black-and-white printer. For example, some colors that are easily discernable on the screen appear much different when printed. If you are designing your application to work with color printers, you should provide alternative logic to accommodate black-and-white printers.

You can determine if the current printer supports printing color by retrieving the *PrinterSettings.SupportsColor* property. If the printer supports color, the *DefaultPageSettings.Color* property will be set to *true*, and the printer will print in color by default. If you want to force black-and-white printing, even if you have a color page and a color printer, set the *DefaultPageSettings.Color* property to *false*. The following code example demonstrates how to provide alternative printing logic based on the *PrinterSettings.SupportsColor* property.

Visual Basic .NET

```
' This example assumes Imports System.Drawing,
' System.Drawing.Drawing2D, and System.Drawing.Printing
Dim BrushOne As Brush
Dim BrushTwo As Brush
If PrintDocument1.PrinterSettings.SupportsColor = True Then
   ' Provides brushes in color for color printing
   BrushOne = Brushes.Red
   BrushTwo = Brushes.Blue
Else
   ' Provides HatchedBrushes for black-and-white printing
   BrushOne = New HatchBrush(HatchStyle.DarkVertical, Color.Black)
   BrushTwo = New HatchBrush(HatchStyle.DashedHorizontal, _
      Color.Black)
End If
```

Visual C#

```
// This example assumes Imports System.Drawing,
// System.Drawing.Drawing2D, and System.Drawing.Printing
Brush BrushOne;
Brush BrushTwo;
if (printDocument1.PrinterSettings.SupportsColor == true)
{
   // Provides brushes in color for color printing
   BrushOne = Brushes.Red;
   BrushTwo = Brushes.Blue;
}
else
{
   // Provides HatchedBrushes for black-and-white printing
   BrushOne = new HatchBrush(HatchStyle.DarkVertical, Color.Black);
   BrushTwo = new HatchBrush(HatchStyle.DashedHorizontal,
      Color.Black);
}
```

To enable printing in your application

1. From the Toolbox, drag an instance of *PrintDocument* to the designer. The *PrintDocument* component appears in the component tray and is automatically configured with the default printer. You can also create a new *PrintDocument* in code.

2. Create a method to handle the *PrintDocument.PrintPage* event.

3. Add application logic to the *PrintPage* event handler to render the content to the printed screen. Use the *PrintPageEventArgs.Graphics* object to render the content to the printer.

4. If working with multipage documents, add logic to your application to keep track of paging.

Using PrintPreviewControl

The .NET Framework provides a *PrintPreviewControl* control to allow you to graphically preview print content before it is sent to the printer. The *PrintPreview-Control* control can be found on the Windows Forms tab of the Toolbox, and you can add an instance of it by dragging it onto your form.

In order to preview a page, the *PrintPreviewControl* control must be associated with a *PrintDocument* instance. This association is created by setting the *Print-PreviewControl.Document* property as follows:

Visual Basic .NET

```
myPrintPreview.Document = myPrintDocument
```

Visual C#

```
myPrintPreview.Document = myPrintDocument;
```

When this association is made, the *PrintPreviewControl* control will display the content that is to be printed in the control. This is accomplished by invoking the method that handles the *PrintDocument.Print* event and capturing the graphics output from that method. This output is then rendered in the *PrintPreviewControl* control.

As program conditions change, the printed document might change as well. You can update the preview by calling the *InvalidatePreview* method as follows:

Visual Basic .NET

```
myPrintPreview.InvalidatePreview()
```

Visual C#

```
myPrintPreview.InvalidatePreview();
```

This causes the page displayed by the *PrintPreviewControl* control to be refreshed.

Another important property of the *PrintPreviewControl* control is the *Zoom* property. *Zoom* specifies the magnification level at which the preview is displayed. A value of 1 causes the preview to be displayed at full size. A fractional value reduces the image, and a value greater than 1 enlarges it.

PrintPreviewDialog

The *PrintPreviewControl* control is a valuable resource for previewing your printed documents and creating custom previews. However, for most applications, a standard suite of print preview functionality is adequate. The .NET Framework provides a standard *PrintPreviewDialog* control that exposes the most commonly used print preview functionality. The dialog box that the *PrintPreviewDialog* control creates is shown in Figure 8.1.

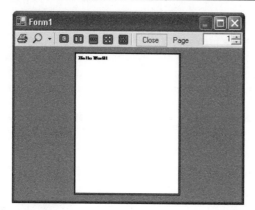

Figure 8.1.   The *PrintPreviewDialog* dialog box.

You can preview a document by setting the *Document* property of the *PrintPreviewDialog* object to the *PrintDocument* object you want to preview. Once displayed, the *PrintPreviewDialog* control provides functionality to view multiple pages of the preview, to zoom, or to print the document. As with any form, you can display a *PrintPreviewDialog* dialog box by calling the *Show* or *ShowDialog* methods. The following example demonstrates how to associate a *PrintPreviewDialog* component with a *PrintDocument* component and display the *PrintPreviewDialog* dialog box.

Visual Basic .NET

```
' Assumes Imports System.Drawing.Printing
Dim myDocument As New PrintDocument()
Dim myDialog As New PrintPreviewDialog()
myDialog.Document = myDocument
myDialog.ShowDialog()
```

Visual C#

```
// Assumes using System.Drawing.Printing;
PrintDocument myDocument = new PrintDocument();
PrintPreviewDialog myDialog = new PrintPreviewDialog();
myDialog.Document = myDocument;
myDialog.ShowDialog();
```

Configuring Printing

The .NET Framework printing interface provides a vast array of configuration options. The *PrintDocument.PrinterSettings* property contains information about the printers available on a system. The *PrintDocument.DefaultPageSettings* property contains the page settings that will be used unless configured otherwise in the *PrintPage* event handler. The properties exposed by these two members are numerous. Fortunately, for the most part they are also self-documenting. Furthermore, when a *PrintDocument* object is created, the default configuration for the default printer is loaded into the *PrinterSettings* property, and the default page settings are loaded into the *DefaultPageSettings* property. Thus, it is possible to create and execute a print job without ever changing the default configuration.

If you want to allow users to set the configuration of their print jobs, Microsoft Visual Studio .NET provides two controls that seamlessly integrate the user interface with the printer configuration: the *PrintDialog* control and the *PageSetupDialog* control.

PrintDialog

The *PrintDialog* dialog box allows users to set the *PrinterSettings* property of a *PrintDocument* object at run time. You can add a *PrintDialog* dialog box to your application by dragging an instance of the *PrintDialog* control from the Windows Forms tab of the Toolbox to the designer. At run time, you can display the *PrintDialog* dialog box by calling the *ShowDialog* method, as follows:

Visual Basic .NET

```
PrintDialog1.ShowDialog()
```

Visual C#

```
PrintDialog1.ShowDialog();
```

The *PrintDialog* dialog box must be associated with a *PrintDocument* object. You can create this association by setting the *PrintDialog.Document* property to the *PrintDocument* you want to use.

When displayed, the *PrintDialog* dialog box binds to the *PrinterSettings* of the *PrintDocument* specified by the *Document* property and provides a graphical interface for user configuration. The *PrintDialog* dialog box is shown in Figure 8.2. The following example demonstrates how to associate a *PrintDialog* component with a *PrintDocument* component and display the *PrintDialog* dialog box.

Visual Basic .NET

```
' Assumes Imports System.Drawing.Printing
Dim myDocument As New PrintDocument()
Dim myDialog As New PrintDialog()
myDialog.Document = myDocument
myDialog.ShowDialog()
```

Visual C#

```
// Assumes using System.Drawing.Printing;
PrintDocument myDocument = new PrintDocument();
PrintDialog myDialog = new PrintDialog();
myDialog.Document = myDocument;
myDialog.ShowDialog();
```

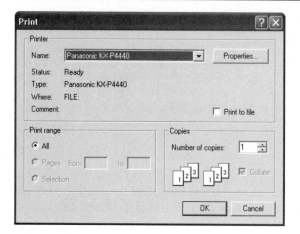

Figure 8.2. The *PrintDialog* dialog box.

PageSetupDialog

The *PageSetupDialog* dialog box is used in a manner similar to the *PrintDialog* dialog box. The *PageSetupDialog* provides a graphical interface that allows the user to configure page settings and printer settings at run time. The user can choose page orientation, paper size, and margins, and configure printer settings as well. The *PageSetupDialog* dialog box is shown in Figure 8.3. The following example demonstrates how to associate a *PageSetupDialog* component with a *PrintDocument* component and display the *PageSetupDialog* dialog box.

Visual Basic .NET

```
' Assumes Imports System.Drawing.Printing
Dim myDocument As New PrintDocument()
Dim myDialog As New PageSetupDialog()
myDialog.Document = myDocument
myDialog.ShowDialog()
```

Visual C#

```
// Assumes using System.Drawing.Printing;
PrintDocument myDocument = new PrintDocument();
PageSetupDialog myDialog = new PageSetupDialog();
myDialog.Document = myDocument;
```

myDialog.ShowDialog();

Like the *PrintDialog*, the *PageSetupDialog* exposes a *Document* property that specifies the *PrintDocument* to use. Setting the *Document* property binds the specified *PrintDocument* to the *PageSetupDialog*, and any changes made in this dialog box are updated in the *PrintDocument.PrinterSettings* and *DefaultPageSettings* properties.

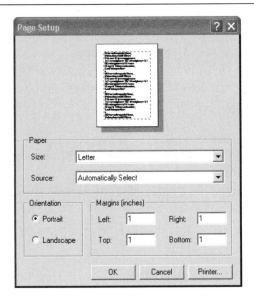

Figure 8.3.   The *PageSetupDialog* dialog box.

Configuring PageSettings at Run Time

You might want to configure individual pages of a multipage document differently from the rest. For example, you might want to print one page in the landscape format and print the rest of the document in the portrait format. You can change the page settings by using the *PrintPageEventArgs.PageSettings* property. This property represents the settings for the page being printed. Changes made to this property are used to print the current page, but are not kept for the rest of the print job. The following code example shows how to change a page layout to landscape at run time:

Visual Basic .NET

```
' This line is excerpted from a PrintPage event handler. The variable
' e represents the PrintPageEventArgs.
e.PageSettings.Landscape = True
```

Visual C#

```
// This line is excerpted from a PrintPage event handler. The variable
// e represents the PrintPageEventArgs.
e.PageSettings.Landscape = true;
```

Lesson Summary

- A printed document is represented by an instance of the *PrintDocument* class. It exposes a *PrinterSettings* property that specifies the settings for the printer and a *DefaultPageSettings* property that specifies the default page properties.

- You print a document by calling the *PrintDocument.Print* method. This method causes the *PrintPage* event to fire. You provide the logic for rendering your document to the printer in the *PrintPage* event handler.

- The *PrintPageEventArgs* object contains all the information and functionality needed to render output to the printer. Printer output is rendered with the *Graphics* object that represents the printer, which is provided in the *PrintPage-EventArgs* object.

- If your document is a multipage document, you must incorporate application logic to handle paging. Set the *PrintEventArgs.HasMorePages* property to *true* to fire the *PrintPage* event again.

- The *PrintPreviewControl* control allows you to preview your print documents before printing them. The *PrintPreviewDialog* dialog box incorporates the most commonly used *PrintPreview* features into an easy-to-use form.

- The *PrintDialog* and the *PageSetupDialog* dialog boxes allow users to configure printer and page properties at run time. You can also configure individual page properties by changing the *PrintPageEventArgs.PageSettings* property during printing.

Lesson 2: Accessing and Invoking Components

Although the .NET Framework provides considerable built-in functionality, from time to time you might want to access external components—for example, an assembly you built using the .NET Framework or an older COM component. You might also need to make a call to a Web service or even interact directly with the Microsoft Windows Application Programming Interface (API). Visual Studio .NET allows you to incorporate these entities into your application with a minimum of effort.

After this lesson, you will be able to

- Explain how to access a .NET Framework assembly
- Describe how to access a COM component or ActiveX control
- Describe how to access a Web service
- Explain how to make a call to the Windows API

Estimated lesson time: 30 minutes

It is likely you will need to access external code at some time. Whether reusing components that you have previously developed, accessing Web services, or making calls to the Windows API, Visual Studio .NET makes it easy to create references to external components and call them in your code.

Accessing .NET and COM Type Libraries

You can access any .NET or COM library on your system without much difficulty. These components might represent other development projects you have created, legacy COM components, or business logic that you need to incorporate into your application. The generalized scheme for accessing .NET or COM components is to create a reference to the type library, *Import* (*use*) the type library in your application, and then declare and instantiate the class you want to use.

You can obtain a list of available type libraries in the Add Reference dialog box. To display the Add Reference dialog box, right-click References in the Solution Explorer under your project, and choose Add Reference from the shortcut menu. The Add Reference dialog box is shown in Figure 8.4.

The Add Reference dialog box has three tabs. Choosing the .NET tab displays available .NET assemblies; the COM tab displays available COM type libraries;

and the Projects tab displays available projects. If the item to which you want to add a reference is not listed, you can browse to the file location by clicking the Browse button. Once you have located the reference you want to add, you can select it with the Select button. The reference is then added to your project in the Solution Explorer.

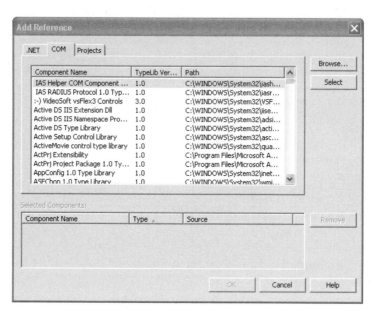

Figure 8.4.   The Add Reference dialog box, showing the COM tab.

Once you have added a reference to an assembly or COM type library, you can us the types contained in that reference in your application by using the fully quali-fied name of the type. If you want to obviate the need to use the fully qualified name, you can use the *Imports* (Visual Basic .NET) or *using* (Visual C#) keywor to make members accessible. Chapter 1 describes how to use the *Imports* and *usin* statements.

Once a reference has been established, you can declare and instantiate the types contained in the type library as you would any other type.

To access a .NET assembly or a COM type library

1. In Solution Explorer, right-click the References node under your project and then choose Add Reference. The Add Reference dialog box opens.

2. Select the reference you want to add. COM type libraries are listed under the COM tab; .NET assemblies are listed under the .NET tab; and projects can be found under the Projects tab.

3. Use the *Imports* (Visual Basic .NET) or *using* (Visual C#) keyword to import the reference into your application.

4. Declare and instantiate the types exposed by your reference as normal.

Instantiating ActiveX Controls

ActiveX is an implementation of COM. As such, you can add a reference to an ActiveX control type library in much the same way that you would add a reference to a COM library. You can then add the ActiveX control to the Toolbox and add it to your applications at design time.

Note   Although ActiveX controls can be hosted in Windows Forms, there are some significant performance drawbacks to doing so. You should use ActiveX controls only when a .NET control with the same functionality is not available.

To instantiate an ActiveX control

1. Add a reference to the type library that contains the ActiveX control, as described previously in this lesson.

2. Add the ActiveX control to the Toolbox by customizing the Toolbox. This is described in greater detail in Chapter 7.

3. Drag an instance of the control from the Toolbox to the designer to add it to your project at design time. Alternatively, you can declare and instantiate the control in code and add it to your application dynamically at run time, as described in Chapter 2.

Accessing a Web Service

An integral feature of the .NET Framework is the Web service. A Web service is a type of class that is hosted on the Internet. You can declare an instance of the Web service in your application, and then call its methods either synchronously or asynchronously.

You can create a reference to a Web service in the Solution Explorer. You can display the Add Web Reference window by right-clicking References under your project and choosing Add Web Reference. This displays a screen that allows you to navigate to the URL of a Web reference or to search online if you do not know the URL. The Add Web Reference window for Visual Studio .NET is shown in Figure 8.5. Visual Studio .NET 2003 has a different window, which is shown in Figure 8.6.

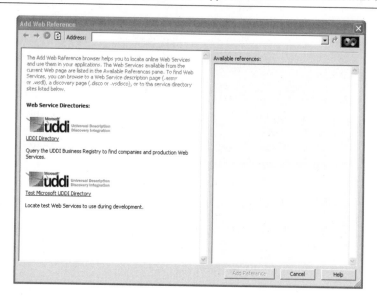

Figure 8.5.   The Add Web Reference window.

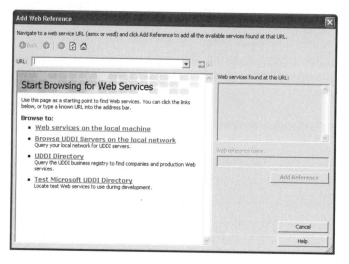

Figure 8.6.   The Visual Studio .NET 2003 Add Web Reference window.

If you do not know the address of the Web service you would like to use, the window displays directories to search. The Universal Description Discovery Integration (UDDI) directory allows you to search Web service registries for companies that provide Web services. When a company is selected, the Web services it offers will be displayed. Choosing a Web service will display the XML contract in the left page of the window and the name of the Web service in the right page. When accessing a Microsoft XML Web service, you can also view a more reader-friendly description of the Web service by removing "?WSDL" from the address displayed in the status bar and reloading the page. Once you have verified the correct Web reference to add, click the Add Reference button to add the reference to your project.

When an instance of a Web service is instantiated, the .NET Framework actually creates an instance of a proxy class that represents the Web service. This class resides in your application and exposes all of the methods provided by the Web service. When one of these methods is called, the call is relayed to the Web service at the address specified on the Internet. You can instantiate a Web service just like any other component. The following code example demonstrates how to instantiate a Web service named *WebService1*:

Visual Basic .NET
```
Dim myService As New WebService1
```

Visual C#
```
WebService1 myService = new WebService1();
```

Calls to Web service methods can be made in two ways: synchronously or asynchronously. Synchronous calls behave just like normal function calls. For instance, the following code example demonstrates how to make a synchronous call to a method named *myMethod* located on *myService*. This example assumes that you have already created a reference and instantiated the Web service:

Visual Basic .NET
```
myService.myMethod()
```

Visual C#
```
myService.myMethod();
```

Synchronous method calls are made just like regular methods calls. However, because they are accessing resources on the Internet, response time can vary, and application execution will pause until a synchronous call to a Web method is completed. If you do not want to pause program execution while you wait for a Web service call to complete, you can make an asynchronous method call. An asynchronous call starts the call to the Web service on a separate thread, allowing program execution to continue while the Web service processes the request. For every method found on a Web service, there are two additional methods for use asynchronously. The names of these methods are the name of the Web method prefixed with *Begin* and *End*. Thus, if a Web service exposes a method named *MyMethod*, the asynchronous methods for *MyMethod* are *BeginMyMethod* and *EndMyMethod*.

You begin an asynchronous method call with the *Begin* method. In addition to requiring the same parameters as a synchronous method call, a *Begin* method call requires an *AsyncCallback* delegate that specifies the method for the Web method to call back on and an object that allows applications to specify custom state information.

Every *Begin* method has a return type of *IAsyncResult*. This interface is used by the corresponding *End* method to retrieve the data returned by the asynchronous call. The callback method specified by the *AsyncCallback* delegate must have a signature that takes an *IAsyncResult* as a parameter. In the callback method, you can call the *End* method to retrieve the data. The following code example demonstrates how to make an asynchronous call to a method named *MyMethod*. The example demonstrates how to make the call, specify a callback method, and retrieve the information returned by the call. This assumes that *MyMethod* is a method on a Web service named *WebService1* and that it returns a string.

Visual Basic .NET

```
Public Class AsyncDemo
   Dim myService As WebService1
   Public Sub CallMethodAsynchronously()
      myService = New WebService1()
      ' The AsyncCallback delegate is created with the AddressOf
      ' operator. The object is required by the method call but not
      ' used in this example.
      myService.BeginMyMethod(AddressOf CallBack, New Object())
   End Sub
   Public Sub CallBack(ByVal e as IAsyncResult)
      Dim myString As String
      ' You retrieve the data by calling the 'End' method,
      ' supplying the IAsyncResult as the parameter
      myString = myService.EndMyMethod(e)
   End Sub
End Class
```

Visual C#

```
public class AsyncDemo
{
   WebService1 myService;
   public void CallMethodAsynchronously()
   {
      myService = new WebService1();
      // Creates the AsyncCallback delegate that will specify the
      // callback method.
      System.AsyncCallback myCallBack = new
         System.AsyncCallback(CallBack);
      // The object is required by the method call but is not
      // used in this example.
      myService.BeginMyMethod(myCallBack, new object());
   }
   public void CallBack(IAsyncResult e)
   {
      string myString;
```

```
    // You retrieve the data by calling the 'End' method,
    // supplying the IAsyncResult as the parameter
    myString = myService.EndMyMethod(e);
  }
}
```

Even though you must specify a callback method, you do not necessarily need to use it. You can retrieve the data in the same method by calling the *End* method directly. If the asynchronous call has to be returned when the call to the *End* method is reached, program execution will pause until it returns. The following code example demonstrates how to retrieve data from an asynchronous call in the same method:

Visual Basic .NET

```
Public Sub AsyncDemo()
    Dim myService As New WebService1
    Dim Async as IAsyncResult
    ' Assigns the IAsyncResult returned by the 'Begin' method to
    ' the local variable. The delegate that specifies the callback
    ' method is required but will not be used to retrieve the data.
    Async = myService.BeginMyMethod(AddressOf SomeMethod, New Object())
    ' Do some processor-intensive stuff here
    Dim myString As String
    ' If the call hasn't yet returned, application execution will pause
    ' here until it does.
    myString = myService.EndMyMethod(Async)
End Sub
```

Visual C#

```
public void AsyncDemo()
{
    WebService1 myService = new WebService1();
    IAsyncResult Async;
    // Creates the delegate to the callback method. This delegate is
    // required by the method call but will not be used to retrieve
    // the data.
    System.AsyncCallback myCallBack = new
        System.AsyncCallback(SomeMethod);
    Async = myService.BeginMyMethod(myCallBack, new object());
    // Do some processor-intensive stuff here
    string myString;
    // If the call hasn't yet returned, application execution will
    // pause here until it does.
    myString = myService.EndMyMethod(Async);
}
```

To create a reference to a Web service

1. In the Solution Explorer, right-click References and choose Add Web Reference.

2. Locate the reference on the Web using either UDDI search or by typing in the address of the Web service. Click the Add Reference button to add the reference to your project.

3. After the reference is added, you can instantiate the Web service just as you would any other class.

To call a method on a Web service synchronously

1. Instantiate the Web service.

2. Call the method as you would call a method of any other class.

To call a method on a Web service asynchronously

1. Create a callback method that takes an *IAsyncResult* as a parameter.

2. Call the *Begin* method of the Web method to invoke the asynchronous call. Supply a delegate to the callback method as a parameter to this method.

3. Either in the callback method or in another method, call the *End* method of the Web method to retrieve the data, specifying the *IAsyncResult* returned by the *Begin* method as the parameter.

Accessing the Windows API

Accessing native functions of the operating system became less important with the introduction of the .NET Framework. Most of the important functions exposed by the Windows API are wrapped in .NET classes, which allow you to access their functionality in a type-safe, robust manner.

Nevertheless, occasionally you might want to make a call to an unmanaged function. You can use the *Declare* keyword in Visual Basic .NET or the *DllImportAttribute* attribute in Visual C# to import a native function. Once you have imported the function, you can use it like any other function in your application. The following code example demonstrates how to declare the Windows API *Beep* function:

Visual Basic .NET

```
Private Declare Function Beep Lib "kernel32" (ByVal dwFreq As _
    Integer, ByVal dwDuration As Integer) As Integer
```

Visual C#

```
[System.Runtime.InteropServices.DllImport("kernel32")]
private static extern int Beep(int dwFreq, int dwDuration);
```

The anatomy of this declaration is as follows: the access modifier (*Private* or *private*) determines the access level that this function is to have in the application. In Visual Basic .NET, you indicate an external function by using the *Declare* keyword. In Visual C#, you indicate an external function by using the *static* and *extern* keywords (both are required on an API declaration). In Visual C#, every external function must be preceded by the *DllImportAttribute* attribute, which specifies the name of the DLL in which the function is located. In Visual Basic .NET, you specify the name of the DLL as a string following the *Lib* keyword. The name of the function (*Beep* in this example) is the name of the external function as found in the DLL. It is case sensitive. In addition, the signature and the return type must exactly match those of the external function.

Note   Many of the type names from Microsoft Visual Basic 6 have changed in Microsoft Visual Basic .NET (for example, the type previously referred to as a Long is now an Integer). You should be especially mindful of this when making declarations to external functions.

Once you declare the external function, you can call it in code as you would any other function.

To declare an external function in Visual Basic .NET

Use the *Declare* keyword to specify an external function. The *Lib* keyword indicates the DLL in which the function is found, and the name and signature must match the name and signature of the external function exactly.

To declare an external function in Visual C#

Use the *DllImportAttribute* attribute found in the *System.Runtime.InteropServices* namespace to specify the DLL that contains your function. You must mark your function with both the *static* and the *extern* keywords, and the name and signature must match the name and signature of the external function exactly.

Lesson Summary

- You can use .NET assemblies or COM type libraries in your application by creating a reference to the type library and instantiating the relevant component. You can use ActiveX controls in the same way. Additionally, you can add them to the Toolbox.

- You can access a Web service by adding a Web reference to your application. Once the Web reference is added, you can declare and instantiate the Web service in code. This will create a wrapper class that exposes the methods of the Web service.

- Synchronous calls to Web service methods can be made like any other method call. Application execution will pause until the result from a synchronous call is returned.

- Asynchronous calls are made in two parts. The *Begin* method requires a delegate to a method that receives an *IAsyncResult* as a parameter. The *End* method of an asynchronous method call uses the *IAsyncResult* returned by the *Begin* method as a parameter to retrieve the data it returns.

- You can declare external functions using the *Declare* keyword in Visual Basic .NET or the *static* and *extern* keywords in Visual C#. You must specify the name of the library that contains the function with the *Lib* keyword in Visual Basic .NET or the *DllImportAttribute* attribute in Visual C#. The name and signature of the function must match the name and signature of the external function exactly.

Lesson 3: Implementing Accessibility

When designing your applications, you must take all potential users into account. For many applications, business and otherwise, this includes people who experience difficulty using the standard user interfaces provided by most Windows Forms applications. By designing your applications to be accessible, you can increase your user base and the usefulness of your programs.

After this lesson, you will be able to

- Describe the basic principles of designing for accessibility
- Explain the accessibility requirements for the Certified for Windows logo program
- Describe the accessibility properties of standard Windows Forms controls and their roles

Estimated lesson time: 20 minutes

People with accessibility requirements are a significant part of the workforce. In order to meet the needs of today's business application programming, applications must be accessible to people with different needs.

Microsoft Windows XP provides a variety of accessibility aids designed to integrate seamlessly with your applications and provide an accessible user experience. For example, SoundSentry allows the user to specify a visual cue whenever the system emits a sound. Additionally, there are accessibility principles you can design into your application.

Accessibility Design

An application begins to be accessible in the design phase. By planning ahead, you can create an application that integrates the principles of accessible design into the user interface. Some of these principles are

- Flexibility
- Choice of input methods
- Choice of output methods
- Consistency
- Compatibility with accessibility aids

Flexibility is a key principle in accessibility design. Users should be able to customize the user interface to their specific needs. They also should be able to choose from a variety of input methods, such as pointing devices or keyboards. The application should provide keyboard access to the application's important features and mouse click access for common tasks. Likewise, users should have a choice of output methods and be able to choose between sound, visual cues, graphics, and text. Your application should interact in a consistent manner with other applications and within its own operation. In addition, your application should be compatible with accessibility aids.

Accessibility and the Certified for Windows Program

In order to provide standard guidelines for designing accessible applications, Microsoft has incorporated five requirements for applications to be certified in the Certified for Windows program. This section discusses the requirements for the Certified for Windows program and how to implement them.

Support Standard System Settings

The first requirement for certification states that applications must support standard system settings for size, color, font, and input. This ensures that all of a user's applications have a consistent user interface that will inherit the look and feel provided by the system settings. Thus, users with accessibility needs can configure their systems once, and all of their applications will automatically adopt a consistent appearance.

You can implement this requirement in your applications by using *System* objects exposed through the .NET Framework. The .NET Framework provides a palette of system colors that can be used to set your application's colors. When the system settings change, the colors of your application's user interface will change. Similarly, you can leave the font determination up to the system by not explicitly setting the *Font* property for your controls. If the *Font* property is not changed from its default value, it will conform to the system font settings. The exception to this is the *Font.Size* property, which can be changed while maintaining accessibility. You should design your application so that it can be used on a screen with 640 x 480 resolution and should not require any special input methods beyond the keyboard and pointing devices.

Ensure Compatibility Using the High Contrast Option

Users requiring a high degree of legibility will select the High Contrast option. This option sets the Windows color scheme to a scheme that provides maximum contrast between light and dark portions of the user interface.

You can ensure that your application conforms to the High Contrast option requirement by only using system colors or colors chosen by the user. Thus, when the High Contrast option is chosen, your application will conform. Additionally, you should avoid using background images for your forms, because they decrease contrast and legibility.

Provide Documented Keyboard Access to All Features

Your application should implement keyboard access for all features, and this access should be documented and discoverable. The use of shortcut keys to access controls and menu items, as well as setting the Tab order, allows you to implement keyboard access for your user interface features. The importance of documentation for these features cannot be overlooked. A user must have some means of discovering keyboard access for features and this should be provided through careful, complete, and well-organized documentation.

Provide Notification of the Keyboard Focus Location

The location of the keyboard focus is used by accessibility aids such as Magnifier and Narrator. Thus, it is important that the user and the application always have a clear understanding of where the focus is. For the most part, this is facilitated by the .NET Framework. When designing your program flow, however, you should always incorporate code to set the focus to the first control on a form when the form is first displayed, and the tab order should be set to provide logical program flow.

Convey No Information by Sound Alone

Your applications should never rely on sound to convey important information. Although sound is an important cue for some users, others might be unable to perceive an audio alert. When using sound to convey information, you should combine the notification with visual cues, such as flashing the background color of the active window, displaying a *MessageBox* notification, or using a non-modal screen that displays information while the application continues to execute.

Accessibility Properties of Windows Forms Controls

In addition to properties that affect the visual interface of a control, each Windows Forms control has five properties related to accessibility that determine how a control interacts with accessibility aids. These properties are summarized in Table 8.2.

Table 8.2.   Accessibility Properties of Windows Forms Controls

Property	Description
AccessibleDescription	Contains the description that is reported to accessibility aids.
AccessibleName	Contains the name that is reported to accessibility aids.
AccessibleRole	Contains the role of the control that is reported to accessibility aids.
AccessibilityObject	Contains an instance of *AccessibleObject*, which provides information about the control to usability aids. This property is read-only and is set by the designer.
AccessibleDefaultAction-Description	Contains a description of the default action of a control. This property cannot be set at design time and must be set in code.

These properties provide information to accessibility aids about the role of the con trol in the application. Accessibility aids can then present this information to the user or use this information to make decisions on how to display the control.

The *AccessibilityObject* property contains the *AccessibleObject* class instance tha provides information to accessibility aids. The *AccessibleName*, *AccessibleDe-scription*, and *AccessibleDefaultActionDescription* properties contain information that accessibility aids can use to describe your user interface. The *AccessibleRole* property contains an enum value that determines how an accessibility aid treats your control. This property is normally set to *(Default)*, which indicates that each control is acting in its usual manner. It is important to set this property, however, when a control is acting in a manner more consistent with another type of control, or for custom controls. For example, if you have a custom control that displays data in a chart form, you would set the *AccessibleRole* property value to *Chart*. The accessibility aids would then treat the control as a chart.

Lesson Summary

- When designing for accessibility, keep the following principles in mind:
  - Flexibility
  - Choice of input methods
  - Choice of output methods
  - Consistency
  - Compatibility with accessibility aids
- The Certified for Windows logo program has the following accessibility requirements for applications:
  - Support standard system settings
  - Be compatible with High Contrast mode
  - Provide documented keyboard access for all user interface features
  - Provide notification of the focus location
  - Convey no information by sound alone
- Windows Forms controls expose the following properties related to accessibility
  - *AccessibleDescription*
  - *AccessibleName*
  - *AccessibleRole*
  - *AccessibilityObject*
  - *AccessibleDefaultActionDescription*

Lesson 4: Implementing Help in Your Application

Too often, the importance of proper program documentation is overlooked. Providing help in your application allows users to learn it more quickly, thereby increasing productivity and saving money. In this lesson, you will learn how to display help in your applications.

After this lesson, you will be able to

- Describe how to use the *Help* class to display help
- Explain how to use the *HelpProvider* component

Estimated lesson time: 20 minutes

For complex or difficult applications, you will want to provide built-in help. You can provide help in the form of HTML files that contain a set of linked help topics or as Compressed HTML (CHM) files that you create with Microsoft HTML Help Workshop. Both of these approaches allow you to display dynamically linked help topics that you can show to your users.

The Help Class

Your application can display HTM or CHM files to users by using the *Help* class. The *Help* class encapsulates the HTML Help 1 engine and provides static methods that allow you to display your help files. The two methods exposed by the *Help* class are *ShowHelp* and *ShowHelpIndex*.

The *ShowHelp* method is used to display a help file for a particular control. This method requires the control that is the parent of the *HelpDialog* dialog box to be displayed as well as the help file URL. The URL can be a file URL (C:\myHelp.htm) or an HTTP URL (http://myserver.com/myHelp.htm). Because the *ShowHelp* method is *Shared* (*static*), you do not need to create an instance of the *Help* class to use it. In fact, the *Help* class cannot be instantiated. The following code example shows how to display help with the *ShowHelp* method:

Visual Basic .NET

```
Help.ShowHelp(MyForm, "C:\myHelpFile.htm")
```

Visual C#

```
Help.ShowHelp(MyForm, @"C:\myHelpFile.htm");
```

You can also specify a *HelpNavigator* parameter. This is a parameter that specifies which elements of the help file to display. You can set this parameter to *TableOf-Contents*, *Find*, *Index*, or *Topic*. You can also specify a keyword to search for, as shown in the following example:

Visual Basic .NET

```
Help.ShowHelp(MyForm, "C:\myHelpFile.htm", "HelpMenu")
```

Visual C#

```
Help.ShowHelp(MyForm, @"C:\myHelpFile.htm", "HelpMenu");
```

The *Help* class also exposes the *ShowHelpIndex* method, which is used to display the index of a specified help file. The call to *ShowHelpIndex* is made the same way as the call to *ShowHelp*.

Visual Basic .NET

```
Help.ShowHelpIndex(MyForm, "C:\myHelpFile.htm")
```

Visual C#

```
Help.ShowHelpIndex(MyForm, @"C:\myHelpFile.htm");
```

You can call the method exposed by the *Help* class in response to a variety of user interface events. For example, many applications include a Help menu item or allow you to right-click a control and choose help for that control from a shortcut menu. You should design your application to provide help where it is most logical and easiest for the user to access.

The HelpProvider Component

The *HelpProvider* component allows you to provide help for the controls on your user interface. The *HelpProvider* is an extender provider; thus, it coordinates and maintains properties for each control as it is added to the form. You can specify a *HelpString* for each control on your form. This string is displayed when the control has the focus and F1 is pressed. You can also specify a *HelpNameSpace* that specifies the URL for the help file associated with the *HelpProvider*.

The *HelpProvider* component provides three properties to each control on the form:

- *HelpString*
- *HelpKeyWord*
- *HelpNavigator*

You can set these properties in the Properties window of each control at design time or in code, as follows:

Visual Basic .NET

```
myHelpProvider.SetHelpString(Button1, _
    "This Button initiates the self-destruct sequence")
```

Visual C#

```
myHelpProvider.SetHelpString(Button1,
    "This Button initiates the self-destruct sequence");
```

If the *HelpNameSpace* property is not set, the *HelpString* is displayed and the other two properties are ignored. If the *HelpNameSpace* property is set to a help file, however, it displays the help file specified using the parameters supplied by the *HelpNavigator* property and the *HelpKeyword* property. The *HelpNavigator* property can be set to any of the following values:

- *TableOfContents.* Displays the table of contents page.
- *Find.* Displays the search page.
- *Index.* Displays the index.
- *Topic.* Displays a help topic.
- *AssociatedIndex.* Displays the index for a specified topic.
- *KeywordIndex.* Displays a keyword search result.

If the *HelpNameSpace* property is set, the *HelpString* no longer displays when F1 is pressed, although it can be accessed in other ways. You can retrieve the *HelpString* associated with a particular control by calling the *HelpProvider* and then calling the *HelpProvider.GetHelpString* method, as shown in the following example:

Visual Basic .NET

```
myHelpProvider.GetHelpString(Button1)
```

Visual C#

```
myHelpProvider.GetHelpString(Button1);
```

Lesson Summary

- The *Help* class provides static methods that allow you to display help for your application. You should call the *Help.ShowHelp* method to display help and design your application in such a way that users can easily access help when they need it.
- The *HelpProvider* component allows you to display either a *HelpString* or a help topic when the F1 key is pressed. You can set individual *HelpString*, *HelpKeyWord*, and *HelpNavigator* properties for each control on your form. If the *HelpNameSpace* is not set, the *HelpString* will be displayed in a pop-up dialog box. If the *HelpNameSpace* is specified, the appropriate help file will be displayed instead.

Lesson 5: Globalization and Localization

The .NET Framework provides unprecedented developer support for globally accessible applications. You can create applications that adapt to different languages, currency formats, date/time formats, and other culture-sensitive information. In this lesson, you will learn how to create globalization and localization in your application.

After this lesson, you will be able to

- Explain what is meant by globalization and what is meant by localization
- Explain how to implement globalization and localization in the user interface
- Describe how to prepare culture-specific formatting
- Describe how to implement right-to-left formatting
- Explain how to convert existing text encoding schemes
- Describe how to validate non-Latin input

Estimated lesson time: 30 minutes

If your company does business in the global marketplace, you must design your applications to accommodate users from a variety of cultures. Users in other parts of the world might be unfamiliar with U.S. formatting standards for currency and dates, or they might be unable to understand the English language. By designing international support into your applications, you increase your application's user base and enable its global use.

Globalization and Localization

Globalization and localization are two different but related processes. Globalization involves applying culture-based formatting to existing data, while localization involves retrieving the appropriate piece of data based on the culture. The following examples illustrate these differences:

- **Globalization.**   Currency is formatted in some countries using a period (.) as a thousand separator and a comma as a decimal separator. A globalized application takes the existing data for currency and formats it appropriately based on location.

- **Localization.**   The title of a form is displayed in a given language depending on the country in which it is deployed. A localized application retrieves the appropriate string and displays it according to the location.

Culture

In your application, culture refers to cultural information about the region in which the application is being used. In the .NET Framework, cultures are identified using a culture code that represents the current language to the framework. A culture code can also specify information about a region. Generally, the culture code is either a two-letter code that specifies the language or a two-letter language code followed by a dash and another two-letter code that specifies the region. Culture codes that only specify the language are known as *neutral cultures*, whereas codes that specify the language and the region are referenced as *specific cultures*. The following list shows examples culture codes:

- **en.**   Specifies English language, no region
- **en-CA.**   Specifies English language, Canada
- **af-ZA.**   Specifies Afrikaans language, South Africa
- **eu.**   Specifies Basque language, no region
- **kn-IN.**   Specifies Kannada language, India
- **tr.**   Specifies Turkish language, no region

A complete list of culture codes can be found in the CultureInfo Class reference topic in the .NET Framework reference documentation.

Although most culture codes follow the format just described, there are some exceptions. For example:

- **uz-UZ-Cyrl.**   Specifies Uzbek language, Uzbekistan, Cyrillic alphabet
- **uz-UZ-Latn.**   Specifies Uzbek language, Uzbekistan, Latin alphabet
- **zh-CHT.**   Specifies traditional Chinese language, no region
- **zh-CHS.**   Specifies simplified Chinese language, no region

Getting and Setting the Current Culture

The application automatically reads the system culture settings and implements them. You can change the current culture of your application programmatically by setting the current culture to a new instance of the *CultureInfo* class. This class holds information about a culture and how it should interact with your application. For example, the *CultureInfo* class contains information on the type of calendar, currency formatting, date formatting, and so on for a specific culture. You can set the culture of an application programmatically by setting the *CurrentThread.CurrentCulture* property to a new instance of the *CultureInfo* class. The *CultureInfo* class constructor takes a string that represents the appropriate culture code as a parameter. The following code example demonstrates how to set the current culture to French-Canadian:

Visual Basic .NET

```
System.Threading.Thread.CurrentThread.CurrentCulture = New _
    System.Globalization.CultureInfo("fr-CA")
```

Visual C#

```
System.Threading.Thread.CurrentThread.CurrentCulture = new
    System.Globalization.CultureInfo("fr-CA");
```

You can retrieve the *CultureInfo* class that represents the *CurrentCulture* by acces
ing the *CultureInfo.CurrentCulture* class, as follows:

Visual Basic .NET

```
' This example assumes Imports System.Globalization
Dim myCurrentCulture As CultureInfo
myCurrentCulture = CultureInfo.CurrentCulture
```

Visual C#

```
// This example assumes using System.Globalization
CultureInfo myCurrentCulture;
myCurrentCulture = CultureInfo.CurrentCulture;
```

Implementing Globalization

When the *Thread.CurrentThread.CurrentCulture* property is set to a new *Culture-Info*, any data formatted by the application is updated with the new format. Data
that is not formatted by the application, however, is unaffected. Consider a form
with a single *Label* control. Suppose that you set the text of this *Label* control in
code like this:

Visual Basic .NET

```
Label1.Text = "$500.00"
```

Visual C#

```
label1.Text = "$500.00";
```

If you then set the current culture to en-GB, which specifies Great Britain, what
would you expect to see displayed in the label? It will read $500.00. The culture
setting has no effect on the label content because no formatting was used. On the
other hand, suppose the value of the *Label* control was set in the following manner:

Visual Basic .NET

```
Label1.Text = Format(500, "Currency")
```

Visual C#

```
label1.Text = (500).ToString("C");
```

When the culture is changed to en-GB, the label reads £500.00. The value is for-matted to the currency format appropriate for the locale. Note that no currency con-version is performed—only the formatting changes.

Implementing Localization

The .NET Framework makes localization easy by creating resource files that hold
data for alternative forms associated with the cultures your application supports. At
run time, the appropriate form is loaded based on the *CultureInfo.CurrentUICul-ture* property.

Getting and Setting the Current UI Culture

The UI culture is represented by an instance of *CultureInfo*, and is distinct from the *CultureInfo.CurrentCulture* property. The *CurrentCulture* setting determines the formatting that will be applied to formatted data, whereas the *CurrentUICulture* determines the resources for localized forms that will be loaded at run time. You can retrieve the *CurrentUICulture* by accessing the *CultureInfo.CurrentUICulture* property, as follows:

Visual Basic .NET

```
' This example assumes Imports System.Globalization
Dim myCurrentCulture As CultureInfo
myCurrentCulture = CultureInfo.CurrentUICulture
```

Visual C#

```
// This example assumes using System.Globalization
CultureInfo myCurrentCulture;
myCurrentCulture = CultureInfo.CurrentUICulture;
```

The current UI culture is set in the same way as the current culture: by accessing the current Thread. For example, the following code sample demonstrates how to set the current UI culture to Thailand:

Visual Basic .NET

```
System.Threading.Thread.CurrentThread.CurrentUICulture = New _
    System.Globalization.CultureInfo("th-TH")
```

Visual C#

```
System.Threading.Thread.CurrentThread.CurrentUICulture = new
    System.Globalization.CultureInfo("th-TH");
```

When the current culture is set, the operating system loads resources specific to that culture if they are available. If culture-specific resources are unavailable, the user interface displays resources for the default culture.

Note   The UI culture must be set before a form is loaded displaying any localized resources. If you want to set the UI culture programmatically, you should set it in the constructor of the main form or in the *main* method of the application. At the very least, it should be set before any important UI elements are displayed.

Creating Localized Forms

Creating localized forms with the .NET Framework is a nearly effortless process. Every form exposes a *Localizable* property that determines if the form is localized or not. Setting this property to *true* enables localization.

When the *Localizable* property of a form is set to *true*, Visual Studio .NET automatically handles the creation of appropriate resource files. This is handled through

the *Language* property of the form. When this property is set to *(Default)*, you ca
edit any of the form's UI properties or controls to provide a representation for the
default UI culture. To create a localized version of the form, you can set the *Language* property to any value other than *(Default)*. Visual Studio .NET will create a
resource file for the new language and store any values you set for the UI in that
file.

Note   Although localized UI elements are usually strings, any property can be
localized. Thus, you can have buttons that adjust in size to accommodate different
text lengths for different languages or a picture box that displays different pictures
based on locale.

You can view the resource files for a form by clicking the Show All Files button in
Solution Explorer, and then expanding the node next to your form. Under your
form, you will see a resource file for every language for which the form has a version. An example of a form with resource files for the default language and
English, French, and German is shown in Figure 8.7.

Figure 8.7.   Localized resource files.

To create localized forms

1. Set the *Localizable* property of your form to *true*.
2. Design the user interface of your form and translate any UI elements into the
   localized languages.
3. Add UI elements for the default culture. This is the culture that will be used if
   no other culture is specified.
4. Set the *Language* property of your form to the appropriate culture.
5. Add the localized UI content to your form.
6. Repeat Steps 4 and 5 for each localized language.
7. Build your application.

When the *CurrentUICulture* is set to a localized culture, your application will load the appropriate version of the form by reading the corresponding resource files. If no resource files exist for a specified culture, the default culture UI will be displayed.

Validating International Input

You might need to incorporate techniques for validating international input into your application. Validating keystroke input can be particularly problematic for international applications. The developer might be unfamiliar with the character system used in a particular locale and, therefore, unable to determine what category keystrokes belong to.

You can use the validation methods provided in the *Char* structure to make these determinations in much the same way as you would for Latin alphabet input. The *Char.IsDigit*, *Char.IsLetter*, and other methods will return appropriate values no matter what input character set is used. Thus, validation code that uses these methods will function correctly without any special modification.

Culture-Specific Formatting

You can supply values for specific members of *CultureInfo* to tailor your application to specific cultural needs. For example, suppose you are writing an application for a client that collaborates with a group in Japan, but the currency used in the application is U.S. dollars. You would need to create an application that uses Japan-specific formatting for most elements, but uses the dollar sign ($) as the currency symbol.

The *CultureInfo* class contains three members that define how globalization formatting is carried out. You can customize these members to provide specific formatting combinations that might be unavailable for standard cultures. These members are summarized in Table 8.3.

Table 8.3.   Formatting Members of CultureInfo

Member	Description
DateTimeFormat	Contains information about how dates and times are formatted, including properties that describe how abbreviated day and month names are rendered, how A.M. and P.M. time is displayed, which calendar and day names to use, and which date and time formats to use when formatting is performed
NumberFormat	Contains information about how numbers and currency are formatted, including properties that describe the decimal and thousand separators to use for numbers and currency, which currency symbol to use, and how percentages are formatted
TextInfo	Contains information about how text is formatted, including which code page to use and the appropriate list separator symbol

You can change the properties of these members to suit specific culture formatting needs. For example, consider the aforementioned example. To create a culture setting that is mostly Japanese, but specifies the dollar symbol ($) for a currency, you would create a new *CultureInfo* object and modify it to the specific case, as demonstrated in the following code example.:

Visual Basic .NET

```
' This example assumes Imports System.Globalization and Imports
' System.Threading
Dim modJPCulture As New CultureInfo("jp-JN")
modJPCulture.NumberFormat.CurrencySymbol = "$"
Thread.CurrentThread.CurrentCulture = modJPCulture
```

Visual C#

```
// This example assumes using System.Globalization and using
// System.Threading
CultureInfo modJPCulture = new CultureInfo("jp-JN");
modJPCulture.NumberFormat.CurrencySymbol = "$";
Thread.CurrentThread.CurrentCulture = modJPCulture;
```

Implementing Right-to-Left Display

Some languages are read from right-to-left instead of left-to-right as in most Latin alphabet languages. Standard Windows Forms provide a *RightToLeft* property that enables implementation of a right-to-left user interface.

The *RightToLeft* property has three settings: *Yes*, *No*, and *Inherit*, with *Inherit* being the default value. When this property is set to *Inherit*, the *RightToLeft* value is determined by the value of the parent control.

Setting a control's *RightToLeft* property to *Yes* does several things, depending on the type of control. Text alignment is reversed. Thus, any text that is normally left-aligned in the control becomes right-aligned. If a form's *RightToLeft* property is set to *Yes*, its caption is right-aligned. Vertical scroll bars are displayed on the left side, and horizontal scroll bars are initialized with the slider right-aligned. Check boxes have their *CheckAlign* property reversed. Tab buttons are reversed, as is the alignment of items in list boxes and combo boxes. In short, formatting for each control becomes a mirror image of itself.

The content contained in a *RightToLeft* control, however, is unchanged. For example, consider a *TextBox* control, shown with standard left-to-right formatting in Figure 8.8.

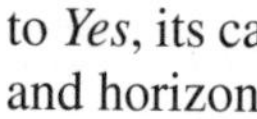

| TextBox1 |

Figure 8.8.   A text box with left-to-right formatting.

In Figure 8.9, the same text box is displayed with right-to-left formatting.

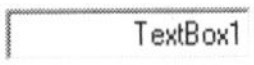

```
TextBox1
```

Figure 8.9.   A text box with right-to-left formatting.

Although control's alignment has changed, the text is still displayed as being read from left to right. Thus, if you create localized resources for cultures that read from right to left, you must format the strings manually.

Setting a form's *RightToLeft* property to *Yes* will cause it and any controls that have a *RightToLeft* value of *Inherit* to become right-aligned. You might want to extend this principle further and create a mirror image of your form for cultures that read from right to left.

You can create a mirror image of your form by creating a localized version and positioning the controls manually to form the mirror image. The position properties of each control will be saved to the resource file for the localized version.

Converting Character Encodings

The .NET Framework uses Unicode UTF-16 character encoding to represent characters. The Unicode character set is a universal standard for representing characters. More than 65,000 characters have a unique representation in this character set, and there is room for the Unicode character set to expand by more than a million more characters. Thus, it is ideal for representing international text content.

Before Unicode, the language requirements for different cultures forced developers to use diverse encodings to represent data internally. Thus, data from different cultures came to be represented in different character sets, such as single-byte editions for European languages, double-byte editions for Asian languages, and bidirectional editions for Middle Eastern languages. This fragmentation made it difficult to share data between cultures and even more difficult to develop world-ready applications that support a multilingual user interface.

The .NET Framework allows you to convert legacy data in other formats to Unicode data. Also, if interaction with legacy components is required, you can convert Unicode data into the legacy-encoding format.

Encoding conversions are carried out by the *Encoding* class, which is found in the *System.Text* namespace. The *Encoding* class cannot be directly instantiated, but you can obtain an instance of this class by using the *Shared* (*static*) method, *Encoding.GetEncoding*, to get an encoding that specifies a particular character code page, as shown in the example to follow:

Visual Basic .NET

```vbnet
' This example assumes Imports System.Text
Dim myEncoding As Encoding
' Code page 932 represents Japanese characters
myEncoding = Encoding.GetEncoding(932)
```

Visual C#

```
// This example assumes using System.Text
Encoding myEncoding;
// Code page 932 represents Japanese characters
myEncoding = Encoding.GetEncoding(932);
```

Once you create an instance of a particular encoding, you can use it to convert characters in that encoding to Unicode format and vice versa. You can convert existing data to Unicode by calling the *Encoding.Convert* method. This method requires as parameters a source encoding, a target encoding, and an array of bytes that represents the data to be converted in the source-encoding format. This method returns an array of bytes in the target-encoding format. To convert to Unicode, you can specify an instance of the *System.Text.UnicodeEncoding* class as the target encoding. The following code example demonstrates how to convert data encoded by code page 932 to data encoded in Unicode:

Visual Basic .NET

```
' This example assumes Imports System.Text. The data to be converted
' is represented as a byte array by the variable name myData
Dim tgtData() As Byte
Dim srcEncoding As Encoding
Dim tgtEncoding As New UnicodeEncoding()
' Code page 932 represents Japanese characters
srcEncoding = Encoding.GetEncoding(932)
' tgtData now contains an array of bytes that represents the Unicode
' encoding of the byte array in myData.
tgtData = Encoding.Convert(srcEncoding, tgtEncoding, myData)
```

Visual C#

```
// This example assumes using System.Text. The data to be converted
// is represented as a byte array by the variable name myData
byte[] tgtData;
Encoding srcEncoding;
UnicodeEncoding tgtEncoding = new UnicodeEncoding();
// Code page 932 represents Japanese characters
srcEncoding = Encoding.GetEncoding(932);
// tgtData now contains an array of bytes that represents the Unicode
// encoding of the byte array in myData.
tgtData = Encoding.Convert(srcEncoding, tgtEncoding, myData);
```

To convert legacy data to an array of bytes in preparation for this conversion, you can call the *GetBytes* method for your encoding to create a *byte* array from a *char* array or a string. For example:

Visual Basic .NET

```
' This example assumes Imports System.Text. The data in the legacy
' format is contained in a variable called myString
Dim myEncoding As Encoding
myEncoding = Encoding.GetEncoding(932)
Dim myBytes() As Byte
myBytes = myEncoding.GetBytes(myString)
```

Visual C#

```
// This example assumes Imports System.Text. The data in the legacy
// format is contained in a variable called myString
Encoding myEncoding;
myEncoding = Encoding.GetEncoding(932);
Byte[] myBytes;
myBytes = myEncoding.GetBytes(myString);
```

Likewise, you can use the *GetChars* method to convert an array of bytes to an array of chars. For example:

Visual Basic .NET

```
' This example assumes Imports System.Text. The data is contained
' in an array of bytes called myBytes.
Dim myEncoding As New UnicodeEncoding()
Dim myChars() As Char
myChars = myEncoding.GetChars(myBytes)
```

Visual C#

```
// This example assumes Imports System.Text. The data is contained
// in an array of bytes called myBytes.
UnicodeEncoding myEncoding = new UnicodeEncoding();
char[] myChars;
myChars = myEncoding.GetChars(myBytes);
```

Lesson Summary

- Globalization refers to formatting data based on locale. Localization refers to displaying a particular set of data based on locale.

- You can implement globalization in your applications by using formatting for your data instead of hard coding the format. Formatting will update when the current culture changes.

- Localization is implemented by providing multiple resource files for localized UI elements. These resource files are created automatically for forms when the *Localizable* property is set to *true* and the *Language* property is changed.

- A culture is represented by an instance of *CultureInfo*. By setting *System.Threading.Thread.CurrentThread.CurrentCulture* to a new *CultureInfo* instance, you set the current culture. You can set the current UI thread by setting *System.Threading.Thread.CurrentThread.CurrentUICulture*.

- You can create custom culture settings by setting individual members of a *CultureInfo* instance.

- You can convert data from code page encodings to Unicode or any other encodings by using the *Encoding.Convert* method. You can obtain an array of bytes from a string or character array by calling the *Encoding.GetBytes* method. Likewise, you can encode an array of bytes to an array of chars by calling the *Encoding.GetChars* method.

Lab 8: Creating a Localized Form with Print Support

In this lab, you will create an application for international use. The application will be a simple forms-based application that accepts orders from the user and adds them to a list box. You will implement globalization for your form and create a localized version for use in Italy. You will also add print support to your form. The solution to this lab is available on the Supplemental Course Materials CD-ROM in the \Labs\Ch08\Solution folder.

Before You Begin

There are no prerequisites to completing this lab.

Estimated lesson time: 60 minutes

Exercise 8.1: Creating the Form

Business is booming! In this exercise, you will create an application to handle orders. The application will allow users to enter values for quantity and price, and add a summary of the order to a list box.

► **To create the form**

1. Create a new Windows Forms project. Add the controls listed in Table 8.4 to the form, and set the properties as indicated.

Table 8.4. Controls and Properties for the Project

Control	Property	Value
Label1	*Name*	lblQuantity
	Text	Quantity
Label2	*Name*	lblPrice
	Text	Price
Label3	*Name*	lblTotal
	Text	Total
TextBox1	*Name*	txtQuantity
	Text	(empty)
TextBox2	*Name*	txtPrice
	Text	(empty)
TextBox3	*Name*	txtTotal

Table 8.4.   Controls and Properties for the Project

Control	Property	Value
	Text	(empty)
	ReadOnly	True
Button1	Name	btnAdd
	Text	Add Order
Button2	Name	btnClear
	Text	Clear Order
Button3	Name	btnClearAll
	Text	Clear All Orders
Button4	Name	btnPrint
	Text	Print
ListBox1	Name	lstOrder

After adding controls, your form should look Figure 8.10.

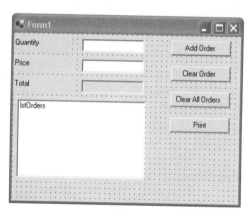

Figure 8.10.   Lab Form1.

2. Using the Events window in the designer (for Visual C#) or the drop-down boxes in the code window (for Visual Basic .NET), implement handlers for the *KeyPress* events of *txtPrice* and *txtQuantity*. They should verify that the keystroke represents a number. The following code example demonstrates an appropriate event handler for txtPrice:

Visual Basic .NET

```
Private Sub txtPrice_KeyPress(ByVal sender As Object, ByVal e As _
    System.Windows.Forms.KeyPressEventArgs) Handles txtPrice.KeyPress
    If Char.IsNumber(e.KeyChar) = False Then
        e.Handled = True
    End If
End Sub
```

Visual C#

```csharp
private void txtPrice_KeyPress(object sender,
    System.Windows.Forms.KeyPressEventArgs e)
{
    if (char.IsNumber(e.KeyChar) == false)
        e.Handled = true;
}
```

3. Add a method to handle the *Click* event of *btnAdd* by double-clicking *btnAdd* in the designer and adding code. This method should multiply the values in *txtQuantity* and *txtPrice* and display the product in currency format in *txtTotal*. It should add a string representation of quantity, price, and total to *lstOrder*. An example follows:

Visual Basic .NET

```vb
Private Sub btnAdd_Click(ByVal sender As System.Object, _
    ByVal e As System.EventArgs) Handles btnAdd.Click
    Dim Total As Single
    Total = Single.Parse(txtQuantity.Text) * _
        Single.Parse(txtPrice.Text)
    txtTotal.Text = Format(Total, "Currency")
    Dim TotalString As String
    TotalString = txtQuantity.Text & " x " & txtPrice.Text & " = " _
        & txtTotal.Text
    lstOrders.Items.Add(TotalString)
End Sub
```

Visual C#

```csharp
private void btnAdd_Click(object sender, System.EventArgs e)
{
    float Total;
    Total = float.Parse(txtQuantity.Text)
        * float.Parse(txtPrice.Text);
    txtTotal.Text = Total.ToString("C");
    string TotalString;
    TotalString = txtQuantity.Text + " x " + txtPrice.Text + " = " +
        txtTotal.Text;
    lstOrders.Items.Add(TotalString);
}
```

4. By double-clicking the appropriate buttons in the designer, create methods to handle the events of *btnClear* and *btnClearAll*. The *btnClear* method should clear the three text boxes, and the *btnClearAll* method should clear the text boxes and the list box as well. For example:

Visual Basic .NET

```vb
Private Sub btnClear_Click(ByVal sender As System.Object, _
    ByVal e As System.EventArgs) Handles btnClear.Click
    txtQuantity.Text = "0"
```

```
      txtPrice.Text = "0"
      txtTotal.Text = Format(0, "Currency")
   End Sub

   Private Sub btnClearAll_Click(ByVal sender As System.Object, _
      ByVal e As System.EventArgs) Handles btnClearAll.Click
         txtQuantity.Text = "0"
         txtPrice.Text = "0"
      txtTotal.Text = Format(0, "Currency")
      lstOrders.Items.Clear()
   End Sub
```

Visual C#

```
private void btnClear_Click(object sender, System.EventArgs e)
{
    txtQuantity.Text = "0";
    txtPrice.Text = "0";
    txtTotal.Text = 0.ToString("C");
}

private void btnClearAll_Click(object sender, System.EventArgs e)
{
    txtQuantity.Text = "0";
    txtPrice.Text = "0";
    txtTotal.Text = 0.ToString("C");
    lstOrders.Items.Clear();
}
```

5. Save and test your work. Your form should carry out a simple adding function and add members to the list box at the bottom.

Exercise 8.2: Localizing the Form

Now that your business is a success, you're going global! In this exercise, you will localize your form to provide the user interface in Italian. You will also implement functionality to allow the user to choose the locale before the application begins.

▶ **To localize the form**

1. In the designer, select Form1. In the Properties window, set *Localizable* to *true*. Notice that the *Language* property is set to *(Default)*. The current UI properties will be used to format the display when the default language is chosen.

2. In the Properties window, change the value of the *Language* property from *(Default)* to Italian (Italy).

3. Using the Properties window, set the properties listed in Table 8.5 to their corresponding values.

Table 8.5.   Resources for the Italian Version of the Form

Property	Value
lblQuantity.Text	Quantità
lblPrice.Text	Prezzo
lblTotal.Text	Totale
btnAdd.Text	Aggiungi ordine
btnClear.Text	Rimuovi ordine
btnClearAll.Text	Rimuovi tutti gli ordini
btnPrint.Text	Stampa

You can generate the à character by holding down the Alt key and typing **0224**. You can also insert the character using the character map tool found in Windows XP. To access the character map tool, click Start, All Programs, Accessories, System Tools.

Note   You might need to adjust the size of some of your controls or your form to accommodate localized content.

---

4. In the Properties window, set the *Language* property of Form1 to *(Default)*. Note that the control texts have reverted to their original settings.

5. From the Project menu, choose Add Windows Form. Name this form **frmLanguage**, and click Open.

6. In the designer, add a combo box to this form. Set the control properties as shown in Table 8.6.

Table 8.6.   Controls and Properties for the Select Locale Form

Control	Property	Value
frmLanguage	*Text*	Choose your locale.
ComboBox1	*Name*	cmbLocale
	Text	Please select a locale.
	Items (add)	United States
	Items (add)	Great Britain
	Items (add)	Italy

7. In the code editor for *frmLanguage*, add an event handler for the *SelectedIndexChanged* event of *cmbLocale*. This method should set the current culture and the current UI culture to the appropriate culture and close the form. For example:

Visual Basic .NET

```
Private Sub cmbLocale_SelectedIndexChanged(ByVal sender As _
    System.Object, ByVal e As System.EventArgs) Handles _
    cmbLocale.SelectedIndexChanged
```

```vb
Dim aString As String
aString = CType(cmbLocale.SelectedItem, String)
Select Case aString
    Case "United States"
    ' Since the default locale is already the United States, no
    ' action is necessary.
    ' action is necessary.
        Me.Close()
    Case "Great Britain"
        System.Threading.Thread.CurrentThread.CurrentCulture = _
            New System.Globalization.CultureInfo("en-GB")
        System.Threading.Thread.CurrentThread.CurrentUICulture _
            = New System.Globalization.CultureInfo("en-GB")
        Me.Close()
    Case "Italy"
        System.Threading.Thread.CurrentThread.CurrentCulture = _
            New System.Globalization.CultureInfo("it-IT")
        System.Threading.Thread.CurrentThread.CurrentUICulture _
            = New System.Globalization.CultureInfo("it-IT")
        Me.Close()
End Select
End Sub
```

Visual C#

```csharp
private void cmbLocale_SelectedIndexChanged(object sender,
    System.EventArgs e)
{
    string aString;
    aString = (string)cmbLocale.SelectedItem;
    switch (aString)
    {
        case "United States":
        // Since the default locale is already the United States, no
        // action is necessary.
            this.Close();
            break;
        case "Great Britain":
            System.Threading.Thread.CurrentThread.CurrentCulture = new
                System.Globalization.CultureInfo("en-GB");
            System.Threading.Thread.CurrentThread.CurrentUICulture =
                new System.Globalization.CultureInfo("en-GB");
            this.Close();
            break;
        case "Italy":
            System.Threading.Thread.CurrentThread.CurrentCulture = new
                System.Globalization.CultureInfo("it-IT");
```

```
System.Threading.Thread.CurrentThread.CurrentUICulture =
    new System.Globalization.CultureInfo("it-IT");
this.Close();
break;
        }
    }
```

8. In the code editor for Form1, locate the constructor. Add the following lines of code immediately after the call to the base class constructor (*MyBase.New()*) in Visual Basic .NET or as the first line of the constructor in Visual C# (before the call to *InitializeComponent*):

Visual Basic .NET

```
Dim aForm As New frmLanguage()
aForm.ShowDialog()
```

Visual C#

```
frmLanguage aForm = new frmLanguage();
aForm.ShowDialog();
```

Note   In Visual Basic, you might have to expand the box labeled Windows Form Designer Generated Code in the code editor to locate the constructor.

---

9. Save and test your application. Choose United States for your locale in the initial form and test the application. Note that currency is formatted using the dollar sign ($). Next close the application and restart, choosing Great Britain as the locale. Currency is now formatted using the pound sign (£). Close the application and restart it one more time, choosing Italy as the locale. Note that the localized version of the form is used and that the appropriate captions are displayed. Currency is formatted using the Euro sign and is formatted in the European style, using the comma (,) as a decimal separator and the period (.) as a thousand separator.

Exercise 8.3: Adding Print Support

In this exercise, you will add print support to your application. You will add a print document and write code to handle the *PrintPage* event. This code will render text to the printer and include support for multipage documents.

▶   **To add print support to your application**

1. In the designer for Form1, drag an instance of *PrintDocument* from the Toolbox to the form. An instance of *PrintDocument* appears in the component tray.

2. Double-click *PrintDocument1* (*printDocument1*) to open the default event handler for the *PrintPage* method. In the default event handler, add the following code to render the contents of *lstOrders* to the printer:

Visual Basic .NET

```
Dim LeftMargin As Single = e.MarginBounds.Left
Dim TopMargin As Single = e.MarginBounds.Top
Dim MyLines As Single = 0
Dim YPosition As Single = 0
Dim Counter As Integer = 0
Dim CurrentLine As String
Dim myFont As New Font("Times New Roman", 16, FontStyle.Regular, _
    GraphicsUnit.Pixel)
' Calculate the number of lines per page.
MyLines = e.MarginBounds.Height / myFont.GetHeight(e.Graphics)
' Prints each line of the file, but stops at the end of a page
While Counter < MyLines And ItemCounter <= lstOrders.Items.Count - 1
    CurrentLine = CType(lstOrders.Items(ItemCounter), String)
    YPosition = TopMargin + Counter * myFont.GetHeight(e.Graphics)
    e.Graphics.DrawString(CurrentLine, myFont, Brushes.Black, _
        LeftMargin, YPosition, New StringFormat())
    Counter += 1
    ItemCounter += 1
End While
' If more lines exist, print another page.
If Not (ItemCounter = lstOrders.Items.Count) Then
    e.HasMorePages = True
Else
    e.HasMorePages = False
End If
```

Visual C#

```
float LeftMargin = e.MarginBounds.Left;
float TopMargin = e.MarginBounds.Top;
float MyLines = 0;
float YPosition = 0;
int Counter = 0;
string CurrentLine;
Font myFont = new Font("Times New Roman", 16, FontStyle.Regular,
    GraphicsUnit.Pixel);
// Calculate the number of lines per page.
MyLines = e.MarginBounds.Height / myFont.GetHeight(e.Graphics);
// Prints each line of the file, but stops at the end of a page
while (Counter < MyLines && ItemCounter <=
    lstOrders.Items.Count - 1)
{
    CurrentLine = (string)lstOrders.Items[ItemCounter];
    YPosition = TopMargin + Counter * myFont.GetHeight(e.Graphics);
    e.Graphics.DrawString(CurrentLine, myFont, Brushes.Black,
        LeftMargin, YPosition, new StringFormat());
    Counter += 1;
    ItemCounter += 1;
}
```

```
// If more lines exist, print another page.
if (!(ItemCounter == lstOrders.Items.Count))
   e.HasMorePages = true;
else
   e.HasMorePages = false;
```

3. Immediately outside of the method declaration, add the *ItemCounter* variable to keep track of the printed items:

Visual Basic .NET

```
Dim ItemCounter As Integer
```

Visual C#

```
int ItemCounter;
```

4. In the designer for Form1, double-click *btnPrint*. As shown in the code example to follow, call the *PrintDocument.Print* method to render your content to the printer. Set the *ItemCounter* variable to 0 so that it prints the entire list each time:

Visual Basic .NET

```
ItemCounter = 0
printDocument1.Print()
```

Visual C#

```
ItemCounter = 0;
printDocument1.Print();
```

5. Save and test your work. Click the Print button to see the order list printed.

Review

These questions are provided as a review for this chapter. If you are unable to answer any of these questions, review the relevant section and try again. Answers to these questions can be found in Appendix A.

1. Briefly describe how to use the *PrintDocument* component to print a document Discuss how to maintain correct line spacing and handle multipage documents

2. Explain how to use the *Begin* and *End* methods on a Web service to make an asynchronous method call.

3. Briefly describe the five accessibility requirements of the Certified for Windows logo program.

4. Explain how to use the *HelpProvider* component to provide help for UI elements.

5. Describe how to create localized versions of a form.

6. Explain how to convert data in legacy code page formats to the Unicode forma

7. Explain the difference between globalization and localization.

8. Explain how to use the *PrintPreviewDialog* control to display a preview of a printed document before it is printed.

C H A P T E R   9

Assemblies, Configuration, and Security

About This Chapter

In this chapter, you will learn about creating, configuring, and securing assemblies. You will learn how to create private, shared, and resource-only assemblies. You will learn how to use the .config file to configure your application and to optimize performance in your code. Finally, you will learn to secure your application against unauthorized users and to protect your code from unauthorized use.

Before You Begin

To complete the lessons in this chapter, you must have completed Chapters 1 through 8.

Lesson 1: Assemblies and Resources

Assemblies are the primary units of deployment in a Microsoft .NET Framework application. Assemblies are collections of types and resources that are bound together to create a logical unit of functionality. Assemblies are also self-describing and contain all the information required by the common language runtime to interpret their contents and configure execution. In this lesson, you will learn how to create an assembly and resource files, retrieve resources dynamically, and share an assembly between applications.

After this lesson, you will be able to

- Describe the parts of an assembly
- Describe how to set identity information for an assembly
- Describe how to create a DLL assembly
- Describe how to retrieve resources programmatically
- Describe how to create a resource-only assembly
- Describe how to apply a strong name to your assembly
- Describe how to install your assembly to the Global Assembly Cache

Estimated lesson time: 45 minutes

Assemblies

Assemblies are the fundamental building blocks of a .NET Framework application. They contain the types and resources that make up an application and describe those contained types to the common language runtime. Assemblies enable code reuse, version control, security, and deployment.

Put simply, an assembly is a project that compiles to an executable file or to a DLL file. Although .NET .exe and .dll files resemble other .exe and .dll files externally, the internal structure of an assembly is quite different from that of .exe or .dll files created with earlier development tools. An assembly consists of four internal parts:

- The assembly manifest, or metadata. This contains information about the assembly that is exposed to the common language runtime.
- The type metadata, which exposes information about the types contained within the assembly.
- The intermediate language code for your assembly.
- The resource files, which are nonexecutable bits of data, such as strings or images for a specific culture.

The assembly manifest contains the metadata that describes the assembly to the common language runtime. The common language runtime then uses the information in the assembly manifest to make decisions about the assembly's execution. An assembly manifest contains the following information:

- **Identity.**   Contains the name and version number of the assembly, and can contain optional information such as locale and signature information.
- **Types and resources.**   Contains a list of all the types that will be exposed to the common language runtime, as well as information about how those types can be accessed.
- **Files.**   Contains a list of all files in the assembly, as well as dependency information for those files.
- **Security permissions.**   Describes the security permissions required by the assembly. If the required permissions conflict with the local security policy, the assembly will fail to execute.

For the most part, the developer does not have to be concerned with the contents of the assembly manifest. It is compiled and presented to the common language runtime automatically. The developer does, however, need to explicitly set the metadata that describes the assembly identity.

The identity of the assembly is contained in the AssemblyInfo.vb or .cs file for your project. You can set identity information for your assembly by right-clicking the AssemblyInfo icon and choosing View Code from the drop-down menu. The code window will open to the AssemblyInfo code page, which contains default null values for several assembly identity attributes. The following code example shows an excerpt from the AssemblyInfo file. Note that Microsoft Visual Basic .NET and Microsoft Visual C# include slightly different attributes by default.

Visual Basic .NET

```
<Assembly: AssemblyTitle("")>
<Assembly: AssemblyDescription("")>
<Assembly: AssemblyCompany("")>
<Assembly: AssemblyProduct("")>
<Assembly: AssemblyCopyright("")>
<Assembly: AssemblyTrademark("")>
<Assembly: CLSCompliant(True)>
```

Visual C#

```
[assembly: AssemblyTitle("")]
[assembly: AssemblyDescription("")]
[assembly: AssemblyConfiguration("")]
[assembly: AssemblyCompany("")]
[assembly: AssemblyProduct("")]
[assembly: AssemblyCopyright("")]
[assembly: AssemblyTrademark("")]
[assembly: AssemblyCulture("")]
```

You can set assembly identity information by setting the value of these attributes in the AssemblyInfo file. The following code example demonstrates how to set the *AssemblyTitle* attribute:

Visual Basic .NET

```
<Assembly: AssemblyTitle("The Best Assembly Ever!")>
```

Visual C#

```
[assembly: AssemblyTitle("The Best Assembly Ever!")]
```

Creating Class Library Assemblies

You will want to create class library assemblies frequently. Class library assemblies represent sets of types that can be referenced and used in other assemblies. For example, you might have a custom control that you want to use in several applications or a component that exposes higher math functions. Such an assembly is not executable itself, but rather must be referenced by an executable application.

You can create class library assemblies and control library assemblies by using the templates provided by Visual Studio .NET. The class library template is designed to help you create an assembly of types that can be exposed to other applications, and the Microsoft Windows control library template is provided to assist you in building assemblies of custom controls.

To create a class library assembly

1. From the File menu, choose New and then choose Project. The New Project window opens.
2. In the New Project window, select Visual Basic Projects or Visual C# Projects, as appropriate, and then choose Class Library or Windows Control Library, as appropriate.
3. Write the code for your class library or Windows control library.
4. Set any required identity information in the AssemblyInfo file of your assembly.
5. From the Build menu, choose Build to build your assembly.

You can switch between a Release version and a Debug version of your assembly by choosing Configuration Manager from the Build menu and setting the appropriate build version. Configuring your assembly is discussed in greater detail in Lesson 2 of this chapter.

Resources and Resource Assemblies

Most production-ready applications use resources. Resources are nonexecutable data that is embedded in an application. Examples of resources include strings displayed in the user interface based on the culture settings of the system or a set of images. Packaging such data into resource files allows you to change the data required by a program without recompiling the entire application. In Chapter 8, you learned how to create resource files and assemblies by localizing your forms. In this section, you will learn how to create resource files manually, how to embed these resource files into assemblies or create resource-only assemblies, and how to use code to retrieve code and objects stored in resource assemblies.

Creating Resource Files

The .NET Framework includes a sample application called ResEditor that can be used for creating text and image resource files. The ResEditor application is not integrated with Visual Studio .NET—it must be run separately. In fact, it is supplied as source code files and must be compiled before it can be used. The ResEditor source files are located in the FrameworkSDK\Samples\Tutorials\resourcesand localization\reseditor folder, found in the folder where Visual Studio .NET is installed. You can build the application using either the batch file supplied in that folder or by adding the source files to an empty Visual Studio project, and then configuring and building them.

Note   If you use the batch file to build the ResEditor, you should run it from the Visual Studio .NET command prompt to ensure that the system path variables include the Visual C# compiler. To open the Visual Studio .NET command prompt in Windows XP, click Start, and then point to All Programs, Visual Studio .NET, Visual Studio .NET Tools.

The ResEditor tool allows you to create .resources or .resx files that contain strings and images. The ResEditor user interface is shown in Figure 9.1.

ResEditor allows you to specify the type and name of the resources in your file. Once entries have been added to the file, you can supply values for the string resources or specify the images to be added for image resources. Once you have created your resource set, you can save it as either a .resources binary file or a .resx XML file.

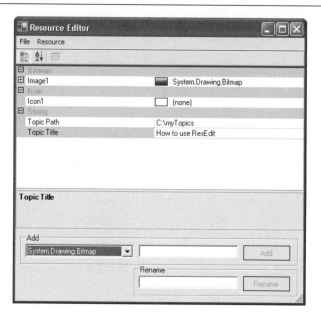

Figure 9.1.   The ResEditor user interface.

To create a resource file with ResEditor

1. If necessary, compile the ResEditor source files. They can be found in the FrameworkSDK\Samples\Tutorials\resourcesandlocalization\reseditor folder, found in the folder in which Visual Studio .NET is installed.

2. Open ResEditor. If you want to edit a preexisting .resources or .resx file, you can open it by choosing File, Open and then browsing to the appropriate file.

3. From the Add drop-down menu, choose the type of resource you want to add. In the Add text box, type the name that the resource will use. Click the Add button to add the resource to the file.

4. In the main pane, click the cell next to the resource name to specify the value. If the resource is a string, type the string into the box. If it is an image, browse to the correct file.

5. If you want to rename any of the resources, highlight the resource you want to rename by clicking it, type the new name in the Rename text box and click the Rename button to apply the new name. If you want to delete a resource, highlight the resource by clicking it and choose Delete from the Resources menu.

6. When you have finished editing your resource file, choose File and then Save As to save your file. You can save it as either a .resources file or a .resx file.

Once created, you can add .resources or .resx files to your project by selecting Project, Add Existing Item and then browsing to the appropriate resource file.

Embedding Resources

Once you have created resource files, you can embed them in your assembly. This allows you to package resources into the same assembly as the code files, thus increasing the portability of your code and reducing its dependence on additional files. To embed an externally created resource into your assembly, all you have to do is add the file to your project. When the project is built, the resource file will be compiled into the assembly.

To embed resources in your assembly

1. Create the resource file. This can be a .resources file or a .resx file. You might find it useful to use a tool such as ResEditor.
2. From the Project menu, choose Add Existing Item. The Add Existing Item window opens.
3. Browse to the correct resource file, and click Open to select it. The file is added to your project.
4. From the Build menu, choose Build to build your solution. The assembly is built with the resource file embedded.

Creating Resource Assemblies

You can create assemblies that only contain resources. You might find this useful in situations where you expect to have to update the data contained in resource files, but do not want to have to recompile your application to update it.

You can create resource assemblies by adding resource files to an empty project. When the project is built, the resources will be compiled into their own assembly that can then be referenced and accessed. Accessing the resources contained in such assemblies is discussed later in this lesson.

To create a resource assembly

1. From the File menu, choose New and then choose Project. The New Project window opens.
2. In the New Project window, choose Visual Basic Projects or Visual C# Projects, as appropriate, and then choose Empty Project. Click OK to create the project. A new empty project is created.
3. From the Project menu, use Add Existing Item to add your resource files to your project.
4. In Solution Explorer, right-click your project and choose Properties. The Project Property Pages open.
5. In the Output Type drop-down menu, change the output type of your project to Class Library.
6. From the Build menu, choose Build <your project>.
7. Your resources are compiled in the assembly.

Creating Satellite Assemblies

When creating international applications, you might want to provide different sets of resources for different cultures. Satellite assemblies allow different sets of resources to load automatically based on the *CurrentUICulture* setting of the thread. You learned how to generate applications for localization in Chapter 8. In this section, you will learn how to create satellite assemblies and incorporate them into your application.

Visual Studio .NET allows you to effortlessly create satellite assemblies by incorporating alternate sets of appropriately named resource files into your application. Visual Studio .NET does the rest upon compilation.

To be incorporated into a satellite assembly, a resource file must follow a specific naming scheme based on the culture for which it is designed. The name of a resource file for a specific culture is the same as the name of the resource file for the invariant culture, and the culture code is inserted between the base name and the extension. Thus, if you have a resource file named MyResources.resx, a resource file containing alternate resources for neutral German UIs would be named MyResources.de.resx. And a version of the file containing German resources specific to Luxembourg would be named MyResources.de-LU.resx.

Once these alternate versions of the file are added to your solution, Visual Studio .NET will compile them into satellite assemblies, and a directory structure for them will be created. At run time, the culture-specific resources contained in these files will be located automatically by the common language runtime.

To create satellite assemblies

1. Create alternate versions of your resource files specific to locales where your application will be run.
2. Name your resource files correctly for their specific culture. Names for resource files for satellite assemblies must contain the culture code separated by periods between the base name and the extension. The base name and extension must be the same as the resource file for the invariant culture.
3. From the Project menu, use Add Exiting Item to add these files to your application.
4. From the Build menu, choose Build Solution to build your solution.
5. Culture-specific resource files are automatically compiled into satellite assemblies and placed in an appropriate directory structure.

Retrieving Resources at Run Time

At run time, you can use the *ResourceManager* class to retrieve embedded resources. A *ResourceManager*, as the name implies, manages access and retrieval of resources embedded in assemblies. Each instance of a *ResourceManager* is associated with an assembly that contains resources.

You can create a *ResourceManager* by specifying two parameters: the base name of the embedded resource file and the assembly in which that file is found. The new *ResourceManager* will be dedicated to the embedded resource file that you specify. The base name is the name of the namespace that contains the file and the file without any extensions. For example, a resource file named myResources.de-DE.resx in a namespace named Namespace1 would have a base name of Namespace1.myResources.

The assembly parameter refers to the assembly in which the resource file is located. If the assembly that contains the resources is the same assembly that contains the object that is creating the *ResourceManager*, you can get a reference to the assembly from the type object of your object. For example:

Visual Basic .NET

```
' This example demonstrates how to create a ResourceManager to
' access resource files in an embedded file named myResources.resx
' in a namespace called myNamespace and the same assembly as the
' current object. This example assumes Imports System.Resources
Dim myManager As New ResourceManager("myNamespace.myResources", _
    Me.GetType.Assembly)
```

Visual C#

```
// This example demonstrates how to create a ResourceManager to
// access resource files in an embedded file named myResources.resx
// in a namespace called myNamespace and the same assembly as the
// current object. This example assumes using System.Resources
    ResourceManager myManager = new ResourceManager
        ("myNamespace.myResources", this.GetType().Assembly);
```

If the resources you are accessing are in a different assembly, such as a resource-only assembly, you must load that assembly before accessing the resources contained there. You can load the assembly by using the *Assembly* object in the *System.Reflection* namespace. For example:

Visual Basic. NET

```
' This example assumes Imports System.Resources
Dim myResources As System.Reflection.Assembly
' The Assembly.Load method requires the name of the assembly as a
' parameter
myResources = System.Reflection.Assembly.Load("ResourceAssembly")
Dim myManager As New ResourceManager("ResourceAssembly.Resources", _
    myResources)
```

Visual C#

```
// This example assumes using System.Resources
System.Reflection.Assembly myResources;
// The Assembly.Load method requires the name of the assembly as a
// parameter
```

```
myResources = System.Reflection.Assembly.Load("ResourceAssembly");
ResourceManager myManager = new
    ResourceManager("ResourceAssembly.Resources",
    myResources);
```

> **Note**   Your project must contain a reference to the assembly you want to access.

Once you have created your resource manager, you can use it to retrieve strings and objects contained in the resource file. To retrieve a string, use the *ResourceManager.GetString* method, specifying the name of the string resource you are retrieving

You can retrieve images and other objects from a resource file by using the *ResourceManager.GetObject* method. This method returns an object corresponding to the name provided. You must perform an explicit conversion to convert the returned object to the correct type. The following code example demonstrates how to retrieve an image using the *ResourceManager*:

Visual Basic .NET

```
' Assumes the existence of a ResourceManager named myManager
Dim myImage As System.Drawing.Image
myImage = CType(myManager.GetObject("ImageResource"), _
    System.Drawing.Image)
```

Visual C#

```
// Assumes the existence of a ResourceManager named myManager
System.Drawing.Image myImage;
myImage = (System.Drawing.Image)myManager.GetObject("ImageResource");
```

Retrieving Culture-Specific Resources from Satellite Assemblies

When culture-specific satellite assemblies exist, a *ResourceManager* will load the correct resources based on the *CurrentUICulture* setting. Thus, if you have an embedded resource file named myResources.resx and a culture-specific file named myResources.de.resx, the *ResourceManager* will load resources from myResources.resx under most conditions, but will load from myResources.de.resx when the *CurrentUICulture* is set to *de*.

To access embedded resources

1. Create an instance of a *ResourceManager* that specifies the namespace and root name of the embedded file that contains the resources, and the assembly in which the embedded file is found.

2. Use the *ResourceManager.GetString* method to retrieve string resources, and the *ResourceManager.GetObject* method to retrieve object resources. You must explicitly convert retrieved objects to the correct type.

Shared Assemblies

Assemblies can be either private or shared. A *private* assembly is an assembly that is used by one application only. A *shared* assembly can be used by multiple applications.

Note   The terms *private* and *shared* have a different meaning for shared assemblies than they do for the *Private* (*private*) and *Shared* access modifiers used with types and members. In the context of shared assemblies, these terms describe whether more than one application can use a particular assembly.

Understanding Private and Shared Assemblies

Most of the assemblies you create will be private assemblies. Private assemblies are the most trouble free for developers and are the assembly created by default. A private assembly is an assembly that can be used by one application only. It is integral to the application, packaged with the application, and available to only that application. Because private assemblies are used by one application only, they do not have version or identity issues. Up to this point, you have created only private assemblies as you worked through the lessons in this guide.

You might disbelieve that last sentence. After all, you learned how to create custom controls in Chapter 7, and you can use the DLL that contains your custom controls in any number of projects. Yet, these controls are described as private assemblies. How can this be?

When you add a reference to a private assembly to your project, Visual Studio .NET creates a copy of the DLL containing that assembly and writes it to your project folder. Thus, multiple projects can reference the same DLL and use the types it contains, but each project has its own copy of the DLL and, therefore, has its own private assembly.

Only one copy of shared assemblies is present per machine, however. Multiple applications can reference and use a shared assembly. You can share an assembly by installing it to the Global Assembly Cache, and there are several reasons why you might want to do so:

- **Shared location.**   If multiple applications need to access the same copy of an assembly, it should be shared.

- **Security.**   The Global Assembly Cache is located in the C:\WINNT (Microsoft Windows 2000) or the WINDOWS (Microsoft Windows XP) folder, which are given the highest level of security by default.

- **Side-by-side versioning.**   Multiple versions of the same assembly can be installed to the Global Assembly Cache, and applications can locate and use the appropriate version.

For the most part, however, assemblies should be private. You should only share an assembly when there is a valid reason to do so. Sharing an assembly and installing it to the Global Assembly Cache further requires that your assembly be signed with a strong name.

Strong Naming

A strong name is a name that guarantees an assembly identity. It consists of information about the assembly, such as its name, version number, any culture information, and the public key of a public/private key pair. This information is encrypted with the private key of the key pair and can be decrypted with the public key of the key pair. Because no one but the developer has access to the private key, the strong name cannot be replicated by anyone but the developer, thereby ensuring the assembly identity.

To sign an assembly with a strong name, you must have access to a public/private key pair. If you do not have a key pair, you can generate one with the strong name utility (sn.exe).

To generate a key pair

1. Open the Visual Studio .NET Command Prompt. In Windows XP, this can be opened from Start, All Programs, Microsoft Visual Studio .NET, Visual Studio .NET Tools.

2. At the prompt, use the *-k* flag with sn.exe to specify an output file for your key pair. Key pair files usually have a .snk extension. An example follows:

```
sn -k myKey.snk
```

A public/private key pair is generated. You can use this key file to sign your assemblies.

To sign your assemblies with a strong name

1. In Solution Explorer, open the AssemblyInfo file for your project.

2. Verify that the version number has been set for your assembly. This is specified in the *AssemblyVersion* attribute as shown in the following example:

Visual Basic .NET

```
<Assembly: AssemblyVersion("1.0.1.1")>
```

Visual C#

```
[assembly: AssemblyVersion("1.0.1.1")]
```

The *AssemblyVersion* attribute is set to *1.0.** by default. The asterisk means that the common language runtime will automatically provide default values for the last two numbers.

3. Use the *AssemblyKeyFileAttribute* to specify the path to the key file for your project. The path can be either an absolute path or a relative path. An example is shown here:

Visual Basic .NET

```
<Assembly: AssemblyKeyFile("..\..\myKey.snk")>
```

Visual C#

```
[assembly: AssemblyKeyFile("..\\..\\myKey.snk")]
```

This attribute appears in Visual C# AssemblyInfo files by default, but must be added manually to Visual Basic .NET AssemblyInfo files.

4. Build your assembly. The strong name will be generated and signed to the assembly.

Installing to the Global Assembly Cache

Once you have signed your assembly with a strong name, it is a small matter to install it to the Global Assembly Cache. You can install your assembly to the Global Assembly Cache by using the Global Assembly Cache utility (gacutil.exe).

To install your assembly to the Global Assembly Cache

1. Sign your assembly with a strong name. (See the previous section for details.)

2. Open the Visual Studio .NET Command Prompt. In Windows XP, this can be opened from Start, All Programs, Microsoft Visual Studio .NET, Visual Studio .NET Tools.

3. Run gacutil.exe with the */i* option to specify the assembly to be installed. The following code example demonstrates how to install an assembly named myAssembly.dll to the Global Assembly Cache:

```
gacutil /i mypath\myAssembly.dll
```

Lesson Summary

- Assemblies are the building blocks of applications. An assembly contains assembly metadata in the assembly manifest, type metadata, code files, and resources. Simply put, any project that compiles to an EXE or DLL file produces an assembly.

- You can create class library assemblies by using the class library or Windows control library templates in Visual Studio .NET.

- Resources are nonexecutable data that is logically deployed in an application. You can add resources to your assembly as .resources files or .resx files. When compiled, the resource files will be embedded in your assembly.

- You can create resource-only assemblies by opening an empty project and only adding resource files to it. When built, the resulting DLL contains resources that can be accessed from other assemblies.

- You can supply alternate versions of resource files for different cultures. These files must be marked with the culture code of the culture. When compiled, these alternate versions will be compiled into satellite assemblies.

- You can retrieve resources at run time using the *ResourceManager* class. Each instance of the *ResourceManager* is associated with a particular resource file embedded within a particular assembly, both of which must be specified when the *ResourceManager* is instantiated. If satellite assemblies exist for a particular culture, the *ResourceManager* will retrieve the appropriate resource when the *CurrentUICulture* is set to that culture.

- Most assemblies are private. A private assembly can be accessed only by the application with which it is associated. When a reference is made in a project to a nonshared assembly, a copy of that assembly is made and added to the project folder.

- A shared assembly can be accessed by multiple programs at once. A shared assembly must be installed to the Global Assembly Cache. To install an assembly to the Global Assembly Cache, you must first sign it with a strong name. You can then use the Global Assembly Cache utility to install the assembly to the Global Assembly Cache.

Lesson 2: Configuring and Optimizing Your Application

The .NET Framework provides tools that you can use to configure and optimize your application after it has been deployed. The configuration file allows you to specify location or version information for dependent assemblies and allows you to configure application properties as well. You can use the performance monitor utility to identify bottlenecks in your application and optimize your code for future builds. In this section, you will learn to create and use a configuration file, to configure your application with dynamic properties, and to use the performance monitor to identify bottlenecks in your code.

After this lesson, you will be able to

- Explain how to create a .config file
- Describe the basic schema of a .config file
- Explain how to set dynamic properties in your application
- Explain how to configure dynamic properties for your application
- Explain how to use the performance monitor to diagnose bottlenecks in your application

Estimated lesson time: 30 minutes

You can provide a configuration file for your application. A configuration file allows you to configure application properties after the application has been deployed without recompiling your code. The configuration file is an XML file that contains information about how your application should be configured. You learned how to use .config files to configure Trace switches in Chapter 5. You can also use configuration files to configure other aspects of your program.

Creating the Configuration File

A configuration file is simply an XML file with the appropriate tags and an appropriate name. A configuration file for an application will have the name *<name>*.*<extension>*.config, where *<name>* is the name of the application, and *<extension>* is the extension of the application (such as .exe). Thus, the .config file for an application named myApplication.exe would be myApplication.exe.config. A configuration file must be located in the same folder as the application assembly that it configures.

The content of a configuration file must be configured in the .config file schema. The basic structure of a configuration file is as follows:

```
<?xml version="1.0" encoding="utf-8" ?>
<configuration>
   <!--configured elements go here -->
</configuration>
```

Aside from the first element, which specifies the XML version and the encoding, and the top-level *<configuration>* element, there is no required content for a configuration file. All other elements are optional and can be added or dispensed with as needed.

In Visual Basic .NET, you can create a configuration file for your assembly by choosing Add New Item from the File menu and selecting Application Configuration File. A file with the structure described earlier is added to your application. You can add elements manually to this file, and it will be appropriately named when the application is built.

In Visual C#, you must manually create the .config file by opening a text editor, such as Notepad, and writing the schema displayed previously, adding any desired elements at the same time. You must then save the file as app.config and add the file to your project.

Note   In Visual C# .NET 2003, you can add a configuration file to your application by choosing Add New Item from the File menu and selecting Application Configuration File.

The .config File Schema

Although an exhaustive discussion of the .config file schema is beyond the scope of this text, this section introduces the higher-level elements of the .config file schema. You are encouraged to consult the Visual Studio .NET documentation for additional reference material on this schema. Table 9.1 provides an overview of high-level schema elements.

Table 9.1.   High-Level .config File Schema Elements

Element	Description
<startup>	Contains only the *<requiredRuntime>* element, which allows you to specify which common language runtime version to use
<runtime>	Allows you to configure information about assembly binding and the behavior of garbage collection
<system.runtime.remoting>	Contains information about the configuration of channels and remote objects
<system.net>	Contains information for Internet applications

Table 9.1.   High-Level .config File Schema Elements

Element	Description
<mscorlib>	Contains the *<cryptographySettings>* element that allows you to configure how the application uses cryptography
<configSections>	Contains custom configuration settings
<system.diagnos-tics>	Contains information on the configuration of the *Trace* and *Debug* classes for your application

To create a configuration file with Visual Basic .NET

1. From the Project menu, choose Add New Item. The Add New Item window opens.

2. In the Add New Item window, choose Application Configuration File. A configuration file is added to your project.

3. Within the *<configuration>* element, add schema elements appropriate to the configuration you would like for your application. Consult the Visual Studio .NET documentation for detailed information on all of the available schema elements.

4. Save your file and build your application.

To create a .config file with Visual C#

1. From the Project menu, choose Add New Item.

2. In the Add New Item window, choose Text File. A new text file is added to your project, and the text editor for it opens.

3. In Solution Explorer, right-click the new text file, and choose Rename. Rename the file **App.config**. In the text editor, add the following XML:

```
<?xml version="1.0" encoding="utf-8" ?>
<configuration>
</configuration>
```

In Solution Explorer, double-click App.config, and choose Yes when asked if you would like to close it. The view reverts to the XML text editor for the App.config file.

Configuring Your Application Using Dynamic Properties

Dynamic properties allow you to configure the startup values of objects in your application. You can map the specific properties of objects to entries in your configuration file and then retrieve them dynamically at run time. Dynamic properties are useful for specifying external resources that might change in the course of an application's lifetime, such as a database connection string. By reading the value of such a property dynamically, you can reconfigure your application without having to recompile and redeploy. Visual Studio .NET allows you to configure dynamic properties using the Properties window at design time, or you can manually add code to retrieve dynamic property values.

Using the Properties Window to Configure Dynamic Properties

You can use the Properties window to set properties of UI elements to be configurable. The Properties window for each control contains an expandable node that allows you to set properties to be read as dynamic properties. Control properties that are likely to be linked to external resources are added to this node by default, or you can add properties by clicking the ellipses next to (Advanced). The Dynam icProperties node is shown in Figure 9.2.

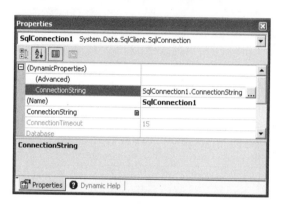

Figure 9.2.   The DynamicProperties node in the Properties window.

In order to read a dynamic property from the .config file, you must supply a key. The key is written to the .config file and corresponds to the appropriate value to return from the .config file. When a key is set for a dynamic property, the key and the value of that property are automatically written to the .config file. The following code example shows the element that is added to the .config file by Visual Studio .NET to make *Button1.Text* configurable:

```
<add key="Button1.Text" value="Button1" />
```

The key value (*Button1.Text*) is used by the application to retrieve the value (*Button1*) at run time. Because key values are read by humans, it is a good idea to create the values according to a consistent pattern. The default pattern used by Visual Studio .NET is *<control>.<propertyname>*, where *control* is the name of the control and *propertyname* is the name of the property.

After the program has been deployed, you can configure any dynamic properties by directly editing the configuration file. For example, to change the value of *Button1.Text* from *Button1* to *myButton*, you would locate the appropriate element in the .config file and change the value represented there. The next time the application starts, the new property value will be read from the configuration file.

To use the Properties window to create a dynamic property

1. In the designer, select the appropriate control.

2. In the Properties window, expand the Dynamic Properties node.

3. If your property is already represented in the Dynamic Properties node, click the ellipses next to the entry for it, select the Map Property to a Key in Configuration File check box, and specify a key for the property. The key and the value for that property are written to the .config file.

4. If your property is not yet represented in the Dynamic Properties node, click the ellipses to the right of the (Advanced) entry. The Dynamic Properties window appears.

5. In the Dynamic Properties window, select the properties you want to be configurable, and set a key using the drop-down menu. The keys and the values for the selected properties are written to the .config file.

Note   Not all properties are available in the Dynamic Properties window. Because property values are stored as strings, you can only configure properties that are represented as strings or types that can be explicitly converted from a string.

To configure a dynamic property of a deployed application

1. Using Notepad or another text editor, open the application configuration file.

2. Locate the node that contains the property value you want to edit.

3. Change the *Value* attribute of the node to the appropriate value.

Note   For properties that are not inherently strings, such as Boolean properties, you must be certain to provide a value that can be parsed to the correct type. For example, when configuring a property with a Boolean data type, you must supply a string that reads either *true* or *false*.

4. Save and close the file. The new property value will be read into the application the next time it is started.

Setting and Retrieving Dynamic Properties Manually

At times, you might want to make properties other than UI properties configurable as well. Consider, for example, a class instantiated at run time. You might want to provide a set of initial properties for that object, but the set of initial properties might vary depending on external factors. You can provide default properties for dynamically created objects in the configuration file and retrieve them dynamically at run time using the *AppSettingsReader* class.

The *AppSettingsReader* class is found in the *System.Configuration* namespace and uses a key to retrieve a value from the configuration file. The main method of this class is the *GetValue* method. The *GetValue* method requires a *String* value for the key, and a *Type* that indicates the type of object to be retrieved. Even though a *Type* is specified, the retrieved value is returned as an *Object* and must be explicitly converted to the correct data type. The following code example demonstrates how to use the *AppSettingsReader* to set the *Text* property of a hypothetical *Widget* object:

Visual Basic .NET

```
' Creates the AppSettingsReader object
Dim myReader As New System.Configuration.AppSettingsReader()
' Creates a new Widget
Dim myWidget As New Widget()
' Retrieves the dynamic property. DynamicWidget.Text is the key,
' and it is returned as a String. It is converted from Object to
' String by the CType function.
myWidget.Text = CType(myReader.GetValue("DynamicWidget.Text", _
    GetType(System.String)), String)
```

Visual C#

```
// Creates the AppSettingsReader object
System.Configuration.AppSettingsReader myReader = new
    System.Configuration.AppSettingsReader();
// Creates a new Widget
Widget myWidget = new Widget();
// Retrieves the dynamic property. DynamicWidget.Text is the key,
// and it is returned as a string. It is converted from object to
// string explicitly.
myWidget.Text = myReader.GetValue("DynamicWidget.Text",
    typeof(System.String)).ToString();
```

If you attempt to use a key not represented in the configuration file, an *InvalidOperationException* will be thrown.

To read data from the configuration file, you must add the elements at design time. Elements containing the key/data pair should be *<add>* elements and should be placed as children of the *<appSettings>* element. The following code example demonstrates how to add an element to the configuration file:

```
<appSettings>
    <!-- User application and configured property settings
        go here.-->
    <!-- Example: <add key="settingName" value="settingValue"/> -->
    <add key="Widget.Visible" value="True" />
    <add key="Widget.Text" value="I love my Widget!" />
</appSettings>
```

To retrieve data from the configuration file manually

1. Create a new instance of *System.Configuration.AppSettingsReader*.

2. Use the *AppSettingsReader.GetValue* method to retrieve the value for the specified key.

3. Convert the object returned by *AppSettingsReader.GetValue* to the appropriate data type.

To add data to the configuration file manually

1. Using Notepad or another text editor, open the application configuration file.

2. Locate the *<appSettings>* element. If the *<appSettings>* element does not exist, add it within the *<configuration>* element.

3. Create *<add>* elements for your data within the *<appSettings>* element. You must specify a value for the key and value attribute, as shown here:

```
<add key="Widget1.Text" value="My Widget">
```

4. Save and close the file.

Optimizing Your Application's Performance

Even after an application is built and deployed, development continues. In business settings, applications are constantly fine-tuned to maximize performance or conserve resources. In this section, you will learn guidelines for optimizing your program.

Optimization Begins During Development

Efficient, optimized code is the result of careful planning and good coding practice. By following coding guidelines, you can create applications that have a measure of optimization built in. Some coding guidelines are as follows:

- **Avoid late binding.**   Avoid the use of *Object* (*object*) data types whenever possible. Unnecessary conversions are expensive in terms of resources and decrease application performance. Visual Basic .NET users should always code with Option Strict On, which enforces strict typing and reduces unnecessary conversions.

- **Avoid global variables.**   Use local variables and constants whenever possible. Local variables are allocated in a memory region that is easier for code to access. Global variables should be used only for truly global needs. The use of constants for frequently used values can make code more efficient.

- **Be wary of loops.**   Because loops can be the most operation-intensive regions of an application, they merit special attention. Take care to design your loops with the fewest operations possible.

Optimization Is an Iterative Process

The general plan for optimizing your code is as follows:

1. Measure performance data.
2. Identify bottlenecks.
3. Tune your code.
4. Repeat.

Once bottlenecks in the code have been identified, those areas should be examined to determine whether performance issues can be corrected. After these issues have been addressed, you should measure performance data again to confirm whether the code optimizations that you just implemented had a performance benefit. Assuming success in this regard, your next round of performance monitoring can identify new or less severe bottlenecks, allowing you to further optimize your application.

Measuring Performance

Windows 2000 and Windows XP include a utility named perfmon.exe that can be used to monitor a wide variety of performance-related issues. You can use this utility to view performance data graphically or to write data to log files.

You can also use *Trace* statements to monitor application execution. Emitted *Trace* statements can be used to pinpoint your application's execution at run time. Cross-referencing this information with performance data allows you narrow down the location of bottlenecks in your code.

Using the Compiler Optimizations

Enabling optimization with the compiler permits automatic optimizations on your application. Although this step does not take the place of careful coding, you can gain a performance benefit in some cases by applying these optimizations.

You can enable optimizations for your application in the Property Pages. To view the optimizations, right-click your project in Solution Explorer and choose Properties. For Visual Basic .NET, choose optimizations in the Configuration Properties folder. The Optimizations Property Page is displayed, as shown in Figure 9.3.

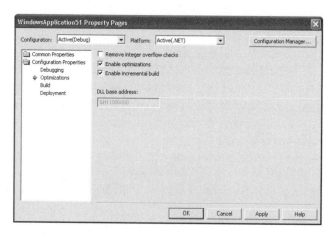

Figure 9.3.   The Optimizations Property Page for Visual Basic .NET.

For Visual C#, choose Build in the Configuration Properties folder to access the optimizations drop-down menu, as shown in Figure 9.4.

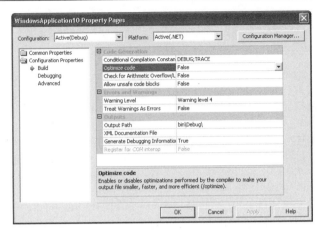

Figure 9.4.   The Build Property Page for Visual C#.

Optimizations are enabled by selecting the check box labeled Enable Optimizations (Visual Basic .NET) or by setting Optimize Code to *true* (Visual C#). This will cause compiler optimizations to be applied when the application is built. Because compiler optimizations can cause code rearrangements at the intermediate language level, applications can be difficult to debug after optimizations have been applied. Thus, you should use compiler optimizations only on release code.

Lesson Summary

- The configuration file contains information that allows you to apply different configurations to your application without recompiling. You can configure applications by making changes in the configuration with a text editor, saving, and then restarting the program.

- Dynamic properties can be useful when they describe external resources that are expected to change in the lifetime of an application. You can configure dynamic applications for UI elements in the designer using the Properties window.

- You can use the *AppSettingsReader* to read data from the .config file manually. The *AppSettingsReader* uses a key to retrieve values stored in *<add>* elements in the configuration file.

- You can use the perfmon.exe utility and *Trace* statements to monitor your application's performance. Use good coding practice and successive rounds of performance monitoring and code tuning to optimize your application.

- You can enable compiler optimizations by selecting Enable Optimizations (Visual Basic .NET) or by setting Optimize Code to *true* (Visual C#) on your application's property pages. This should only be done for release builds.

Lesson 3: Securing Your Application

When writing an application, it is important to protect your code. Hackers and malicious users cause significant damage to businesses every year. It is your responsibility to ensure that your code is secure from attack. In addition, sensitive information, such as company databases and personal information, must be kept secure from unauthorized users. The .NET Framework provides ample tools to secure your applications from unauthorized use. In this lesson, you will learn how to use imperative and declarative security checks to secure your application. You will learn how to protect against unauthorized users, unauthorized code groups, and unidentified code. You will also learn to implement custom security checks.

After this lesson, you will be able to

- Explain what a permission is and how it is used
- Explain the difference between declarative and imperative security
- Explain how to configure role-based security
- Explain how to configure code access security

Estimated lesson time: 40 minutes

Security is about protection. You can use the security features provided by the .NET Framework to protect your code from unauthorized users and to protect the system from unauthorized use of your code. The system administrator sets the overall system security policy. The administrator decides what kind of code a machine will be allowed to execute, whether a particular assembly is trusted, and if so, what kind of trust is extended to the assembly. The security policy set by the system administrator cannot be overridden by your code: it is the highest level of security on a given machine.

Security further protects your application within the bounds set by the system administrator. You can use role-based security to authorize users and code access security to protect your code from misuse by unauthorized callers. Security authorizations can be either *imperative* or *declarative*. In imperative security, permission to execute is demanded at run time. Declarative security, on the other hand, specifies permissions required by the assembly in the assembly manifest. If the required permissions are in conflict with the security policy, the assembly is not allowed to execute. *Permission* objects are the central objects in code security.

Note Unless otherwise specified, all of the code examples in this lesson use *Imports System.Security.Permissions* for Visual Basic .NET or *using System.Security.Permissions* for Visual C#.

Permissions

A permission is a code object that represents a user, an identity, or a code resource. *Permission* objects are used for a variety of security-related functions, such as to represent security clearances and to enforce security policy.

The IPermission Interface

All security permissions in the .NET Framework must implement the *IPermission* interface, which provides a common level of functionality for all security objects, though you will rarely, if ever need to implement this interface as the security permissions provided by the .NET Framework have already implemented it. Nevertheless, an examination of the methods described by the *IPermission* interface give insight into how the objects it implements work. The member methods of the *IPermission* interface are described in Table 9.2.

Table 9.2.   Methods of the IPermission Interface

Method	Description
Copy	Creates and returns an identical copy of the permission
Demand	Walks the call stack and throws a *SecurityException* if any callers in the stack lack the permission
Intersect	Creates and returns a permission that is the intersection of two permissions
IsSubsetOf	Determines whether the current permission is a subset of a specified permission
Union	Creates a permission that is the union of the current permission and the specified permission

Permissions can use the *Demand* method to enforce security. The method requires that callers must have been granted the appropriate permission to access the protected code. If the appropriate permission has not been granted, a *SecurityException* is thrown. The *Copy* method creates an identical copy of the permission, and the *IsSubsetOf* method determines whether the current permission is a subset of a specified permission. The *Union* and *Intersect* methods are used to create a new permission from two specified permissions of the same type. The permission returned by a *Union* method represents the sum of the two permissions specified, and the permission returned by the *Intersect* method represents only those resources that both permissions have in common. In the following sections, you will learn how to use these methods as implemented in the *Permission* objects provided by the .NET Framework.

Configuring Role-Based Authorization

Role-based security is security that grants or denies access to an application or resource based on the identity and role of the user. For example, suppose you have an application that is used by both managers and clerks. You might want to allow everyone to access some parts of the application, but make sensitive parts of the application, such as payroll or personal information, available to managers only. Role-based authorization implements this kind of security.

The Principal

In the .NET Framework, authenticated users are represented by a *Principal* object. The *Principal* object contains information about a user's identity and role, and can be used to validate identity against a *PrincipalPermission* object, which is used to protect sensitive parts of an application from unauthenticated users.

When writing a Windows application, you can use the built-in security to verify the identity and role of the current user. You can associate the *WindowsPrincipal* object that represents the current user with your application by setting the principal policy for the current application domain as follows:

Visual Basic .NET

```
AppDomain.CurrentDomain.SetPrincipalPolicy _
    (PrincipalPolicy.WindowsPrincipal)
Visual C#
AppDomain.CurrentDomain.SetPrincipalPolicy
    (PrincipalPolicy.WindowsPrincipal);
```

The *WindowsPrincipal* contains a reference to the *WindowsIdentity* object that represents the current user. You can obtain information about your current user by accessing the *WindowsIdentity* exposed by the current *WindowsPrincipal*. Because the *WindowsPrincipal* returns the *Identity* property as an *IIdentity* interface, you must explicitly convert it to a *WindowsIdentity* object. For example:

Visual Basic .NET

```
' This example assumes that the Principal policy has been set to
' WindowsPrincipal.
Dim myPrincipal As WindowsPrincipal
' Gets a reference to the current WindowsPrincipal
myPrincipal = CType(Threading.Thread.CurrentPrincipal, _
    WindowsPrincipal)
Dim myIdentity As WindowsIdentity
' Gets the WindowsIdentity of the current principal
myIdentity = CType(myPrincipal.Identity, WindowsIdentity)
' Displays the username of the current user
MessageBox.Show(myIdentity.Name)
```

Visual C#

```
// This example assumes that the Principal policy has been set to
// WindowsPrincipal
WindowsPrincipal myPrincipal;
// Gets a reference to the current WindowsPrincipal
myPrincipal = (WindowsPrincipal)
    System.Threading.Thread.CurrentPrincipal;
```

```
WindowsIdentity myIdentity;
// Gets the WindowsIdentity of the current principal
myIdentity = (WindowsIdentity)myPrincipal.Identity;
// Displays the username of the current user
MessageBox.Show(myIdentity.Name);
```

Imperative Role-Based Security

You can use a *PrincipalPermission* object to perform imperative security checks. A *PrincipalPermission* object can specify an identity and a role, and can demand that the current user match the name and role specified by the *PrincipalPermission*. The *Demand* method checks the current *Principal* against the name and role specified in the *PrincipalPermission*. The following code example demonstrates how to create a *PrincipalPermission* and use it to validate the current user:

Visual Basic .NET

```
' The PrincipalPermission constructor requires the name and role
' as strings
Dim myPermission As New PrincipalPermission("Megan", "Manager")
' Demands that the CurrentPrincipal be named Megan in the role of
' Manager
myPermission.Demand()
```

Visual C#

```
// The PrincipalPermission constructor requires the name and role
// as strings
PrincipalPermission myPermission = new PrincipalPermission("Megan",
    "Manager");
// Demands that the CurrentPrincipal be named Megan in the role of
// Manager
myPermission.Demand();
```

You can use the *Union* method to create a permission that combines two permissions. For example, the following code example creates a new permission that combines two others:

Visual Basic .NET

```
Dim Permission1 As New PrincipalPermission("Megan", "Manager")
Dim Permission2 As New PrincipalPermission("Ann", "Group Manager")
Dim Permission3 As PrincipalPermission
' Creates a union of Permission1 and Permission2
Permission3 = Permission2.Union(Permission1)
' Requires that either Ann:Group Manager, or Megan:Manager be the
' current Principal to access this code
Permission3.Demand()
```

Visual C#

```
PrincipalPermission Permission1 = new PrincipalPermission("Megan",
    "Manager");
PrincipalPermission Permission2 = new PrincipalPermission("Ann",
    "Group Manager");
PrincipalPermission Permission3;
// Creates a union of Permission1 and Permission2
Permission3 = (PrincipalPermission)Permission2.Union(Permission1);
// Requires that either Ann:Group Manager, or Megan:Manager be the
// current Principal to access this code
Permission3.Demand();
```

When creating a *PrincipalPermission* object, you can specify *Nothing* (*null*) for either the name or the role. This allows you to create a permission that validates only the name or only the role of the permission. For example, the following lines of code create a *PrincipalPermission* object that validates only the role of the current *Principal*:

Visual Basic .NET

```
' Creates a permission that checks only if you are a manager
Dim myPermission As New PrincipalPermission(Nothing, "Manager")
```

Visual C#

```
// Creates a permission that checks only if you are a manager
PrincipalPermission myPermission = new
    PrincipalPermission(null, "Manager");
```

You can use the *Intersect* method to create a new permission that encompasses only the intersection of two other permissions, as shown in the following example:

Visual Basic .NET

```
Dim Permission1 As New PrincipalPermission(Nothing, "Manager")
Dim Permission2 As New PrincipalPermission("Megan", Nothing)
Dim Permission3 As PrincipalPermission
' Creates a new permission that represents the intersection of
' Permission1 and Permission2
Permission3 = Permission2.Intersect(Permission1)
' Requires that the Principal who accesses this code be named Megan
' in the role of Manager
Permission3.Demand()
```

Visual C#

```
PrincipalPermission Permission1 = new PrincipalPermission(null,
    "Manager");
PrincipalPermission Permission2 = new PrincipalPermission("Megan",
    null);
PrincipalPermission Permission3;
// Creates a new permission that represents the intersection of
```

```
// Permission1 and Permission2
Permission3 = (PrincipalPermission)Permission2.Intersect(Permission1);
// Requires that the Principal who accesses this code be named Megan
// in the role of Manager
Permission3.Demand();
```

You can also use *PrincipalPermissions* to authenticate membership in the Windows built-in roles such as Administrators. When specifying a built-in role, you must precede it with BUILTIN\ as follows:

Visual Basic .NET

```
Dim myPermission as New PrincipalPermission("Rob", _
    "BUILTIN\Administrators")
```

Visual C#

```
// Two backslashes (\\) are required for C# because a single
// backslash specifies an escape sequence.
PrincipalPermission myPermission = new
    PrincipalPermission("Rob", "BUILTIN\\Administrators");
```

Declarative Role-Based Security

Every *Permission* object has a corresponding attribute. These attributes can be attached to classes and members and used to control access to those classes or members. Attributes play a key role in declarative security. In the declarative security model, permission attributes are attached to the members they protect to specify the level of access. Additionally, the attributes are emitted into the type metadata so that the metadata for the assembly can be examined. The administrator can make a decision to allow the assembly to execute or not based on that metadata. Each permission attribute requires a *SecurityAction* in the constructor that indicates the action to be taken. In role-based security, this is usually a *Demand* action. You can set properties for permission attributes at creation by using the *:=* operator (Visual Basic .NET) or the = operator (Visual C#). The following code example demonstrates how to implement declarative role-based security for a method named *myMethod*:

Visual Basic .NET

```
<PrincipalPermission(SecurityAction.Demand, Name:="Joe", _
    Role:="Clerk")> Public Sub MyMethod()
' Method implementation omitted
End Sub
```

Visual C#

```
[PrincipalPermission(SecurityAction.Demand, Name="Joe",
    Role="Clerk")]
public void myMethod()
{
    // Method implementation omitted
}
```

Configuring Code Access Security

Code access security prevents your code from being misused by unauthorized cal
ers. You can also use code access security to communicate security requirements t
the system administrator.

Like role-based security, code access security is based on permissions. In role-
based security, a permission represents the identity or role of the user. In code
access security, a permission represents system resources and control access to
those resources. A good example is the file system. If you have an application tha
writes to files, you should ensure that unauthorized callers are unable to use that
resource to maliciously inflict damage to your file structure. A *FileIOPermission*
object protects any code that accesses the file system by ensuring that all callers
have the appropriate level of permission.

Code Access Permissions

Each code access permission represents a particular resource. Most permissions ar
found in the *System.Security* namespace, but some specialized permissions are sup
plied by other namespaces. Table 9.3 lists and briefly describes some of the code
access permissions supplied by the .NET Framework. This list is by no means
exhaustive, but provides a sampling of the kinds of permissions you can use to cor
trol security in your applications.

Table 9.3.   Code Access Permissions

Permission	Description
DirectoryServicesPermission	Controls the ability to access Active Directory
EnvironmentPermission	Controls the ability to read and set environment variables
EventLogPermission	Controls the ability to read and write to event logs
FileDialogPermission	Controls the ability to access files or folders through a file dialog box
FileIOPermission	Controls the ability to create, read, and write to the file sys tem
OleDbPermission	Controls the ability to access an OleDb database
PrintingPermission	Controls access to the printer
ReflectionPermission	Controls the ability to use the *System.Reflection* classes to discover information about types at run time
RegistryPermission	Controls the ability to read and write to the registry
SecurityPermission	Controls several rights, including the ability to execute code, manipulate threads and principals, and call into unmanaged code
SQLClientPermission	Controls the ability to access a Microsoft SQL Server data base
UIPermission	Controls the ability to access the user interface

Creating Code Access Permissions

Every code access permission exposes a different set of overloaded constructors that allow you to specifically configure the resources that the code access permission protects. You can create a permission that represents access to all of the resources it protects or a subset based on the parameters supplied at instantiation.

You can create a permission that provides unrestricted access to the resource it represents by using the *PermissionState.Unrestricted* flag. You can also use the *PermissionState.None* flag to create a permission that represents no access. Examples of both follow:

Visual Basic .NET

```
' Represents unrestricted access to Reflection resources
Dim myPermission As New _
    ReflectionPermission(PermissionState.Unrestricted)
' Represents completely restricted access to UI resources
Dim anotherPermission As New _
    UIPermission(PermissionState.None)
```

Visual C#

```
// Represents unrestricted access to Reflection resources
ReflectionPermission myPermission = new
    ReflectionPermission(PermissionState.Unrestricted);
// Represents completely restricted access to UI resources
UIPermission anotherPermission = new
    UIPermission(PermissionState.None);
```

Each permission also exposes additional constructors that allow you to specifically configure the permission. Although it is beyond the scope of this book to detail each constructor, you should be aware of the level of fine-tuning that each permission can provide. The following code example demonstrates how to create a permission that represents the right to write to only a single file in the file system:

Visual Basic .NET

```
Dim myPermission As New _
    FileIOPermission(FileIOPermissionAccess.Write, "C:\myFile.txt")
```

Visual C#

```
FileIOPermission myPermission = new
    FileIOPermission(FileIOPermissionAccess.Write, "C:\\myFile.txt");
```

CodeAccessPermission Members

All code access permissions inherit from the base class *CodeAccessPermission*. As such, they all expose a similar set of methods that can be used to validate and enforce security policy. Table 9.4 lists and describes some of the common members that are important for enforcing security policy. The next section discusses how to use these methods to enforce code access security.

Table 9.4.   CodeAccessPermission Methods

Method	Description
Assert	Asserts that the code calling this method can access the resource represented by the permission even if callers higher in the call stack do not have that permission
Demand	Requires that all callers higher in the call stack have permission to access the resource represented by this permission
Deny	Denies code that calls this method permission to access the resource represented by this permission
PermitOnly	Denies code that calls this method permission to access the resource represented by this permission except for the subset of that resource that the permission instance specifies.
RevertAll	Removes all previous *Assert*, *Deny*, and *PermitOnly* overrides
RevertAssert	Removes all previous *Assert* overrides
RevertDeny	Removes all previous *Deny* overrides
RevertPermitOnly	Removes all previous *PermitOnly* overrides

Imperative Code Access Security

Like role-based security, code access security can be used imperatively or declaratively. When using imperative code access security, security is enforced at run time.

The *Demand* method is the primary method for enforcing code access security. Permission to access protected resources is granted by the common language runtime, which checks the security policy for the assembly set by the system administrator. When the *Demand* method of a permission object is called, it walks the call stack to verify that each and every caller higher in the stack has been granted permission to access the resource represented by the permission. Thus, a trusted assembly might have a method that calls another method protected by a code access permission. If the call to the second method originates in a trusted assembly, the call will succeed and the protected resource can be used. However, if an untrusted assembly calls the method in the trusted assembly, which then calls the protected method, the *Permission* object will walk the stack to verify that every caller has permission to access this resource. Because the untrusted assembly does not have the appropriate permission, the call will fail.

The following code example demonstrates how to use the *Demand* method:

Visual Basic .NET

```
' Creates a permission object that represents unrestricted
' access to the file system
Dim myPermission As New _
    FileIOPermission(PermissionState.Unrestricted)
' Demands that all callers to this code have permission for
' unrestricted access to the file system
myPermission.Demand()
```

Visual C#

```
// Creates a permission object that represents unrestricted
// access to the file system
FileIOPermission myPermission = new
    FileIOPermission(PermissionState.Unrestricted);
// Demands that all callers to this code have permission for
// unrestricted access to the file system
myPermission.Demand();
```

You can also use code access permissions to protect code above and beyond the security policy. The *Deny* method denies callers to your code permission to access the protected resource even if they have been granted that permission by the common language runtime. For example:

Visual Basic .NET

```
' Creates a permission object that represents unrestricted
' access to the file system
Dim myPermission As New _
    FileIOPermission(PermissionState.Unrestricted)
' Denies access to the file system to this method
myPermission.Deny()
```

Visual C#

```
// Creates a permission object that represents unrestricted
// access to the file system
FileIOPermission myPermission = new
    FileIOPermission(PermissionState.Unrestricted);
// Denies access to the file system to this method
myPermission.Deny();
```

Similar to the *Deny* method is the *PermitOnly* method. This method allows you to deny access to the resource except for the resource explicitly represented by the permission. For example, suppose you create a *FileIOPermission* object that only represents the ability to write to a particular file. Calling the *PermitOnly* method of this permission will cause any attempt to access the file system to fail unless it is an attempt to write to that particular file. The following code example demonstrates how to use the *PermitOnly* method:

Visual Basic .NET

```
' Creates a permission object that represents access to a
' specific file
Dim myPermission As New _
    FileIOPermission(FileIOPermissionAccess.Write, "C:\myFile.txt")
' Permits only access to this file, and denies all other
' permission
myPermission.PermitOnly()
```

Visual C#

```
// Creates a permission object that represents access to a
// specific file
FileIOPermission myPermission = new
    FileIOPermission(FileIOPermissionAccess.Write, "C:\\myFile.txt");
// Permits only access to this file, and denies all other
// permission
myPermission.PermitOnly();
```

The *Assert* method is used to declare that a method has permission to access the specified resource. This causes any *Demand* stack walks to cease checking for permission from callers higher in the stack. Thus, if an untrusted assembly calls a method containing an *Assert* call, which then attempts to call a method protected by a *Demand*, the *Demand* will be satisfied by the *Assert* and will allow the call to proceed even though it originated in an untrusted assembly. However, using *Assert* calls is risky because they can allow untrusted code to access protected resources. Therefore, you should be careful when making *Assert* calls. You should also note that *Assert* calls cannot be used to bypass the system security policy. An assembly must be given the appropriate permission to make *Assert* calls for them to be valid. The following code example demonstrates how to *Assert* a permission:

Visual Basic .NET

```
' Creates a permission object that represents unrestricted
' access to the file system
Dim myPermission As New _
    FileIOPermission(PermissionState.Unrestricted)
' Asserts permission to access the file system
myPermission.Assert()
```

Visual C#

```
// Creates a permission object that represents unrestricted
// access to the file system
FileIOPermission myPermission = new
    FileIOPermission(PermissionState.Unrestricted);
// Asserts permission to access the file system
myPermission.Assert();
```

You can use the *Revert* methods provided by each permission class to remove any previous *Deny*, *Assert*, or *PermitOnly* calls. The *Revert* methods are static methods belonging to the class as opposed to any one instance of the class, and thus affect all objects of that type. The following code example shows how to use the *Revert* methods:

Visual Basic .NET

```
' Reverts all ReflectionPermission overrides
ReflectionPermission.RevertAll()
' Reverts EnvironmentPermission Deny calls
EnvironmentPermission.RevertDeny()
```

```
' Reverts FileIOPermission Assert calls
FileIOPermission.RevertAssert()
' Reverts MessageQueuePermission PermitOnly calls
MessageQueuePermission.RevertPermitOnly()
```

Visual C#

```
// Reverts all ReflectionPermission overrides
ReflectionPermission.RevertAll();
// Reverts EnvironmentPermission Deny calls
EnvironmentPermission.RevertDeny();
// Reverts FileIOPermission Assert calls
FileIOPermission.RevertAssert();
// Reverts MessageQueuePermission PermitOnly calls
MessageQueuePermission.RevertPermitOnly();
```

Declarative Code Access Security

You can use declarative code access security instead of imperative code access security to configure access to system resources. As in role-based security, each code access permission has a corresponding attribute that can be attached to methods or classes to specify security actions. Additionally, you can use declarative code access security to request permissions for the entire assembly.

You can attach a code access permission attribute to a class or method in the same way you specify a role-based security attribute. However, instead of specifying a role, you must specify the SecurityAction represented by the attribute. The following code example demonstrates how to deny the *FileIOPermission* to a class using declarative security:

Visual Basic .NET

```
<FileIOPermission(SecurityAction.Deny)>Public Class aClass
    ' Class implementation omitted
End Class
```

Visual C#

```
[FileIOPermission(SecurityAction.Deny)]
public class aClass
{
    // Class implementation omitted
}
```

The *SecurityAction.Demand*, *SecurityAction.Deny*, *SecurityAction.Assert*, and *SecurityAction.PermitOnly* flags respectively correspond to the *Demand*, *Deny*, *Assert*, and *PermitOnly* methods of the relevant permission. There are additional security actions that can be applied to classes and methods with declarative security. If you specify *SecurityAction.LinkDemand*, you only require the immediate caller to this class or method to have been granted the appropriate permission. Specifying *SecurityAction.InheritanceDemand* requires that any derived class inheriting this class or overriding this method must have the appropriate permission.

You can also use permission attributes to make security requests for the entire assembly. There are three *SecurityAction* flags that can be specified in an assembly-wide directive. When *SecurityAction.RequestMinimum* is specified, it makes request to the common language runtime to be granted the requested permission. the requested permission is not granted by the security policy, the assembly will no execute. A *SecurityAction.RequestOptional* is similar, but the assembly will still run even if the requested permission is not granted. Specifying *SecurityAction.RequestRefuse* requests that the assembly be denied the specified permission You must use the *Assembly* (*assembly*) directive when specifying these actions, a shown in the following example:

Visual Basic .NET

```
<Assembly: FileIOPermission(SecurityAction.RequestMinimum)>
```

Visual C#

```
[assembly: FileIOPermission(SecurityAction.RequestMinimum)]
```

As in role-based declarative security, you can set any properties for the permission attribute upon initialization by using the := operator (Visual Basic .NET) or the = operator (Visual C#). The following code example demonstrates how to create an *Assert* for permission to access a single file using declarative security:

Visual Basic .NET

```
<FileIOPermission(SecurityAction.Assert, _
    Write:="C:\myFile.txt")>Public Sub WriteFile()
    ' Method implementation omitted
End Sub
```

Visual C#

```
[FileIOPermission(SecurityAction.Assert,
    Write="C:\\myFile.txt")]
public void WriteFile()
{
    // Method implementation omitted
}
```

Using Exception Handling with Imperative Security

Your applications should anticipate possible error conditions and appropriately handle any exceptions that might be thrown. Because a security failure will throw a *SecurityException*, imperative security demands should be wrapped in appropriate exception handling that allows your application to degrade gracefully if security permissions are not granted. You must decide on the appropriate course of action when a requested permission is not granted. An appropriate course of action is to allow the user to save data and then end the program, or else to proceed with program execution, bypassing the protected resource. Whatever route you decide for your application, good programming practice directs that foreseeable exceptions should never go unhandled.

Configuring Network and Machine Code Access Security Policy

Code access security is enforced by the machine's code access security policy. This policy consists of a hierarchical set of policy levels and code groups, and it assigns code access security permissions to assemblies based on where the code originated from as well as any evidence that it is trustworthy. Policy levels represent levels of code execution within which permissions can be granted, while code groups represent code with common characteristics that can be grouped on the basis of permissions granted to them.

Policy Levels

The .NET Framework provides four security policy levels. They are described in Table 9.5.

Table 9.5.   Security Policy Levels

Policy Level	Description
Enterprise	The Enterprise policy applies to every computer on the network. It can be changed only by a domain or network administrator. Any managed code that is executed in a network or distributed context is subject to the Enterprise security policy, as well as the Machine and User policies.
Machine	The Machine policy applies to the individual computer. It can be changed by a domain or machine administrator. The machine policy contains most of the default security policy for a computer. All managed code executed on the local computer is subject to the Machine policy.
User	The User policy applies to processes associated with the current user, and can be modified by that user or an administrator. All managed code executed in processes associated with the current user is subject to the User policy.
Application Domain	The Application Domain policy applies to managed code executed in the host's application domain.

These policy levels are arranged hierarchically, with Enterprise level at the top, then Machine, User, and Application Domain. Permissions granted at a higher level, cannot be increased by security policy at a lower level, but can be further restricted. Thus, for example, if Machine policy grants permission to access the file system, but not the registry, User policy cannot allow access to the registry, but it can further restrict access to the file system. Granting and denying permissions at the security policy level is accomplished through the administration of that policy's code groups and their associated permission sets.

Code Groups

Each policy level has its own associated set of code groups. A code group is a logi
cal set of code with similar characteristics. Each code group can encompass any
number of assemblies, and an assembly can belong to multiple code groups. Each
code group has its own set of permissions that are granted and denied to assemblies
affected by that code group.

Assemblies are placed in code groups upon the examination of *evidence*. Evidence
is information about an assembly collected by the run time, including the Strong
Name, the URL that the code originated from, the publisher of the code, and security certificates. The .NET Framework provides the code groups and associated
permission sets listed in Table 9.6.

Table 9.6.   Code Groups Provided by the .NET Framework

Code Group	Membership Criteria
All code	All code is included in this code group.
Application Directory	All code installed in the application directory represented by this code group.
Cryptographic Hash	Code that has an MD5, SHA1, or another cryptographic hash.
Software Publisher	All code signed with the public key of a valid Authenticode signature.
Site Membership	All code that originates from a particular HTTP, HTTPS, or FTP site.
Strong Name	All code that has a cryptographically strong name.
URL	All code that originates from a particular URL.
Zone	All code that originates from the zone represented by this code group.

Note that most of these code groups usually have multiple instances. For example,
there is an Application Directory code group for each directory that has an installed
managed code assembly. All code groups and their associated permissions can be
administered through the Code Access Security Policy utility (caspol.exe).

The Code Access Security Policy Utility (caspol.exe)

Caspol.exe is a command-line utility used to view and modify code groups. To run
caspol.exe, open the command prompt then type **caspol** followed by any appropriate flags. If you type caspol without any flags you will view information describing
how to use the utility.

Note   Using Caspol from the command line requires a valid path to the utility. To ensure that the path to the utility is set, you should use the Visual Studio .NET command prompt accessed from the Visual Studio .NET entry in your operating system's Start menu.

Viewing Code Groups and Permission Sets

You can view the code groups present on your machine by using the *-listgroups* flag, as shown in the following code example (typed in the Command Prompt window):

```
caspol.exe -listgroups
```

This command writes a list of all the code groups in the current security policy level to the console output. You can also use the *-all* flag if you want to view all code groups in all security policy levels, as shown in the example that follows:

```
caspol.exe -all -listgroups
```

Note that each code group can be expressed numerically when configuring security policy for your machine. For example, All Code is group 1. Similarly, you can view the named permission sets on your machine by using the *-lp* flag:

```
caspol.exe -lp
```

Adding, Removing, and Changing Security Policy

You can use caspol to add, remove, and alter the security policy of code groups, but this powerful tool should be used with caution. Incorrect settings can allow malicious users to attack and exploit your machine. You can add a new code group by using the *-addgroup* flag. In this following example, the website *www.microsoft.com* is added as a code group subordinate to code group 1. The new code group is created with Full Trust, meaning that any code downloaded from *www.microsoft.com* will be granted full security permissions, as shown here:

```
caspol.exe -addgroup 1 -site www.microsoft.com FullTrust
```

You can view the newly created code group with the *-listgroups* flag.

Note   Each time you use caspol to alter your computer's security policy, you will be prompted to confirm that is what you want to do. Altering security policy should be undertaken with great care.

After creating a new code group, you might decide to change the policy of the group. For example, you might reconsider granting Full Trust to a code group or want to increase permissions of another. You can use the *-chggroup* flag to alter permissions. The following code example changes the permission set associated with the code group created in the last example to the LocalIntranet permission set

```
caspol.exe -chggroup 1.6 LocalIntranet
```

You can also remove entire groups with the *-remgroup* flag, as shown:

```
caspol.exe -remgroup 1.6
```

Lesson Summary

- There are two basic types of code security: role-based security, which authenti-cates users and roles, and code access security, which protects system resources from unauthorized calls.

- The ability to access code and system resources is represented by *Permission* objects. All *Permission* objects implement the *IPermission* interface, which provides a basic set of functionality required by all *Permission* objects.

- Role-based authorization verifies the role and/or identity of the current *Princi-pal* object. You can use the built-in Windows authentication to validate against the *WindowsPrincipal* by setting the *PrincipalPolicy* of the current *AppDo-main*.

- Access to system resources is represented by code access *Permission* objects. Code access permissions can represent all access to the specified resource or a specific subset of that resource.

- Security checks can be applied imperatively or declaratively. Declarative secu-rity is applied by associating attribute declarations that specify a security action with classes or methods. Imperative security is applied by calling the appropri-ate methods of a *Permission* object that represents the *Principal* (for role-based security) or system resource (for code access security).

- You can use declarative security to request permissions for the entire assembly. You can use the *Assembly* (*assembly*) directive to make a declarative security request for the entire assembly.

- Code groups represent collections of code with common characteristics, such has a URL of origin or certificate credentials. Each code group has an associ-ated set of permissions that it grants to the code that is a member of that group. Code that exists on a particular machine can belong to many code groups at once and is subject to the security policy of each of those code groups.

- Caspol.exe is a command-line utility that can be used to view and alter code access security policy on a machine.

ab 9: Configuring and Securing an
Application

In this lab, you will modify the international business application you created in Lab 8. You will add code to allow the user to set the culture by editing the configuration file. You will then configure role-based security for your application to prevent unauthorized users from using it. Finally, you will configure code access security to prevent unauthorized printing. The solution to this lab is available on the Supplemental Course Materials CD-ROM in the \Labs\Ch09\Solution folder.

Before You Begin

Before you begin this lab, you must have either completed the Chapter 8 lab or loaded the Chapter 8 lab solution from the CD-ROM. Additionally, you must use a computer where you are a member of the Windows Administrators group.

Estimated lesson time: 45 minutes

Exercise 9.1: Adding the Configuration File

In this exercise, you will add a configuration file to your application, and then add code that reads a culture value from the configuration file and sets the *CurrentCulture* and the *CurrentUICulture* to that value. This exercise begins with the solution to the Chapter 8 lab already loaded into Visual Studio .NET.

▶ **To add the configuration file**

1. In Solution Explorer, right-click *frmLanguage* and choose Delete. Click OK in response to the dialog box. *frmLanguage* is deleted from the project.

2. In Solution Explorer, right-click Form1 and choose View Code. The code window for Form1 opens.

3. Locate the constructor for *Form1*. Note that in Visual Basic .NET, you will have to open the Windows Form Designer generated code region. In the constructor, delete the following two lines of code:

Visual Basic .NET

```
Dim aForm As New frmLanguage()
aForm.ShowDialog()
```

Visual C#

```
frmLanguage aForm = new frmLanguage();
aForm.ShowDialog();
```

4. Add a configuration file to your application. The method for doing this differs depending on the language you use.

Visual Basic .NET

1. From the Project menu, choose Add New Item.
2. In the Add New Item window, choose Application Configuration File. An application configuration file is added to your project.

Visual C#

1. From the Project menu, choose Add New Item.
2. In the Add New Item window, choose Text File. A new text file is added to your project and the text editor for it opens.
3. In Solution Explorer, right-click the new text file, and choose Rename. Rename the file **App.config**. In the text editor, add the following XML:

```
<?xml version="1.0" encoding="utf-8" ?>
<configuration>
</configuration>
```

4. In Solution Explorer, double-click App.config, and choose Yes when asked if you would like to close it. The view reverts to the XML text editor for the App.config file.
5. In the XML text editor for the App.config file, add the following XML code. This code should be nested within the *<configuration>* element:

```
<appSettings>
    <!-- Change the value of Culture to set the current culture -->
    <!-- Change the value of UICulture to set the current
        UI culture -->
    <add key="Culture" value="it-IT" />
    <add key="UICulture" value="it-IT" />
</appSettings>
```

6. In Solution Explorer, right-click Form1 and choose View Code. The code editor for Form1 opens.
7. In the constructor for *Form1*, add the following code to read the values from the configuration file and set the *CurrentCulture* and *CurrentUICulture*.

Visual Basic .NET

```
Dim Reader As New System.Configuration.AppSettingsReader()
Threading.Thread.CurrentThread.CurrentCulture = New _
    Globalization.CultureInfo(CType(Reader.GetValue("Culture", _
    GetType(String)), String))
Threading.Thread.CurrentThread.CurrentUICulture = New _
    Globalization.CultureInfo(CType(Reader.GetValue("UICulture", _
    GetType(String)), String))
```

Visual C#

```
System.Configuration.AppSettingsReader reader = new
    System.Configuration.AppSettingsReader();
System.Threading.Thread.CurrentThread.CurrentCulture = new
```

```
     System.Globalization.CultureInfo((string)
     (reader.GetValue("Culture", typeof(string)))));
System.Threading.Thread.CurrentThread.CurrentUICulture = new
     System.Globalization.CultureInfo((string)
     (reader.GetValue("UICulture", typeof(string)))));
```

8. Press F5 to test your application. When Form1 opens, note that the user interface is displayed in Italian and the Euro symbol is used to format currency in
   the list box.

Exercise 9.2: Securing Your Application

In this exercise, you will add security code to your application. You will use imperative security to verify the role of the user, and then add a declarative security
check to protect access to the printer.

▶   **To add security to your application**

1. In Solution Explorer, right-click Form1 and choose View Code. The code editor
   for Form1 opens.

2. In the constructor for *Form1*, add the following code to restrict access to the
   application to members of the Windows built-in Administrators role:

Visual Basic .NET

```
AppDomain.CurrentDomain.SetPrincipalPolicy _
    (System.Security.Principal.PrincipalPolicy.WindowsPrincipal)
Dim myPerm As New _
    System.Security.Permissions.PrincipalPermission(Nothing, _
    "BUILTIN\Administrators")
Try
     myPerm.Demand()
Catch se As System.Security.SecurityException
    MessageBox.Show _
        ("You do not have permission to run this program!")
    End
End Try
```

Visual C#

```
AppDomain.CurrentDomain.SetPrincipalPolicy
    (System.Security.Principal.PrincipalPolicy.WindowsPrincipal);
System.Security.Permissions.PrincipalPermission myPerm = new
    System.Security.Permissions.PrincipalPermission(null,
    "BUILTIN\\Administrators");
try
{
     myPerm.Demand();
}
catch(System.Security.SecurityException se)
{
```

```
MessageBox.Show
    ("You do not have permission to run this program!");
throw se;
}
```

3. Locate the *btnPrint_Click* method. Attach the following security attribute to this method to ensure that only trusted code is allowed to use the printer:

Visual Basic .NET

```
<Drawing.Printing.PrintingPermission _
    (Security.Permissions.SecurityAction.Demand, _
    Level:=Drawing.Printing.PrintingPermissionLevel.AllPrinting)>
```

Visual C#

```
[System.Drawing.Printing.PrintingPermission
    (System.Security.Permissions.SecurityAction.Demand,
    Level=System.Drawing.Printing.PrintingPermissionLevel.AllPrinting)]
```

4. In the *btnPrint_Click* method, add exception handling to wrap the printing attempt. For example:

Visual Basic .NET

```
Try
    PrintDocument1.Print()
Catch
    MessageBox.Show("You do not have permission to print!")
End Try
```

Visual C#

```
try
{
    printDocument1.Print();
}
catch
{
    MessageBox.Show("You do not have permission to print!");
}
```

5. Press F5 to test your application. The application should run normally.

Note   Your code will fail to run if you are not a member of the Administrators group. In this case, set the specified role to a Windows built-in group in which you are a member. If you receive a security exception when attempting to print, you should adjust the security policy for this assembly or ask the system administrator to do so.

---

6. In the line that creates the *PrincipalPermission*, change the specified role from BUILTIN\Administrators to a nonexistent Windows role, such as BUILTIN\Administratorss. Press F5 to build and run the program.

The application denies you permission and fails to execute. In Visual Basic .NET, the application ends. In Visual C#, the application breaks on an unhandled exception that is rethrown. Change the specified role back to BUILTIN\Administrators.

7. In the attribute specifying the *PrintingPermission*, change the security action from *Demand* to *Deny*. Press F5 to build and run the application and attempt to print.

   Permission to print is denied, and the user is informed. Return the security action to its original value and build the application.

8. From the File menu, choose Save All to save your work.

Review

The following questions are intended to reinforce key concepts and information presented in this chapter. If you are unable to answer a question, return to the appropriate lesson to review, and then try the question again. Answers to the questions can be found in Appendix A.

1. Describe how to sign your assembly with a strong name. Why would you want to do this?

2. Describe how to use code to retrieve resources at run time.

3. Explain how to retrieve information from the configuration file at run time. How would you store information in the configuration file at design time?

4. You are creating a solution that must be accessed by members of a group called Developers and Administrators on the local machine. Describe a plan to implement this security scheme.

5. Briefly highlight the differences between imperative and declarative security as they pertain to code access security.

6. What is a shared assembly? How would you create one?

C H A P T E R   1 0

Deploying Your Application

About This Chapter

In this chapter, you will learn how to plan and execute the deployment of your project. You will learn how to plan deployments from a network, from the Internet, and from removable media. In addition, you will learn how to create a setup project for your application and deploy your application to a host computer.

Before You Begin

To complete the lessons in this chapter, you must have completed Chapters 1 through 9.

Lesson 1: Planning the Deployment of Your Project

For an application to be successful, it must reach the intended audience. Microsoft Visual Studio .NET provides many different options for deploying your project, from simple XCOPY deployment (copying a directory and its subdirectories) to fully configurable Microsoft Windows Installer options. In this lesson, you will learn how to choose the best deployment option for your project.

After this lesson, you will be able to

- Explain how to use XCOPY to deploy a Microsoft Windows Forms application
- Describe how to create and configure a setup project for your application using the Setup Project Wizard
- Explain how to plan a deployment from removable media
- Explain how to plan a deployment from a network share
- Explain how to plan a deployment from a Web server

Estimated lesson time: 45 minutes

Once an application has been developed, tested, and debugged, it is ready for deployment to client machines. The goal of a deployment is the simple and easy installation of application files and any other required files to a client machine. For simple programs, the Microsoft .NET Framework allows you to deploy your application by copying the application directory to the target machine. For more complex applications, Visual Studio .NET provides Windows Installer technology, which allows you to make fully configurable setup projects for your application.

XCOPY Deployment

XCOPY deployment is a simple and straightforward deployment scenario that uses the MS-DOS XCOPY command to copy the contents of a directory and subdirectories to a target directory. XCOPY deployments have severe limitations, however.

XCOPY deployment is accomplished from the command prompt. You use the XCOPY command to specify the source directory and the target directory. The /s flag indicates that subdirectories are to be copied as well. For example, the following command-line command is used to copy the MyApplication directory and all subdirectories from drive D to drive C:

```
XCOPY D:\MyApplication C:\MyApplication /s
```

You can obtain information about additional XCOPY command-line flags by typing **HELP XCOPY** at the command prompt.

XCOPY deployment dictates that all files required by the application are located in the application directory. This includes the compiled .exe files and any other required files, such as .dll files representing components or controls and resource files. XCOPY deployment also requires installation of the .NET Framework on the target machine. Additionally, an application to be deployed in this manner cannot require any files or resources, such as databases or shared components, that are not already installed on each and every client machine on which the program will be installed.

As a rule, you should use XCOPY deployment only for applications that have no external dependencies outside of the .NET Framework and only if the .NET Framework is guaranteed to be installed on every target machine.

To deploy your application using XCOPY

1. Verify that your application meets the requirements for XCOPY deployment.
2. Open the command window. To locate the command window in Microsoft Windows XP, click Start, All Programs, Accessories.
3. Run XCOPY from the command prompt, specifying the source and destination directories and including any command-line flags, such as the */s* example cited previously.

Creating Setup Projects

For applications that cannot be deployed by XCOPY, you can use Visual Studio .NET to create Windows Installer setup projects. Windows Installer projects are fully configurable for a variety of deployment plans. You can create a setup project for your application by adding a setup project to an existing solution.

There are two kinds of setup projects related to Windows Forms: *setup projects* and *merge module projects*. Setup projects are used for deploying executable applications. A compiled setup project contains a setup application capable of installing your program to a target computer. A merge module, on the other hand, deploys controls or components that do not exist as stand-alone applications and cannot be deployed directly. A merge module is a redistributable package that can be merged with an existing setup project. It contains all the appropriate information concerning how and where to install the assembly, but it must be installed along with an application.

Using the Setup Project Wizard

To choose the appropriate type of setup application for your project, Visual Studio .NET provides the Setup Project Wizard. The Setup Project Wizard walks you through the task of creating your setup project and quickly creates the base setup project, which then can be further configured in the integrated development environment (IDE).

To add a setup project to your solution, click File, Add Project, New Project to display the Add New Project dialog box. To access the Setup Project Wizard, choose Setup And Deployment Projects in the Project Types pane and Setup Project Wizard in the Templates window. This launches the Setup Project Wizard shown in Figure 10.1.

Figure 10.1.   The Setup Project Wizard.

Click Next to open the Choose A Project Type page, as shown in Figure 10.2. This page allows you to specify the type of setup project to create. If you are creating a setup project for an application, choose Create A Setup For A Windows Application. If you are creating a setup project for a DLL file (in other words, a nonexecutable assembly), choose Create A Merge Module For Windows Installer. Click Next

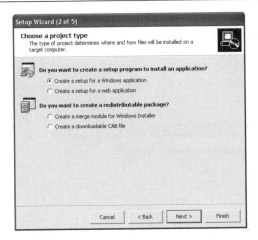

Figure 10.2.   Choosing the project type in the Setup Wizard.

The Choose Project Outputs To Include page allows you to choose the files from your solution that will be included in your setup project. Normally, you will see five check boxes (six for Visual C#) for each project in your solution, each of which specifies a type of content to be added to the setup project. As each entry is clicked, a description of that entry is shown in the Description box. The Visual Basic .NET page is shown in Figure 10.3.

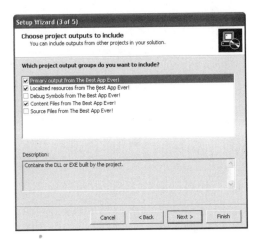

Figure 10.3.   Using the Setup Wizard to choose project outputs to include in your setup project.

Select the Primary Output check box if you want to include the .exe or .dll files represented by the project. Source Files and Debug Symbols can be useful in a test deployment but are usually not needed for a release deployment. Click Next.

Figure 10.4 shows the Choose Files To Include page of the Setup Project Wizard. This page allows you to specify additional files to be included in your setup project. Additional files can be text files that consist of "readme" information, HTML pages containing application help, or other kinds of support files that normally are not included with the application. You can specify a file by clicking the Add button and browsing to the appropriate file. Click Next.

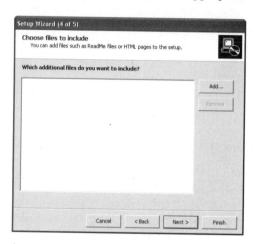

Figure 10.4.   Using the Setup Wizard to choose other files to include in your setup project

The Create Project page of the Setup Project Wizard, shown in Figure 10.5, provides a detailed summary of your choices for the setup project. Click Finish to create the setup project and add it to your solution. At any time after it is created, you can add additional content to your setup project by right-clicking the project in Solution Explorer and choosing the appropriate option from the Add menu.

Figure 10.5.   The Setup Project Wizard summary.

To create a setup project for your application with the Setup Project Wizard

1. From the File menu, choose Add Project, New Project. The Add New Project dialog box opens.

2. In the Project Types pane, choose Setup And Deployment Projects. In the Templates pane, choose Setup Wizard.

3. After the title pane, choose the type of setup project. Choose Merge Module for a DLL or Setup For A Windows Application for an application.

4. Use the next two screens to specify the project output and any additional files that you want to include in your setup project.

5. On the Summary screen, click Finish to create your setup project.

Once you create your setup project, it is added to your solution and can be viewed in Solution Explorer, as shown in Figure 10.6. In addition to the files you specify for inclusion, Visual Studio .NET automatically detects any dependencies the setup project might have and adds them to the Detected Dependencies folder. For example, in Figure 10.6, a dependency on the .NET Framework redistributable package has been detected. Dependencies that are not explicitly included in the setup project are excluded from the build process by default. You can include an excluded dependency file by right-clicking the file in Solution Explorer and clearing the check mark from Exclude in the pop-up menu. Note that including the .NET Framework redistributable files dramatically increases the size of your application. You should only include redistributable files if the target machine for your application does not have the .NET Framework already installed.

Figure 10.6.   A detected dependency.

Configuring Build Properties of Your Setup Project

Once your setup project has been added to your solution, you can configure the output it produces by setting the Build properties. Normally, a setup project produces at least one Windows Installer file (with an .msi extension), which contains all the information and content needed to install your application to a target computer. Depending on how the Build properties are configured, however, you can create additional files to package content or install Windows Installer on target machines that do not have it already. You can access the Build properties of your project by right-clicking your project in Solution Explorer and choosing Properties. This displays the Property Pages dialog box for your setup application. An example is shown in Figure 10.7.

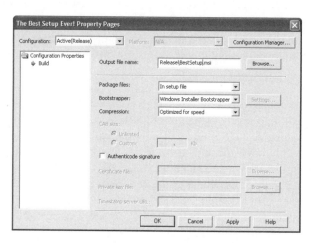

Figure 10.7.   The Setup Property Pages dialog box.

The Build properties determine how the output of your setup project is configured. You might want to provide different values for these properties based on the deployment plan for your project. The Build properties are discussed in detail in the following sections. Refer to Figure 10.7 throughout this discussion.

Output File Name

The Output File Name option represents the location where the Windows Installer file will be placed when built and the name it will have. The default value for this property is *<configuration>\<project name>.<extension>*, where *<configuration>* is a subdirectory for the selected configuration located in the project directory, *<project name>* defaults to the name of the project, and *<extension>* is .msi for Windows Installer applications and .msm for Windows Installer merge modules. You can alter the build path by clicking the Browse button and choosing a new build directory.

Package Files

The Package Files option determines how the output files for your solution will be packaged into the setup project. The default setting is to package output files in the setup file itself. This allows for the greatest level of compression and the lowest level of complexity because all the information needed to deploy your application is contained within a single file.

In some cases, however, you might want to package your application in Cabinet (CAB) files. When you package your output into CAB files, you can choose the size of the CAB files you produce. This is useful if you have a size limitation for your output files. For example, if you plan to distribute your application on floppy disks, you would want to package your output files into CAB files and set the CAB file size (see the next section for more information) to 1440 KB. You could then copy the resulting CAB files to floppy disks.

Another option for this property is to package your output in loose, uncompressed files. With this option, no compression is applied, and the project output files are simply copied to the same directory as the .msi file.

CAB Size

If you choose to package your files in CAB files, the CAB Size property becomes enabled. You can choose between two options for this property. Choosing Unlimited causes the setup project to create a single CAB file that contains all your project output. If you choose Custom, you can specify the maximum size of your CAB files. This is particularly useful if you are planning to distribute your application on floppy disks or other removable media.

Bootstrapper

The Bootstrapper option for your setup project allows you to specify whether to generate a bootstrapping application along with your setup project. A bootstrapping application installs Windows Installer 1.5 to the target machine before your application is installed. Windows Installer 1.5 is the default version of Windows Installer for Windows XP. If you choose to create a bootstrapping application, your setup project will generate additional files that will be used by your setup application to install Windows Installer 1.5 when necessary. Any deployment to Windows XP will not require the use of a bootstrapping application. If you are deploying to a prior version of Windows, you will need to run the bootstrapping application the first time a Windows Installer project is used.

If you are only planning to deploy your application to machines running Windows XP or machines that have already had Windows Installer 1.5 installed, you can choose None to generate no bootstrapping application. Otherwise, you would choose Windows Installer Bootstrapper for most distribution plans. Choosing Windows Installer causes four additional files to be generated and placed in the Build directory. These files are summarized in Table 10.1.

Table 10.1.   Windows Installer Bootstrapper Files

File	Description
Setup.exe	This file serves as the entry point for the installation process. When th application is run, it checks to see if the target machine already has Windows Installer 1.5 installed. If not, it invokes InstMsiA.exe or Ins MsiW.exe as appropriate to install Windows Installer. It then installs th application from the MSI file.
InstMsiA.exe	Installs Windows Installer 1.5 on a Windows 95 or Windows 98 machine.
InstMsiW.exe	Installs Windows Installer 1.5 on a Windows NT or Windows 2000 machine.
Setup.ini	Contains the name of the .msi file to be run by Setup.exe after installa tion of Windows Installer is verified.

If you plan to make your application downloadable from the Web, however, you should choose the Web Bootstrapper option for your setup project. Choosing Wel Bootstrapper causes three additional files to be generated and placed in your outpu folder. The InstMsiA.exe and InstMsiW.exe files function in the same manner as was described for the Windows Installer Bootstrapper option: they install Window Installer to the machine as appropriate. The third file is also called Setup.exe, but i has slightly different functionality than the Setup.exe produced with the Windows Installer Bootstrapper option. The Setup.exe file determines if Windows Installer i already installed on the target machine, and if not, it downloads the appropriate executable to install it. Then it downloads and executes the .msi file containing your application.

Choosing the Web Bootstrapper option opens the Web Bootstrapper Settings dialog box, which allows you to set two additional properties. The Setup Folder URL specifies the Web folder that contains the setup installer program and any files associated with that program. You can specify a different URL for the Web Boot- strapper files (InstMsiA.exe and InstMsiW.exe) by setting the Windows Installer Upgrade Folder URL. This allows you to put the bootstrapping application in a dif ferent Web folder than the setup application. If you do not specify a different folder, the Web Bootstrapper executable files should be installed to the same Web folder as the setup files.

Compression

The Compression property determines which compression scheme will be applied to the setup project. If you chose to package your files as loose, uncompressed files, this option is unavailable. Otherwise, you can choose between three settings None indicates that no compression will be applied to the files. This generally results in the fastest install time but can dramatically increase the size of your setu project. Optimized For Speed applies compression to your project but will optimize for a fast install, resulting in a larger setup project as well. Optimized For Size results in a setup project of the smallest possible size, but it might require more time to install.

Authenticode Signature

If you want to use Authenticode signing to sign your setup project, select the check box next to Authenticode Signature in the Setup Property Pages dialog box. This enables three properties relating to your Authenticode signature that can be set. The Certificate File box allows you to specify the folder that contains an Authenticode certificate, which can be used to sign your files. The Browse button allows you to browse to the folder containing the certificate. Similarly, in the Private Key File box, you can specify the folder that contains the private key for digital encryption of the signed files, and you can use the Browse button to browse to the appropriate folder. Additionally, the Timestamp Server URL box lets you specify the Web location for a timestamp server used to sign the files. If you specify Authenticode Signature, you must specify a folder for your certificate file and your private key. Specifying a Timestamp Server URL is optional.

Building, Distributing, and Deploying a Setup Project

Once you have specified the output to be included in your setup project and have set the relevant properties, you can build and distribute it. Once distributed, your setup project can be deployed to client machines.

Building the Project

To build the setup project, select the project in Solution Explorer and choose Build *<project name>* from the Build menu. This invokes the build process for your setup project. The resultant files from the setup build are located in the folder specified by Output File Name in the Setup Property Pages. These files can then be copied to the distribution platform you have chosen.

Distributing the Setup Project

Your distribution plan should ensure that your application is capable of deploying to the target computers. The many options for distributing your application include distributing with removable media, distributing via a network share, or distributing by download from the Web.

Distribution via Removable Media

Removable media is the traditional method for distributing applications. When planning a distribution with removable media, it is important to keep the capacity of the chosen medium in mind. Floppy disks have a maximum capacity of 1.44 MB, so they might not have enough capacity for many setup projects. The capacity of a CD-ROM is considerably larger, but it still might fall short for large setup projects. If your setup application needs to be larger than the capacity of your chosen medium, package your output files in CAB files and copy the resultant CAB files to multiple disks or to a DVD.

To distribute your application via removable media

1. Analyze the size requirements for your setup project, and choose how the files will be packaged on the Property Pages for your application. If you are planning a distribution via floppy disks, choose CAB files and set the CAB file maximum size to 1440 KB.

2. Build your setup project.

3. Copy the setup project output files from the Build folder to the removable media. If you are distributing via floppy disks and have created multiple CAB files, copy the .msi file to the first disk and then copy each CAB file to a separate disk.

Distribution via a Network Share

If your application is designed for use by a group of users on a common network, you can distribute your application by placing it on a network share. In general, this is the simplest method of distribution. All you need to do to distribute your application via a network share is share a folder on the network server and copy the output files to the shared folder. You can then publish the address of the network share to your intended users, who can then download the installation files to the target machines. Additionally, the network administrator can set security properties for the network share folder so that only the intended recipients of the application can download the installer files. If a bootstrapper application is to be included with the setup project, choose a Windows Installer Bootstrapper on the Property Pages.

To distribute your application via a network share

1. If you are including a bootstrapper application with your setup project, choose Windows Installer Bootstrapper on the Property Pages for your setup project.

2. Build your setup project.

3. Share a folder on the network server, and set any appropriate access restrictions.

4. Copy the project setup output files from the Build folder to the network share folder.

5. Publish the network address of the setup files to the end users.

Distribution via a Network Share Using Administrative Installation

You can also deploy your application to a network share via administrative installation. This allows you to create an image of the application and the setup file in a shared folder. End users can then download the setup file from the share and install it on their own machines. Administrative installation allows you greater flexibility in configuring the installation properties for the application on the target computers. As you will see in Lesson 2, during administrative installation, you can set options for your application that are then carried over to the client installations.

To distribute your application via a network share using administrative installation

1. If you are including a bootstrapper application with your setup project, choose Windows Installer Bootstrapper on the Property Pages for your setup project.

2. Build your setup project.

3. Share a folder on the network server, and set any appropriate access restrictions.

4. Open the command window.

5. Change the directory in the command window to the directory that contains the setup project.

6. Invoke administrative installation by using the following command, where *<setup>* is the name of your setup program:

   ```
   msiexec.exe /A <setup>.msi
   ```

7. Follow the instructions given by the Setup Project Wizard. Choose the shared folder as the target folder for installation.

8. Publish the network address of the setup files to the end users.

Distribution via the World Wide Web

For a project with a wide distribution audience, you might want to distribute your application via an Internet download. The procedure for making your application accessible over the Internet is fundamentally the same as distributing via a network share. Rather than copy your installer files to a shared directory, however, you copy them to a virtual Web directory. If you are including a bootstrapper application with your setup project, you can copy the bootstrapper application to another directory, as specified by the Windows Installer Upgrade Folder URL setting on the Property Pages. If you are including a bootstrapper, set the Bootstrapper property to Web Bootstrapper for built-in authentication.

To distribute your application via the Web

1. If you are including a bootstrapper application with your setup project, choose Web Bootstrapper on the Property Pages for your setup project. Set the Setup Folder URL property to the URL to which you plan to copy your setup application. If desired, you can specify an additional URL for the bootstrapper program in the Windows Installer Upgrade Folder URL property.

2. Build your setup project.

3. Copy the project setup output files from the Build folder to the virtual folder that will host your application. If you specified a Setup Folder URL property for a Web Bootstrapper in Step 1, you should copy the output files to the folder represented by that URL.

4. Publish the URL to your intended audience.

Deploying Your Project

Once the setup program has been created and distributed, deploying an application is an easy process. If you chose not to create a bootstrapper application, you simply double-click on the .msi file created by your setup project. If a bootstrapper application is included, you can launch the process by double-clicking the Setup.exe file, which will install Windows Installer if necessary. Either approach ultimately will open the .msi file created by your setup project, which will launch the Setup Wizard. The wizard will automatically install your application to the correct directories. In Lesson 2 of this chapter, you will learn to configure the Setup Wizard to create seamless installations.

Lesson Summary

- Under rare conditions, you can deploy a .NET application by using XCOPY to copy the application directory and all subdirectories to a target computer. This is possible only when the .NET Framework is installed on all target machines and the application has no dependencies on shared assemblies or resources. In most circumstances, XCOPY deployment is not a viable possibility.

- You can use Visual Studio .NET to create Windows Installer setup projects and merge modules. A setup project must be executed on a computer that has Windows Installer 1.5 installed and contains all the content and information needed to install an application to a client computer. A merge module is used to package DLL files and cannot be installed by itself—it must be merged with a setup project.

- The Setup Project Wizard allows you to specify the content to add to your setup project and choose the kind of setup project to create.

- You can configure the Build properties of your setup project by using the Setup Property Pages. You can configure how the files are packaged, compression settings, whether to create a bootstrapper, the output file directory, and Authenticode settings.

- Once the project is built, you can distribute it in a variety of ways. You should configure the Build properties of your setup project to be optimized for your distribution plan.

Lesson 2: Configuring Your Setup Project

Windows Installer setup projects are highly configurable. You can specify locations for files on target computers, create file associations, check for preexisting conditions, or execute custom actions. In this lesson, you will learn how to create a fully configured Windows Installer setup application.

After this lesson, you will be able to

- Explain how to use the Setup Project properties to provide information about your application
- Describe how to configure the directory structure of the deployed application with the File System Editor
- Explain how to create registry keys upon installation with the Registry Editor
- Explain how to create file associations with the File Types Editor
- Describe how to edit the deployment user interface with the User Interface Editor
- Explain how to create a custom action for your setup project
- Describe how to specify a launch condition for your setup project
- Explain how to use Ngen.exe to create a native image of your application on the client machine
- Describe how to verify the security policies for an installed application

Estimated lesson time: 45 minutes

You can create, compile, and distribute a setup project using only what you learned in Lesson 1 of this chapter. For many applications, this will be adequate. For most applications, however, you will want to provide some degree of customization for your setup project. A series of editors in Visual Studio .NET allow you to set installation properties and actions to be taken by the setup program. After your application is installed, you can use command-line utilities to create a precompiled image of your application in the native image cache and to verify the security policies for an installed application.

Setting the Setup Project Properties

The Setup Project properties provide information about your project and set actions relating to versions of your project. The Setup Project properties are set in the Properties window. Note that this is the Properties window in the IDE, not the Properties page covered in Lesson 1. Many Setup Project properties can provide descriptive information about your application. These properties include

- **AddRemoveProgramsIcon.**   Specifies an icon for the Add/Remove Programs dialog box on the client computer

- **Author.**   Contains information about the author of the program
- **Description.**   Contains a description of the application
- **Keywords.**   Contains keywords to be associated with the application
- **Localization.**   Provides the locale information for the application
- **Manufacturer.**   Contains information about the manufacturer of the application
- **ManufacturerURL.**   Contains the URL of the manufacturer's Web site
- **ProductName.**   Contains the name of the product
- **Subject.**   Contains information about the subject of the application
- **SupportPhone.**   Provides a phone number for support for the application
- **SupportURL.**   Contains a URL for support for the application
- **Title.**   Contains the title of the application

Other properties of the setup project are used to determine the behavior of the setup project at install time. These properties include

- **DetectNewerInstall.**   The setup project looks for a more recent version of the application on the target computer and aborts the installation if one is found.
- **RemovePreviousVersion.**   The setup project looks for earlier versions of the application and uninstalls them in favor of the new version if one is found.
- **Version.**   This property holds the information used by the previous two properties to determine versioning.

There are two additional properties: ProductCode and UpgradeCode. These are used by the setup program and should never be altered manually.

These properties are editable in the Properties window at design time. You can also set properties for individual files in your setup project.

Registering Components at Installation

If your setup project includes a font, COM component, or any other component that requires registration, you can register it upon installation by setting the file's *Register* property in the Properties window. The possible settings for this property are

- **vsdrpDoNotRegister.**   Indicates that this object requires no registration
- **vsdrpCOM.**   Indicates that this object will be registered as a COM object
- **vsdrpCOMRelativePath.**   Indicates that this object will be registered as an isolated COM object
- **vsdrpCOMSelfReg.**   Indicates that this item will be self-registered as a COM object when installed
- **vsdrpFont.**   Indicates that this item will be registered as a Font upon installation

Note that some of these options might be unavailable for some component types. No registration is required for .NET assemblies and components, so the *Register* property for these elements should be set to *vsdrpDoNotRegister*. Fonts should be set to *vsdrpFont*, and COM files with *OleSelfRegister* in their version information will default to *vsdrpCOMSelfReg*.

To register a component upon installation

In Solution Explorer, select your component. In the Properties window, set the *Register* property to the appropriate value.

The Installation Editors

Visual Studio .NET provides six installation editors that allow you to impart a high degree of configuration to your setup project. The editors are

- **File System Editor.**   Allows you to configure the installation of your application to the file system of the target computer
- **Registry Editor.**   Allows you to write entries to the registry upon installation
- **File Types Editor.**   Allows you to set associations between applications and file types
- **User Interface Editor.**   Allows you to edit the user interface seen during installation for both regular installation and administrative installation
- **Custom Actions Editor.**   Allows you to define custom actions to be performed during installation
- **Launch Conditions Editor.**   Allows you to set conditions for launching the installation of your setup project

File System Editor

The File System Editor is used to manipulate the file system on the target computer. You can add output files to various directories, create new directories on the target machine, or create and add shortcuts to the target machine. You can access the File System Editor by selecting your setup project in Solution Explorer and choosing View, Editor, File System Editor.

The File System Editor window is split into two panes, as shown in Figure 10.8.

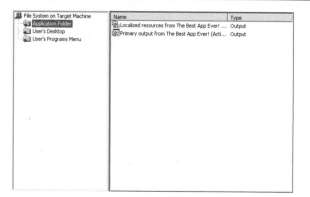

Figure 10.8.   The File System Editor.

The right pane of the File System Editor lists all the output files in your setup project. The left pane represents the directory structure of the target computer. Initially, the File System Editor consists of three folders: the Application Folder, the User's Desktop, and the User's Program Menu. By default, the output files are initially stored in the Application Folder. You can change the folder for a particular file by selecting the file in the right pane and dragging it to the appropriate folder.

You can add additional folders to the File System Editor by right-clicking the left pane and choosing Add Special Folder. The shortcut menu pictured in Figure 10.9 appears.

Figure 10.9.   The Add Special Folder shortcut menu.

Using this menu, you can add a special folder to the File System Editor or create your own custom folder. If you choose a custom folder, this folder will be created in the target computer's File System upon installation.

Adding a Loose File to Your Setup Application Using the File System Editor

You can use the File System Editor to add loose files and assemblies to your setup project. These files will be incorporated into the setup project and installed upon execution of the setup project, but they will not be compressed and packaged with the rest of the project output.

To add a loose file or assembly to your setup project

1. If the folder to which you want your file to be added is not present in the left pane of the File System Editor, right-click the left pane and choose the appropriate folder from the shortcut menu. You can also create subfolders under existing folders by right-clicking on an existing folder and choosing Add, Folder.

2. In the left pane of the File System Editor, right-click the folder to which you want the file to be added upon installation and choose File. If you are adding an assembly, choose Assembly.

3. Browse to the item you want to add and select it. Click OK (for assemblies) or Open (for files). The file or assembly is added to your setup project and will be installed to the specified folder at installation.

Installing an Assembly to the Global Assembly Cache upon Installation

You can use the File System Editor to install an assembly to the Global Assembly Cache upon installation. To do so, the assembly must be incorporated in the setup project as a loose file and not compressed with the other project output. To install the assembly to the Global Assembly Cache, you must first sign your assembly with a strong name. See Chapter 9 for more information on strongly naming your assembly. Once your assembly has been strongly named, all you need to do is add a Global Assembly Cache folder to the File System Editor and add your assembly to that folder. Upon installation, your assembly will be added to the Global Assembly Cache.

To install an assembly to the Global Assembly Cache upon installation

1. Sign your assembly with a strong name.

2. After creating your setup project, open the File System Editor.

3. Right-click the left pane, and choose Add Special Folder. In the shortcut menu, choose the Global Assembly Cache folder.

4. In the left pane, right-click the Global Assembly Cache folder. Choose Add, and then choose Assembly from the shortcut menu. Choose the appropriate assembly or browse to its location and click OK to add the assembly. The assembly will be added to the Global Assembly Cache upon installation. If the assembly was not already a part of your setup project, it is added to it.

Adding a Shortcut Using the File System Editor

You might want to configure your setup application to add a shortcut to the installed application on the target machine's desktop or another location. You can use the File System Editor to create shortcuts to files and add them to folders on the client machine.

To create a shortcut and add it to the target computer

1. In Solution Explorer, right-click the file for which you want to create a shortcut. Choose Find In Editor. The right pane of the File System Editor switches to the folder that contains that file.

2. In the right pane of the File System Editor, right-click the file for which you want to create a shortcut and choose Create Shortcut. A shortcut to the file is created and added to the pane.

3. Drag the shortcut from the right pane to the appropriate folder in the left pane.

Registry Editor

You can use the Registry Editor to write registry entries upon installation. You can create new registry key entries or write new values to existing registry key entries. The Registry Editor is shown in Figure 10.10.

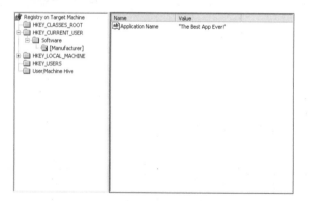

Figure 10.10.   The Registry Editor.

Like the File System Editor, the Registry Editor window is divided into two panes. The left pane represents the registry on the target computer, and the right pane represents registry key values.

To add a new registry key

Right-click the key that you want to contain the new registry key, and choose New Key. A new subkey is added to that registry key. Name the key appropriately.

To add a new registry key value

1. In the left pane of the Registry Editor, right-click the registry key you want to add a value to, choose New, and then choose String Value, Environment String Value, Binary Value, or DWORD Value, depending on the type of key value you want to add. A new key value entry is added to the right pane.

2. In the Properties window, set the *Value* property of the new key value to an appropriate value.

File Types Editor

The File Types Editor allows you to create associations between files with a particular extension and your application. An example of a file association might be the association between files with the .txt extension and the Notepad application. When a .txt file is double-clicked, it is automatically opened with Notepad. The File Types Editor shown in Figure 10.11 allows you to create these associations.

Figure 10.11. The File Types Editor.

You can create a new file association by right-clicking the File Types Editor and choosing Add File Type. This causes a new blank file type to be added to the window. Beneath the new file type, *&Open* is added as an action. You can add additional actions by right-clicking the file type and choosing Add Action.

You can configure the file association in the Properties window for the file type and the action. The *Name* property of the file association is the name of the file types that it represents. You can add file types to this file association by setting the *Extensions* property to the extension of the file type you want to add. If you want to associate more than one file type with your application, you can add multiple file types separated by semicolons to this property. It is not necessary to prefix file extensions with a period.

The *Command* property for the association represents the application to launch when an action is taken. For example, if you are creating an association between your application and a file with the extension .tew, set the *Command* property to your application. Whenever an action is invoked on a .tew file, your application launches and performs the appropriate action.

Actions associated with a file type have three properties. The *Name* property is the text that appears in the context menu when a file with this extension is right-clicked. The *Verb* property specifies the verb that is used to invoke an action for the file type. The *Arguments* property allows you to supply any required command-line arguments to the application.

When a document that has a file association with your application is right-clicked, a context menu appears presenting the *Name* property of any defined actions. When one of the actions is chosen, the executable represented by the action is launched. The executable receives the path of the chosen document and any other parameters specified in the *Arguments* property as command-line parameters. The path of the document is always the first member of the argument array. These arguments are passed to the *Main* method of the application. You must add any appropriate program logic to cause the application to perform the desired task. The following example demonstrates how you would use the command-line argument to open a file with an application's *Open* command:

Visual Basic .NET

```
Shared Sub Main(ByVal args() As String)
    If Not args.Length = 0 Then
        ' Assumes that the application's Open command takes a
        ' string that contains the path of the file to open. The
        ' Open method must also be Shared, as you cannot call an
        ' instance method from a Shared method.
        Open(args(0))
    Else
        Application.Run(New Form1())
    End If
End Sub
```

Visual C#

```
static void Main(string[] args)
{
    if(args.Length!=0)
    {
        // Assumes that the application's Open command takes a
        // string that contains the path of the file to open. The
        // Open method must also be static, as you cannot call an
        // instance method from a static method.
        Open(args[0]);
    }
     else
    {
        Application.Run(new Form1());
    }
}
```

Note   Visual Basic Windows Forms applications do not contain a *Sub Main* by default; it must be added manually. You must then set the startup object to *Sub Main* in the Property Pages for your project. For Visual C# applications, you must manually modify the *static void Main* declaration to accept the array of strings as an argument.

User Interface Editor

The User Interface Editor allows you to alter the visual interface that the user sees when installing your application. The User Interface Editor, shown in Figure 10.12, consists of two tree-view displays: Install and Administrative Install.

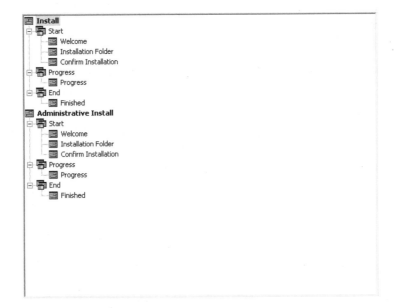

Figure 10.12.   The User Interface Editor.

Each tree view graphically represents the dialog boxes that the user views during installation and is divided into three sections: Start, Progress, and End. Each section contains a series of preset dialog boxes appropriate to that phase of deployment.

In the Start phase, Windows Installer gathers information about the program installation from the machine and the user. Any dialog boxes requiring user choices (such as a dialog box for choosing the installation directory) should be in the Start phase. At the end of the Start phase, Windows Installer checks for available disk space. If there is insufficient disk space, the deployment aborts.

The Progress phase occurs while the application is installing. There is normally no user interaction during the Progress phase, and only a single dialog box indicating installation progress is displayed.

The End phase is entered after the application has installed. This phase is normally used to present information about the installation to the user.

You can change the properties of each dialog box by selecting it in the User Interface Editor and editing the properties in the Properties window. For example, you can set the *BannerBitmap* property of the Welcome dialog box to display a custom bitmap image for your company.

You can change the order that the dialog boxes are viewed during installation by selecting a dialog box and dragging it to the desired spot in the tree view. Although it is technically possible for any dialog box to appear in any position, there are some practical limitations. For example, a Finished dialog box cannot appear at the start of an application.

Administrative Installation vs. Regular Installation

When configuring the setup project for administrative installation (see Lesson 1 of this chapter), you might want to afford the administrator options that are unavailable during regular installation. For example, you might not want end users to choose the installation directory for an application, preferring instead to set the directory during administrative installation. In this case, you would remove the Installation Folder dialog box from the regular install tree but leave it in the administrative installation tree. Thus, the administrator chooses the folder for installation, and it is installed to that directory when the end users install the application.

Adding Dialog Boxes

Customizable dialog boxes that accept user input can be added to your installation—choose check boxes, radio buttons, or text boxes. Editing the box properties in the Properties window allows you to customize their appearance. In addition to properties that control the appearance of the dialog box, such as *BannerBitmap*, *BannerText*, and *BodyText*, other properties allow the application to retrieve input from the user. For example, consider a dialog box of the type *RadioButtons (2 buttons)*. You can add this dialog box to a node in your tree view by right-clicking the node, choosing Add Dialog, and then selecting RadioButtons (2 buttons) from the Add Dialog dialog box. This dialog box also exposes the following:

- *Button1Label*
- *Button2Label*
- *Button1Value*
- *Button2Value*
- *DefaultValue*
- *ButtonProperty*

The properties called *ButtonNLabel*, where *N* is the number of the button, represent the text that will appear next to the radio button. Similarly, *ButtonNValue* represents the value that is returned by the button group when that button is chosen. *DefaultValue* indicates the start value for the button group.

The *ButtonProperty* value is a string that represents the property name used by the installer to retrieve the value of the button group. This property can be referenced by custom launch conditions (as described later in this lesson) to make decisions concerning application installation. For example, if the *ButtonProperty* is set to *Buttons*, you create a launch condition that examines the value of the *Buttons* property. If the first radio button is selected, *Buttons* takes the value contained in the *Button1Value* property. Likewise, if the second radio button is selected, *Buttons* takes the value contained in the *Button2Value* property. Many of the customizable dialog boxes have similarly configurable properties, which allow you to create a rich and complex installation experience for your users.

Custom Actions Editor

Custom actions are an advanced installation technology. With the Custom Actions Editor, you can configure code to be executed during installation. Custom action code must be contained in an *Installer* class. You can use custom actions to execute code upon four *Installer* events: *Install*, *Commit*, *Rollback*, or *Uninstall*. *Install* actions occur after the files have been installed but before the installation has been committed. *Commit* actions occur when an installation is committed on the target machine. *Rollback* actions are executed when an installation fails and is rolled back, and *Uninstall* actions are executed when an application is being uninstalled. You can use the Custom Actions Editor, shown in Figure 10.13, to associate code with these Windows Installer events.

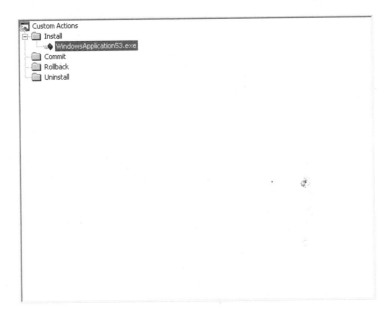

Figure 10.13.   The Custom Actions Editor.

Any executable code can be executed as a custom action. You can add a new custom action in the Custom Action Editor by right-clicking the event in which you want your custom action to run and choosing Add Custom Action from the context menu. This opens the Select Item In Project dialog box, which allows you to select an item in your project to set as a custom action. A new custom action representing the item you selected is added to your setup project. You can configure the custom action by setting the properties in the Properties window. These properties are summarized in Table 10.2.

Table 10.2.   Custom Action Properties

Property	Description
(Name)	This is the name of the selected custom action.
Arguments	Supplies any required command-line arguments to the application represented by the custom action. This property is applicable only when the custom action is implemented as an executable (.exe).
Condition	Enters a Boolean statement that will be evaluated before the custom action is executed. If the statement is *true*, the custom action will execute. If the statement is *false*, the action will not execute. You can use the *Condition* property to evaluate properties chosen in custom dialog boxes.
CustomActionData	Passes any additional required data to the custom action.
EntryPoint	Specifies the name of the method to execute for the custom action. If left blank, the custom action will attempt to execute a method with the same name as the event with which the custom action is associated (for example, *Install*). This property applies only to custom actions implemented in DLLs.
InstallerClass	A Boolean value that represents whether your custom action is implemented in an *Installer* class. This property must be *true* if the custom action is implemented in an *Installer* and *false* if it is not.
SourcePath	Contains the actual path on the developer's machine to the file that implements the custom action. This property is read-only.

To create a custom action

1. Write, test, and debug the code for the custom action you want to add to your setup project.
2. From the View menu, choose Editors, Custom Actions Editor.
3. Right-click the installation event that you want to associate with your custom action, and choose Add Custom Action. The Select Item In Project window opens.
4. Browse to the file that implements your custom action, and select it.
5. In the Properties window, configure the properties of the custom action.

Launch Conditions Editor

You can use the Launch Conditions Editor to create conditions that must be met by the target machine before the installation will execute. For example, you can determine that the appropriate version of Windows is running or that an up-to-date version of a required component has been installed. You can search for files, search the registry, or search for Windows Installer components, and then make decisions based on whether the correct files were found. The Launch Conditions Editor is shown in Figure 10.14.

The Launch Conditions Editor window is divided into two parts. You can add a search that searches for a file, a registry key, or a Windows Installer component on the target computer. You can then add a condition based on the outcome of that search. If the condition is met, installation will proceed normally. If the condition is not met, installation will be rolled back.

Figure 10.14.   The Launch Conditions Editor.

Creating Searches

You can create a search by right-clicking Search Target Machine in the Launch Conditions Editor and choosing the appropriate kind of search. The search types are summarized in Table 10.3.

Table 10.3.   Launch Condition Search Types

Search Type	Description
File	Searches the target computer's file system for a specified file. You can configure the search to look for a specific version of the file, as well as specify minimum and maximum file sizes and dates for the object of the search.
Registry	Searches the registry of the target computer for a specified registry entry. You can specify a search for the root, the key, and the value.
Windows Installer	Searches the target computer for a specified Windows Installer component.

Each search has a *Property* property. This property specifies the property name tha can be used to retrieve the Boolean value that indicates whether a search was suc- cessful. You use the name created in the *Property* property to create launch condi tions, as addressed later in this section.

To create a search for requirements on the target machine

1. From the View menu, choose Editor, Launch Conditions.
2. In the Launch Conditions Editor, right-click Search Target Machine, and choose the option representing the kind of search you would like to add from the context menu.
3. In the Properties window, configure the conditions of your search.

Creating Launch Conditions

Once you have created a search, you can evaluate the results of that search and use them to create a launch condition. A launch condition represents an all-or-nothing decision about the fate of an installation. If the launch condition is met, the installa tion continues. If the launch condition fails, the installation aborts.

You can add a launch condition to a setup project by right-clicking Launch Condi- tions in the Launch Conditions Editor and choosing Add Launch Condition. A launch condition has three properties, which are summarized in Table 10.4.

Table 10.4.   Launch Condition Properties

Property	Description
Name	The name of the launch condition as seen in the Launch Conditions Editor.
Condition	A string that contains a valid Boolean expression. The expression is evaluated at install time. If *true*, the installa- tion continues. If *false*, the installation aborts. The string can also contain more than one Boolean expression con- nected by logical operators (AND, OR, and so on).
Message	Contains the message to be displayed in the event that the installation fails.

To create a launch condition

1. From the View menu, choose Editor, Launch Conditions Editor.
2. In the Launch Conditions Editor, right-click Launch Conditions and choose Add Launch Condition.
3. In the Properties window, configure the properties for your launch condition.

Installing a Native Assembly Image

Applications and assemblies developed in the .NET Framework are generally deployed as Microsoft intermediate language (MSIL) files. At run time, these files are just-in-time compiled to native code, which allows maximum efficiency and use of resources coupled with excellent application speed. In situations where performance is critical, you might be able to achieve a somewhat higher level of performance by precompiling your application to native code. You can use the Ngen.exe utility to create a native image for your application.

Ngen.exe is a command-line utility that generates a native image of your application or assembly and installs it to the Native Image Cache. After you have generated a native image, the runtime will locate and execute the native image whenever the assembly is called.

To create a native image of your assembly or application

1. Open the Visual Studio .NET command prompt. This can be accessed by opening the Windows Start menu and then choosing All Programs, then Microsoft Visual Studio .NET, and then Microsoft Visual Studio .NET Tools.
2. Change directories to the directory that contains your assembly or application.
3. Use the Ngen.exe utility as shown in the following code. For DLL assemblies, you must specify the name of the assembly. For executable applications, you must specify the path to the executable file. For example:

```
Ngen myAssembly
Ngen C:\myApp.exe
```

Verifying Installed Assembly Security Policies

Once your assembly is installed, you can use the Permview.exe utility to view the permissions it requests. To use the Permview.exe utility, open the Visual Studio .NET Command Prompt and type the following code:

```
Permview myAssembly.dll
Permview myApp.exe
```

In the code lines, myAssembly is the name of the DLL while myApp is the name of the executable you want to examine. This assumes that the assembly manifest is contained in the specified file. If the assembly manifest is separate from the rest of the assembly, you should specify the file containing the assembly manifest in the command line instead.

Running this utility displays a list of all requested assembly level permissions. If you want to examine all declared permissions, including at the class and method level, use the */DECL* flag as shown here:

```
Permview /DECL myAssembly.dll
```

You can also write the output to a file instead of the console. To write the output to a file, use the */OUTPUT* flag to specify the output file, as follows:

```
Permview /OUTPUT myTextFile.text myAssembly.dll
```

Lesson Summary

- Setup applications are highly configurable. You can set setup properties that provide information about the origin of your application and behavior of your application at design time in the Properties window.
- Use the *Register* property to register a COM component or a font at install time.
- Use the File System Editor to edit the file system on the target computer.
- Use the Registry Editor to write registry entries to the target computer.
- Use the File Types Editor to create file associations on the target computer.
- Use the User Interface Editor to customize the installation user interface.
- Use the Custom Actions Editor to add a custom action.
- Use the Launch Conditions Editor to add a search and a launch condition.
- Use Ngen.exe to create a native code image of your application or assembly.
- Use Permview.exe to view the permissions granted to an assembly.

Lab 10: Creating an Installer Application

In this lab, you will create a setup project for the application you created in Chapter 8 and Chapter 9. You will use the Setup Project Wizard to create a setup project and configure the project with the Property Pages. You will add a shortcut to the desktop of the target computer and add a launch condition to verify that the operating system is Windows 2000 or later. In addition, you will build your setup project and install your application to your computer. Once installed, you will verify the security permissions for your application. The solution to this lab is available on the Supplemental Course Materials CD-ROM in the \Labs\Ch10\Solution folder.

Before You Begin

Before you begin this lab, you must have completed the Chapter 8 and Chapter 9 labs or loaded the Chapter 10 lab partial solution from the \Labs\Ch10\Partial folder on the CD-ROM.

Estimated lesson time: 30 minutes

Exercise 10.1: Creating the Setup Project

In this exercise, you will use the Setup Project Wizard to create a setup project for your application.

▶ **To create the setup project**

1. From the File menu, choose Add Project and then choose New Project. The Add New Project dialog box opens.

2. In the left pane of the Add New Project dialog box, choose Setup And Deployment Projects. In the right pane, choose Setup Wizard. Name your project **InternationalSales**, and click OK to continue.

3. In the Setup wizard, click Next to go to the Choose A Project Type page.

4. Choose Create A Setup For A Windows Application. Click Next to go to the Choose Project Outputs To Include page.

5. Choose Primary Output, Localized Resources, and Content Files for inclusion in the setup project. Click Next to continue.

6. Click Next in the next step of the wizard, and then click Finish on the final step to create your setup project.

7. In Solution Explorer, right-click InternationalSales and choose Properties. The InternationalSales Property Page opens.

8. In the Bootstrapper drop-down menu, choose None to skip creating a bootstrapper application.

> **Note**   If you are using a machine running Windows 2000, you should choose a Windows bootstrapper application instead of None.

9. Click OK to close the property page.

10. From the File menu, choose Save All to save your work.

Exercise 10.2: Configuring Your Application

In this exercise, you will create a shortcut for your application and add a launch condition to verify that the target machine is running Windows 2000 or later.

▶ **To add a shortcut to your application**

1. In Solution Explorer, click and highlight the setup project. From the View menu, choose Editor, File System to open the File System Editor.

2. In the left pane of the File System Editor, click Application Folder to open the Application Folder. The output from your setup project should appear in this folder in the right pane of the File System Editor.

3. In the right pane, right-click Primary Output and choose Create Shortcut. A new shortcut is created. Name the shortcut **International Sales**.

4. Drag the shortcut to the User's Desktop Folder.

5. From the View menu, choose Editors, Launch Conditions Editor to open the Launch Conditions Editor.

6. Right-click Launch Conditions, and choose Add Launch Condition to add a new launch condition. Name the Launch Condition **Windows2000**.

7. In the Properties window, set the *Condition* property to **VersionNT>=500** to specify Windows 2000 or later. Set the *Message* property to **You must be running Windows 2000 or later to install this application**.

8. In Solution Explorer, highlight the International Sales project, and from the Build menu, choose Build International Sales to build your setup application.

9. From the File menu, choose Save All.

10. Close Visual Studio .NET.

Exercise 10.3: Installing Your Application

In this exercise, you will install your application to your computer. You will test the shortcut added by your setup application, and you will verify the security policy for your assembly.

▶ **To install your application**

1. In Windows, browse to the folder containing your setup project. It should be in the Debug folder of your Setup Project folder.

2. Double-click the International Sales icon, and follow the directions provided by the Windows Installer.

3. After the Windows Installer has finished, locate the shortcut named International Sales on your desktop. Double-click the shortcut to open your application.

4. Close your application.

5. Open the Visual Studio .NET Command Prompt. Use the DOS cd command to change the current directory to the directory where your application is installed.

6. Use the Permview.exe utility to view the security policy for your assembly. Use the */DECL* flag to view all security declarations in the assembly. An example follows. (Note that the name of your application might differ, depending on how you named it.)

```
Permview /DECL Chapter10.exe
```

Note   If your file name contains any spaces, you will be unable to use it with Permview.exe on the command line. In this case, you should enclose the file name in quotation marks to use Permview.exe.

Review

The following questions are intended to reinforce key concepts and information presented in this chapter. If you are unable to answer a question, return to the appropriate lesson to review, and then try the question again. Answers to the questions can be found in Appendix A.

1. Describe XCOPY deployment. Under what conditions is it useful? When can it not be used?

2. Imagine that you have created an application for a client who wants to distribute the application to his workforce via a network share. He wants to ensure that everyone who downloads the application will download it to the same folder. Describe a plan that would accomplish this goal.

3. You have written documentation for your application and have provided it in the form of several HTML files. Describe two ways you can include this content in your setup project.

4. What is a native image? How do you create one?

5. What is the purpose of a bootstrapper application? When do you not need to create one?

6. Describe a general strategy for creating a setup project that terminates installation if a specific file is not already installed on the target machine.

7. How would you ensure that all relevant registry entries were removed in the event that installation of your application failed?

APPENDIX   A

Questions and Answers

Chapter 1: Introduction to the .NET Framework

Page 39

1. Briefly describe the major components of the .NET Framework and describe what each component does.

   The .NET Framework consists of two primary parts: the common language runtime, which manages application execution, enforces type safety, and manages memory reclamation, and the .NET base class library, which consists of thousands of predeveloped classes that can be used to build applications.

2. Briefly explain what is meant by a reference type and a value type.

   A value type holds all of the data represented by the variable within the variable itself. A reference type contains a reference to a memory address that holds the data instead of the actual data itself.

3. How do you enable your application to use .NET base class library members without referencing their fully qualified names?

   Use the *Imports* keyword (Visual Basic .NET) or the *using* keyword (Visual C#) to make a .NET Framework namespace visible to your application.

4. Briefly describe how garbage collection works.

   The garbage collector is a thread that runs in the background of managed .NET applications. It constantly traces the reference tree and attempts to find objects that are no longer referenced. When a nonreferenced object is found, its memory is reclaimed for later use.

5. Briefly describe what members are, and list the four types of members.

   Members are the parts of a class or a structure that hold data or implement functionality. The primary member types are fields, properties, methods, and events.

6. Explain what constructors and destructors are and describe what they are used for.

   The constructor is the method that initializes a class or structure and is run when a type is first instantiated. It is used to set default values and perform other tasks required by the class. A destructor is the method that is

run as the object is being reclaimed by garbage collection. It contains any code that is required for cleanup of the object.

7. Briefly explain the difference between *Public* (*public*), *Friend* (*internal*), and *Private* (*private*) access levels as they apply to user-defined types and member.

In user-defined types, *Public* (*public*) classes can be instantiated by any ele ment of the application. *Friend* (*internal*) classes can be instantiated only by members of the same assembly, and *Private* (*private*) classes can be instantiated only by themselves or types they are nested in. Likewise, a *Public* (*public*) member can be accessed by any client in the application, a *Friend* (*internal*) member can be accessed only from members of the same assembly, and *Private* (*private*) members can be accessed only from within the type.

8. Do you need to instantiate a class before accessing a *Shared* (*static*) member? Why or why not?

Because a *Shared* (*static*) member belongs to the type rather than to any instance of the type, you can access the member without first creating an instance of the type.

9. Briefly describe how a class is similar to a structure. How are they different?

Both classes and structures can have members such as methods, proper- ties, and fields, both use a constructor for initialization, and both inherit from *System.Object*. Both classes and structures can be used to model real world objects.

Classes are reference types, and the memory that holds class instances is allocated on the heap. Structures are value types, and the memory that holds structure instances is allocated on the stack.

Chapter 2: Creating the User Interface

Page 107

1. You are creating an application for a major bank. The application should inte- grate seamlessly with Microsoft Office XP, be easy to learn, and instill a sense of corporate pride in the users. Name two ways you might approach these goals in the user interface.

Design the user interface to mimic the look and feel of Microsoft Office XP which will allow users of Office XP to immediately feel comfortable with the new application. Integration of the corporate logo and other visual ele ments associated with the company will aid in identification of the pro- gram with the company.

2. You are writing an application that needs to display a common set of controls on several different forms. What is the fastest way to approach this problem?

Create a single form that incorporates the common controls, and use visual inheritance to create derived forms.

3. If you wanted to prompt a user for input every time a form received the focus, what would be the best strategy for implementing this functionality?

Write an event handler for the *Activated* event that implements the relevant functionality.

4. Describe two ways to set the tab order of controls on your form.

You can set the tab order in Visual Studio by choosing Tab Index from the View menu and clicking each control in the order you desire. Alternatively, you can set the *TabIndex* property either in code or in the Properties window.

5. What is an extender provider, and what does one do?

Extender providers are components that provide additional properties to controls on a form. Examples include the *ErrorProvider*, *HelpProvider*, and *ToolTip* components. They can be used to provide additional information about particular controls to the user in the user interface.

6. Explain when you might implement a shortcut menu instead of a main menu.

If every possible option is exposed on a main menu, the menu can become busy and hard to use. Shortcut menus allow less frequently used options to be exposed only in situations where they are likely to be used.

7. Describe what is meant by field-level validation and form-level validation.

Field-level validation is the process of validating each individual field as it is entered into a form. Form-level validation describes the process of validating all of the data on a form before submitting the form.

8. Describe how to retrieve the ASCII key code from a keystroke. How would you retrieve key combinations for non-ASCII keys?

Keystrokes can be intercepted by handling the *KeyPress* and *KeyDown* events. Both of these events relay information to their handling methods in the form of their *EventArgs*. The *KeyPressEventArgs*, relayed by the *KeyPress* event, exposes the ASCII value of the key pressed in the *KeyPressEventArgs.KeyChar* property. The *KeyEventArgs*, relayed by the *KeyDown* event, exposes properties that indicate whether non-ASCII keys such as ALT, CTRL, or Shift have been pressed. To retrieve the ASCII key code from a keystroke, you would handle the *KeyPress* event and get that information from the *KeyPressEventArgs.KeyChar* property. To retrieve non-ASCII information, you would handle the *KeyDown* event and use the properties exposed by the *KeyEventArgs* instance.

9. Describe in general terms how to add a control to a form at run time.

You must first declare and instantiate a new instance of the control. Then, you must add the control to the form's *Controls* collection. Once the control has been added to the *Controls* collection, you must manually set properties that govern the control's position and appearance.

Chapter 3: Types and Members

Page 170

1. Explain when a type conversion will undergo an implicit cast and when you must perform an explicit cast. What are the dangers associated with explicit casts?

   Types can be implicitly converted when the conversion can always take place without any potential loss of data. When a potential loss of data is possible, an explicit cast is required. If an explicit cast is improperly performed, a loss of data precision can result, or an exception can be thrown

2. Explain why you might use enums and constants instead of their associated literal values.

   Enums and constants make code easier to read and maintain by substituting human-legible tokens for frequently used constant values.

3. Briefly summarize the similarities and differences between arrays and collections.

   Arrays and collections allow you to manage groups of objects. You can access a particular object by index in both arrays and collections, and you can use *For Each...Next (foreach)* syntax to iterate through the members of arrays and most collections. Arrays are fixed in length, and members must be initialized before use. Members of collections must be declared and initialized outside of the collection, and then added to the collection. Collections provided in the *System.Collections* namespace can grow or shrink dynamically, and items can be added or removed at run time.

4. Explain how properties differ from fields. Why would you expose public data through properties instead of fields?

   Properties allow validation code to execute when values are accessed or changed. This allows you to impose some measure of control over when and how values are read or changed. Fields cannot perform validation when being read or set.

5. Explain what a delegate is and how one works.

   A delegate acts like a strongly typed function pointer. Delegates can invoke the methods that they reference without making explicit calls to those methods.

6. Briefly explain how to convert a string representation of a number to a numeric type, such as an *Integer* or a *Double*.

   All numeric data types have a *Parse* method that accepts a string parameter and returns the value represented by that string cast to the appropriate data type. You can use the *Parse* method of each data type to convert strings to that type.

7. What are the two kinds of multidimensional arrays? Briefly describe each.

   Multidimensional arrays can be either rectangular arrays or jagged arrays. A rectangular array can be thought of as a table, where each row has the same number of columns. Rectangular arrays with more than two

dimensions continue this concept, where each member of each dimension has the same number of members of each other dimension. Jagged arrays can be thought of as an array of arrays. A two-dimensional jagged array is like a table where each row might have a different number of columns.

Chapter 4: Object-Oriented Programming and Polymorphism

ge 215

1. Briefly explain encapsulation and why it is important in object-oriented programming.

   Encapsulation is the principle that all of the data and functionality required by an object be contained by that object. This allows objects to exist as independent, interchangeable units of functionality without maintaining dependencies on other units of code.

2. What is method overloading, and when is it useful?

   Method overloading allows you to create several methods with the same name but different signatures. Overloading is useful when you want to provide the same or similar functionality to different sets of parameters.

3. You need to create several unrelated classes that each expose a common set of methods. Briefly outline a strategy that will allow these classes to polymorphically expose that functionality to other classes.

   Factor the common set of methods into an interface, and then implement that interface in each class. Each class can then be implicitly cast to that interface and can polymorphically interact with other classes.

4. You need to create several classes that provide a core set of functionality but each must be able to interact with a different set of objects. Outline a strategy for developing these classes with the least development time.

   Create a single class that implements all of the common functionality required by these classes. Then, use inheritance to create derived classes that are specific for each individual case.

5. Describe an abstract class and explain when one might be useful.

   An abstract class is a class that cannot be instantiated but must be inherited. It can contain both implemented methods and abstract methods, which must be implemented in an inheriting class. Thus, it can define common functionality for some methods, a common interface for other methods, and leave more detailed implementation up to the inheriting class.

Chapter 5: Testing and Debugging Your Application

ge 267

1. Describe Break mode and some of the available methods for navigating in Break mode.

   Break mode allows you to observe program execution on a line-by-line basis. You can navigate program execution in Break mode by using Step Into, Step Over, Step Out, Run To Cursor, and Set Next Statement.

2. When would you use the Watch window?

You would use the Watch window to observe the values of application va ables while in Break mode.

3. You are deploying a beta version of a large application and want to collect pe formance data in text files while the application is in use. Briefly describe a strategy for enabling this scenario.

Place *Trace* statements that report the data of interest throughout the application. Create a *TextWriterTraceListener* and add it to the *Listeners* collection. Create *Trace* switches that control when *Trace* statements are executed. Configure the *TextWriterTraceListener* to write output to a text file. Then, compile and deploy the application with *Trace* defined, and enable the *Trace* switches in the application .config file.

4. When testing a method, should you test data that is known to be outside of th bounds of normal operation? Why or why not?

Yes. In addition to testing normal data operation, you must test known ba input to ensure that your application can recover from input errors with out a catastrophic application failure.

5. Briefly explain what each segment of a *Try...Catch...Finally* (*try...catch...finally*) block does.

The *Try* (*try*) block encloses code that is to be executed. If an exception is thrown, it can be caught in an appropriate *Catch* (*catch*) block where cod that will allow the application to handle the execution will be executed. Th *Finally* (*finally*) block contains any code that must be executed whether o not the exception is handled.

Chapter 6: Data Access Using ADO.NET

Page 357

1. What are the major components of a Data Provider, and what function does each fulfill?

An ADO.NET Data Provider is a suite of components designed to facili- tate data access. Every Data Provider minimally includes a *Connection* object that provides the actual connection to the data source, a *Comman* object that represents a direct command to the data source, a *DataReade* object that provides connected, forward-only, read-only access to a data- base, and a *DataAdapter* that facilitates disconnected data access.

2. Briefly contrast connected and disconnected data access in ADO.NET.

In ADO.NET, connected data access is available through the *DataReader* which is a lightweight class designed to provide very fast and efficient dat access. It is severely limited, however, in that it can only provide forward only data access, it does not allow editing, and it requires the exclusive us of a *Connection* object. In contrast, disconnected data access is facilitated by a *DataAdapter*, which manages the commands required for selecting

and updating data. The *DataAdapter* executes a SELECT command against a database, opening a data connection just long enough to retrieve the data, and loads the data into a *DataSet*, which is an in-memory copy of the data. When the data is ready to be updated, the Data Provider manages the updates in the same way, generating the appropriate commands to update the database and keeping the connection open just long enough to execute those commands.

3. What are the three possible settings for the *CommandType* property of a *SqlCommand* object or an *OleDbCommand* object, and what does each mean?

    A *Command* object can have a *CommandType* property setting of *Text*, *StoredProcedure*, or *TableDirect*. When set to *Text*, the command executes the SQL string that is stored in the *Command* object's *CommandText* property. When set to *StoredProcedure*, the command accesses a procedure stored on the database and returns the results. A *CommandText* setting of *TableDirect* indicates that the command should return the entire contents of the table indicated by the *CommandText* property.

4. How could you execute DDL commands, such as ALTER or CREATE TABLE, against a database with ADO.NET?

    You must use a *Command* object to execute DDL commands. You can set the *CommandType* property to *Text* and enter the appropriate DDL command in the *CommandText* property. Then call *Command.ExecuteNonQuery* to execute the command.

5. Briefly discuss the advantages and disadvantages of using typed *DataSet* objects.

    Typed *DataSet* objects allow you to work with data that is represented as members of the .NET common type system. This allows your applications to be aware of the types of data returned in a *DataSet* and serves to eliminate errors resulting from invalid casts, as any type mismatches are caught at compile time. Untyped *DataSet* objects, however, are useful if you do not know the structure of your data, and can be used with any data source.

6. How can you manage data currency on a form with several bound controls?

    Every data source on a form has an associated *CurrencyManager* object that keeps that of the "current" record with respect to bound controls. For convenience, all of the *CurrencyManager* objects represented on a form are exposed through the form's *BindingContext* property. The *Position* of the *CurrencyManager* can be changed, allowing navigation through the records.

7. Describe how to use a *DataView* to filter or sort data.

    You can apply sort criteria to a *DataView* by setting the *Sort* property to the name of a column or columns to be sorted by. The data represented in a *DataView* object can be filtered by setting the *RowFilter* property to a valid filter expression.

8. Briefly describe an *XmlDataDocument* and how it relates to a *DataSet*.

   An *XmlDataDocument* is an in-memory representation of data in a hierar-chical XML format. Each *XmlDataDocument* is synchronized with a *DataSet*. Whenever changes are made to one object, the other is instantly updated. Thus, you can use the *XmlDataDocument* to perform XML manipulations on a *DataSet*.

9. What are the four major parts of a SQL SELECT statement? Briefly describe each one.

   The four major parts of a SELECT statement are SELECT, FROM, WHERE, and ORDER BY. SELECT specifies the fields to be retrieved. FROM specifies the table from which the records are to be retrieved. WHERE allows you to specify filter criteria for the records to be retrieved and ORDER BY allows you to specify a sort order for the records.

10. In Visual Basic .NET or Visual C# programming, when would you use Struc-tured Query Language (SQL) statements? How are they executed?

    ADO.NET handles most of the database communication for you behind the scenes. You would only use SQL statements when generating ad hoc queries for the database. You execute SQL statements by using a *DataCom-mand* object. Statements the return records, such as SELECT statements are executed using the *ExecuteQuery* method. You can also return a single value with a SELECT statement by using the *ExecuteScalar* method. To execute non–value returning statements, such as DELETE, INSERT INTO, or UPDATE statements, use the *ExecuteNonQuery* method.

11. What is meant by a SQL injection attack? How can you prevent them from occurring in your application?

    SQL injection attacks occur when a malicious user attempts to execute SQL code by passing a SQL string to the application through user input. You can guard against SQL injection attacks by validating the format of all strings derived from user input that are used to form ad hoc SQL statements.

12. How can you read XML data into a dataset? How would you write data in a dataset to an XML file? How would you retrieve a string representation of the XML contained within a dataset? Describe each in general terms.

    To read data from an XML file into a dataset, you can use the *ReadXML* method of the dataset, specifying the stream or file that contains the XML data. To write data to a file, you can use the *WriteXML* method of the dataset, again specifying either the file or the stream that represents the file. The *GetXML* method of the dataset can be used to retrieve a string representation of the XML data contained by a dataset.

Chapter 7: Creating Controls Using the .NET Framework

Page 399

1. Briefly describe the three types of user-developed controls and how they differ

The three types of user-developed controls are inherited controls, user controls, and custom controls. An inherited control derives from a standard Windows Forms control and inherits the look, feel, and functionality of that control. User controls allow you to combine standard Windows Forms controls and bind them together with common functionality. Custom controls inherit from *Control* and are the most development-intensive kind of control. Custom controls must implement all their own code for painting and inherit only generic control functionality. All specific functionality must be implemented by the developer.

2. Describe the roles of *Graphics*, *Brush*, *Pen*, and *GraphicsPath* objects in graphics rendering.

   The *Graphics* object represents a drawing surface and encapsulates methods that allow graphics to be rendered to that surface. A *Brush* is an object that is used to fill solid shapes, and a *Pen* is used to render lines. A *GraphicsPath* object represents a complex shape that can be rendered by a *Graphics* object.

3. Describe the general procedure for rendering text to a drawing surface.

   You must first obtain a reference to a *Graphics* object. Next, create an instance of a *GraphicsPath* object. Use the *GraphicsPath.AddString* method to add text to the *GraphicsPath*. Then, call the *Graphics.DrawPath* or *Graphics.FillPath* to render the text.

4. Describe the role of the *LicenseProvider* in control licensing.

   The *LicenseProvider* controls license validation and grants run-time licenses to validly licensed components. The *LicenseManager.Validate* method checks for an available license file and checks against the validation logic provided by the specific implementation of *LicenseProvider*. You specify which *LicenseProvider* to use by applying the *LicenseProviderAttribute*.

5. Describe how to create a form or control with a nonrectangular shape.

   Set the *Region* property of the form or control to a *Region* object that contains the irregular shape. You can create a *Region* object from a *GraphicsPath* object.

Chapter 8: Advanced .NET Framework Topics

Page 454

1. Briefly describe how to use the *PrintDocument* component to print a document. Discuss maintaining correct line spacing and multipage documents.

   The *PrintDocument* class exposes the *Print* method, which raises the *PrintPage* event. Code to render printed items to the printer should be placed in the *PrintPage* event handler. The *PrintPage* event handler provides the objects required to render to the printer in an instance of the *PagePrintEventArgs* class. Content is rendered to the printer using the *Graphics* object provided by *PagePrintEventArgs*. You can calculate correct line spacing by dividing the height of the *MarginBounds* property by the height of the font you are rendering. If your document has multiple pages, you must set the *PagePrintEventArgs.HasMorePages* property to *true*, which causes the *PrintPage* event to fire again. Because the *PrintPage* event handler retains no inherent memory of how many pages have been printed, you must incorporate all logic for printing multiple pages into your event handler.

2. Explain how to use the *Begin* and *End* methods on a Web Service to make an asynchronous method call.

Every public Web method on a Web Service can be called either synchronously or asynchronously. To make an asynchronous call to a Web method, you call the method named *Begin*<webmethod>, where <webmethod> is the name of the method. This method requires a delegate to an appropriate callback method and returns a value of *IAsyncResult*. This value is returned as a parameter in the callback method. To retrieve the data returned by the Web method, call *End*<webmethod>, supplying a reference to the *IAsyncResult* returned by *Begin*<webmethod>. This will allow you to retrieve the actual data returned by the Web method.

3. Briefly describe the five accessibility requirements of the Certified for Windows logo program.

The five requirements are

- **Support standard system settings. This requires your application to be able to conform to system settings for colors, fonts, and other UI elements.**

- **Be compatible with High Contrast mode. This requirement can be met by using only the System palette for UI colors.**

- **Provide documented keyboard access for all UI features. Key points in this requirement are shortcut keys and accessible documentation.**

- **Provide notification of the focus location. This requirement is handled primarily by the .NET Framework.**

- **Convey no information by sound alone. This requirement can be met by providing redundant means of conveying information.**

4. Explain how to use the *HelpProvider* component to provide help for UI elements.

You can provide either a *HelpString* or a help topic for UI elements with the *HelpProvider*. The *HelpProvider* provides *HelpString*, *HelpKeyWord*, and *HelpNavigator* properties for each control on the form. If no value for the *HelpProvider.HelpNameSpace* is set, the *HelpString* will be provided as help. If the *HelpNameSpace* is set, the *HelpProvider* will display the appropriate help topic as configured by the *HelpKeyWord* and *HelpNavigator* properties. Help for a particular element is displayed when the element has the focus and the F1 key is pressed.

5. Describe how to create localized versions of a form.

   To create a localized version of a form, set the *Localizable* property to *true*. Then set the *Language* property to the language/region for which you want to create the localized form. Make any localization-related changes in the UI. The changed property values will automatically be stored in resource files and loaded when the *CurrentUICulture* is set to the appropriate *CultureInfo*.

6. Explain how to convert data in legacy code page formats to the Unicode format.

   You can use the *Encoding.Convert* method to convert data between encoding types. This method requires instances of both encoding types and an array of bytes that represents the data to be converted. It returns an array of bytes in the target format. You can convert a string or array of chars to an array of bytes with the *Encoding.GetBytes* method and can convert an array of bytes back to chars with the *Encoding.GetChars* method.

7. Explain the difference between Globalization and Localization.

   Globalization refers to the application of culture-specific format to existing data. Localization refers to providing new culture-specific resources and retrieving the appropriate resources based on the culture setting.

8. Explain how to use the *PrintPreviewDialog* control to display a preview of a printed document before it is printed.

   You display a preview of a printed document with the *PrintPreviewDialog* control by first setting the *PrintDocument* property of the *PrintPreviewDialog* instance to the *PrintDocument* you want to preview, then by calling the *PrintPreviewDialog.Show* command to display the dialog box.

Chapter 9: Assemblies, Configuration, and Security

age 500

1. Describe how to sign your assembly with a strong name. Why would you want to do this?

   To sign your assembly with a strong name, you must have access to a key file or create one with the strong name utility (sn.exe). You then specify the key file in the AssemblyInfo file and verify that the version number is correct. The assembly will be signed with a strong name when built. In addition to identifying your assembly and ensuring version identity, a strong name is required if you want to install your assembly to the Global Assembly Cache.

2. Describe how to use code to retrieve resources at run time.

   You must first create an instance of the *ResourceManager* class that is associated with the assembly that contains the desired resource. You can then use the *GetString* method to retrieve string resources or the *GetObject* method to retrieve object resources.

3. Explain how to retrieve information from the configuration file at run time. How would you store information in the configuration file at design time?

You must first create an instance of *AppSettingsReader* to read the configu ration file. You can then call the *GetValue* method to read values repre- sented in the configuration file. To add configuration file entries, you should create *<add>* elements in the *<appSettings>* node of the configura- tion file. In the *<add>* element, you should specify a value for the entry and a key that can be used to retrieve the entry. The value can be changed between executions of the application.

4. You are creating a solution that must be accessed by members of a group called Developers and Administrators on the local machine. Describe a plan to imple ment this security scheme.

Create one *PrincipalPermission* that represents the Developers group and another *PrincipalPermission* that represents the BUILTIN\Administrators group. Then, create a third permission that represents the union of the two by calling the *Union* method and demand that permission.

5. Briefly highlight the differences between imperative and declarative security as they pertain to code access security.

Imperative security is implemented by calling methods of *Permission* objects in code at run time. Declarative security is configured by attaching attributes representing permissions to classes and methods. Imperative security allows a finer control over the point in execution where permis- sions are demanded, but declarative security is emitted into metadata, and required permissions can be discovered through the classes in the *Sys- tem.Reflection* namespace. Additionally, you can request assembly-wide per missions using the *Assembly* (*assembly*) directive with declarative security.

6. What is a shared assembly? How would you create one?

An assembly is an assembly of which only a single copy is installed per machine. This copy can be shared by multiple applications. To make an assembly a shared assembly, you must first assign it a strong name, and then install it to the global assembly cache.

Chapter 10: Deploying Your Application

Page 534

1. Describe XCOPY deployment. Under what conditions is it useful? When can it not be used?

XCOPY deployment is a simple method of deployment where the DOS command XCOPY is used to copy the application directory and any subdi- rectories to the target machine. You can use XCOPY deployment if your application has no dependency on shared files and requires no special actions to be taken upon deployment. If an application requires a more complex deployment or references shared assemblies, you cannot use XCOPY.

2. You have created an application for a client who wants to distribute your application to his workforce via a network share. He wants to ensure that everyone who downloads the application will download it to the same folder. Describe a plan that would accomplish this goal.

   Create a setup project for the application. Using the User Interface Editor, provide a dialog box that allows the file directory to be set during administrative installation, but removes this box from regular installation. Use administrative installation to install the application to the network share.

3. You have written documentation for your application and have provided it in the form of several HTML files. Describe two ways you could include this content in your setup project.

   You can include loose HTML files along with your application by either including them when you create the setup project with the Setup wizard or by adding them to the project after creation with the File System Editor.

4. What is a native image? How do you create one?

   A native image is a precompiled version of a .NET assembly. You can create a native image of your application by using the Ngen.exe utility.

5. What is the purpose of a bootstrapper application? When do you not need to create one?

   A bootstrapper application automatically detects if Windows Installer is installed on the target machine. If Windows Installer is not present, it installs Windows Installer before proceeding with the rest of the installation. You should create a bootstrapper application unless all of your target machines are running Windows XP (which has Microsoft Windows Installer 1.5 already installed) or have had Microsoft Installer 1.5 installed previously.

6. Describe a general strategy for creating a setup project that terminates installation if a specific file is not already installed on the target machine.

   First, create a file search to search the file system for the specific file. Then create a launch condition to evaluate the results of the search. You can connect the launch condition to the results of the search by evaluating the value returned by the property specified in the search's *Property* property in the expression specified by the launch condition's *Condition* property.

7. How would you ensure that all relevant registry entries were removed in the event that installation of your application failed?

   You can ensure that registry entries are removed, as well as perform any other "clean-up" tasks, by creating an *Installer* class and writing the appropriate code in the *Rollback* event handler. Then create a new Custom Action and set the *InstallerClass*, and *EntryPoint* properties to appropriate values.

Glossary

abstract class A class that cannot be instantiated but is used as a base from which other classes can be derived. In Microsoft Visual Basic .NET, abstract classes are declared using the *MustInherit* keyword. In Microsoft Visual C#, abstract classes are declared using the *abstract* keyword.

abstraction Representing real-world objects as programmatic constructs.

abstract members A member of a base class that cannot be invoked, but instead provides a template for members of a derived class. In Visual Basic .NET, abstract members are declared using the *MustOverride* keyword. In Visual C#, abstract members are declared using the *abstract* keyword.

ADO.NET The data access architecture for the Microsoft .NET Framework. ADO.NET is built around a disconnected data access model that uses a set of classes called a Data Provider to retrieve data from a data source.

alias The name you use to identify resources on the Web. Aliases represent physical resources on the Web server, such as a Web form, an HTML page, or a graphic.

anchoring In Windows Forms controls, the resizing and repositioning of a control when its parent form is resized. You can anchor a control by setting the *Anchor* property.

assembly The primary unit of deployment for a .NET application. An assembly is either an executable application (EXE) or a class library (DLL).

assembly manifest The metadata for the assembly. It contains all of the information needed to describe the assembly to the common language runtime.

authentication The process of determining the identity of a user. In effect, authentication validates that the users are who they say they are. *See also* authorization.

authorization The process of allowing access to an application or resource based on credentials supplied by the user. *See also* authentication.

B

base class A class that provides properties and methods as a foundation for a derived class. In objected-oriented programming, one class can be based on another through inheritance. Using this technique, the base class provides characteristics (such as properties and methods) to a derived class. The derived class can reuse, modify, or add to the members of the base class.

Bezier A curve specified by four points. Two points specify the ends of the curve, and the other two points influence the shape of the curve between the end points.

Boolean A data type that can represent a value of either true or false.

bootstrapper In deployment, an application that installs Microsoft Windows Installer on machines that do not currently have it installed.

boundary condition In testing, test conditions at the limit of normal operation and just over or under those limits.

boxing The act of wrapping a Value type, such as an Integer, inside an object so that it can be treated like a Reference type.

Break mode In debugging, a state of suspended execution wherein the application can be executed in a line-by-line manner, and individual program variables can be examined.

breakpoint In debugging, a predetermined point where execution of an application will halt and enter Break mode.

C

cast An explicit conversion from one type to another.

circular reference A condition that occurs when two objects refer to each other but do not have an external reference. Circular references are automatically detected and disposed of by the garbage collector.

class A user-defined Reference type that serves as a template for an object of that type.

CLR *See* common language runtime.

code access security Verification that all callers to code have appropriate permission to access it.

code tuning The act of examining application code and optimizing for faster execution. Code tuning is usually an iterative process that involves several successive rounds of planning, improvement, and assessment of the results.

common language runtime (CLR) The environment in which managed code executes. The common language runtime provides just-in-time compilation, enforces type safety, and manages memory through garbage collection.

Common Type System A set of types that are used by all .NET languages, thus ensuring .NET language type compatibility.

complex binding In data binding, binding more than one column to a single control. The *DataGrid* is an example of a control that can be complexly bound.

component Strictly speaking, a class that implements *IComponent* or inherits *System.Component*. More generally, any class that provides a reusable set of functionality.

connected data access Data access that requires a data connection that is always open.

constant A type that represents a value that doe not change in the course of an application's exec tion and cannot be changed.

constraint In ADO.NET, an object that represen a rule that enforces referential integrity, such as constraint that specifies a primary key.

constructor The method that executes when a class is instantiated. The constructor usually con tains initialization code to set member variables initial values.

container controls Controls that can host other controls. Examples include *Forms*, *Panels*, and *TabPages*.

control A class that inherits *System.Control*. Co trols usually have a visual representation, intera with the user as a part of the user interface, and a hosted in a container control.

controls collection The collection of a containe control that manages the controls it hosts.

custom control A user-designed control that directly inherits *System.Control*.

D

data binding A way to link data (such as a data set) in your application to the properties of a co trol.

data consumer A control that is bound to a data source.

Data Provider A set of classes that work togethe to provide managed data access.

DataSet A class that contains an application cop of data that has been retrieved from a data sourc

delegate An object that acts as a type-safe func tion pointer. Delegates can be used to invoke the method they point to.

eploying Installing an application on the computer where it will run.

erived class A class that is based on another class (called a base class) through inheritance. A derived class inherits the members of its base class and can override or shadow those members.

esign time Represents the state of the application while being designed. Applications at design time consist of noncompiled code that can be manipulated in the code editor or designer window.

estructor The method that is run just before a class is removed from memory. Generally, a destructor contains any code required to "clean up" after the class. *See also* finalizer.

sconnected data access Data access that uses a data connection only when executing database operations. This is the default kind of data access implemented by ADO.NET.

ocking In Windows Forms, attaching a control to the edge of the form. You can dock a control by setting the *Dock* property.

ncapsulation In component programming, separating the implementation of a component from the interface. Only the public interface of a component is made accessible to the rest of the application. Component data should never be accessible to outside callers.

vent A notification raised by a control or component that a specified condition has occurred.

vent handler A method that is executed when a particular event is raised.

xception Any class that derives from *System.Exception*. Exceptions are thrown in response to run-time errors. *See also* throwing.

exception handling The process of dealing with unusual occurrences within code so that it does not cause the program to crash or lose data.

explicit conversion A conversion of one type to another that cannot be performed automatically. An explicit conversion usually presents some danger of a failed conversion or a loss of data.

extender provider A specialized type of control that provides design time properties to other controls. *ErrorProvider* and *HelpProvider* are examples of extender providers.

F

field A member variable of a class or structure.

finalizer In Visual Basic .NET, the method that is called just before an instance of a class is destroyed. *See also* destructor.

floating-point numbers A number that has a decimal component. *See also* floating-point types.

floating-point types Types capable of representing floating-point numbers. Floating-point types include Single (float) and Double (double). *See also* floating-point numbers.

focus When referring to a control, the condition of being able to receive user input through the keyboard or other input devices. A control that is capable of receiving input is said to have the focus.

foreign key In a data table, a column that contains a key value that uniquely identifies a record in a related table.

form The primary unit of the user interface in a Windows Forms application. A form serves as a nexus for data display and user input, and can host controls.

G

GAC *See* Global Assembly Cache.

garbage collection Automatic memory management provided by the common language runtime. Unused memory is automatically reclaimed by garbage collection without interaction with the application.

GDI+ *See* Graphic Device Interface.

getter The code segment of a property that returns the value the property contains.

Global Assembly Cache (GAC) A machine-wide cache that stores assemblies that have been specifically designated to be shared between several applications.

globalization Applying culture-based formatting to existing data, for example, using culture-specific currency symbols and formatting.

Graphic Device Interface (GDI) In Windows, a graphics display system used by applications to display or print bitmapped text (TrueType fonts), images, and other graphical elements. GDI+ is the name given to the .NET Framework's managed implementation of the GDI.

I

implicit conversion A conversion between types that can be performed automatically by the common language runtime. An implicit conversion will always succeed and never pose a danger of data loss.

inheritance In object-oriented programming, creating a new class that incorporates and extends all of the characteristics and functionality of a base class.

inherited control A user-created control that inherits an existing control. An inherited control inherits all of the functionality of the base control and can incorporate custom functionality as well.

interface A contract for behavior that can be implemented by a class. Classes that implement the same interface can be expected to provide th members defined by the interface.

L

localization Providing multiple sets of data specific to different cultures and retrieving the data appropriate to the current culture setting.

logical error An error that compiles and execute correctly but produces unexpected results. These can be the most difficult errors to detect in application testing.

M

managed code Code that runs under the commo language runtime. The common language runtim handles many tasks that would formerly have bee handled in the application's executable. Manage code solves the Windows programming problem of component registration and versioning (sometimes called DLL Hell) because managed code contains all the versioning and type information that the common language runtime needs to run the application. The common language runtime handles registration dynamically at run time rathe than statically through the system registry, as is done with applications based on the Component Object Model (COM).

metadata Data about data. For example, the name version, security information, and size of a file constitute metadata about the file.

Microsoft Intermediate Language (MSIL) A low-level language that is just-in-time compiled to native code at run time. All .NET assemblies are represented in the MSIL.

MSIL *See* Microsoft Intermediate Language.

multidimensional array An array that contains more than one dimension.

namespace A logical organization of types that perform related functions.

.NET Framework A managed environment for the development and execution of code. It consists of the common language runtime and .NET Framework base class library.

.NET Framework base class library A collection of object-oriented types and interfaces that provides object models to assist in the development of your applications.

O

object The base class for all types in the .NET framework. More generically, any instance of a class or structure.

object-oriented programming The process of creating applications by using programmatic constructs to represent real-world objects.

operator overloading In Visual C#, defining custom behavior for an operator when interacting with custom types.

optimization The process of examining your application and modifying it to be more efficient in terms of either speed or size of the deployed application.

overloading Creating multiple methods with the same name but different signatures.

overriding When inheriting from a base class, providing a new method for one of the base class methods.

P

parent-child relationship In data access, a relationship between two tables wherein a record from the parent table can be used to retrieve one or more related records from a child table. A parent-child relationship can be defined by using a *DataRelation* object.

polymorphism The ability of classes to provide different implementations of the same public interface. Thus, two classes that exhibit polymorphism might contain different implementations, but because the interfaces are identical, they can be treated the same in code.

primary key In a data table, the column that uniquely identifies a record in the table.

private assembly An assembly that is used by only one application. In .NET Framework programming, most assemblies are private assemblies.

project The collection of Visual Studio .NET source files that make up an application.

R

reference type A type, such as a class, whose instance data is allocated on the heap. Variables that represent reference types contain a reference to the object on the heap as opposed to the object's data itself. *See also* value type.

registry The system repository for information about a computer's settings. The registry can contain configuration information about programs and system components.

resource Nonexecutable data, such as a string or image, that is deployed in an application.

role-based security Code that ensures that users of your application have appropriate permission to access your application based on the identity of the user.

run time Represents the state of the application while executing. At run time, the application consists of executing code.

run-time error An error that causes an invalid result or attempts an invalid operation at run time.

S

satellite assembly When localizing an application, assemblies that contain alternate sets of resources to be used in the application for different cultures.

setter The code segment of a property that sets the property's value.

shadowing Hiding a member in a base class with a member in an inherited class that has a different signature.

shared assembly An assembly that is referenced by several applications on a single machine. A shared assembly must be installed to the Global Assembly Cache (GAC).

shared members In Visual Basic .NET, members that belong to the class instead of any one instance of the class. Shared members can be accessed before an instance of a class is created. Shared members are called static members in Visual C#.

simple binding In data binding, binding a control to a single data column. A *TextBox* is an example of a control that can be simply bound.

solution A group of Visual Studio .NET projects that make up a single functional unit.

SQL *See* Structured Query Language.

static members In Visual C#, members that belong to the class instead of any one instance of the class. Shared members can be accessed before an instance of a class is created. Static members are called shared members in Visual Basic .NET.

Step Into Moving from a calling procedure to a called procedure during debugging. Also used in reference to setting breakpoints to stop execution in a specific procedure during debugging.

Step Out In Break mode, resuming execution of function call until the call returns.

Step Over In Break mode, executing a procedure call as a single statement during debugging.

strong name A name that uniquely identifies an assembly. It consists of the assembly's name, version, and culture information as well as a public key encrypted by a private key. An assembly must have a strong name to be installed to the Global Assembly Cache (GAC).

strongly typed Refers to types for all variables being explicitly declared. Strong typing eliminate the possibility of type mismatch errors, which are discovered at compile time. Visual C# is inherently strongly typed, and Visual Basic .NET is strongly typed when Option Strict is set to On.

Struct In Visual C#, a user-defined Value type that serves as a template for an instance of that type. *See also* Structure.

Structure In Visual Basic .NET, a user-defined Value type that serves as a template for an instanc of that type. *See also* Struct.

structured exception handling Using *Try...Catch...Finally* blocks to handle errors that might occur during code execution. When exceptions are thrown, they are handled in the *Catch* block before code in the *Finally* block is executed

Structured Query Language (SQL) The standard language used for issuing commands to databases.

syntax error An error that occurs because of typographical errors or nonsensical code. In the .NET Framework, syntax errors prevent compilation and are thus discovered at compile time.

T

target audience The group of end users for whom an application is designed.

reads The basic unit to which the server alloates processor time. A single process can have
multiple threads.

rowing The act of passing an exception to the
ext caller in the call stack. *See also* exception.

acing A programming technique for recording
vents, such as exceptions, in an application. Tracng is used during debugging and in the testing
hase of application deployment.

ansaction A group of commands (treated as a
ingle unit) that change the data stored in a dataase. The transaction ensures that the commands
re handled in an all-or-nothing fashion—if one of
he commands fails, all of the commands fail, and
ny data that was written to the database by the
ommands is backed out. In this way, transactions
maintain the integrity of data in a database.

ning The process of making adjustments to a
eployed application that do not affect code.

J

nicode The universal character encoding scheme
or characters and text. Each character is repreented by a unique numeric value.

nmanaged code Code that is not managed by the
ommon language runtime. Unmanaged code is
ot checked for type-safety and must be used with
xtreme care.

ser control A user-defined control that encapsuates other Windows Forms controls with custom
unctionality in a common container.

V

value type A type, such as an Integer, Decimal, or
Structure, whose instance data is allocated on the
stack. Variables that represent value types contain
the object's instance data itself as opposed to a reference to that data. *See also* reference type.

W

Watch window When debugging, the window that
allows you to examine the values of predetermined watch variables.

Web service A service or component that is
implemented by a Web server and can be instantiated and accessed programmatically as a component over the World Wide Web.

X

XML Schema A description of the data elements
contained in an XML file. The XML Schema provides the names of the elements, their types,
whether or not they are key fields, and other information.

ndex

ymbol

colon), implementing interfaces, 185–187

D

S

X-Y-Z

PowerTools

At Microsoft Press, we use tools to illustrate our books for software developers and IT professionals. Tools very simply and powerfully symbolize human inventiveness. They're a metaphor for people extending their capabilities, precision, and reach. From simple calipers and pliers to digital micrometers and lasers, these stylized illustrations give each book a visual identity, and a personality to the series. With tools and knowledge, there's no limit to creativity and innovation. Our tagline says it all: *the tools you need to put technology to work.*

MICROSOFT LICENSE AGREEMENT
Book Companion CD

- **Support Services.** Microsoft may, but is not obligated to, provide you with support services related to the SOFTWARE PRODUCT ("Support Services"). Use of Support Services is governed by the Microsoft policies and programs described user manual, in "online" documentation, and/or in other Microsoft-provided materials. Any supplemental software code provided to you as part of the Support Services shall be considered part of the SOFTWARE PRODUCT and subject to the and conditions of this EULA. With respect to technical information you provide to Microsoft as part of the Support Servic Microsoft may use such information for its business purposes, including for product support and development. Microsoft not utilize such technical information in a form that personally identifies you.

- **Software Transfer.** You may permanently transfer all of your rights under this EULA, provided you retain no copies, yo transfer all of the SOFTWARE PRODUCT (including all component parts, the media and printed materials, any upgrades EULA, and, if applicable, the Certificate of Authenticity), **and** the recipient agrees to the terms of this EULA.

- **Termination.** Without prejudice to any other rights, Microsoft may terminate this EULA if you fail to comply with the te and conditions of this EULA. In such event, you must destroy all copies of the SOFTWARE PRODUCT and all of its component parts.

3. **COPYRIGHT.** All title and copyrights in and to the SOFTWARE PRODUCT (including but not limited to any images, photographs, animations, video, audio, music, text, SAMPLE CODE, REDISTRIBUTABLES, and "applets" incorporated ir SOFTWARE PRODUCT) and any copies of the SOFTWARE PRODUCT are owned by Microsoft or its suppliers. The SOF WARE PRODUCT is protected by copyright laws and international treaty provisions. Therefore, you must treat the SOFTW PRODUCT like any other copyrighted material **except** that you may install the SOFTWARE PRODUCT on a single compui provided you keep the original solely for backup or archival purposes. You may not copy the printed materials accompanyin SOFTWARE PRODUCT.

4. **U.S. GOVERNMENT RESTRICTED RIGHTS.** The SOFTWARE PRODUCT and documentation are provided with RESTRICTED RIGHTS. Use, duplication, or disclosure by the Government is subject to restrictions as set forth in subparag (c)(1)(ii) of the Rights in Technical Data and Computer Software clause at DFARS 252.227-7013 or subparagraphs (c)(1) an of the Commercial Computer Software—Restricted Rights at 48 CFR 52.227-19, as applicable. Manufacturer is Microsoft Corporation/One Microsoft Way/Redmond, WA 98052-6399.

5. **EXPORT RESTRICTIONS.** You agree that you will not export or re-export the SOFTWARE PRODUCT, any part thereof any process or service that is the direct product of the SOFTWARE PRODUCT (the foregoing collectively referred to as the "Restricted Components"), to any country, person, entity, or end user subject to U.S. export restrictions. You specifically agr to export or re-export any of the Restricted Components (i) to any country to which the U.S. has embargoed or restricted the of goods or services, which currently include, but are not necessarily limited to, Cuba, Iran, Iraq, Libya, North Korea, Sudan, Syria, or to any national of any such country, wherever located, who intends to transmit or transport the Restricted Compone back to such country; (ii) to any end user who you know or have reason to know will utilize the Restricted Components in the design, development, or production of nuclear, chemical, or biological weapons; or (iii) to any end user who has been prohib from participating in U.S. export transactions by any federal agency of the U.S. government. You warrant and represent that neither the BXA nor any other U.S. federal agency has suspended, revoked, or denied your export privileges.

DISCLAIMER OF WARRANTY

NO WARRANTIES OR CONDITIONS. MICROSOFT EXPRESSLY DISCLAIMS ANY WARRANTY OR CONDITION FOR SOFTWARE PRODUCT. THE SOFTWARE PRODUCT AND ANY RELATED DOCUMENTATION ARE PROVIDED "AS IS" WITHOUT WARRANTY OR CONDITION OF ANY KIND, EITHER EXPRESS OR IMPLIED, INCLUDING, WITHOUT LIMI TION, THE IMPLIED WARRANTIES OF MERCHANTABILITY, FITNESS FOR A PARTICULAR PURPOSE, OR NONINFRINGEMENT. THE ENTIRE RISK ARISING OUT OF USE OR PERFORMANCE OF THE SOFTWARE PRODUCT REMAINS WITH YOU.

LIMITATION OF LIABILITY. TO THE MAXIMUM EXTENT PERMITTED BY APPLICABLE LAW, IN NO EVENT SHAL MICROSOFT OR ITS SUPPLIERS BE LIABLE FOR ANY SPECIAL, INCIDENTAL, INDIRECT, OR CONSEQUENTIAL DAN AGES WHATSOEVER (INCLUDING, WITHOUT LIMITATION, DAMAGES FOR LOSS OF BUSINESS PROFITS, BUSINES INTERRUPTION, LOSS OF BUSINESS INFORMATION, OR ANY OTHER PECUNIARY LOSS) ARISING OUT OF THE USE OR INABILITY TO USE THE SOFTWARE PRODUCT OR THE PROVISION OF OR FAILURE TO PROVIDE SUPPORT SERVICES, EVEN IF MICROSOFT HAS BEEN ADVISED OF THE POSSIBILITY OF SUCH DAMAGES. IN ANY CASE, MICROSOFT'S ENTIRE LIABILITY UNDER ANY PROVISION OF THIS EULA SHALL BE LIMITED TO THE GREATER C THE AMOUNT ACTUALLY PAID BY YOU FOR THE SOFTWARE PRODUCT OR US$5.00; PROVIDED, HOWEVER, IF YC HAVE ENTERED INTO A MICROSOFT SUPPORT SERVICES AGREEMENT, MICROSOFT'S ENTIRE LIABILITY REGAR SUPPORT SERVICES SHALL BE GOVERNED BY THE TERMS OF THAT AGREEMENT. BECAUSE SOME STATES AND JURISDICTIONS DO NOT ALLOW THE EXCLUSION OR LIMITATION OF LIABILITY, THE ABOVE LIMITATION MAY P APPLY TO YOU.

MISCELLANEOUS

This EULA is governed by the laws of the State of Washington USA, except and only to the extent that applicable law mandates ge ing law of a different jurisdiction.

Should you have any questions concerning this EULA, or if you desire to contact Microsoft for any reason, please contact the Mic subsidiary serving your country, or write: Microsoft Sales Information Center/One Microsoft Way/Redmond, WA 98052-6399.